HEALTH INSURANCE PORTABILITY AND ACCOUNTABILITY ACT OF 1996

JULY 31, 1996.—Ordered to be printed

Mr. HASTERT, from the committee of conference,
submitted the following

CONFERENCE REPORT

[To accompany H.R. 3103]

The committee of conference on the disagreeing votes of the two Houses on the amendment of the Senate to the bill (H.R. 3103), to amend the Internal Revenue Code of 1986 to improve portability and continuity of health insurance coverage in the group and individual markets, to combat waste, fraud, and abuse in health insurance and health care delivery, to promote the use of medical savings accounts, to improve access to long-term care services and coverage, to simplify the administration of health insurance, and for other purposes, having met, after full and free conference, and agreed to recommend and do recommend to their respective Houses as follows:

That the House recede from its disagreement to the amendment of the Senate and agree to the same with an amendment as follows:

In lieu of the matter proposed to be inserted by the Senate amendment, insert the following:

SECTION 1. SHORT TITLE; TABLE OF CONTENTS.

(a) SHORT TITLE.—This Act may be cited as the "Health Insurance Portability and Accountability Act of 1996".

(b) TABLE OF CONTENTS.—The table of contents of this Act is as follows:

26–252

TITLE I—HEALTH CARE ACCESS, PORTABILITY, AND RENEWABILITY

Subtitle A—Group Market Rules

PART 1—PORTABILITY, ACCESS, AND RENEWABILITY REQUIREMENTS

SEC. 101. THROUGH THE EMPLOYEE RETIREMENT INCOME SECURITY ACT OF 1974.

(a) IN GENERAL.—Subtitle B of title I of the Employee Retirement Income Security Act of 1974 is amended by adding at the end the following new part:

"PART 7—GROUP HEALTH PLAN PORTABILITY, ACCESS, AND RENEWABILITY REQUIREMENTS

"SEC. 701. INCREASED PORTABILITY THROUGH LIMITATION ON PREEXISTING CONDITION EXCLUSIONS.

"(a) LIMITATION ON PREEXISTING CONDITION EXCLUSION PERIOD; CREDITING FOR PERIODS OF PREVIOUS COVERAGE.—Subject to subsection (d), a group health plan, and a health insurance issuer offering group health insurance coverage, may, with respect to a participant or beneficiary, impose a preexisting condition exclusion only if—

"(1) such exclusion relates to a condition (whether physical or mental), regardless of the cause of the condition, for which medical advice, diagnosis, care, or treatment was recommended or received within the 6-month period ending on the enrollment date;

"(2) such exclusion extends for a period of not more than 12 months (or 18 months in the case of a late enrollee) after the enrollment date; and

"(3) the period of any such preexisting condition exclusion is reduced by the aggregate of the periods of creditable coverage (if any, as defined in subsection (c)(1)) applicable to the participant or beneficiary as of the enrollment date.

"(b) DEFINITIONS.—For purposes of this part—

"(1) PREEXISTING CONDITION EXCLUSION.—

"(A) IN GENERAL.—The term 'preexisting condition exclusion' means, with respect to coverage, a limitation or exclusion of benefits relating to a condition based on the fact that the condition was present before the date of enrollment for such coverage, whether or not any medical advice, diag-

nosis, care, or treatment was recommended or received before such date.

"(B) TREATMENT OF GENETIC INFORMATION.—Genetic information shall not be treated as a condition described in subsection (a)(1) in the absence of a diagnosis of the condition related to such information.

"(2) ENROLLMENT DATE.—The term 'enrollment date' means, with respect to an individual covered under a group health plan or health insurance coverage, the date of enrollment of the individual in the plan or coverage or, if earlier, the first day of the waiting period for such enrollment.

"(3) LATE ENROLLEE.—The term 'late enrollee' means, with respect to coverage under a group health plan, a participant or beneficiary who enrolls under the plan other than during—

"(A) the first period in which the individual is eligible to enroll under the plan, or

"(B) a special enrollment period under subsection (f).

"(4) WAITING PERIOD.—The term 'waiting period' means, with respect to a group health plan and an individual who is a potential participant or beneficiary in the plan, the period that must pass with respect to the individual before the individual is eligible to be covered for benefits under the terms of the plan.

"(c) RULES RELATING TO CREDITING PREVIOUS COVERAGE.—

"(1) CREDITABLE COVERAGE DEFINED.—For purposes of this part, the term 'creditable coverage' means, with respect to an individual, coverage of the individual under any of the following:

"(A) A group health plan.

"(B) Health insurance coverage.

"(C) Part A or part B of title XVIII of the Social Security Act.

"(D) Title XIX of the Social Security Act, other than coverage consisting solely of benefits under section 1928.

"(E) Chapter 55 of title 10, United States Code.

"(F) A medical care program of the Indian Health Service or of a tribal organization.

"(G) A State health benefits risk pool.

"(H) A health plan offered under chapter 89 of title 5, United States Code.

"(I) A public health plan (as defined in regulations).

"(J) A health benefit plan under section 5(e) of the Peace Corps Act (22 U.S.C. 2504(e)).

Such term does not include coverage consisting solely of coverage of excepted benefits (as defined in section 706(c)).

"(2) NOT COUNTING PERIODS BEFORE SIGNIFICANT BREAKS IN COVERAGE.—

"(A) IN GENERAL.—A period of creditable coverage shall not be counted, with respect to enrollment of an individual under a group health plan, if, after such period and before the enrollment date, there was a 63-day period during all of which the individual was not covered under any creditable coverage.

"(B) WAITING PERIOD NOT TREATED AS A BREAK IN COVERAGE.—For purposes of subparagraph (A) and subsection

(d)(4), any period that an individual is in a waiting period for any coverage under a group health plan (or for group health insurance coverage) or is in an affiliation period (as defined in subsection (g)(2)) shall not be taken into account in determining the continuous period under subparagraph (A).

"(3) METHOD OF CREDITING COVERAGE.—

"(A) STANDARD METHOD.—Except as otherwise provided under subparagraph (B), for purposes of applying subsection (a)(3), a group health plan, and a health insurance issuer offering group health insurance coverage, shall count a period of creditable coverage without regard to the specific benefits covered during the period.

"(B) ELECTION OF ALTERNATIVE METHOD.—A group health plan, or a health insurance issuer offering group health insurance coverage, may elect to apply subsection (a)(3) based on coverage of benefits within each of several classes or categories of benefits specified in regulations rather than as provided under subparagraph (A). Such election shall be made on a uniform basis for all participants and beneficiaries. Under such election a group health plan or issuer shall count a period of creditable coverage with respect to any class or category of benefits if any level of benefits is covered within such class or category.

"(C) PLAN NOTICE.—In the case of an election with respect to a group health plan under subparagraph (B) (whether or not health insurance coverage is provided in connection with such plan), the plan shall—

"(i) prominently state in any disclosure statements concerning the plan, and state to each enrollee at the time of enrollment under the plan, that the plan has made such election, and

"(ii) include in such statements a description of the effect of this election.

"(4) ESTABLISHMENT OF PERIOD.—Periods of creditable coverage with respect to an individual shall be established through presentation of certifications described in subsection (e) or in such other manner as may be specified in regulations.

"(d) EXCEPTIONS.—

"(1) EXCLUSION NOT APPLICABLE TO CERTAIN NEWBORNS.—Subject to paragraph (4), a group health plan, and a health insurance issuer offering group health insurance coverage, may not impose any preexisting condition exclusion in the case of an individual who, as of the last day of the 30-day period beginning with the date of birth, is covered under creditable coverage.

"(2) EXCLUSION NOT APPLICABLE TO CERTAIN ADOPTED CHILDREN.—Subject to paragraph (4), a group health plan, and a health insurance issuer offering group health insurance coverage, may not impose any preexisting condition exclusion in the case of a child who is adopted or placed for adoption before attaining 18 years of age and who, as of the last day of the 30-day period beginning on the date of the adoption or placement for adoption, is covered under creditable coverage. The previous

sentence shall not apply to coverage before the date of such adoption or placement for adoption.

"(3) EXCLUSION NOT APPLICABLE TO PREGNANCY.—A group health plan, and health insurance issuer offering group health insurance coverage, may not impose any preexisting condition exclusion relating to pregnancy as a preexisting condition.

"(4) LOSS IF BREAK IN COVERAGE.—Paragraphs (1) and (2) shall no longer apply to an individual after the end of the first 63-day period during all of which the individual was not covered under any creditable coverage.

"(e) CERTIFICATIONS AND DISCLOSURE OF COVERAGE.—

"(1) REQUIREMENT FOR CERTIFICATION OF PERIOD OF CREDITABLE COVERAGE.—

"(A) IN GENERAL.—A group health plan, and a health insurance issuer offering group health insurance coverage, shall provide the certification described in subparagraph (B)—

"(i) at the time an individual ceases to be covered under the plan or otherwise becomes covered under a COBRA continuation provision,

"(ii) in the case of an individual becoming covered under such a provision, at the time the individual ceases to be covered under such provision, and

"(iii) on the request on behalf of an individual made not later than 24 months after the date of cessation of the coverage described in clause (i) or (ii), whichever is later.

The certification under clause (i) may be provided, to the extent practicable, at a time consistent with notices required under any applicable COBRA continuation provision.

"(B) CERTIFICATION.—The certification described in this subparagraph is a written certification of—

"(i) the period of creditable coverage of the individual under such plan and the coverage (if any) under such COBRA continuation provision, and

"(ii) the waiting period (if any) (and affiliation period, if applicable) imposed with respect to the individual for any coverage under such plan.

"(C) ISSUER COMPLIANCE.—To the extent that medical care under a group health plan consists of group health insurance coverage, the plan is deemed to have satisfied the certification requirement under this paragraph if the health insurance issuer offering the coverage provides for such certification in accordance with this paragraph.

"(2) DISCLOSURE OF INFORMATION ON PREVIOUS BENEFITS.—In the case of an election described in subsection (c)(3)(B) by a group health plan or health insurance issuer, if the plan or issuer enrolls an individual for coverage under the plan and the individual provides a certification of coverage of the individual under paragraph (1)—

"(A) upon request of such plan or issuer, the entity which issued the certification provided by the individual shall promptly disclose to such requesting plan or issuer in-

formation on coverage of classes and categories of health benefits available under such entity's plan or coverage, and

"(B) such entity may charge the requesting plan or issuer for the reasonable cost of disclosing such information.

"(3) REGULATIONS.—The Secretary shall establish rules to prevent an entity's failure to provide information under paragraph (1) or (2) with respect to previous coverage of an individual from adversely affecting any subsequent coverage of the individual under another group health plan or health insurance coverage.

"(f) SPECIAL ENROLLMENT PERIODS.—

"(1) INDIVIDUALS LOSING OTHER COVERAGE.—A group health plan, and a health insurance issuer offering group health insurance coverage in connection with a group health plan, shall permit an employee who is eligible, but not enrolled, for coverage under the terms of the plan (or a dependent of such an employee if the dependent is eligible, but not enrolled, for coverage under such terms) to enroll for coverage under the terms of the plan if each of the following conditions is met:

"(A) The employee or dependent was covered under a group health plan or had health insurance coverage at the time coverage was previously offered to the employee or dependent.

"(B) The employee stated in writing at such time that coverage under a group health plan or health insurance coverage was the reason for declining enrollment, but only if the plan sponsor or issuer (if applicable) required such a statement at such time and provided the employee with notice of such requirement (and the consequences of such requirement) at such time.

"(C) The employee's or dependent's coverage described in subparagraph (A)—

"(i) was under a COBRA continuation provision and the coverage under such provision was exhausted; or

"(ii) was not under such a provision and either the coverage was terminated as a result of loss of eligibility for the coverage (including as a result of legal separation, divorce, death, termination of employment, or reduction in the number of hours of employment) or employer contributions towards such coverage were terminated.

"(D) Under the terms of the plan, the employee requests such enrollment not later than 30 days after the date of exhaustion of coverage described in subparagraph (C)(i) or termination of coverage or employer contribution described in subparagraph (C)(ii).

"(2) FOR DEPENDENT BENEFICIARIES.—

"(A) IN GENERAL.—If—

"(i) a group health plan makes coverage available with respect to a dependent of an individual,

"(ii) the individual is a participant under the plan (or has met any waiting period applicable to becoming a participant under the plan and is eligible to be en-

rolled under the plan but for a failure to enroll during a previous enrollment period), and

    "(iii) a person becomes such a dependent of the individual through marriage, birth, or adoption or placement for adoption,

the group health plan shall provide for a dependent special enrollment period described in subparagraph (B) during which the person (or, if not otherwise enrolled, the individual) may be enrolled under the plan as a dependent of the individual, and in the case of the birth or adoption of a child, the spouse of the individual may be enrolled as a dependent of the individual if such spouse is otherwise eligible for coverage.

    "(B) DEPENDENT SPECIAL ENROLLMENT PERIOD.—A dependent special enrollment period under this subparagraph shall be a period of not less than 30 days and shall begin on the later of—

        "(i) the date dependent coverage is made available, or

        "(ii) the date of the marriage, birth, or adoption or placement for adoption (as the case may be) described in subparagraph (A)(iii).

    "(C) NO WAITING PERIOD.—If an individual seeks to enroll a dependent during the first 30 days of such a dependent special enrollment period, the coverage of the dependent shall become effective—

        "(i) in the case of marriage, not later than the first day of the first month beginning after the date the completed request for enrollment is received;

        "(ii) in the case of a dependent's birth, as of the date of such birth; or

        "(iii) in the case of a dependent's adoption or placement for adoption, the date of such adoption or placement for adoption.

"(g) USE OF AFFILIATION PERIOD BY HMOS AS ALTERNATIVE TO PREEXISTING CONDITION EXCLUSION.—

    "(1) IN GENERAL.—In the case of a group health plan that offers medical care through health insurance coverage offered by a health maintenance organization, the plan may provide for an affiliation period with respect to coverage through the organization only if—

        "(A) no preexisting condition exclusion is imposed with respect to coverage through the organization,

        "(B) the period is applied uniformly without regard to any health status-related factors, and

        "(C) such period does not exceed 2 months (or 3 months in the case of a late enrollee).

    "(2) AFFILIATION PERIOD.—

        "(A) DEFINED.—For purposes of this part, the term 'affiliation period' means a period which, under the terms of the health insurance coverage offered by the health maintenance organization, must expire before the health insurance coverage becomes effective. The organization is not required to provide health care services or benefits during such pe-

riod and no premium shall be charged to the participant or beneficiary for any coverage during the period.

"(B) BEGINNING.—Such period shall begin on the enrollment date.

"(C) RUNS CONCURRENTLY WITH WAITING PERIODS.—An affiliation period under a plan shall run concurrently with any waiting period under the plan.

"(3) ALTERNATIVE METHODS.—A health maintenance organization described in paragraph (1) may use alternative methods, from those described in such paragraph, to address adverse selection as approved by the State insurance commissioner or official or officials designated by the State to enforce the requirements of part A of title XXVII of the Public Health Service Act for the State involved with respect to such issuer.

"SEC. 702. PROHIBITING DISCRIMINATION AGAINST INDIVIDUAL PARTICIPANTS AND BENEFICIARIES BASED ON HEALTH STATUS.

"(a) IN ELIGIBILITY TO ENROLL.—

"(1) IN GENERAL.—Subject to paragraph (2), a group health plan, and a health insurance issuer offering group health insurance coverage in connection with a group health plan, may not establish rules for eligibility (including continued eligibility) of any individual to enroll under the terms of the plan based on any of the following health status-related factors in relation to the individual or a dependent of the individual:

"(A) Health status.

"(B) Medical condition (including both physical and mental illnesses).

"(C) Claims experience.

"(D) Receipt of health care.

"(E) Medical history.

"(F) Genetic information.

"(G) Evidence of insurability (including conditions arising out of acts of domestic violence).

"(H) Disability.

"(2) NO APPLICATION TO BENEFITS OR EXCLUSIONS.—To the extent consistent with section 701, paragraph (1) shall not be construed—

"(A) to require a group health plan, or group health insurance coverage, to provide particular benefits other than those provided under the terms of such plan or coverage, or

"(B) to prevent such a plan or coverage from establishing limitations or restrictions on the amount, level, extent, or nature of the benefits or coverage for similarly situated individuals enrolled in the plan or coverage.

"(3) CONSTRUCTION.—For purposes of paragraph (1), rules for eligibility to enroll under a plan include rules defining any applicable waiting periods for such enrollment.

"(b) IN PREMIUM CONTRIBUTIONS.—

"(1) IN GENERAL.—A group health plan, and a health insurance issuer offering health insurance coverage in connection with a group health plan, may not require any individual (as a condition of enrollment or continued enrollment under the plan) to pay a premium or contribution which is greater than

12

such premium or contribution for a similarly situated individual enrolled in the plan on the basis of any health status-related factor in relation to the individual or to an individual enrolled under the plan as a dependent of the individual.

"(2) CONSTRUCTION.—Nothing in paragraph (1) shall be construed—

"(A) to restrict the amount that an employer may be charged for coverage under a group health plan; or

"(B) to prevent a group health plan, and a health insurance issuer offering group health insurance coverage, from establishing premium discounts or rebates or modifying otherwise applicable copayments or deductibles in return for adherence to programs of health promotion and disease prevention.

"SEC. 703. GUARANTEED RENEWABILITY IN MULTIEMPLOYER PLANS AND MULTIPLE EMPLOYER WELFARE ARRANGEMENTS.

"A group health plan which is a multiemployer plan or which is a multiple employer welfare arrangement may not deny an employer whose employees are covered under such a plan continued access to the same or different coverage under the terms of such a plan, other than—

"(1) for nonpayment of contributions;

"(2) for fraud or other intentional misrepresentation of material fact by the employer;

"(3) for noncompliance with material plan provisions;

"(4) because the plan is ceasing to offer any coverage in a geographic area;

"(5) in the case of a plan that offers benefits through a network plan, there is no longer any individual enrolled through the employer who lives, resides, or works in the service area of the network plan and the plan applies this paragraph uniformly without regard to the claims experience of employers or any health status-related factor in relation to such individuals or their dependents; and

"(6) for failure to meet the terms of an applicable collective bargaining agreement, to renew a collective bargaining or other agreement requiring or authorizing contributions to the plan, or to employ employees covered by such an agreement.

"SEC. 704. PREEMPTION; STATE FLEXIBILITY; CONSTRUCTION.

"(a) CONTINUED APPLICABILITY OF STATE LAW WITH RESPECT TO HEALTH INSURANCE ISSUERS.—

"(1) IN GENERAL.—Subject to paragraph (2) and except as provided in subsection (b), this part shall not be construed to supersede any provision of State law which establishes, implements, or continues in effect any standard or requirement solely relating to health insurance issuers in connection with group health insurance coverage except to the extent that such standard or requirement prevents the application of a requirement of this part.

"(2) CONTINUED PREEMPTION WITH RESPECT TO GROUP HEALTH PLANS.—Nothing in this part shall be construed to affect or modify the provisions of section 514 with respect to group health plans.

"(b) SPECIAL RULES IN CASE OF PORTABILITY REQUIREMENTS.—

"(1) IN GENERAL.—Subject to paragraph (2), the provisions of this part relating to health insurance coverage offered by a health insurance issuer supersede any provision of State law which establishes, implements, or continues in effect a standard or requirement applicable to imposition of a preexisting condition exclusion specifically governed by section 701 which differs from the standards or requirements specified in such section.

"(2) EXCEPTIONS.—Only in relation to health insurance coverage offered by a health insurance issuer, the provisions of this part do not supersede any provision of State law to the extent that such provision—

"(i) substitutes for the reference to '6-month period' in section 701(a)(1) a reference to any shorter period of time;

"(ii) substitutes for the reference to '12 months' and '18 months' in section 701(a)(2) a reference to any shorter period of time;

"(iii) substitutes for the references to '63' days in sections 701(c)(2)(A) and 701(d)(4)(A) a reference to any greater number of days;

"(iv) substitutes for the reference to '30-day period' in sections 701(b)(2) and 701(d)(1) a reference to any greater period;

"(v) prohibits the imposition of any preexisting condition exclusion in cases not described in section 701(d) or expands the exceptions described in such section;

"(vi) requires special enrollment periods in addition to those required under section 701(f); or

"(vii) reduces the maximum period permitted in an affiliation period under section 701(g)(1)(B).

"(c) RULES OF CONSTRUCTION.—Nothing in this part shall be construed as requiring a group health plan or health insurance coverage to provide specific benefits under the terms of such plan or coverage.

"(d) DEFINITIONS.—For purposes of this section—

"(1) STATE LAW.—The term 'State law' includes all laws, decisions, rules, regulations, or other State action having the effect of law, of any State. A law of the United States applicable only to the District of Columbia shall be treated as a State law rather than a law of the United States.

"(2) STATE.—The term 'State' includes a State, the Northern Mariana Islands, any political subdivisions of a State or such Islands, or any agency or instrumentality of either.

"SEC. 705. SPECIAL RULES RELATING TO GROUP HEALTH PLANS.

"(a) GENERAL EXCEPTION FOR CERTAIN SMALL GROUP HEALTH PLANS.—The requirements of this part shall not apply to any group health plan (and group health insurance coverage offered in connection with a group health plan) for any plan year if, on the first day of such plan year, such plan has less than 2 participants who are current employees.

"(b) EXCEPTION FOR CERTAIN BENEFITS.—The requirements of this part shall not apply to any group health plan (and group health insurance coverage) in relation to its provision of excepted benefits described in section 706(c)(1).

"(c) EXCEPTION FOR CERTAIN BENEFITS IF CERTAIN CONDITIONS MET.—

"(1) LIMITED, EXCEPTED BENEFITS.—The requirements of this part shall not apply to any group health plan (and group health insurance coverage offered in connection with a group health plan) in relation to its provision of excepted benefits described in section 706(c)(2) if the benefits—

"(A) are provided under a separate policy, certificate, or contract of insurance; or

"(B) are otherwise not an integral part of the plan.

"(2) NONCOORDINATED, EXCEPTED BENEFITS.—The requirements of this part shall not apply to any group health plan (and group health insurance coverage offered in connection with a group health plan) in relation to its provision of excepted benefits described in section 706(c)(3) if all of the following conditions are met:

"(A) The benefits are provided under a separate policy, certificate, or contract of insurance.

"(B) There is no coordination between the provision of such benefits and any exclusion of benefits under any group health plan maintained by the same plan sponsor.

"(C) Such benefits are paid with respect to an event without regard to whether benefits are provided with respect to such an event under any group health plan maintained by the same plan sponsor.

"(3) SUPPLEMENTAL EXCEPTED BENEFITS.—The requirements of this part shall not apply to any group health plan (and group health insurance coverage) in relation to its provision of excepted benefits described in section 706(c)(4) if the benefits are provided under a separate policy, certificate, or contract of insurance.

"(d) TREATMENT OF PARTNERSHIPS.—For purposes of this part—

"(1) TREATMENT AS A GROUP HEALTH PLAN.—Any plan, fund, or program which would not be (but for this subsection) an employee welfare benefit plan and which is established or maintained by a partnership, to the extent that such plan, fund, or program provides medical care (including items and services paid for as medical care) to present or former partners in the partnership or to their dependents (as defined under the terms of the plan, fund, or program), directly or through insurance, reimbursement, or otherwise, shall be treated (subject to paragraph (2)) as an employee welfare benefit plan which is a group health plan.

"(2) EMPLOYER.—In the case of a group health plan, the term 'employer' also includes the partnership in relation to any partner.

"(3) PARTICIPANTS OF GROUP HEALTH PLANS.—In the case of a group health plan, the term 'participant' also includes—

"(A) in connection with a group health plan maintained by a partnership, an individual who is a partner in relation to the partnership, or

"(B) in connection with a group health plan maintained by a self-employed individual (under which one or

15

more employees are participants), the self-employed individ-ual,

if such individual is, or may become, eligible to receive a benefit under the plan or such individual's beneficiaries may be eligible to receive any such benefit.

"SEC. 706. DEFINITIONS.

"(a) GROUP HEALTH PLAN.—*For purposes of this part—*

"(1) IN GENERAL.—*The term 'group health plan' means an employee welfare benefit plan to the extent that the plan provides medical care (as defined in paragraph (2) and including items and services paid for as medical care) to employees or their dependents (as defined under the terms of the plan) directly or through insurance, reimbursement, or otherwise.*

"(2) MEDICAL CARE.—*The term 'medical care' means amounts paid for—*

"(A) *the diagnosis, cure, mitigation, treatment, or prevention of disease, or amounts paid for the purpose of affecting any structure or function of the body,*

"(B) *amounts paid for transportation primarily for and essential to medical care referred to in subparagraph (A), and*

"(C) *amounts paid for insurance covering medical care referred to in subparagraphs (A) and (B).*

"(b) DEFINITIONS RELATING TO HEALTH INSURANCE.—*For purposes of this part—*

"(1) HEALTH INSURANCE COVERAGE.—*The term 'health insurance coverage' means benefits consisting of medical care (provided directly, through insurance or reimbursement, or otherwise and including items and services paid for as medical care) under any hospital or medical service policy or certificate, hospital or medical service plan contract, or health maintenance organization contract offered by a health insurance issuer.*

"(2) HEALTH INSURANCE ISSUER.—*The term 'health insurance issuer' means an insurance company, insurance service, or insurance organization (including a health maintenance organization, as defined in paragraph (3)) which is licensed to engage in the business of insurance in a State and which is subject to State law which regulates insurance (within the meaning of section 514(b)(2)). Such term does not include a group health plan.*

"(3) HEALTH MAINTENANCE ORGANIZATION.—*The term 'health maintenance organization' means—*

"(A) *a Federally qualified health maintenance organization (as defined in section 1301(a) of the Public Health Service Act (42 U.S.C. 300e(a))),*

"(B) *an organization recognized under State law as a health maintenance organization, or*

"(C) *a similar organization regulated under State law for solvency in the same manner and to the same extent as such a health maintenance organization.*

"(4) GROUP HEALTH INSURANCE COVERAGE.—*The term 'group health insurance coverage' means, in connection with a group health plan, health insurance coverage offered in connection with such plan.*

"(c) EXCEPTED BENEFITS.—For purposes of this part, the term 'excepted benefits' means benefits under one or more (or any combination thereof) of the following:

"(1) BENEFITS NOT SUBJECT TO REQUIREMENTS.—

"(A) Coverage only for accident, or disability income insurance, or any combination thereof.

"(B) Coverage issued as a supplement to liability insurance.

"(C) Liability insurance, including general liability insurance and automobile liability insurance.

"(D) Workers' compensation or similar insurance.

"(E) Automobile medical payment insurance.

"(F) Credit-only insurance.

"(G) Coverage for on-site medical clinics.

"(H) Other similar insurance coverage, specified in regulations, under which benefits for medical care are secondary or incidental to other insurance benefits.

"(2) BENEFITS NOT SUBJECT TO REQUIREMENTS IF OFFERED SEPARATELY.—

"(A) Limited scope dental or vision benefits.

"(B) Benefits for long-term care, nursing home care, home health care, community-based care, or any combination thereof.

"(C) Such other similar, limited benefits as are specified in regulations.

"(3) BENEFITS NOT SUBJECT TO REQUIREMENTS IF OFFERED AS INDEPENDENT, NONCOORDINATED BENEFITS.—

"(A) Coverage only for a specified disease or illness.

"(B) Hospital indemnity or other fixed indemnity insurance.

"(4) BENEFITS NOT SUBJECT TO REQUIREMENTS IF OFFERED AS SEPARATE INSURANCE POLICY.—Medicare supplemental health insurance (as defined under section 1882(g)(1) of the Social Security Act), coverage supplemental to the coverage provided under chapter 55 of title 10, United States Code, and similar supplemental coverage provided to coverage under a group health plan.

"(d) OTHER DEFINITIONS.—For purposes of this part—

"(1) COBRA CONTINUATION PROVISION.—The term 'COBRA continuation provision' means any of the following:

"(A) Part 6 of this subtitle.

"(B) Section 4980B of the Internal Revenue Code of 1986, other than subsection (f)(1) of such section insofar as it relates to pediatric vaccines.

"(C) Title XXII of the Public Health Service Act.

"(2) HEALTH STATUS-RELATED FACTOR.—The term 'health status-related factor' means any of the factors described in section 702(a)(1).

"(3) NETWORK PLAN.—The term 'network plan' means health insurance coverage offered by a health insurance issuer under which the financing and delivery of medical care (including items and services paid for as medical care) are provided, in whole or in part, through a defined set of providers under contract with the issuer.

"(4) PLACED FOR ADOPTION.—The term 'placement', or being 'placed', for adoption, has the meaning given such term in section 609(c)(3)(B).

"SEC. 707. REGULATIONS.

"The Secretary, consistent with section 104 of the Health Care Portability and Accountability Act of 1996, may promulgate such regulations as may be necessary or appropriate to carry out the provisions of this part. The Secretary may promulgate any interim final rules as the Secretary determines are appropriate to carry out this part.".

(b) ENFORCEMENT WITH RESPECT TO HEALTH INSURANCE ISSUERS.—Section 502(b) of such Act (29 U.S.C. 1132(b)) is amended by adding at the end the following new paragraph:

"(3) The Secretary is not authorized to enforce under this part any requirement of part 7 against a health insurance issuer offering health insurance coverage in connection with a group health plan (as defined in section 706(a)(1)). Nothing in this paragraph shall affect the authority of the Secretary to issue regulations to carry out such part.".

(c) DISCLOSURE OF INFORMATION TO PARTICIPANTS AND BENEFICIARIES.—

(1) IN GENERAL.—Section 104(b)(1) of such Act (29 U.S.C. 1024(b)(1)) is amended in the matter following subparagraph (B)—

(A) by striking "102(a)(1)," and inserting "102(a)(1) (other than a material reduction in covered services or benefits provided in the case of a group health plan (as defined in section 706(a)(1))),"; and

(B) by adding at the end the following new sentences: "If there is a modification or change described in section 102(a)(1) that is a material reduction in covered services or benefits provided under a group health plan (as defined in section 706(a)(1)), a summary description of such modification or change shall be furnished to participants and beneficiaries not later than 60 days after the date of the adoption of the modification or change. In the alternative, the plan sponsors may provide such description at regular intervals of not more than 90 days. The Secretary shall issue regulations within 180 days after the date of enactment of the Health Insurance Portability and Accountability Act of 1996, providing alternative mechanisms to delivery by mail through which group health plans (as so defined) may notify participants and beneficiaries of material reductions in covered services or benefits.".

(2) PLAN DESCRIPTION AND SUMMARY.—Section 102(b) of such Act (29 U.S.C. 1022(b)) is amended—

(A) by inserting "in the case of a group health plan (as defined in section 706(a)(1)), whether a health insurance issuer (as defined in section 706(b)(2)) is responsible for the financing or administration (including payment of claims) of the plan and (if so) the name and address of such issuer;" after "type of administration of the plan;"; and

(B) by inserting "including the office at the Department of Labor through which participants and beneficiaries may *seek assistance or information regarding their rights under this Act and the Health Insurance Portability and Accountability Act of 1996 with respect to health benefits that are offered through a group health plan (as defined in section 706(a)(1))" after "benefits under the plan".*

(d) TREATMENT OF HEALTH INSURANCE ISSUERS OFFERING HEALTH INSURANCE COVERAGE TO NONCOVERED PLANS.—Section 4(b) of such Act (29 U.S.C. 1003(b)) is amended by adding at the end (after and below paragraph (5)) the following:

"The provisions of part 7 of subtitle B shall not apply to a health insurance issuer (as defined in section 706(b)(2)) solely by reason of health insurance coverage (as defined in section 706(b)(1)) provided by such issuer in connection with a group health plan (as defined in section 706(a)(1)) if the provisions of this title do not apply to such group health plan.".

(e) REPORTING AND ENFORCEMENT WITH RESPECT TO CERTAIN ARRANGEMENTS.—

(1) IN GENERAL.—Section 101 of such Act (29 U.S.C. 1021) is amended—

(A) by redesignating subsection (g) as subsection (h), and

(B) by inserting after subsection (f) the following new subsection:

"(g) REPORTING BY CERTAIN ARRANGEMENTS.—The Secretary may, by regulation, require multiple employer welfare arrangements providing benefits consisting of medical care (within the meaning of section 706(a)(2)) which are not group health plans to report, not more frequently than annually, in such form and such manner as the Secretary may require for the purpose of determining the extent to which the requirements of part 7 are being carried out in connection with such benefits.".

(2) ENFORCEMENT.—

(A) IN GENERAL.—Section 502 of such Act (29 U.S.C. 1132) is amended—

(i) in subsection (a)(6), by striking "under subsection (c)(2) or (i) or (l)" and inserting "under paragraph (2), (4), or (5) of subsection (c) or under subsection (i) or (l)"; and

(ii) in the last 2 sentences of subsection (c), by striking "For purposes of this paragraph" and all that follows through "The Secretary and" and inserting the following:

"(5) The Secretary may assess a civil penalty against any person of up to $1,000 a day from the date of the person's failure or refusal to file the information required to be filed by such person with the Secretary under regulations prescribed pursuant to section 101(g).

"(6) The Secretary and".

(B) TECHNICAL AND CONFORMING AMENDMENT.—Section 502(c)(1) of such Act (29 U.S.C. 1132(c)(1)) is amended by adding at the end the following sentence: "For purposes of this paragraph, each violation described in subparagraph (A) with respect to any single participant, and each violation described in subparagraph (B) with respect to any

single participant or beneficiary, shall be treated as a separate violation.".

(3) COORDINATION.—Section 506 of such Act (29 U.S.C. 1136) is amended by adding at the end the following new subsection:

"(c) COORDINATION OF ENFORCEMENT WITH STATES WITH RESPECT TO CERTAIN ARRANGEMENTS.—A State may enter into an agreement with the Secretary for delegation to the State of some or all of the Secretary's authority under sections 502 and 504 to enforce the requirements under part 7 in connection with multiple employer welfare arrangements, providing medical care (within the meaning of section 706(a)(2)), which are not group health plans.".

(f) CONFORMING AMENDMENTS.—

(1) Section 514(b) of such Act (29 U.S.C. 1144(b)) is amended by adding at the end the following new paragraph:

"(9) For additional provisions relating to group health plans, see section 704.".

(2)(A) Part 6 of subtitle B of title I of such Act (29 U.S.C. 1161 et seq.) is amended by striking the heading and inserting the following:

"PART 6—CONTINUATION COVERAGE AND ADDITIONAL STANDARDS FOR GROUP HEALTH PLANS".

(B) The table of contents in section 1 of such Act is amended by striking the item relating to the heading for part 6 of subtitle B of title I and inserting the following:

"PART 6—CONTINUATION COVERAGE AND ADDITIONAL STANDARDS FOR GROUP HEALTH PLANS".

(3) The table of contents in section 1 of such Act (as amended by the preceding provisions of this section) is amended by inserting after the items relating to part 6 the following new items:

(g) EFFECTIVE DATES.—

(1) IN GENERAL.—Except as provided in this section, this section (and the amendments made by this section) shall apply with respect to group health plans for plan years beginning after June 30, 1997.

(2) DETERMINATION OF CREDITABLE COVERAGE.—

(A) PERIOD OF COVERAGE.—

(i) IN GENERAL.—Subject to clause (ii), no period before July 1, 1996, shall be taken into account under part 7 of subtitle B of title I of the Employee Retire-

ment Income Security Act of 1974 (as added by this section) in determining creditable coverage.

(ii) SPECIAL RULE FOR CERTAIN PERIODS.—The Secretary of Labor, consistent with section 104, shall provide for a process whereby individuals who need to establish creditable coverage for periods before July 1, 1996, and who would have such coverage credited but for clause (i) may be given credit for creditable coverage for such periods through the presentation of documents or other means.

(B) CERTIFICATIONS, ETC.—

(i) IN GENERAL.—Subject to clauses (ii) and (iii), subsection (e) of section 701 of the Employee Retirement Income Security Act of 1974 (as added by this section) shall apply to events occurring after June 30, 1996.

(ii) NO CERTIFICATION REQUIRED TO BE PROVIDED BEFORE JUNE 1, 1997.—In no case is a certification required to be provided under such subsection before June 1, 1997.

(iii) CERTIFICATION ONLY ON WRITTEN REQUEST FOR EVENTS OCCURRING BEFORE OCTOBER 1, 1996.—In the case of an event occurring after June 30, 1996, and before October 1, 1996, a certification is not required to be provided under such subsection unless an individual (with respect to whom the certification is otherwise required to be made) requests such certification in writing.

(C) TRANSITIONAL RULE.—In the case of an individual who seeks to establish creditable coverage for any period for which certification is not required because it relates to an event occurring before June 30, 1996—

(i) the individual may present other credible evidence of such coverage in order to establish the period of creditable coverage; and

(ii) a group health plan and a health insurance issuer shall not be subject to any penalty or enforcement action with respect to the plan's or issuer's crediting (or not crediting) such coverage if the plan or issuer has sought to comply in good faith with the applicable requirements under the amendments made by this section.

(3) SPECIAL RULE FOR COLLECTIVE BARGAINING AGREEMENTS.—Except as provided in paragraph (2), in the case of a group health plan maintained pursuant to 1 or more collective bargaining agreements between employee representatives and one or more employers ratified before the date of the enactment of this Act, part 7 of subtitle B of title I of Employee Retirement Income Security Act of 1974 (other than section 701(e) thereof) shall not apply to plan years beginning before the later of—

(A) the date on which the last of the collective bargaining agreements relating to the plan terminates (determined without regard to any extension thereof agreed to after the date of the enactment of this Act), or

(B) July 1, 1997.

For purposes of subparagraph (A), any plan amendment made pursuant to a collective bargaining agreement relating to the plan which amends the plan solely to conform to any requirement of such part shall not be treated as a termination of such collective bargaining agreement.

(4) TIMELY REGULATIONS.—The Secretary of Labor, consistent with section 104, shall first issue by not later than April 1, 1997, such regulations as may be necessary to carry out the amendments made by this section.

(5) LIMITATION ON ACTIONS.—No enforcement action shall be taken, pursuant to the amendments made by this section, against a group health plan or health insurance issuer with respect to a violation of a requirement imposed by such amendments before January 1, 1998, or, if later, the date of issuance of regulations referred to in paragraph (4), if the plan or issuer has sought to comply in good faith with such requirements.

SEC. 102. THROUGH THE PUBLIC HEALTH SERVICE ACT.

(a) IN GENERAL.—The Public Health Service Act is amended by adding at the end the following new title:

"TITLE XXVII—ASSURING PORTABILITY, AVAILABILITY, AND RENEWABILITY OF HEALTH INSURANCE COVERAGE

"PART A—GROUP MARKET REFORMS

"SUBPART 1—PORTABILITY, ACCESS, AND RENEWABILITY REQUIREMENTS

"SEC. 2701. INCREASED PORTABILITY THROUGH LIMITATION ON PRE-EXISTING CONDITION EXCLUSIONS.

"(a) LIMITATION ON PREEXISTING CONDITION EXCLUSION PERIOD; CREDITING FOR PERIODS OF PREVIOUS COVERAGE.—Subject to subsection (d), a group health plan, and a health insurance issuer offering group health insurance coverage, may, with respect to a participant or beneficiary, impose a preexisting condition exclusion only if—

"(1) such exclusion relates to a condition (whether physical or mental), regardless of the cause of the condition, for which medical advice, diagnosis, care, or treatment was recommended or received within the 6-month period ending on the enrollment date;

"(2) such exclusion extends for a period of not more than 12 months (or 18 months in the case of a late enrollee) after the enrollment date; and

"(3) the period of any such preexisting condition exclusion is reduced by the aggregate of the periods of creditable coverage (if any, as defined in subsection (c)(1)) applicable to the participant or beneficiary as of the enrollment date.

"(b) DEFINITIONS.—For purposes of this part—

"(1) PREEXISTING CONDITION EXCLUSION.—

"*(A) IN GENERAL.—The term 'preexisting condition exclusion' means, with respect to coverage, a limitation or exclusion of benefits relating to a condition based on the fact that the condition was present before the date of enrollment for such coverage, whether or not any medical advice, diagnosis, care, or treatment was recommended or received before such date.*

"*(B) TREATMENT OF GENETIC INFORMATION.—Genetic information shall not be treated as a condition described in subsection (a)(1) in the absence of a diagnosis of the condition related to such information.*

"*(2) ENROLLMENT DATE.—The term 'enrollment date' means, with respect to an individual covered under a group health plan or health insurance coverage, the date of enrollment of the individual in the plan or coverage or, if earlier, the first day of the waiting period for such enrollment.*

"*(3) LATE ENROLLEE.—The term 'late enrollee' means, with respect to coverage under a group health plan, a participant or beneficiary who enrolls under the plan other than during—*

"*(A) the first period in which the individual is eligible to enroll under the plan, or*

"*(B) a special enrollment period under subsection (f).*

"*(4) WAITING PERIOD.—The term 'waiting period' means, with respect to a group health plan and an individual who is a potential participant or beneficiary in the plan, the period that must pass with respect to the individual before the individual is eligible to be covered for benefits under the terms of the plan.*

"*(c) RULES RELATING TO CREDITING PREVIOUS COVERAGE.—*

"*(1) CREDITABLE COVERAGE DEFINED.—For purposes of this title, the term 'creditable coverage' means, with respect to an individual, coverage of the individual under any of the following:*

"*(A) A group health plan.*

"*(B) Health insurance coverage.*

"*(C) Part A or part B of title XVIII of the Social Security Act.*

"*(D) Title XIX of the Social Security Act, other than coverage consisting solely of benefits under section 1928.*

"*(E) Chapter 55 of title 10, United States Code.*

"*(F) A medical care program of the Indian Health Service or of a tribal organization.*

"*(G) A State health benefits risk pool.*

"*(H) A health plan offered under chapter 89 of title 5, United States Code.*

"*(I) A public health plan (as defined in regulations).*

"*(J) A health benefit plan under section 5(e) of the Peace Corps Act (22 U.S.C. 2504(e)).*

Such term does not include coverage consisting solely of coverage of excepted benefits (as defined in section 2791(c)).

"*(2) NOT COUNTING PERIODS BEFORE SIGNIFICANT BREAKS IN COVERAGE.—*

"*(A) IN GENERAL.—A period of creditable coverage shall not be counted, with respect to enrollment of an individual under a group health plan, if, after such period and before the enrollment date, there was a 63-day period during all of which the individual was not covered under any creditable coverage.*

"(B) WAITING PERIOD NOT TREATED AS A BREAK IN COVERAGE.—For purposes of subparagraph (A) and subsection (d)(4), any period that an individual is in a waiting period for any coverage under a group health plan (or for group health insurance coverage) or is in an affiliation period (as defined in subsection (g)(2)) shall not be taken into account in determining the continuous period under subparagraph (A).

"(3) METHOD OF CREDITING COVERAGE.—

"(A) STANDARD METHOD.—Except as otherwise provided under subparagraph (B), for purposes of applying subsection (a)(3), a group health plan, and a health insurance issuer offering group health insurance coverage, shall count a period of creditable coverage without regard to the specific benefits covered during the period.

"(B) ELECTION OF ALTERNATIVE METHOD.—A group health plan, or a health insurance issuer offering group health insurance, may elect to apply subsection (a)(3) based on coverage of benefits within each of several classes or categories of benefits specified in regulations rather than as provided under subparagraph (A). Such election shall be made on a uniform basis for all participants and beneficiaries. Under such election a group health plan or issuer shall count a period of creditable coverage with respect to any class or category of benefits if any level of benefits is covered within such class or category.

"(C) PLAN NOTICE.—In the case of an election with respect to a group health plan under subparagraph (B) (whether or not health insurance coverage is provided in connection with such plan), the plan shall—

"(i) prominently state in any disclosure statements concerning the plan, and state to each enrollee at the time of enrollment under the plan, that the plan has made such election, and

"(ii) include in such statements a description of the effect of this election.

"(D) ISSUER NOTICE.—In the case of an election under subparagraph (B) with respect to health insurance coverage offered by an issuer in the small or large group market, the issuer—

"(i) shall prominently state in any disclosure statements concerning the coverage, and to each employer at the time of the offer or sale of the coverage, that the issuer has made such election, and

"(ii) shall include in such statements a description of the effect of such election.

"(4) ESTABLISHMENT OF PERIOD.—Periods of creditable coverage with respect to an individual shall be established through presentation of certifications described in subsection (e) or in such other manner as may be specified in regulations.

"(d) EXCEPTIONS.—

"(1) EXCLUSION NOT APPLICABLE TO CERTAIN NEWBORNS.—Subject to paragraph (4), a group health plan, and a health insurance issuer offering group health insurance coverage, may not impose any preexisting condition exclusion in the case of an individual who, as of the last day of the 30-day period beginning with the date of birth, is covered under creditable coverage.

"(2) EXCLUSION NOT APPLICABLE TO CERTAIN ADOPTED CHILDREN.—Subject to paragraph (4), a group health plan, and a health insurance issuer offering group health insurance coverage, may not impose any preexisting condition exclusion in the case of a child who is adopted or placed for adoption before attaining 18 years of age and who, as of the last day of the 30-day period beginning on the date of the adoption or placement for adoption, is covered under creditable coverage. The previous sentence shall not apply to coverage before the date of such adoption or placement for adoption.

"(3) EXCLUSION NOT APPLICABLE TO PREGNANCY.—A group health plan, and health insurance issuer offering group health insurance coverage, may not impose any preexisting condition exclusion relating to pregnancy as a preexisting condition.

"(4) LOSS IF BREAK IN COVERAGE.—Paragraphs (1) and (2) shall no longer apply to an individual after the end of the first 63-day period during all of which the individual was not covered under any creditable coverage.

"(e) CERTIFICATIONS AND DISCLOSURE OF COVERAGE.—

"(1) REQUIREMENT FOR CERTIFICATION OF PERIOD OF CREDITABLE COVERAGE.—

"(A) IN GENERAL.—A group health plan, and a health insurance issuer offering group health insurance coverage, shall provide the certification described in subparagraph (B)—

"(i) at the time an individual ceases to be covered under the plan or otherwise becomes covered under a COBRA continuation provision,

"(ii) in the case of an individual becoming covered under such a provision, at the time the individual ceases to be covered under such provision, and

"(iii) on the request on behalf of an individual made not later than 24 months after the date of cessation of the coverage described in clause (i) or (ii), whichever is later.

The certification under clause (i) may be provided, to the extent practicable, at a time consistent with notices required under any applicable COBRA continuation provision.

"(B) CERTIFICATION.—The certification described in this subparagraph is a written certification of—

"(i) the period of creditable coverage of the individual under such plan and the coverage (if any) under such COBRA continuation provision, and

"(ii) the waiting period (if any) (and affiliation period, if applicable) imposed with respect to the individual for any coverage under such plan.

"(C) ISSUER COMPLIANCE.—To the extent that medical care under a group health plan consists of group health insurance coverage, the plan is deemed to have satisfied the certification requirement under this paragraph if the health insurance issuer offering the coverage provides for such certification in accordance with this paragraph.

"(2) DISCLOSURE OF INFORMATION ON PREVIOUS BENEFITS.—In the case of an election described in subsection (c)(3)(B) by a group health plan or health insurance issuer, if the plan or issuer enrolls an individual for coverage under the plan and the individual provides a certification of coverage of the individual under paragraph (1)—

"(A) upon request of such plan or issuer, the entity which issued the certification provided by the individual shall promptly disclose to such requesting plan or issuer information on coverage of classes and categories of health benefits available under such entity's plan or coverage, and

"(B) such entity may charge the requesting plan or issuer for the reasonable cost of disclosing such information.

"(3) REGULATIONS.—The Secretary shall establish rules to prevent an entity's failure to provide information under paragraph (1) or (2) with respect to previous coverage of an individual from adversely affecting any subsequent coverage of the individual under another group health plan or health insurance coverage.

"(f) SPECIAL ENROLLMENT PERIODS.—

"(1) INDIVIDUALS LOSING OTHER COVERAGE.—A group health plan, and a health insurance issuer offering group health insurance coverage in connection with a group health plan, shall permit an employee who is eligible, but not enrolled, for coverage under the terms of the plan (or a dependent of such an employee if the dependent is eligible, but not enrolled, for coverage under such terms) to enroll for coverage under the terms of the plan if each of the following conditions is met:

"(A) The employee or dependent was covered under a group health plan or had health insurance coverage at the time coverage was previously offered to the employee or dependent.

"(B) The employee stated in writing at such time that coverage under a group health plan or health insurance coverage was the reason for declining enrollment, but only if the plan sponsor or issuer (if applicable) required such a statement at such time and provided the employee with notice of such requirement (and the consequences of such requirement) at such time.

"(C) The employee's or dependent's coverage described in subparagraph (A)—

"(i) was under a COBRA continuation provision and the coverage under such provision was exhausted; or

"(ii) was not under such a provision and either the coverage was terminated as a result of loss of eligibility for the coverage (including as a result of legal separation, divorce, death, termination of employment, or re-

duction in the number of hours of employment) or employer contributions towards such coverage were terminated.

"(D) Under the terms of the plan, the employee requests such enrollment not later than 30 days after the date of exhaustion of coverage described in subparagraph (C)(i) or termination of coverage or employer contribution described in subparagraph (C)(ii).

"(2) FOR DEPENDENT BENEFICIARIES.—

"(A) IN GENERAL.—If—

"(i) a group health plan makes coverage available with respect to a dependent of an individual,

"(ii) the individual is a participant under the plan (or has met any waiting period applicable to becoming a participant under the plan and is eligible to be enrolled under the plan but for a failure to enroll during a previous enrollment period), and

"(iii) a person becomes such a dependent of the individual through marriage, birth, or adoption or placement for adoption,

the group health plan shall provide for a dependent special enrollment period described in subparagraph (B) during which the person (or, if not otherwise enrolled, the individual) may be enrolled under the plan as a dependent of the individual, and in the case of the birth or adoption of a child, the spouse of the individual may be enrolled as a dependent of the individual if such spouse is otherwise eligible for coverage.

"(B) DEPENDENT SPECIAL ENROLLMENT PERIOD.—A dependent special enrollment period under this subparagraph shall be a period of not less than 30 days and shall begin on the later of—

"(i) the date dependent coverage is made available, or

"(ii) the date of the marriage, birth, or adoption or placement for adoption (as the case may be) described in subparagraph (A)(iii).

"(C) NO WAITING PERIOD.—If an individual seeks to enroll a dependent during the first 30 days of such a dependent special enrollment period, the coverage of the dependent shall become effective—

"(i) in the case of marriage, not later than the first day of the first month beginning after the date the completed request for enrollment is received;

"(ii) in the case of a dependent's birth, as of the date of such birth; or

"(iii) in the case of a dependent's adoption or placement for adoption, the date of such adoption or placement for adoption.

"(g) USE OF AFFILIATION PERIOD BY HMOS AS ALTERNATIVE TO PREEXISTING CONDITION EXCLUSION.—

"(1) IN GENERAL.—A health maintenance organization which offers health insurance coverage in connection with a group health plan and which does not impose any preexisting

condition exclusion allowed under subsection (a) with respect to any particular coverage option may impose an affiliation period for such coverage option, but only if—

"(A) such period is applied uniformly without regard to any health status-related factors; and

"(B) such period does not exceed 2 months (or 3 months in the case of a late enrollee).

"(2) AFFILIATION PERIOD.—

"(A) DEFINED.—For purposes of this title, the term 'affiliation period' means a period which, under the terms of the health insurance coverage offered by the health maintenance organization, must expire before the health insurance coverage becomes effective. The organization is not required to provide health care services or benefits during such period and no premium shall be charged to the participant or beneficiary for any coverage during the period.

"(B) BEGINNING.—Such period shall begin on the enrollment date.

"(C) RUNS CONCURRENTLY WITH WAITING PERIODS.—An affiliation period under a plan shall run concurrently with any waiting period under the plan.

"(3) ALTERNATIVE METHODS.—A health maintenance organization described in paragraph (1) may use alternative methods, from those described in such paragraph, to address adverse selection as approved by the State insurance commissioner or official or officials designated by the State to enforce the requirements of this part for the State involved with respect to such issuer.

"SEC. 2702. PROHIBITING DISCRIMINATION AGAINST INDIVIDUAL PARTICIPANTS AND BENEFICIARIES BASED ON HEALTH STATUS.

"(a) IN ELIGIBILITY TO ENROLL.—

"(1) IN GENERAL.—Subject to paragraph (2), a group health plan, and a health insurance issuer offering group health insurance coverage in connection with a group health plan, may not establish rules for eligibility (including continued eligibility) of any individual to enroll under the terms of the plan based on any of the following health status-related factors in relation to the individual or a dependent of the individual:

"(A) Health status.

"(B) Medical condition (including both physical and mental illnesses).

"(C) Claims experience.

"(D) Receipt of health care.

"(E) Medical history.

"(F) Genetic information.

"(G) Evidence of insurability (including conditions arising out of acts of domestic violence).

"(H) Disability.

"(2) NO APPLICATION TO BENEFITS OR EXCLUSIONS.—To the extent consistent with section 701, paragraph (1) shall not be construed—

"(A) to require a group health plan, or group health insurance coverage, to provide particular benefits other than those provided under the terms of such plan or coverage, or

"(B) to prevent such a plan or coverage from establishing limitations or restrictions on the amount, level, extent, or nature of the benefits or coverage for similarly situated individuals enrolled in the plan or coverage.

"(3) CONSTRUCTION.—For purposes of paragraph (1), rules for eligibility to enroll under a plan include rules defining any applicable waiting periods for such enrollment.

"(b) IN PREMIUM CONTRIBUTIONS.—

"(1) IN GENERAL.—A group health plan, and a health insurance issuer offering health insurance coverage in connection with a group health plan, may not require any individual (as a condition of enrollment or continued enrollment under the plan) to pay a premium or contribution which is greater than such premium or contribution for a similarly situated individual enrolled in the plan on the basis of any health status-related factor in relation to the individual or to an individual enrolled under the plan as a dependent of the individual.

"(2) CONSTRUCTION.—Nothing in paragraph (1) shall be construed—

"(A) to restrict the amount that an employer may be charged for coverage under a group health plan; or

"(B) to prevent a group health plan, and a health insurance issuer offering group health insurance coverage, from establishing premium discounts or rebates or modifying otherwise applicable copayments or deductibles in return for adherence to programs of health promotion and disease prevention.

"SUBPART 2—PROVISIONS APPLICABLE ONLY TO HEALTH INSURANCE ISSUERS

"SEC. 2711. GUARANTEED AVAILABILITY OF COVERAGE FOR EMPLOYERS IN THE GROUP MARKET.

"(a) ISSUANCE OF COVERAGE IN THE SMALL GROUP MARKET.—

"(1) IN GENERAL.—Subject to subsections (c) through (f), each health insurance issuer that offers health insurance coverage in the small group market in a State—

"(A) must accept every small employer (as defined in section 2791(e)(4)) in the State that applies for such coverage; and

"(B) must accept for enrollment under such coverage every eligible individual (as defined in paragraph (2)) who applies for enrollment during the period in which the individual first becomes eligible to enroll under the terms of the group health plan and may not place any restriction which is inconsistent with section 2702 on an eligible individual being a participant or beneficiary.

"(2) ELIGIBLE INDIVIDUAL DEFINED.—For purposes of this section, the term 'eligible individual' means, with respect to a health insurance issuer that offers health insurance coverage to a small employer in connection with a group health plan in the

small group market, such an individual in relation to the employer as shall be determined—

"(A) in accordance with the terms of such plan,

"(B) as provided by the issuer under rules of the issuer which are uniformly applicable in a State to small employers in the small group market, and

"(C) in accordance with all applicable State laws governing such issuer and such market.

"(b) ASSURING ACCESS IN THE LARGE GROUP MARKET.—

"(1) REPORTS TO HHS.—The Secretary shall request that the chief executive officer of each State submit to the Secretary, by not later December 31, 2000, and every 3 years thereafter a report on—

"(A) the access of large employers to health insurance coverage in the State, and

"(B) the circumstances for lack of access (if any) of large employers (or one or more classes of such employers) in the State to such coverage.

"(2) TRIENNIAL REPORTS TO CONGRESS.—The Secretary, based on the reports submitted under paragraph (1) and such other information as the Secretary may use, shall prepare and submit to Congress, every 3 years, a report describing the extent to which large employers (and classes of such employers) that seek health insurance coverage in the different States are able to obtain access to such coverage. Such report shall include such recommendations as the Secretary determines to be appropriate.

"(3) GAO REPORT ON LARGE EMPLOYER ACCESS TO HEALTH INSURANCE COVERAGE.—The Comptroller General shall provide for a study of the extent to which classes of large employers in the different States are able to obtain access to health insurance coverage and the circumstances for lack of access (if any) to such coverage. The Comptroller General shall submit to Congress a report on such study not later than 18 months after the date of the enactment of this title.

"(c) SPECIAL RULES FOR NETWORK PLANS.—

"(1) IN GENERAL.—In the case of a health insurance issuer that offers health insurance coverage in the small group market through a network plan, the issuer may—

"(A) limit the employers that may apply for such coverage to those with eligible individuals who live, work, or reside in the service area for such network plan; and

"(B) within the service area of such plan, deny such coverage to such employers if the issuer has demonstrated, if required, to the applicable State authority that—

"(i) it will not have the capacity to deliver services adequately to enrollees of any additional groups because of its obligations to existing group contract holders and enrollees, and

"(ii) it is applying this paragraph uniformly to all employers without regard to the claims experience of those employers and their employees (and their dependents) or any health status-related factor relating to such employees and dependents.

"(2) 180-DAY SUSPENSION UPON DENIAL OF COVERAGE.—An issuer, upon denying health insurance coverage in any service area in accordance with paragraph (1)(B), may not offer coverage in the small group market within such service area for a period of 180 days after the date such coverage is denied.

"(d) APPLICATION OF FINANCIAL CAPACITY LIMITS.—

"(1) IN GENERAL.—A health insurance issuer may deny health insurance coverage in the small group market if the issuer has demonstrated, if required, to the applicable State authority that—

"(A) it does not have the financial reserves necessary to underwrite additional coverage; and

"(B) it is applying this paragraph uniformly to all employers in the small group market in the State consistent with applicable State law and without regard to the claims experience of those employers and their employees (and their dependents) or any health status-related factor relating to such employees and dependents.

"(2) 180-DAY SUSPENSION UPON DENIAL OF COVERAGE.—A health insurance issuer upon denying health insurance coverage in connection with group health plans in accordance with paragraph (1) in a State may not offer coverage in connection with group health plans in the small group market in the State for a period of 180 days after the date such coverage is denied or until the issuer has demonstrated to the applicable State authority, if required under applicable State law, that the issuer has sufficient financial reserves to underwrite additional coverage, whichever is later. An applicable State authority may provide for the application of this subsection on a service-area-specific basis.

"(e) EXCEPTION TO REQUIREMENT FOR FAILURE TO MEET CERTAIN MINIMUM PARTICIPATION OR CONTRIBUTION RULES.—

"(1) IN GENERAL.—Subsection (a) shall not be construed to preclude a health insurance issuer from establishing employer contribution rules or group participation rules for the offering of health insurance coverage in connection with a group health plan in the small group market, as allowed under applicable State law.

"(2) RULES DEFINED.—For purposes of paragraph (1)—

"(A) the term 'employer contribution rule' means a requirement relating to the minimum level or amount of employer contribution toward the premium for enrollment of participants and beneficiaries; and

"(B) the term 'group participation rule' means a requirement relating to the minimum number of participants or beneficiaries that must be enrolled in relation to a specified percentage or number of eligible individuals or employees of an employer.

"(f) EXCEPTION FOR COVERAGE OFFERED ONLY TO BONA FIDE ASSOCIATION MEMBERS.—Subsection (a) shall not apply to health insurance coverage offered by a health insurance issuer if such coverage is made available in the small group market only through one or more bona fide associations (as defined in section 2791(d)(3)).

"SEC. 2712. GUARANTEED RENEWABILITY OF COVERAGE FOR EMPLOYERS IN THE GROUP MARKET.

"(a) IN GENERAL.—Except as provided in this section, if a health insurance issuer offers health insurance coverage in the small or large group market in connection with a group health plan, the issuer must renew or continue in force such coverage at the option of the plan sponsor of the plan.

"(b) GENERAL EXCEPTIONS.—A health insurance issuer may nonrenew or discontinue health insurance coverage offered in connection with a group health plan in the small or large group market based only on one or more of the following:

"(1) NONPAYMENT OF PREMIUMS.—The plan sponsor has failed to pay premiums or contributions in accordance with the terms of the health insurance coverage or the issuer has not received timely premium payments.

"(2) FRAUD.—The plan sponsor has performed an act or practice that constitutes fraud or made an intentional misrepresentation of material fact under the terms of the coverage.

"(3) VIOLATION OF PARTICIPATION OR CONTRIBUTION RULES.—The plan sponsor has failed to comply with a material plan provision relating to employer contribution or group participation rules, as permitted under section 2711(e) in the case of the small group market or pursuant to applicable State law in the case of the large group market.

"(4) TERMINATION OF COVERAGE.—The issuer is ceasing to offer coverage in such market in accordance with subsection (c) and applicable State law.

"(5) MOVEMENT OUTSIDE SERVICE AREA.—In the case of a health insurance issuer that offers health insurance coverage in the market through a network plan, there is no longer any enrollee in connection with such plan who lives, resides, or works in the service area of the issuer (or in the area for which the issuer is authorized to do business) and, in the case of the small group market, the issuer would deny enrollment with respect to such plan under section 2711(c)(1)(A).

"(6) ASSOCIATION MEMBERSHIP CEASES.—In the case of health insurance coverage that is made available in the small or large group market (as the case may be) only through one or more bona fide associations, the membership of an employer in the association (on the basis of which the coverage is provided) ceases but only if such coverage is terminated under this paragraph uniformly without regard to any health status-related factor relating to any covered individual.

"(c) REQUIREMENTS FOR UNIFORM TERMINATION OF COVERAGE.—

"(1) PARTICULAR TYPE OF COVERAGE NOT OFFERED.—In any case in which an issuer decides to discontinue offering a particular type of group health insurance coverage offered in the small or large group market, coverage of such type may be discontinued by the issuer in accordance with applicable State law in such market only if—

"(A) the issuer provides notice to each plan sponsor provided coverage of this type in such market (and participants and beneficiaries covered under such coverage) of *such discontinuation at least 90 days prior to the date of the discontinuation of such coverage;*

"(B) the issuer offers to each plan sponsor provided coverage of this type in such market, the option to purchase all (or, in the case of the large group market, any) other health insurance coverage currently being offered by the issuer to a group health plan in such market; and

"(C) in exercising the option to discontinue coverage of this type and in offering the option of coverage under subparagraph (B), the issuer acts uniformly without regard to the claims experience of those sponsors or any health status-related factor relating to any participants or beneficiaries covered or new participants or beneficiaries who may become eligible for such coverage.

"(2) DISCONTINUANCE OF ALL COVERAGE.—

"(A) IN GENERAL.—In any case in which a health insurance issuer elects to discontinue offering all health insurance coverage in the small group market or the large group market, or both markets, in a State, health insurance coverage may be discontinued by the issuer only in accordance with applicable State law and if—

"(i) the issuer provides notice to the applicable State authority and to each plan sponsor (and participants and beneficiaries covered under such coverage) of such discontinuation at least 180 days prior to the date of the discontinuation of such coverage; and

"(ii) all health insurance issued or delivered for issuance in the State in such market (or markets) are discontinued and coverage under such health insurance coverage in such market (or markets) is not renewed.

"(B) PROHIBITION ON MARKET REENTRY.—In the case of a discontinuation under subparagraph (A) in a market, the issuer may not provide for the issuance of any health insurance coverage in the market and State involved during the 5-year period beginning on the date of the discontinuation of the last health insurance coverage not so renewed.

"(d) EXCEPTION FOR UNIFORM MODIFICATION OF COVERAGE.— At the time of coverage renewal, a health insurance issuer may modify the health insurance coverage for a product offered to a group health plan—

"(1) in the large group market; or

"(2) in the small group market if, for coverage that is available in such market other than only through one or more bona fide associations, such modification is consistent with State law and effective on a uniform basis among group health plans with that product.

"(e) APPLICATION TO COVERAGE OFFERED ONLY THROUGH ASSOCIATIONS.—In applying this section in the case of health insurance coverage that is made available by a health insurance issuer in the small or large group market to employers only through one or more associations, a reference to 'plan sponsor' is deemed, with respect to coverage provided to an employer member of the association, to include a reference to such employer.

"SEC. 2713. DISCLOSURE OF INFORMATION.

"*(a) DISCLOSURE OF INFORMATION BY HEALTH PLAN ISSUERS.—In connection with the offering of any health insurance coverage to a small employer, a health insurance issuer—*

"*(1) shall make a reasonable disclosure to such employer, as part of its solicitation and sales materials, of the availability of information described in subsection (b), and*

"*(2) upon request of such a small employer, provide such information.*

"*(b) INFORMATION DESCRIBED.—*

"*(1) IN GENERAL.—Subject to paragraph (3), with respect to a health insurance issuer offering health insurance coverage to a small employer, information described in this subsection is information concerning—*

"*(A) the provisions of such coverage concerning issuer's right to change premium rates and the factors that may affect changes in premium rates;*

"*(B) the provisions of such coverage relating to renewability of coverage;*

"*(C) the provisions of such coverage relating to any pre-existing condition exclusion; and*

"*(D) the benefits and premiums available under all health insurance coverage for which the employer is qualified.*

"*(2) FORM OF INFORMATION.—Information under this subsection shall be provided to small employers in a manner determined to be understandable by the average small employer, and shall be sufficient to reasonably inform small employers of their rights and obligations under the health insurance coverage.*

"*(3) EXCEPTION.—An issuer is not required under this section to disclose any information that is proprietary and trade secret information under applicable law.*

"*SUBPART 3—EXCLUSION OF PLANS; ENFORCEMENT; PREEMPTION*

"SEC. 2721. EXCLUSION OF CERTAIN PLANS.

"*(a) EXCEPTION FOR CERTAIN SMALL GROUP HEALTH PLANS.—The requirements of subparts 1 and 2 shall not apply to any group health plan (and health insurance coverage offered in connection with a group health plan) for any plan year if, on the first day of such plan year, such plan has less than 2 participants who are current employees.*

"*(b) LIMITATION ON APPLICATION OF PROVISIONS RELATING TO GROUP HEALTH PLANS.—*

"*(1) IN GENERAL.—The requirements of subparts 1 and 2 shall apply with respect to group health plans only—*

"*(A) subject to paragraph (2), in the case of a plan that is a nonfederal governmental plan, and*

"*(B) with respect to health insurance coverage offered in connection with a group health plan (including such a plan that is a church plan or a governmental plan).*

"*(2) TREATMENT OF NONFEDERAL GOVERNMENTAL PLANS.—*

"*(A) ELECTION TO BE EXCLUDED.—If the plan sponsor of a nonfederal governmental plan which is a group health plan to which the provisions of subparts 1 and 2 otherwise*

34

apply makes an election under this subparagraph (in such form and manner as the Secretary may by regulations prescribe), then the requirements of such subparts insofar as they apply directly to group health plans (and not merely to group health insurance coverage) shall not apply to such governmental plans for such period except as provided in this paragraph.

"(B) PERIOD OF ELECTION.—An election under subparagraph (A) shall apply—

"(i) for a single specified plan year, or

"(ii) in the case of a plan provided pursuant to a collective bargaining agreement, for the term of such agreement.

An election under clause (i) may be extended through subsequent elections under this paragraph.

"(C) NOTICE TO ENROLLEES.—Under such an election, the plan shall provide for—

"(i) notice to enrollees (on an annual basis and at the time of enrollment under the plan) of the fact and consequences of such election, and

"(ii) certification and disclosure of creditable coverage under the plan with respect to enrollees in accordance with section 2701(e).

"(c) EXCEPTION FOR CERTAIN BENEFITS.—The requirements of subparts 1 and 2 shall not apply to any group health plan (or group health insurance coverage) in relation to its provision of excepted benefits described in section 2791(c)(1).

"(d) EXCEPTION FOR CERTAIN BENEFITS IF CERTAIN CONDITIONS MET.—

"(1) LIMITED, EXCEPTED BENEFITS.—The requirements of subparts 1 and 2 shall not apply to any group health plan (and group health insurance coverage offered in connection with a group health plan) in relation to its provision of excepted benefits described in section 2791(c)(2) if the benefits—

"(A) are provided under a separate policy, certificate, or contract of insurance; or

"(B) are otherwise not an integral part of the plan.

"(2) NONCOORDINATED, EXCEPTED BENEFITS.—The requirements of subparts 1 and 2 shall not apply to any group health plan (and group health insurance coverage offered in connection with a group health plan) in relation to its provision of excepted benefits described in section 2791(c)(3) if all of the following conditions are met:

"(A) The benefits are provided under a separate policy, certificate, or contract of insurance.

"(B) There is no coordination between the provision of such benefits and any exclusion of benefits under any group health plan maintained by the same plan sponsor.

"(C) Such benefits are paid with respect to an event without regard to whether benefits are provided with respect to such an event under any group health plan maintained by the same plan sponsor.

"(3) SUPPLEMENTAL EXCEPTED BENEFITS.—The requirements of this part shall not apply to any group health plan

(and group health insurance coverage) in relation to its provision of excepted benefits described in section 27971(c)(4) if the benefits are provided under a separate policy, certificate, or contract of insurance.

"(e) TREATMENT OF PARTNERSHIPS.—For purposes of this part—

"(1) TREATMENT AS A GROUP HEALTH PLAN.—Any plan, fund, or program which would not be (but for this subsection) an employee welfare benefit plan and which is established or maintained by a partnership, to the extent that such plan, fund, or program provides medical care (including items and services paid for as medical care) to present or former partners in the partnership or to their dependents (as defined under the terms of the plan, fund, or program), directly or through insurance, reimbursement, or otherwise, shall be treated (subject to paragraph (2)) as an employee welfare benefit plan which is a group health plan.

"(2) EMPLOYER.—In the case of a group health plan, the term 'employer' also includes the partnership in relation to any partner.

"(3) PARTICIPANTS OF GROUP HEALTH PLANS.—In the case of a group health plan, the term 'participant' also includes—

"(A) in connection with a group health plan maintained by a partnership, an individual who is a partner in relation to the partnership, or

"(B) in connection with a group health plan maintained by a self-employed individual (under which one or more employees are participants), the self-employed individual,

if such individual is, or may become, eligible to receive a benefit under the plan or such individual's beneficiaries may be eligible to receive any such benefit.

"SEC. 2722. ENFORCEMENT.

"(a) STATE ENFORCEMENT.—

"(1) STATE AUTHORITY.—Subject to section 2723, each State may require that health insurance issuers that issue, sell, renew, or offer health insurance coverage in the State in the small or large group markets meet the requirements of this part with respect to such issuers.

"(2) FAILURE TO IMPLEMENT PROVISIONS.—In the case of a determination by the Secretary that a State has failed to substantially enforce a provision (or provisions) in this part with respect to health insurance issuers in the State, the Secretary shall enforce such provision (or provisions) under subsection (b) insofar as they relate to the issuance, sale, renewal, and offering of health insurance coverage in connection with group health plans in such State.

"(b) SECRETARIAL ENFORCEMENT AUTHORITY.—

"(1) LIMITATION.—The provisions of this subsection shall apply to enforcement of a provision (or provisions) of this part only—

"(A) as provided under subsection (a)(2); and

"(B) with respect to group health plans that are non-federal governmental plans.

"(2) IMPOSITION OF PENALTIES.—In the cases described in paragraph (1)—

"(A) IN GENERAL.—Subject to the succeeding provisions of this subsection, any nonfederal governmental plan that is a group health plan and any health insurance issuer that fails to meet a provision of this part applicable to such plan or issuer is subject to a civil money penalty under this subsection.

"(B) LIABILITY FOR PENALTY.—In the case of a failure by—

"(i) a health insurance issuer, the issuer is liable for such penalty, or

"(ii) a group health plan that is a nonfederal governmental plan which is—

"(I) sponsored by 2 or more employers, the plan is liable for such penalty, or

"(II) not so sponsored, the employer is liable for such penalty.

"(C) AMOUNT OF PENALTY.—

"(i) IN GENERAL.—The maximum amount of penalty imposed under this paragraph is $100 for each day for each individual with respect to which such a failure occurs.

"(ii) CONSIDERATIONS IN IMPOSITION.—In determining the amount of any penalty to be assessed under this paragraph, the Secretary shall take into account the previous record of compliance of the entity being assessed with the applicable provisions of this part and the gravity of the violation.

"(iii) LIMITATIONS.—

"(I) PENALTY NOT TO APPLY WHERE FAILURE NOT DISCOVERED EXERCISING REASONABLE DILIGENCE.—No civil money penalty shall be imposed under this paragraph on any failure during any period for which it is established to the satisfaction of the Secretary that none of the entities against whom the penalty would be imposed knew, or exercising reasonable diligence would have known, that such failure existed.

"(II) PENALTY NOT TO APPLY TO FAILURES CORRECTED WITHIN 30 DAYS.—No civil money penalty shall be imposed under this paragraph on any failure if such failure was due to reasonable cause and not to willful neglect, and such failure is corrected during the 30-day period beginning on the first day any of the entities against whom the penalty would be imposed knew, or exercising reasonable diligence would have known, that such failure existed.

"(D) ADMINISTRATIVE REVIEW.—

"(i) OPPORTUNITY FOR HEARING.—The entity assessed shall be afforded an opportunity for hearing by the Secretary upon request made within 30 days after the date of the issuance of a notice of assessment. In

such hearing the decision shall be made on the record pursuant to section 554 of title 5, United States Code. If no hearing is requested, the assessment shall constitute a final and unappealable order.

"(ii) HEARING PROCEDURE.—If a hearing is requested, the initial agency decision shall be made by an administrative law judge, and such decision shall become the final order unless the Secretary modifies or vacates the decision. Notice of intent to modify or vacate the decision of the administrative law judge shall be issued to the parties within 30 days after the date of the decision of the judge. A final order which takes effect under this paragraph shall be subject to review only as provided under subparagraph (E).

"(E) JUDICIAL REVIEW.—

"(i) FILING OF ACTION FOR REVIEW.—Any entity against whom an order imposing a civil money penalty has been entered after an agency hearing under this paragraph may obtain review by the United States district court for any district in which such entity is located or the United States District Court for the District of Columbia by filing a notice of appeal in such court within 30 days from the date of such order, and simultaneously sending a copy of such notice by registered mail to the Secretary.

"(ii) CERTIFICATION OF ADMINISTRATIVE RECORD.—The Secretary shall promptly certify and file in such court the record upon which the penalty was imposed.

"(iii) STANDARD FOR REVIEW.—The findings of the Secretary shall be set aside only if found to be unsupported by substantial evidence as provided by section 706(2)(E) of title 5, United States Code.

"(iv) APPEAL.—Any final decision, order, or judgment of the district court concerning such review shall be subject to appeal as provided in chapter 83 of title 28 of such Code.

"(F) FAILURE TO PAY ASSESSMENT; MAINTENANCE OF ACTION.—

"(i) FAILURE TO PAY ASSESSMENT.—If any entity fails to pay an assessment after it has become a final and unappealable order, or after the court has entered final judgment in favor of the Secretary, the Secretary shall refer the matter to the Attorney General who shall recover the amount assessed by action in the appropriate United States district court.

"(ii) NONREVIEWABILITY.—In such action the validity and appropriateness of the final order imposing the penalty shall not be subject to review.

"(G) PAYMENT OF PENALTIES.—Except as otherwise provided, penalties collected under this paragraph shall be paid to the Secretary (or other officer) imposing the penalty and shall be available without appropriation and until expended for the purpose of enforcing the provisions with respect to which the penalty was imposed.

"SEC. 2723. PREEMPTION; STATE FLEXIBILITY; CONSTRUCTION.

"(a) CONTINUED APPLICABILITY OF STATE LAW WITH RESPECT TO HEALTH INSURANCE ISSUERS.—

"(1) IN GENERAL.—Subject to paragraph (2) and except as provided in subsection (b), this part and part C insofar as it relates to this part shall not be construed to supersede any provision of State law which establishes, implements, or continues in effect any standard or requirement solely relating to health insurance issuers in connection with group health insurance coverage except to the extent that such standard or requirement prevents the application of a requirement of this part.

"(2) CONTINUED PREEMPTION WITH RESPECT TO GROUP HEALTH PLANS.—Nothing in this part shall be construed to affect or modify the provisions of section 514 of the Employee Retirement Income Security Act of 1974 with respect to group health plans.

"(b) SPECIAL RULES IN CASE OF PORTABILITY REQUIREMENTS.—

"(1) IN GENERAL.—Subject to paragraph (2), the provisions of this part relating to health insurance coverage offered by a health insurance issuer supersede any provision of State law which establishes, implements, or continues in effect a standard or requirement applicable to imposition of a preexisting condition exclusion specifically governed by section 701 which differs from the standards or requirements specified in such section.

"(2) EXCEPTIONS.—Only in relation to health insurance coverage offered by a health insurance issuer, the provisions of this part do not supersede any provision of State law to the extent that such provision—

"(i) substitutes for the reference to '6-month period' in section 2701(a)(1) a reference to any shorter period of time;

"(ii) substitutes for the reference to '12 months' and '18 months' in section 2701(a)(2) a reference to any shorter period of time;

"(iii) substitutes for the references to '63' days in sections 2701(c)(2)(A) and 2701(d)(4)(A) a reference to any greater number of days;

"(iv) substitutes for the reference to '30-day period' in sections 2701(b)(2) and 2701(d)(1) a reference to any greater period;

"(v) prohibits the imposition of any preexisting condition exclusion in cases not described in section 2701(d) or expands the exceptions described in such section;

"(vi) requires special enrollment periods in addition to those required under section 2701(f); or

"(vii) reduces the maximum period permitted in an affiliation period under section 2701(g)(1)(B).

"(c) RULES OF CONSTRUCTION.—Nothing in this part shall be construed as requiring a group health plan or health insurance coverage to provide specific benefits under the terms of such plan or coverage.

"(d) DEFINITIONS.—For purposes of this section—

"(1) STATE LAW.—The term 'State law' includes all laws, decisions, rules, regulations, or other State action having the effect of law, of any State. A law of the United States applicable

only to the District of Columbia shall be treated as a State law rather than a law of the United States.

"(2) STATE.—The term 'State' includes a State (including the Northern Mariana Islands), any political subdivisions of a State or such Islands, or any agency or instrumentality of either.

"PART C—DEFINITIONS; MISCELLANEOUS PROVISIONS

"SEC. 2791. DEFINITIONS.

"(a) GROUP HEALTH PLAN.—

"(1) DEFINITION.—The term 'group health plan' means an employee welfare benefit plan (as defined in section 3(1) of the Employee Retirement Income Security Act of 1974) to the extent that the plan provides medical care (as defined in paragraph (2)) and including items and services paid for as medical care) to employees or their dependents (as defined under the terms of the plan) directly or through insurance, reimbursement, or otherwise.

"(2) MEDICAL CARE.—The term 'medical care' means amounts paid for—

"(A) the diagnosis, cure, mitigation, treatment, or prevention of disease, or amounts paid for the purpose of affecting any structure or function of the body,

"(B) amounts paid for transportation primarily for and essential to medical care referred to in subparagraph (A), and

"(C) amounts paid for insurance covering medical care referred to in subparagraphs (A) and (B).

"(3) TREATMENT OF CERTAIN PLANS AS GROUP HEALTH PLAN FOR NOTICE PROVISION.—A program under which creditable coverage described in subparagraph (C), (D), (E), or (F) of section 2701(c)(1) is provided shall be treated as a group health plan for purposes of applying section 2701(e).

"(b) DEFINITIONS RELATING TO HEALTH INSURANCE.—

"(1) HEALTH INSURANCE COVERAGE.—The term 'health insurance coverage' means benefits consisting of medical care (provided directly, through insurance or reimbursement, or otherwise and including items and services paid for as medical care) under any hospital or medical service policy or certificate, hospital or medical service plan contract, or health maintenance organization contract offered by a health insurance issuer.

"(2) HEALTH INSURANCE ISSUER.—The term 'health insurance issuer' means an insurance company, insurance service, or insurance organization (including a health maintenance organization, as defined in paragraph (3)) which is licensed to engage in the business of insurance in a State and which is subject to State law which regulates insurance (within the meaning of section 514(b)(2) of the Employee Retirement Income Security Act of 1974). Such term does not include a group health plan.

"(3) HEALTH MAINTENANCE ORGANIZATION.—The term 'health maintenance organization' means—

"(A) a Federally qualified health maintenance organization (as defined in section 1301(a)),

"(B) an organization recognized under State law as a health maintenance organization, or

"(C) a similar organization regulated under State law for solvency in the same manner and to the same extent as such a health maintenance organization.

"(4) GROUP HEALTH INSURANCE COVERAGE.—The term 'group health insurance coverage' means, in connection with a group health plan, health insurance coverage offered in connection with such plan.

"(5) INDIVIDUAL HEALTH INSURANCE COVERAGE.—The term 'individual health insurance coverage' means health insurance coverage offered to individuals in the individual market, but does not include short-term limited duration insurance.

"(c) EXCEPTED BENEFITS.—For purposes of this title, the term 'excepted benefits' means benefits under one or more (or any combination thereof) of the following:

"(1) BENEFITS NOT SUBJECT TO REQUIREMENTS.—

"(A) Coverage only for accident, or disability income insurance, or any combination thereof.

"(B) Coverage issued as a supplement to liability insurance.

"(C) Liability insurance, including general liability insurance and automobile liability insurance.

"(D) Workers' compensation or similar insurance.

"(E) Automobile medical payment insurance.

"(F) Credit-only insurance.

"(G) Coverage for on-site medical clinics.

"(H) Other similar insurance coverage, specified in regulations, under which benefits for medical care are secondary or incidental to other insurance benefits.

"(2) BENEFITS NOT SUBJECT TO REQUIREMENTS IF OFFERED SEPARATELY.—

"(A) Limited scope dental or vision benefits.

"(B) Benefits for long-term care, nursing home care, home health care, community-based care, or any combination thereof.

"(C) Such other similar, limited benefits as are specified in regulations.

"(3) BENEFITS NOT SUBJECT TO REQUIREMENTS IF OFFERED AS INDEPENDENT, NONCOORDINATED BENEFITS.—

"(A) Coverage only for a specified disease or illness.

"(B) Hospital indemnity or other fixed indemnity insurance.

"(4) BENEFITS NOT SUBJECT TO REQUIREMENTS IF OFFERED AS SEPARATE INSURANCE POLICY.—Medicare supplemental health insurance (as defined under section 1882(g)(1) of the Social Security Act), coverage supplemental to the coverage provided under chapter 55 of title 10, United States Code, and similar supplemental coverage provided to coverage under a group health plan.

"(d) OTHER DEFINITIONS.—

"(1) APPLICABLE STATE AUTHORITY.—The term 'applicable State authority' means, with respect to a health insurance issuer in a State, the State insurance commissioner or official or

officials designated by the State to enforce the requirements of this title for the State involved with respect to such issuer.

"(2) BENEFICIARY.—The term 'beneficiary' has the meaning given such term under section 3(8) of the Employee Retirement Income Security Act of 1974.

"(3) BONA FIDE ASSOCIATION.—The term 'bona fide association' means, with respect to health insurance coverage offered in a State, an association which—

"(A) has been actively in existence for at least 5 years;

"(B) has been formed and maintained in good faith for purposes other than obtaining insurance;

"(C) does not condition membership in the association on any health status-related factor relating to an individual (including an employee of an employer or a dependent of an employee);

"(D) makes health insurance coverage offered through the association available to all members regardless of any health status-related factor relating to such members (or individuals eligible for coverage through a member);

"(E) does not make health insurance coverage offered through the association available other than in connection with a member of the association; and

"(F) meets such additional requirements as may be imposed under State law.

"(4) COBRA CONTINUATION PROVISION.—The term 'COBRA continuation provision' means any of the following:

"(A) Section 4980B of the Internal Revenue Code of 1986, other than subsection (f)(1) of such section insofar as it relates to pediatric vaccines.

"(B) Part 6 of subtitle B of title I of the Employee Retirement Income Security Act of 1974, other than section 609 of such Act.

"(C) Title XXII of this Act.

"(5) EMPLOYEE.—The term 'employee' has the meaning given such term under section 3(6) of the Employee Retirement Income Security Act of 1974.

"(6) EMPLOYER.—The term 'employer' has the meaning given such term under section 3(5) of the Employee Retirement Income Security Act of 1974, except that such term shall include only employers of two or more employees.

"(7) CHURCH PLAN.—The term 'church plan' has the meaning given such term under section 3(33) of the Employee Retirement Income Security Act of 1974.

"(8) GOVERNMENTAL PLAN.—(A) The term 'governmental plan' has the meaning given such term under section 3(32) of the Employee Retirement Income Security Act of 1974 and any Federal governmental plan.

"(B) FEDERAL GOVERNMENTAL PLAN.—The term 'Federal governmental plan' means a governmental plan established or maintained for its employees by the Government of the United States or by any agency or instrumentality of such Government.

"(C) NONFEDERAL GOVERNMENTAL PLAN.—The term 'nonfederal governmental plan' means a governmental plan that is not a Federal governmental plan.

"(9) HEALTH STATUS-RELATED FACTOR.—The term 'health status-related factor' means any of the factors described in section 2702(a)(1).

"(10) NETWORK PLAN.—The term 'network plan' means health insurance coverage of a health insurance issuer under which the financing and delivery of medical care (including items and services paid for as medical care) are provided, in whole or in part, through a defined set of providers under contract with the issuer.

"(11) PARTICIPANT.—The term 'participant' has the meaning given such term under section 3(7) of the Employee Retirement Income Security Act of 1974.

"(12) PLACED FOR ADOPTION DEFINED.—The term 'placement', or being 'placed', for adoption, in connection with any placement for adoption of a child with any person, means the assumption and retention by such person of a legal obligation for total or partial support of such child in anticipation of adoption of such child. The child's placement with such person terminates upon the termination of such legal obligation.

"(13) PLAN SPONSOR.—The term 'plan sponsor' has the meaning given such term under section 3(16)(B) of the Employee Retirement Income Security Act of 1974.

"(14) STATE.—The term 'State' means each of the several States, the District of Columbia, Puerto Rico, the Virgin Islands, Guam, American Samoa, and the Northern Mariana Islands.

"(e) DEFINITIONS RELATING TO MARKETS AND SMALL EMPLOYERS.—For purposes of this title:

"(1) INDIVIDUAL MARKET.—

"(A) IN GENERAL.—The term 'individual market' means the market for health insurance coverage offered to individuals other than in connection with a group health plan.

"(B) TREATMENT OF VERY SMALL GROUPS.—

"(i) IN GENERAL.—Subject to clause (ii), such terms includes coverage offered in connection with a group health plan that has fewer than two participants as current employees on the first day of the plan year.

"(ii) STATE EXCEPTION.—Clause (i) shall not apply in the case of a State that elects to regulate the coverage described in such clause as coverage in the small group market.

"(2) LARGE EMPLOYER.—The term 'large employer' means, in connection with a group health plan with respect to a calendar year and a plan year, an employer who employed an average of at least 51 employees on business days during the preceding calendar year and who employs at least 2 employees on the first day of the plan year.

"(3) LARGE GROUP MARKET.—The term 'large group market' means the health insurance market under which individuals obtain health insurance coverage (directly or through any arrangement) on behalf of themselves (and their dependents) through a group health plan maintained by a large employer.

"(4) SMALL EMPLOYER.—The term 'small employer' means, in connection with a group health plan with respect to a calendar year and a plan year, an employer who employed an average of at least 2 but not more than 50 employees on business days during the preceding calendar year and who employs at least 2 employees on the first day of the plan year.

"(5) SMALL GROUP MARKET.—The term 'small group market' means the health insurance market under which individuals obtain health insurance coverage (directly or through any arrangement) on behalf of themselves (and their dependents) through a group health plan maintained by a small employer.

"(6) APPLICATION OF CERTAIN RULES IN DETERMINATION OF EMPLOYER SIZE.—For purposes of this subsection—

"(A) APPLICATION OF AGGREGATION RULE FOR EMPLOYERS.—all persons treated as a single employer under subsection (b), (c), (m), or (o) of section 414 of the Internal Revenue Code of 1986 shall be treated as 1 employer.

"(B) EMPLOYERS NOT IN EXISTENCE IN PRECEDING YEAR.—In the case of an employer which was not in existence throughout the preceding calendar year, the determination of whether such employer is a small or large employer shall be based on the average number of employees that it is reasonably expected such employer will employ on business days in the current calendar year.

"(C) PREDECESSORS.—Any reference in this subsection to an employer shall include a reference to any predecessor of such employer.

"SEC. 2792. REGULATIONS.

"The Secretary, consistent with section 104 of the Health Care Portability and Accountability Act of 1996, may promulgate such regulations as may be necessary or appropriate to carry out the provisions of this title. The Secretary may promulgate any interim final rules as the Secretary determines are appropriate to carry out this title.".

(b) APPLICATION OF RULES BY CERTAIN HEALTH MAINTENANCE ORGANIZATIONS.—Section 1301 of such Act (42 U.S.C. 300e) is amended by adding at the end the following new subsection:

"(d) An organization that offers health benefits coverage shall not be considered as failing to meet the requirements of this section notwithstanding that it provides, with respect to coverage offered in connection with a group health plan in the small or large group market (as defined in section 2791(e)), an affiliation period consistent with the provisions of section 2701(g).".

(c) EFFECTIVE DATE.—

(1) IN GENERAL.—Except as provided in this subsection, part A of title XXVII of the Public Health Service Act (as added by subsection (a)) shall apply with respect to group health plans, and health insurance coverage offered in connection with group health plans, for plan years beginning after June 30, 1997.

(2) DETERMINATION OF CREDITABLE COVERAGE.—

(A) PERIOD OF COVERAGE.—

(i) IN GENERAL.—Subject to clause (ii), no period before July 1, 1996, shall be taken into account under part A of title XXVII of the Public Health Service Act *(as added by this section) in determining creditable coverage.*

(ii) SPECIAL RULE FOR CERTAIN PERIODS.—The Secretary of Health and Human Services, consistent with section 104, shall provide for a process whereby individuals who need to establish creditable coverage for periods before July 1, 1996, and who would have such coverage credited but for clause (i) may be given credit for creditable coverage for such periods through the presentation of documents or other means.

(B) CERTIFICATIONS, ETC.—

(i) IN GENERAL.—Subject to clauses (ii) and (iii), subsection (e) of section 2701 of the Public Health Service Act (as added by this section) shall apply to events occurring after June 30, 1996.

(ii) NO CERTIFICATION REQUIRED TO BE PROVIDED BEFORE JUNE 1, 1997.—In no case is a certification required to be provided under such subsection before June 1, 1997.

(iii) CERTIFICATION ONLY ON WRITTEN REQUEST FOR EVENTS OCCURRING BEFORE OCTOBER 1, 1996.—In the case of an event occurring after June 30, 1996, and before October 1, 1996, a certification is not required to be provided under such subsection unless an individual (with respect to whom the certification is otherwise required to be made) requests such certification in writing.

(C) TRANSITIONAL RULE.—In the case of an individual who seeks to establish creditable coverage for any period for which certification is not required because it relates to an event occurring before June 30, 1996—

(i) the individual may present other credible evidence of such coverage in order to establish the period of creditable coverage; and

(ii) a group health plan and a health insurance issuer shall not be subject to any penalty or enforcement action with respect to the plan's or issuer's crediting (or not crediting) such coverage if the plan or issuer has sought to comply in good faith with the applicable requirements under the amendments made by this section.

(3) SPECIAL RULE FOR COLLECTIVE BARGAINING AGREEMENTS.—Except as provided in paragraph (2)(B), in the case of a group health plan maintained pursuant to 1 or more collective bargaining agreements between employee representatives and one or more employers ratified before the date of the enactment of this Act, part A of title XXVII of the Public Health Service Act (other than section 2701(e) thereof) shall not apply to plan years beginning before the later of—

(A) the date on which the last of the collective bargaining agreements relating to the plan terminates (determined without regard to any extension thereof agreed to after the date of the enactment of this Act), or

(B) July 1, 1997.

For purposes of subparagraph (A), any plan amendment made pursuant to a collective bargaining agreement relating to the plan which amends the plan solely to conform to any requirement of such part shall not be treated as a termination of such collective bargaining agreement.

(4) TIMELY REGULATIONS.—The Secretary of Health and Human Services, consistent with section 104, shall first issue by not later than April 1, 1997, such regulations as may be necessary to carry out the amendments made by this section and section 111.

(5) LIMITATION ON ACTIONS.—No enforcement action shall be taken, pursuant to the amendments made by this section, against a group health plan or health insurance issuer with respect to a violation of a requirement imposed by such amendments before January 1, 1998, or, if later, the date of issuance of regulations referred to in paragraph (4), if the plan or issuer has sought to comply in good faith with such requirements.

(d) MISCELLANEOUS CORRECTION.—Section 2208(1) of the Public Health Service Act (42 U.S.C. 300bb–8(1)) is amended by striking "section 162(i)(2)" and inserting "5000(b)".

SEC. 103. REFERENCE TO IMPLEMENTATION THROUGH THE INTERNAL REVENUE CODE OF 1986.

For provisions amending the Internal Revenue Code of 1986 to provide for application and enforcement of rules for group health plans similar to those provided under the amendments made by section 101(a), see section 401.

SEC. 104. ASSURING COORDINATION.

The Secretary of the Treasury, the Secretary of Health and Human Services, and the Secretary of Labor shall ensure, through the execution of an interagency memorandum of understanding among such Secretaries, that—

(1) regulations, rulings, and interpretations issued by such Secretaries relating to the same matter over which two or more such Secretaries have responsibility under this subtitle (and the amendments made by this subtitle and section 401) are administered so as to have the same effect at all times; and

(2) coordination of policies relating to enforcing the same requirements through such Secretaries in order to have a coordinated enforcement strategy that avoids duplication of enforcement efforts and assigns priorities in enforcement.

Subtitle B—Individual Market Rules

SEC. 111. AMENDMENT TO PUBLIC HEALTH SERVICE ACT.

(a) IN GENERAL.—Title XXVII of the Public Health Service Act, as added by section 102(a) of this Act, is amended by inserting after part A the following new part:

"PART B—INDIVIDUAL MARKET RULES

"SEC. 2741. GUARANTEED AVAILABILITY OF INDIVIDUAL HEALTH INSURANCE COVERAGE TO CERTAIN INDIVIDUALS WITH PRIOR GROUP COVERAGE.

"(a) GUARANTEED AVAILABILITY.—

"(1) IN GENERAL.—Subject to the succeeding subsections of this section and section 2744, each health insurance issuer that offers health insurance coverage (as defined in section 2791(b)(1)) in the individual market in a State may not, with respect to an eligible individual (as defined in subsection (b)) desiring to enroll in individual health insurance coverage—

"(A) decline to offer such coverage to, or deny enrollment of, such individual; or

"(B) impose any preexisting condition exclusion (as defined in section 2701(b)(1)(A)) with respect to such coverage.

"(2) SUBSTITUTION BY STATE OF ACCEPTABLE ALTERNATIVE MECHANISM.—The requirement of paragraph (1) shall not apply to health insurance coverage offered in the individual market in a State in which the State is implementing an acceptable alternative mechanism under section 2744.

"(b) ELIGIBLE INDIVIDUAL DEFINED.—In this part, the term 'eligible individual' means an individual—

"(1)(A) for whom, as of the date on which the individual seeks coverage under this section, the aggregate of the periods of creditable coverage (as defined in section 2701(c)) is 18 or more months and (B) whose most recent prior creditable coverage was under a group health plan, governmental plan, or church plan (or health insurance coverage offered in connection with any such plan);

"(2) who is not eligible for coverage under (A) a group health plan, (B) part A or part B of title XVIII of the Social Security Act, or (C) a State plan under title XIX of such Act (or any successor program), and does not have other health insurance coverage;

"(3) with respect to whom the most recent coverage within the coverage period described in paragraph (1)(A) was not terminated based on a factor described in paragraph (1) or (2) of section 2712(b) (relating to nonpayment of premiums or fraud);

"(4) if the individual had been offered the option of continuation coverage under a COBRA continuation provision or under a similar State program, who elected such coverage; and

"(5) who, if the individual elected such continuation coverage, has exhausted such continuation coverage under such provision or program.

"(c) ALTERNATIVE COVERAGE PERMITTED WHERE NO STATE MECHANISM.—

"(1) IN GENERAL.—In the case of health insurance coverage offered in the individual market in a State in which the State is not implementing an acceptable alternative mechanism under section 2744, the health insurance issuer may elect to limit the coverage offered under subsection (a) so long as it offers at least two different policy forms of health insurance coverage both of which—

"(A) are designed for, made generally available to, and actively marketed to, and enroll both eligible and other individuals by the issuer; and

"(B) meet the requirement of paragraph (2) or (3), as elected by the issuer.

For purposes of this subsection, policy forms which have different cost-sharing arrangements or different riders shall be considered to be different policy forms.

"(2) CHOICE OF MOST POPULAR POLICY FORMS.—The requirement of this paragraph is met, for health insurance coverage policy forms offered by an issuer in the individual market, if the issuer offers the policy forms for individual health insurance coverage with the largest, and next to largest, premium volume of all such policy forms offered by the issuer in the State or applicable marketing or service area (as may be prescribed in regulation) by the issuer in the individual market in the period involved.

"(3) CHOICE OF 2 POLICY FORMS WITH REPRESENTATIVE COVERAGE.—

"(A) IN GENERAL.—The requirement of this paragraph is met, for health insurance coverage policy forms offered by an issuer in the individual market, if the issuer offers a lower-level coverage policy form (as defined in subparagraph (B)) and a higher-level coverage policy form (as defined in subparagraph (C)) each of which includes benefits substantially similar to other individual health insurance coverage offered by the issuer in that State and each of which is covered under a method described in section 2744(c)(3)(A) (relating to risk adjustment, risk spreading, or financial subsidization).

"(B) LOWER-LEVEL OF COVERAGE DESCRIBED.—A policy form is described in this subparagraph if the actuarial value of the benefits under the coverage is at least 85 percent but not greater than 100 percent of a weighted average (described in subparagraph (D)).

"(C) HIGHER-LEVEL OF COVERAGE DESCRIBED.—A policy form is described in this subparagraph if—

"(i) the actuarial value of the benefits under the coverage is at least 15 percent greater than the actuarial value of the coverage described in subparagraph (B) offered by the issuer in the area involved; and

"(ii) the actuarial value of the benefits under the coverage is at least 100 percent but not greater than 120 percent of a weighted average (described in subparagraph (D)).

"(D) WEIGHTED AVERAGE.—For purposes of this paragraph, the weighted average described in this subparagraph is the average actuarial value of the benefits provided by all the health insurance coverage issued (as elected by the issuer) either by that issuer or by all issuers in the State in the individual market during the previous year (not including coverage issued under this section), weighted by enrollment for the different coverage.

"(4) ELECTION.—The issuer elections under this subsection shall apply uniformly to all eligible individuals in the State for that issuer. Such an election shall be effective for policies offered during a period of not shorter than 2 years.

"(5) ASSUMPTIONS.—For purposes of paragraph (3), the actuarial value of benefits provided under individual health in-

surance coverage shall be calculated based on a standardized population and a set of standardized utilization and cost factors.

"(d) SPECIAL RULES FOR NETWORK PLANS.—

"(1) IN GENERAL.—In the case of a health insurance issuer that offers health insurance coverage in the individual market through a network plan, the issuer may—

"(A) limit the individuals who may be enrolled under such coverage to those who live, reside, or work within the service area for such network plan; and

"(B) within the service area of such plan, deny such coverage to such individuals if the issuer has demonstrated, if required, to the applicable State authority that—

"(i) it will not have the capacity to deliver services adequately to additional individual enrollees because of its obligations to existing group contract holders and enrollees and individual enrollees, and

"(ii) it is applying this paragraph uniformly to individuals without regard to any health status-related factor of such individuals and without regard to whether the individuals are eligible individuals.

"(2) 180-DAY SUSPENSION UPON DENIAL OF COVERAGE.—An issuer, upon denying health insurance coverage in any service area in accordance with paragraph (1)(B), may not offer coverage in the individual market within such service area for a period of 180 days after such coverage is denied.

"(e) APPLICATION OF FINANCIAL CAPACITY LIMITS.—

"(1) IN GENERAL.—A health insurance issuer may deny health insurance coverage in the individual market to an eligible individual if the issuer has demonstrated, if required, to the applicable State authority that—

"(A) it does not have the financial reserves necessary to underwrite additional coverage; and

"(B) it is applying this paragraph uniformly to all individuals in the individual market in the State consistent with applicable State law and without regard to any health status-related factor of such individuals and without regard to whether the individuals are eligible individuals.

"(2) 180-DAY SUSPENSION UPON DENIAL OF COVERAGE.—An issuer upon denying individual health insurance coverage in any service area in accordance with paragraph (1) may not offer such coverage in the individual market within such service area for a period of 180 days after the date such coverage is denied or until the issuer has demonstrated, if required under applicable State law, to the applicable State authority that the issuer has sufficient financial reserves to underwrite additional coverage, whichever is later. A State may provide for the application of this paragraph on a service-area-specific basis.

"(e) MARKET REQUIREMENTS.—

"(1) IN GENERAL.—The provisions of subsection (a) shall not be construed to require that a health insurance issuer offering health insurance coverage only in connection with group health plans or through one or more bona fide associations, or both, offer such health insurance coverage in the individual market.

"(2) CONVERSION POLICIES.—A health insurance issuer offering health insurance coverage in connection with group health plans under this title shall not be deemed to be a health insurance issuer offering individual health insurance coverage solely because such issuer offers a conversion policy.

"(f) CONSTRUCTION.—Nothing in this section shall be construed—

"(1) to restrict the amount of the premium rates that an issuer may charge an individual for health insurance coverage provided in the individual market under applicable State law; or

"(2) to prevent a health insurance issuer offering health insurance coverage in the individual market from establishing premium discounts or rebates or modifying otherwise applicable copayments or deductibles in return for adherence to programs of health promotion and disease prevention.

"SEC. 2742. GUARANTEED RENEWABILITY OF INDIVIDUAL HEALTH INSURANCE COVERAGE.

"(a) IN GENERAL.—Except as provided in this section, a health insurance issuer that provides individual health insurance coverage to an individual shall renew or continue in force such coverage at the option of the individual.

"(b) GENERAL EXCEPTIONS.—A health insurance issuer may nonrenew or discontinue health insurance coverage of an individual in the individual market based only on one or more of the following:

"(1) NONPAYMENT OF PREMIUMS.—The individual has failed to pay premiums or contributions in accordance with the terms of the health insurance coverage or the issuer has not received timely premium payments.

"(2) FRAUD.—The individual has performed an act or practice that constitutes fraud or made an intentional misrepresentation of material fact under the terms of the coverage.

"(3) TERMINATION OF PLAN.—The issuer is ceasing to offer coverage in the individual market in accordance with subsection (c) and applicable State law.

"(4) MOVEMENT OUTSIDE SERVICE AREA.—In the case of a health insurance issuer that offers health insurance coverage in the market through a network plan, the individual no longer resides, lives, or works in the service area (or in an area for which the issuer is authorized to do business) but only if such coverage is terminated under this paragraph uniformly without regard to any health status-related factor of covered individuals.

"(5) ASSOCIATION MEMBERSHIP CEASES.—In the case of health insurance coverage that is made available in the individual market only through one or more bona fide associations, the membership of the individual in the association (on the basis of which the coverage is provided) ceases but only if such coverage is terminated under this paragraph uniformly without regard to any health status-related factor of covered individuals.

"(c) REQUIREMENTS FOR UNIFORM TERMINATION OF COVERAGE.—

"(1) PARTICULAR TYPE OF COVERAGE NOT OFFERED.—In any case in which an issuer decides to discontinue offering a par-

ticular type of health insurance coverage offered in the individual market, coverage of such type may be discontinued by the issuer only if—

"(A) the issuer provides notice to each covered individual provided coverage of this type in such market of such discontinuation at least 90 days prior to the date of the discontinuation of such coverage;

"(B) the issuer offers to each individual in the individual market provided coverage of this type, the option to purchase any other individual health insurance coverage currently being offered by the issuer for individuals in such market; and

"(C) in exercising the option to discontinue coverage of this type and in offering the option of coverage under subparagraph (B), the issuer acts uniformly without regard to any health status-related factor of enrolled individuals or individuals who may become eligible for such coverage.

"(2) DISCONTINUANCE OF ALL COVERAGE.—

"(A) IN GENERAL.—Subject to subparagraph (C), in any case in which a health insurance issuer elects to discontinue offering all health insurance coverage in the individual market in a State, health insurance coverage may be discontinued by the issuer only if—

"(i) the issuer provides notice to the applicable State authority and to each individual of such discontinuation at least 180 days prior to the date of the expiration of such coverage, and

"(ii) all health insurance issued or delivered for issuance in the State in such market are discontinued and coverage under such health insurance coverage in such market is not renewed.

"(B) PROHIBITION ON MARKET REENTRY.—In the case of a discontinuation under subparagraph (A) in the individual market, the issuer may not provide for the issuance of any health insurance coverage in the market and State involved during the 5-year period beginning on the date of the discontinuation of the last health insurance coverage not so renewed.

"(d) EXCEPTION FOR UNIFORM MODIFICATION OF COVERAGE.— At the time of coverage renewal, a health insurance issuer may modify the health insurance coverage for a policy form offered to individuals in the individual market so long as such modification is consistent with State law and effective on a uniform basis among all individuals with that policy form.

"(e) APPLICATION TO COVERAGE OFFERED ONLY THROUGH ASSOCIATIONS.—In applying this section in the case of health insurance coverage that is made available by a health insurance issuer in the individual market to individuals only through one or more associations, a reference to an 'individual' is deemed to include a reference to such an association (of which the individual is a member).

"SEC. 2743. CERTIFICATION OF COVERAGE.

"The provisions of section 2701(e) shall apply to health insurance coverage offered by a health insurance issuer in the individual market in the same manner as it applies to health insurance cov-

erage offered by a health insurance issuer in connection with a group health plan in the small or large group market.

"SEC. 2744. STATE FLEXIBILITY IN INDIVIDUAL MARKET REFORMS.

"(a) WAIVER OF REQUIREMENTS WHERE IMPLEMENTATION OF ACCEPTABLE ALTERNATIVE MECHANISM.—

"(1) IN GENERAL.—The requirements of section 2741 shall not apply with respect to health insurance coverage offered in the individual market in the State so long as a State is found to be implementing, in accordance with this section and consistent with section 2746(b), an alternative mechanism (in this section referred to as an 'acceptable alternative mechanism')—

"(A) under which all eligible individuals are provided a choice of health insurance coverage;

"(B) under which such coverage does not impose any preexisting condition exclusion with respect to such coverage;

"(C) under which such choice of coverage includes at least one policy form of coverage that is comparable to comprehensive health insurance coverage offered in the individual market in such State or that is comparable to a standard option of coverage available under the group or individual health insurance laws of such State; and

"(D) in a State which is implementing—

"(i) a model act described in subsection (c)(1),

"(ii) a qualified high risk pool described in subsection (c)(2), or

"(iii) a mechanism described in subsection (c)(3).

"(2) PERMISSIBLE FORMS OF MECHANISMS.—A private or public individual health insurance mechanism (such as a health insurance coverage pool or programs, mandatory group conversion policies, guaranteed issue of one or more plans of individual health insurance coverage, or open enrollment by one or more health insurance issuers), or combination of such mechanisms, that is designed to provide access to health benefits for individuals in the individual market in the State in accordance with this section may constitute an acceptable alternative mechanism.

"(b) APPLICATION OF ACCEPTABLE ALTERNATIVE MECHANISMS.—

"(1) PRESUMPTION.—

"(A) IN GENERAL.—Subject to the succeeding provisions of this subsection, a State is presumed to be implementing an acceptable alternative mechanism in accordance with this section as of July 1, 1997, if, by not later than April 1, 1997, the chief executive officer of a State—

"(i) notifies the Secretary that the State has enacted or intends to enact (by not later than January 1, 1998, or July 1, 1998, in the case of a State described in subparagraph (B)(ii)) any necessary legislation to provide for the implementation of a mechanism reasonably designed to be an acceptable alternative mechanism as of January 1, 1998 (or, in the case of a State described in subparagraph (B)(ii), July 1, 1998); and

"(ii) provides the Secretary with such information as the Secretary may require to review the mechanism *and its implementation (or proposed implementation) under this subsection.*

"(B) DELAY PERMITTED FOR CERTAIN STATES.—

"(i) EFFECT OF DELAY.—In the case of a State described in clause (ii) that provides notice under subparagraph (A)(i), for the presumption to continue on and after July 1, 1998, the chief executive officer of the State by April 1, 1998—

"(I) must notify the Secretary that the State has enacted any necessary legislation to provide for the implementation of a mechanism reasonably designed to be an acceptable alternative mechanism as of July 1, 1998; and

"(II) must provide the Secretary with such information as the Secretary may require to review the mechanism and its implementation (or proposed implementation) under this subsection.

"(ii) STATES DESCRIBED.—A State described in this clause is a State that has a legislature that does not meet within the 12-month period beginning on the date of enactment of this Act.

"(C) CONTINUED APPLICATION.—In order for a mechanism to continue to be presumed to be an acceptable alternative mechanism, the State shall provide the Secretary every 3 years with information described in subparagraph (A)(ii) or (B)(i)(II) (as the case may be).

"(2) NOTICE.—If the Secretary finds, after review of information provided under paragraph (1) and in consultation with the chief executive officer of the State and the insurance commissioner or chief insurance regulatory official of the State, that such a mechanism is not an acceptable alternative mechanism or is not (or no longer) being implemented, the Secretary—

"(A) shall notify the State of—

"(i) such preliminary determination, and

"(ii) the consequences under paragraph (3) of a failure to implement such a mechanism; and

"(B) shall permit the State a reasonable opportunity in which to modify the mechanism (or to adopt another mechanism) in a manner so that may be an acceptable alternative mechanism or to provide for implementation of such a mechanism.

"(3) FINAL DETERMINATION.—If, after providing notice and opportunity under paragraph (2), the Secretary finds that the mechanism is not an acceptable alternative mechanism or the State is not implementing such a mechanism, the Secretary shall notify the State that the State is no longer considered to be implementing an acceptable alternative mechanism and that the requirements of section 2741 shall apply to health insurance coverage offered in the individual market in the State, effective as of a date specified in the notice.

"(4) LIMITATION ON SECRETARIAL AUTHORITY.—The Secretary shall not make a determination under paragraph (2) or (3) on any basis other than the basis that a mechanism is not

an acceptable alternative mechanism or is not being implemented.

"(5) FUTURE ADOPTION OF MECHANISMS.—If a State, after January 1, 1997, submits the notice and information described in paragraph (1), unless the Secretary makes a finding described in paragraph (3) within the 90-day period beginning on the date of submission of the notice and information, the mechanism shall be considered to be an acceptable alternative mechanism for purposes of this section, effective 90 days after the end of such period, subject to the second sentence of paragraph (1).

"(c) PROVISION RELATED TO RISK.—

"(1) ADOPTION OF NAIC MODELS.—The model act referred to in subsection (a)(1)(D)(i) is the Small Employer and Individual Health Insurance Availability Model Act (adopted by the National Association of Insurance Commissioners on June 3, 1996) insofar as it applies to individual health insurance coverage or the Individual Health Insurance Portability Model Act (also adopted by such Association on such date).

"(2) QUALIFIED HIGH RISK POOL.—For purposes of subsection (a)(1)(D)(ii), a 'qualified high risk pool' described in this paragraph is a high risk pool that—

"(A) provides to all eligible individuals health insurance coverage (or comparable coverage) that does not impose any preexisting condition exclusion with respect to such coverage for all eligible individuals, and

"(B) provides for premium rates and covered benefits for such coverage consistent with standards included in the NAIC Model Health Plan for Uninsurable Individuals Act (as in effect as of the date of the enactment of this title).

"(3) OTHER MECHANISMS.—For purposes of subsection (a)(1)(D)(iii), a mechanism described in this paragraph—

"(A) provides for risk adjustment, risk spreading, or a risk spreading mechanism (among issuers or policies of an issuer) or otherwise provides for some financial subsidization for eligible individuals, including through assistance to participating issuers; or

"(B) is a mechanism under which each eligible individual is provided a choice of all individual health insurance coverage otherwise available.

"SEC. 2745. ENFORCEMENT.

"(a) STATE ENFORCEMENT.—

"(1) STATE AUTHORITY.—Subject to section 2746, each State may require that health insurance issuers that issue, sell, renew, or offer health insurance coverage in the State in the individual market meet the requirements established under this part with respect to such issuers.

"(2) FAILURE TO IMPLEMENT REQUIREMENTS.—In the case of a State that fails to substantially enforce the requirements set forth in this part with respect to health insurance issuers in the State, the Secretary shall enforce the requirements of this part under subsection (b) insofar as they relate to the issuance, sale, renewal, and offering of health insurance coverage in the individual market in such State.

"(b) SECRETARIAL ENFORCEMENT AUTHORITY.—The Secretary shall have the same authority in relation to enforcement of the provisions of this part with respect to issuers of health insurance coverage in the individual market in a State as the Secretary has under section 2722(b)(2) in relation to the enforcement of the provisions of part A with respect to issuers of health insurance coverage in the small group market in the State.

"SEC. 2746. PREEMPTION.

"(a) IN GENERAL.—Subject to subsection (b), nothing in this part (or part C insofar as it applies to this part) shall be construed to prevent a State from establishing, implementing, or continuing in effect standards and requirements unless such standards and requirements prevent the application of a requirement of this part.

"(b) RULES OF CONSTRUCTION.—Nothing in this part (or part C insofar as it applies to this part) shall be construed to affect or modify the provisions of section 514 of the Employee Retirement Income Security Act of 1974 (29 U.S.C. 1144).

"SEC. 2747. GENERAL EXCEPTIONS.

"(a) EXCEPTION FOR CERTAIN BENEFITS.—The requirements of this part shall not apply to any health insurance coverage in relation to its provision of excepted benefits described in section 2791(c)(1).

"(b) EXCEPTION FOR CERTAIN BENEFITS IF CERTAIN CONDITIONS MET.—The requirements of this part shall not apply to any health insurance coverage in relation to its provision of excepted benefits described in paragraph (2), (3), or (4) of section 2791(c) if the benefits are provided under a separate policy, certificate, or contract of insurance.".

(b) EFFECTIVE DATE.—

    (1) IN GENERAL.—Except as provided in this subsection, part B of title XXVII of the Public Health Service Act (as inserted by subsection (a)) shall apply with respect to health insurance coverage offered, sold, issued, renewed, in effect, or operated in the individual market after June 30, 1997, regardless of when a period of creditable coverage occurs.

    (2) APPLICATION OF CERTIFICATION RULES.—The provisions of section 102(d)(2) of this Act shall apply to section 2743 of the Public Health Service Act in the same manner as it applies to section 2701(e) of such Act.

Subtitle C—General and Miscellaneous Provisions

SEC. 191. HEALTH COVERAGE AVAILABILITY STUDIES.

(a) STUDIES.—

    (1) STUDY ON EFFECTIVENESS OF REFORMS.—The Secretary of Health and Human Services shall provide for a study on the effectiveness of the provisions of this title and the various State laws, in ensuring the availability of reasonably priced health coverage to employers purchasing group coverage and individuals purchasing coverage on a non-group basis.

(2) STUDY ON ACCESS AND CHOICE.—The Secretary also shall provide for a study on—

(A) the extent to which patients have direct access to, and choice of, health care providers, including specialty providers, within a network plan, as well as the opportunity to utilize providers outside of the network plan, under the various types of coverage offered under the provisions of this title; and

(B) the cost and cost-effectiveness to health insurance issuers of providing access to out-of-network providers, and the potential impact of providing such access on the cost and quality of health insurance coverage offered under provisions of this title.

(3) CONSULTATION.—The studies under this subsection shall be conducted in consultation with the Secretary of Labor, representatives of State officials, consumers, and other representatives of individuals and entities that have expertise in health insurance and employee benefits.

(b) REPORTS.—Not later than January 1, 2000, the Secretary shall submit to the appropriate committees of Congress a report on each of the studies under subsection (a).

SEC. 192. REPORT ON MEDICARE REIMBURSEMENT OF TELEMEDICINE.

The Health Care Financing Administration shall complete its ongoing study of medicare reimbursement of all telemedicine services and submit a report to Congress on medicare reimbursement of telemedicine services by not later than March 1, 1997. The report shall—

(1) utilize data compiled from the current demonstration projects already under review and gather data from other ongoing telemedicine networks;

(2) include an analysis of the cost of services provided via telemedicine; and

(3) include a proposal for medicare reimbursement of such services.

SEC. 193. ALLOWING FEDERALLY-QUALIFIED HMOS TO OFFER HIGH DEDUCTIBLE PLANS.

Section 1301(b) of the Public Health Service Act (42 U.S.C. 300e(b)) is amended by adding at the end the following new paragraph:

"(6) A health maintenance organization that otherwise meets the requirements of this title may offer a high-deductible health plan (as defined in section 220(c)(2) of the Internal Revenue Code of 1986).".

SEC. 194. VOLUNTEER SERVICES PROVIDED BY HEALTH PROFESSIONALS AT FREE CLINICS.

Section 224 of the Public Health Service Act (42 U.S.C. 233) is amended by adding at the end the following subsection:

"(o)(1) For purposes of this section, a free clinic health professional shall in providing a qualifying health service to an individual be deemed to be an employee of the Public Health Service for a calendar year that begins during a fiscal year for which a transfer was made under paragraph (6)(D). The preceding sentence is subject to the provisions of this subsection.

"(2) In providing a health service to an individual, a health care practitioner shall for purposes of this subsection be considered to be a free clinic health professional if the following conditions are met:

"(A) The service is provided to the individual at a free clinic, or through offsite programs or events carried out by the free clinic.

"(B) The free clinic is sponsoring the health care practitioner pursuant to paragraph (5)(C).

"(C) The service is a qualifying health service (as defined in paragraph (4)).

"(D) Neither the health care practitioner nor the free clinic receives any compensation for the service from the individual or from any third-party payor (including reimbursement under any insurance policy or health plan, or under any Federal or State health benefits program). With respect to compliance with such condition:

"(i) The health care practitioner may receive repayment from the free clinic for reasonable expenses incurred by the health care practitioner in the provision of the service to the individual.

"(ii) The free clinic may accept voluntary donations for the provision of the service by the health care practitioner to the individual.

"(E) Before the service is provided, the health care practitioner or the free clinic provides written notice to the individual of the extent to which the legal liability of the health care practitioner is limited pursuant to this subsection (or in the case of an emergency, the written notice is provided to the individual as soon after the emergency as is practicable). If the individual is a minor or is otherwise legally incompetent, the condition under this subparagraph is that the written notice be provided to a legal guardian or other person with legal responsibility for the care of the individual.

"(F) At the time the service is provided, the health care practitioner is licensed or certified in accordance with applicable law regarding the provision of the service.

"(3)(A) For purposes of this subsection, the term 'free clinic' means a health care facility operated by a nonprofit private entity meeting the following requirements:

"(i) The entity does not, in providing health services through the facility, accept reimbursement from any third-party payor (including reimbursement under any insurance policy or health plan, or under any Federal or State health benefits program).

"(ii) The entity, in providing health services through the facility, either does not impose charges on the individuals to whom the services are provided, or imposes a charge according to the ability of the individual involved to pay the charge.

"(iii) The entity is licensed or certified in accordance with applicable law regarding the provision of health services.

"(B) With respect to compliance with the conditions under subparagraph (A), the entity involved may accept voluntary donations for the provision of services.

"(4) For purposes of this subsection, the term 'qualifying health service' means any medical assistance required or authorized to be provided in the program under title XIX of the Social Security Act, without regard to whether the medical assistance is included in the plan submitted under such program by the State in which the health care practitioner involved provides the medical assistance. References in the preceding sentence to such program shall as applicable be considered to be references to any successor to such program.

"(5) Subsection (g) (other than paragraphs (3) through (5)) and subsections (h), (i), and (l) apply to a health care practitioner for purposes of this subsection to the same extent and in the same manner as such subsections apply to an officer, governing board member, employee, or contractor of an entity described in subsection (g)(4), subject to paragraph (6) and subject to the following:

"(A) The first sentence of paragraph (1) applies in lieu of the first sentence of subsection (g)(1)(A).

"(B) This subsection may not be construed as deeming any free clinic to be an employee of the Public Health Service for purposes of this section.

"(C) With respect to a free clinic, a health care practitioner is not a free clinic health professional unless the free clinic sponsors the health care practitioner. For purposes of this subsection, the free clinic shall be considered to be sponsoring the health care practitioner if—

"(i) with respect to the health care practitioner, the free clinic submits to the Secretary an application meeting the requirements of subsection (g)(1)(D); and

"(ii) the Secretary, pursuant to subsection (g)(1)(E), determines that the health care practitioner is deemed to be an employee of the Public Health Service.

"(D) In the case of a health care practitioner who is determined by the Secretary pursuant to subsection (g)(1)(E) to be a free clinic health professional, this subsection applies to the health care practitioner (with respect to the free clinic sponsoring the health care practitioner pursuant to subparagraph C)) for any cause of action arising from an act or omission of the health care practitioner occurring on or after the date on which the Secretary makes such determination.

"(E) Subsection (g)(1)(F) applies to a health care practitioner for purposes of this subsection only to the extent that, in providing health services to an individual, each of the conditions specified in paragraph (2) is met.

"(6)(A) For purposes of making payments for judgments against the United States (together with related fees and expenses of witnesses) pursuant to this section arising from the acts or omissions of free clinic health professionals, there is authorized to be appropriated $10,000,000 for each fiscal year.

"(B) The Secretary shall establish a fund for purposes of this subsection. Each fiscal year amounts appropriated under subparagraph (A) shall be deposited in such fund.

"(C) Not later than May 1 of each fiscal year, the Attorney General, in consultation with the Secretary, shall submit to the Congress a report providing an estimate of the amount of claims (to-

gether with related fees and expenses of witnesses) that, by reason of the acts or omissions of free clinic health professionals, will be paid pursuant to this section during the calendar year that begins in the following fiscal year. Subsection (k)(1)(B) applies to the estimate under the preceding sentence regarding free clinic health professionals to the same extent and in the same manner as such subsection applies to the estimate under such subsection regarding officers, governing board members, employees, and contractors of entities described in subsection (g)(4).

"(D) Not later than December 31 of each fiscal year, the Secretary shall transfer from the fund under subparagraph (B) to the appropriate accounts in the Treasury an amount equal to the estimate made under subparagraph (C) for the calendar year beginning in such fiscal year, subject to the extent of amounts in the fund.

"(7)(A) This subsection takes effect on the date of the enactment of the first appropriations Act that makes an appropriation under paragraph (6)(A), except as provided in subparagraph (B)(i).

"(B)(i) Effective on the date of the enactment of the Health Insurance Portability and Accountability Act of 1996—

"(I) the Secretary may issue regulations for carrying out this subsection, and the Secretary may accept and consider applications submitted pursuant to paragraph (5)(C); and

"(II) reports under paragraph (6)(C) may be submitted to the Congress.

"(ii) For the first fiscal year for which an appropriation is made under subparagraph (A) of paragraph (6), if an estimate under subparagraph (C) of such paragraph has not been made for the calendar year beginning in such fiscal year, the transfer under subparagraph (D) of such paragraph shall be made notwithstanding the lack of the estimate, and the transfer shall be made in an amount equal to the amount of such appropriation.".

SEC. 195. FINDINGS; SEVERABILITY.

(a) FINDINGS RELATING TO EXERCISE OF COMMERCE CLAUSE AUTHORITY.—Congress finds the following in relation to the provisions of this title:

(1) Provisions in group health plans and health insurance coverage that impose certain preexisting condition exclusions impact the ability of employees to seek employment in interstate commerce, thereby impeding such commerce.

(2) Health insurance coverage is commercial in nature and is in and affects interstate commerce.

(3) It is a necessary and proper exercise of Congressional authority to impose requirements under this title on group health plans and health insurance coverage (including coverage offered to individuals previously covered under group health plans) in order to promote commerce among the States.

(4) Congress, however, intends to defer to States, to the maximum extent practicable, in carrying out such requirements with respect to insurers and health maintenance organizations that are subject to State regulation, consistent with the provisions of the Employee Retirement Income Security Act of 1974.

(b) SEVERABILITY.—If any provision of this title or the application of such provision to any person or circumstance is held to be unconstitutional, the remainder of this title and the application of

the provisions of such to any person or circumstance shall not be affected thereby.

TITLE II—PREVENTING HEALTH CARE FRAUD AND ABUSE; ADMINISTRATIVE SIMPLIFICATION

SEC. 200. REFERENCES IN TITLE.

Except as otherwise specifically provided, whenever in this title an amendment is expressed in terms of an amendment to or repeal of a section or other provision, the reference shall be considered to be made to that section or other provision of the Social Security Act.

Subtitle A—Fraud and Abuse Control Program

SEC. 201. FRAUD AND ABUSE CONTROL PROGRAM.

(a) ESTABLISHMENT OF PROGRAM.—Title XI (42 U.S.C. 1301 et seq.) is amended by inserting after section 1128B the following new section:

"FRAUD AND ABUSE CONTROL PROGRAM

"SEC. 1128C. (a) ESTABLISHMENT OF PROGRAM.—
"(1) IN GENERAL.—Not later than January 1, 1997, the Secretary, acting through the Office of the Inspector General of the Department of Health and Human Services, and the Attorney General shall establish a program—
"(A) to coordinate Federal, State, and local law enforcement programs to control fraud and abuse with respect to health plans,
"(B) to conduct investigations, audits, evaluations, and inspections relating to the delivery of and payment for health care in the United States,
"(C) to facilitate the enforcement of the provisions of sections 1128, 1128A, and 1128B and other statutes applicable to health care fraud and abuse,
"(D) to provide for the modification and establishment of safe harbors and to issue advisory opinions and special fraud alerts pursuant to section 1128D, and
"(E) to provide for the reporting and disclosure of certain final adverse actions against health care providers, suppliers, or practitioners pursuant to the data collection system established under section 1128E.
"(2) COORDINATION WITH HEALTH PLANS.—In carrying out the program established under paragraph (1), the Secretary and the Attorney General shall consult with, and arrange for the sharing of data with representatives of health plans.
"(3) GUIDELINES.—
"(A) IN GENERAL.—The Secretary and the Attorney General shall issue guidelines to carry out the program under paragraph (1). The provisions of sections 553, 556,

and 557 of title 5, United States Code, shall not apply in the issuance of such guidelines.

    "(B) INFORMATION GUIDELINES.—

        "(i) IN GENERAL.—Such guidelines shall include guidelines relating to the furnishing of information by health plans, providers, and others to enable the Secretary and the Attorney General to carry out the program (including coordination with health plans under paragraph (2)).

        "(ii) CONFIDENTIALITY.—Such guidelines shall include procedures to assure that such information is provided and utilized in a manner that appropriately protects the confidentiality of the information and the privacy of individuals receiving health care services and items.

        "(iii) QUALIFIED IMMUNITY FOR PROVIDING INFORMATION.—The provisions of section 1157(a) (relating to limitation on liability) shall apply to a person providing information to the Secretary or the Attorney General in conjunction with their performance of duties under this section.

    "(4) ENSURING ACCESS TO DOCUMENTATION.—The Inspector General of the Department of Health and Human Services is authorized to exercise such authority described in paragraphs (3) through (9) of section 6 of the Inspector General Act of 1978 (5 U.S.C. App.) as necessary with respect to the activities under the fraud and abuse control program established under this subsection.

    "(5) AUTHORITY OF INSPECTOR GENERAL.—Nothing in this Act shall be construed to diminish the authority of any Inspector General, including such authority as provided in the Inspector General Act of 1978 (5 U.S.C. App.).

"(b) ADDITIONAL USE OF FUNDS BY INSPECTOR GENERAL.—

    "(1) REIMBURSEMENTS FOR INVESTIGATIONS.—The Inspector General of the Department of Health and Human Services is authorized to receive and retain for current use reimbursement for the costs of conducting investigations and audits and for monitoring compliance plans when such costs are ordered by a court, voluntarily agreed to by the payor, or otherwise.

    "(2) CREDITING.—Funds received by the Inspector General under paragraph (1) as reimbursement for costs of conducting investigations shall be deposited to the credit of the appropriation from which initially paid, or to appropriations for similar purposes currently available at the time of deposit, and shall remain available for obligation for 1 year from the date of the deposit of such funds.

"(c) HEALTH PLAN DEFINED.—For purposes of this section, the term 'health plan' means a plan or program that provides health benefits, whether directly, through insurance, or otherwise, and includes—

    "(1) a policy of health insurance;

    "(2) a contract of a service benefit organization; and

    "(3) a membership agreement with a health maintenance organization or other prepaid health plan.".

(b) ESTABLISHMENT OF HEALTH CARE FRAUD AND ABUSE CONTROL ACCOUNT IN FEDERAL HOSPITAL INSURANCE TRUST FUND.— Section 1817 (42 U.S.C. 1395i) is amended by adding at the end the following new subsection:

"*(k) HEALTH CARE FRAUD AND ABUSE CONTROL ACCOUNT.—*

"*(1) ESTABLISHMENT.—*There is hereby established in the Trust Fund an expenditure account to be known as the 'Health Care Fraud and Abuse Control Account' (in this subsection referred to as the 'Account').

"*(2) APPROPRIATED AMOUNTS TO TRUST FUND.—*

"*(A) IN GENERAL.—*There are hereby appropriated to the Trust Fund—

"*(i)* such gifts and bequests as may be made as provided in subparagraph (B);

"*(ii)* such amounts as may be deposited in the Trust Fund as provided in sections 242(b) and 249(c) of the Health Insurance Portability and Accountability Act of 1996, and title XI; and

"*(iii)* such amounts as are transferred to the Trust Fund under subparagraph (C).

"*(B) AUTHORIZATION TO ACCEPT GIFTS.—*The Trust Fund is authorized to accept on behalf of the United States money gifts and bequests made unconditionally to the Trust Fund, for the benefit of the Account or any activity financed through the Account.

"*(C) TRANSFER OF AMOUNTS.—*The Managing Trustee shall transfer to the Trust Fund, under rules similar to the rules in section 9601 of the Internal Revenue Code of 1986, an amount equal to the sum of the following:

"*(i)* Criminal fines recovered in cases involving a Federal health care offense (as defined in section 982(a)(6)(B) of title 18, United States Code).

"*(ii)* Civil monetary penalties and assessments imposed in health care cases, including amounts recovered under titles XI, XVIII, and XIX, and chapter 38 of title 31, United States Code (except as otherwise provided by law).

"*(iii)* Amounts resulting from the forfeiture of property by reason of a Federal health care offense.

"*(iv)* Penalties and damages obtained and otherwise creditable to miscellaneous receipts of the general fund of the Treasury obtained under sections 3729 through 3733 of title 31, United States Code (known as the False Claims Act), in cases involving claims related to the provision of health care items and services (other than funds awarded to a relator, for restitution or otherwise authorized by law).

"*(D) APPLICATION.—*Nothing in subparagraph (C)(iii) shall be construed to limit the availability of recoveries and forfeitures obtained under title I of the Employee Retirement Income Security Act of 1974 for the purpose of providing equitable or remedial relief for employee welfare benefit plans, and for participants and beneficiaries under such plans, as authorized under such title.

"(3) APPROPRIATED AMOUNTS TO ACCOUNT FOR FRAUD AND ABUSE CONTROL PROGRAM, ETC.—

"(A) DEPARTMENTS OF HEALTH AND HUMAN SERVICES AND JUSTICE.—

"(i) IN GENERAL.—There are hereby appropriated to the Account from the Trust Fund such sums as the Secretary and the Attorney General certify are necessary to carry out the purposes described in subparagraph (C), to be available without further appropriation, in an amount not to exceed—

"(I) for fiscal year 1997, $104,000,000,

"(II) for each of the fiscal years 1998 through 2003, the limit for the preceding fiscal year, increased by 15 percent; and

"(III) for each fiscal year after fiscal year 2003, the limit for fiscal year 2003.

"(ii) MEDICARE AND MEDICAID ACTIVITIES.—For each fiscal year, of the amount appropriated in clause (i), the following amounts shall be available only for the purposes of the activities of the Office of the Inspector General of the Department of Health and Human Services with respect to the medicare and medicaid programs—

"(I) for fiscal year 1997, not less than $60,000,000 and not more than $70,000,000;

"(II) for fiscal year 1998, not less than $80,000,000 and not more than $90,000,000;

"(III) for fiscal year 1999, not less than $90,000,000 and not more than $100,000,000;

"(IV) for fiscal year 2000, not less than $110,000,000 and not more than $120,000,000;

"(V) for fiscal year 2001, not less than $120,000,000 and not more than $130,000,000;

"(VI) for fiscal year 2002, not less than $140,000,000 and not more than $150,000,000; and

"(VII) for each fiscal year after fiscal year 2002, not less than $150,000,000 and not more than $160,000,000.

"(B) FEDERAL BUREAU OF INVESTIGATION.—There are hereby appropriated from the general fund of the United States Treasury and hereby appropriated to the Account for transfer to the Federal Bureau of Investigation to carry out the purposes described in subparagraph (C), to be available without further appropriation—

"(i) for fiscal year 1997, $47,000,000;

"(ii) for fiscal year 1998, $56,000,000;

"(iii) for fiscal year 1999, $66,000,000;

"(iv) for fiscal year 2000, $76,000,000;

"(v) for fiscal year 2001, $88,000,000;

"(vi) for fiscal year 2002, $101,000,000; and

"(vii) for each fiscal year after fiscal year 2002, $114,000,000.

"(C) USE OF FUNDS.—The purposes described in this subparagraph are to cover the costs (including equipment, salaries and benefits, and travel and training) of the administration and operation of the health care fraud and abuse control program established under section 1128C(a), including the costs of—

"(i) prosecuting health care matters (through criminal, civil, and administrative proceedings);

"(ii) investigations;

"(iii) financial and performance audits of health care programs and operations;

"(iv) inspections and other evaluations; and

"(v) provider and consumer education regarding compliance with the provisions of title XI.

"(4) APPROPRIATED AMOUNTS TO ACCOUNT FOR MEDICARE INTEGRITY PROGRAM.—

"(A) IN GENERAL.—There are hereby appropriated to the Account from the Trust Fund for each fiscal year such amounts as are necessary to carry out the Medicare Integrity Program under section 1893, subject to subparagraph (B) and to be available without further appropriation.

"(B) AMOUNTS SPECIFIED.—The amount appropriated under subparagraph (A) for a fiscal year is as follows:

"(i) For fiscal year 1997, such amount shall be not less than $430,000,000 and not more than $440,000,000.

"(ii) For fiscal year 1998, such amount shall be not less than $490,000,000 and not more than $500,000,000.

"(iii) For fiscal year 1999, such amount shall be not less than $550,000,000 and not more than $560,000,000.

"(iv) For fiscal year 2000, such amount shall be not less than $620,000,000 and not more than $630,000,000.

"(v) For fiscal year 2001, such amount shall be not less than $670,000,000 and not more than $680,000,000.

"(vi) For fiscal year 2002, such amount shall be not less than $690,000,000 and not more than $700,000,000.

"(vii) For each fiscal year after fiscal year 2002, such amount shall be not less than $710,000,000 and not more than $720,000,000.

"(5) ANNUAL REPORT.—Not later than January 1, the Secretary and the Attorney General shall submit jointly a report to Congress which identifies—

"(A) the amounts appropriated to the Trust Fund for the previous fiscal year under paragraph (2)(A) and the source of such amounts; and

"(B) the amounts appropriated from the Trust Fund for such year under paragraph (3) and the justification for the expenditure of such amounts.

"(6) GAO REPORT.—Not later than January 1 of 2000, 2002, and 2004, the Comptroller General of the United States shall submit a report to Congress which—

"(A) identifies—

"(i) the amounts appropriated to the Trust Fund for the previous two fiscal years under paragraph (2)(A) and the source of such amounts; and

"(ii) the amounts appropriated from the Trust Fund for such fiscal years under paragraph (3) and the justification for the expenditure of such amounts;

"(B) identifies any expenditures from the Trust Fund with respect to activities not involving the Medicare program under title XVIII;

"(C) identifies any savings to the Trust Fund, and any other savings, resulting from expenditures from the Trust Fund; and

"(D) analyzes such other aspects of the operation of the Trust Fund as the Comptroller General of the United States considers appropriate.".

SEC. 202. MEDICARE INTEGRITY PROGRAM.

(a) ESTABLISHMENT OF MEDICARE INTEGRITY PROGRAM.—Title XVIII is amended by adding at the end the following new section:

"MEDICARE INTEGRITY PROGRAM

"SEC. 1893. (a) ESTABLISHMENT OF PROGRAM.—There is hereby established the Medicare Integrity Program (in this section referred to as the 'Program') under which the Secretary shall promote the integrity of the Medicare program by entering into contracts in accordance with this section with eligible entities to carry out the activities described in subsection (b).

"(b) ACTIVITIES DESCRIBED.—The activities described in this subsection are as follows:

"(1) Review of activities of providers of services or other individuals and entities furnishing items and services for which payment may be made under this title (including skilled nursing facilities and home health agencies), including medical and utilization review and fraud review (employing similar standards, processes, and technologies used by private health plans, including equipment and software technologies which surpass the capability of the equipment and technologies used in the review of claims under this title as of the date of the enactment of this section).

"(2) Audit of cost reports.

"(3) Determinations as to whether payment should not be, or should not have been, made under this title by reason of section 1862(b), and recovery of payments that should not have been made.

"(4) Education of providers of services, beneficiaries, and other persons with respect to payment integrity and benefit quality assurance issues.

"(5) Developing (and periodically updating) a list of items of durable medical equipment in accordance with section

1834(a)(15) which are subject to prior authorization under such section.

"(c) ELIGIBILITY OF ENTITIES.—An entity is eligible to enter into a contract under the Program to carry out any of the activities described in subsection (b) if—

"(1) the entity has demonstrated capability to carry out such activities;

"(2) in carrying out such activities, the entity agrees to cooperate with the Inspector General of the Department of Health and Human Services, the Attorney General, and other law enforcement agencies, as appropriate, in the investigation and deterrence of fraud and abuse in relation to this title and in other cases arising out of such activities;

"(3) the entity complies with such conflict of interest standards as are generally applicable to Federal acquisition and procurement; and

"(4) the entity meets such other requirements as the Secretary may impose.

In the case of the activity described in subsection (b)(5), an entity shall be deemed to be eligible to enter into a contract under the Program to carry out the activity if the entity is a carrier with a contract in effect under section 1842.

"(d) PROCESS FOR ENTERING INTO CONTRACTS.—The Secretary shall enter into contracts under the Program in accordance with such procedures as the Secretary shall by regulation establish, except that such procedures shall include the following:

"(1) Procedures for identifying, evaluating, and resolving organizational conflicts of interest that are generally applicable to Federal acquisition and procurement.

"(2) Competitive procedures to be used—

"(A) when entering into new contracts under this section;

"(B) when entering into contracts that may result in the elimination of responsibilities of an individual fiscal intermediary or carrier under section 202(b) of the Health Insurance Portability and Accountability Act of 1996; and

"(C) at any other time considered appropriate by the Secretary,

except that the Secretary may continue to contract with entities that are carrying out the activities described in this section pursuant to agreements under section 1816 or contracts under section 1842 in effect on the date of the enactment of this section.

"(3) Procedures under which a contract under this section may be renewed without regard to any provision of law requiring competition if the contractor has met or exceeded the performance requirements established in the current contract.

The Secretary may enter into such contracts without regard to final rules having been promulgated.

"(e) LIMITATION ON CONTRACTOR LIABILITY.—The Secretary shall by regulation provide for the limitation of a contractor's liability for actions taken to carry out a contract under the Program, and such regulation shall, to the extent the Secretary finds appropriate,

employ the same or comparable standards and other substantive and procedural provisions as are contained in section 1157.".

(b) ELIMINATION OF FI AND CARRIER RESPONSIBILITY FOR CARRYING OUT ACTIVITIES SUBJECT TO PROGRAM.—

(1) RESPONSIBILITIES OF FISCAL INTERMEDIARIES UNDER PART A.—Section 1816 (42 U.S.C. 1395h) is amended by adding at the end the following new subsection:

"(l) No agency or organization may carry out (or receive payment for carrying out) any activity pursuant to an agreement under this section to the extent that the activity is carried out pursuant to a contract under the Medicare Integrity Program under section 1893.".

(2) RESPONSIBILITIES OF CARRIERS UNDER PART B.—Section 1842(c) (42 U.S.C. 1395u(c)) is amended by adding at the end the following new paragraph:

"(6) No carrier may carry out (or receive payment for carrying out) any activity pursuant to a contract under this subsection to the extent that the activity is carried out pursuant to a contract under the Medicare Integrity Program under section 1893. The previous sentence shall not apply with respect to the activity described in section 1893(b)(5) (relating to prior authorization of certain items of durable medical equipment under section 1834(a)(15)).".

SEC. 203. BENEFICIARY INCENTIVE PROGRAMS.

(a) CLARIFICATION OF REQUIREMENT TO PROVIDE EXPLANATION OF MEDICARE BENEFITS.—The Secretary of Health and Human Services (in this section referred to as the "Secretary") shall provide an explanation of benefits under the medicare program under title XVIII of the Social Security Act with respect to each item or service for which payment may be made under the program which is furnished to an individual, without regard to whether or not a deductible or coinsurance may be imposed against the individual with respect to the item or service.

(b) PROGRAM TO COLLECT INFORMATION ON FRAUD AND ABUSE.—

(1) ESTABLISHMENT OF PROGRAM.—Not later than 3 months after the date of the enactment of this Act, the Secretary shall establish a program under which the Secretary shall encourage individuals to report to the Secretary information on individuals and entities who are engaging in or who have engaged in acts or omissions which constitute grounds for the imposition of a sanction under section 1128, 1128A, or 1128B of the Social Security Act, or who have otherwise engaged in fraud and abuse against the medicare program under title XVIII of such act for which there is a sanction provided under law. The program shall discourage provision of, and not consider, information which is frivolous or otherwise not relevant or material to the imposition of such a sanction.

(2) PAYMENT OF PORTION OF AMOUNTS COLLECTED.—If an individual reports information to the Secretary under the program established under paragraph (1) which serves as the basis for the collection by the Secretary or the Attorney General of any amount of at least $100 (other than any amount paid as a penalty under section 1128B of the Social Security Act), the Secretary may pay a portion of the amount collected to the individ-

ual (under procedures similar to those applicable under section 7623 of the Internal Revenue Code of 1986 to payments to individuals providing information on violations of such Code).

(c) PROGRAM TO COLLECT INFORMATION ON PROGRAM EFFICIENCY.—

(1) ESTABLISHMENT OF PROGRAM.—Not later than 3 months after the date of the enactment of this Act, the Secretary shall establish a program under which the Secretary shall encourage individuals to submit to the Secretary suggestions on methods to improve the efficiency of the medicare program.

(2) PAYMENT OF PORTION OF PROGRAM SAVINGS.—If an individual submits a suggestion to the Secretary under the program established under paragraph (1) which is adopted by the Secretary and which results in savings to the program, the Secretary may make a payment to the individual of such amount as the Secretary considers appropriate.

SEC. 204. APPLICATION OF CERTAIN HEALTH ANTI-FRAUD AND ABUSE SANCTIONS TO FRAUD AND ABUSE AGAINST FEDERAL HEALTH CARE PROGRAMS.

(a) IN GENERAL.—Section 1128B (42 U.S.C. 1320a–7b) is amended as follows:

(1) In the heading, by striking "MEDICARE OR STATE HEALTH CARE PROGRAMS" and inserting "FEDERAL HEALTH CARE PROGRAMS".

(2) In subsection (a)(1), by striking "a program under title XVIII or a State health care program (as defined in section 1128(h))" and inserting "a Federal health care program (as defined in subsection (f))".

(3) In subsection (a)(5), by striking "a program under title XVIII or a State health care program" and inserting "a Federal health care program".

(4) In the second sentence of subsection (a)—

(A) by striking "a State plan approved under title XIX" and inserting "a Federal health care program", and

(B) by striking "the State may at its option (notwithstanding any other provision of that title or of such plan)" and inserting "the administrator of such program may at its option (notwithstanding any other provision of such program)".

(5) In subsection (b), by striking "title XVIII or a State health care program" each place it appears and inserting "a Federal health care program".

(6) In subsection (c), by inserting "(as defined in section 1128(h))" after "a State health care program".

(7) By adding at the end the following new subsection:

"(f) For purposes of this section, the term 'Federal health care program' means—

"(1) any plan or program that provides health benefits, whether directly, through insurance, or otherwise, which is funded directly, in whole or in part, by the United States Government (other than the health insurance program under chapter 89 of title 5, United States Code); or

"(2) any State health care program, as defined in section 1128(h).".

(b) EFFECTIVE DATE.—The amendments made by this section shall take effect on January 1, 1997.

SEC. 205. GUIDANCE REGARDING APPLICATION OF HEALTH CARE FRAUD AND ABUSE SANCTIONS.

Title XI (42 U.S.C. 1301 et seq.), as amended by section 201, is amended by inserting after section 1128C the following new section:

"GUIDANCE REGARDING APPLICATION OF HEALTH CARE FRAUD AND ABUSE SANCTIONS

"SEC. 1128D. (a) SOLICITATION AND PUBLICATION OF MODIFICATIONS TO EXISTING SAFE HARBORS AND NEW SAFE HARBORS.—

"(1) IN GENERAL.—

"(A) SOLICITATION OF PROPOSALS FOR SAFE HARBORS.—Not later than January 1, 1997, and not less than annually thereafter, the Secretary shall publish a notice in the Federal Register soliciting proposals, which will be accepted during a 60-day period, for—

"(i) modifications to existing safe harbors issued pursuant to section 14(a) of the Medicare and Medicaid Patient and Program Protection Act of 1987 (42 U.S.C. 1320a–7b note);

"(ii) additional safe harbors specifying payment practices that shall not be treated as a criminal offense under section 1128B(b) and shall not serve as the basis for an exclusion under section 1128(b)(7);

"(iii) advisory opinions to be issued pursuant to subsection (b); and

"(iv) special fraud alerts to be issued pursuant to subsection (c).

"(B) PUBLICATION OF PROPOSED MODIFICATIONS AND PROPOSED ADDITIONAL SAFE HARBORS.—After considering the proposals described in clauses (i) and (ii) of subparagraph (A), the Secretary, in consultation with the Attorney General, shall publish in the Federal Register proposed modifications to existing safe harbors and proposed additional safe harbors, if appropriate, with a 60-day comment period. After considering any public comments received during this period, the Secretary shall issue final rules modifying the existing safe harbors and establishing new safe harbors, as appropriate.

"(C) REPORT.—The Inspector General of the Department of Health and Human Services (in this section referred to as the 'Inspector General') shall, in an annual report to Congress or as part of the year-end semiannual report required by section 5 of the Inspector General Act of 1978 (5 U.S.C. App.), describe the proposals received under clauses (i) and (ii) of subparagraph (A) and explain which proposals were included in the publication described in subparagraph (B), which proposals were not included in that publication, and the reasons for the rejection of the proposals that were not included.

"(2) CRITERIA FOR MODIFYING AND ESTABLISHING SAFE HARBORS.—In modifying and establishing safe harbors under para-

graph (1)(B), the Secretary may consider the extent to which providing a safe harbor for the specified payment practice may result in any of the following:

"(A) *An increase or decrease in access to health care services.*

"(B) *An increase or decrease in the quality of health care services.*

"(C) *An increase or decrease in patient freedom of choice among health care providers.*

"(D) *An increase or decrease in competition among health care providers.*

"(E) *An increase or decrease in the ability of health care facilities to provide services in medically underserved areas or to medically underserved populations.*

"(F) *An increase or decrease in the cost to Federal health care programs (as defined in section 1128B(f)).*

"(G) *An increase or decrease in the potential overutilization of health care services.*

"(H) *The existence or nonexistence of any potential financial benefit to a health care professional or provider which may vary based on their decisions of—*

"(i) *whether to order a health care item or service; or*

"(ii) *whether to arrange for a referral of health care items or services to a particular practitioner or provider.*

"(I) *Any other factors the Secretary deems appropriate in the interest of preventing fraud and abuse in Federal health care programs (as so defined).*

"(b) ADVISORY OPINIONS.—

"(1) ISSUANCE OF ADVISORY OPINIONS.—*The Secretary, in consultation with the Attorney General, shall issue written advisory opinions as provided in this subsection.*

"(2) MATTERS SUBJECT TO ADVISORY OPINIONS.—*The Secretary shall issue advisory opinions as to the following matters:*

"(A) *What constitutes prohibited remuneration within the meaning of section 1128B(b).*

"(B) *Whether an arrangement or proposed arrangement satisfies the criteria set forth in section 1128B(b)(3) for activities which do not result in prohibited remuneration.*

"(C) *Whether an arrangement or proposed arrangement satisfies the criteria which the Secretary has established, or shall establish by regulation for activities which do not result in prohibited remuneration.*

"(D) *What constitutes an inducement to reduce or limit services to individuals entitled to benefits under title XVIII or title XIX within the meaning of section 1128B(b).*

"(E) *Whether any activity or proposed activity constitutes grounds for the imposition of a sanction under section 1128, 1128A, or 1128B.*

"(3) MATTERS NOT SUBJECT TO ADVISORY OPINIONS.—*Such advisory opinions shall not address the following matters:*

"(A) *Whether the fair market value shall be, or was paid or received for any goods, services or property.*

"(B) Whether an individual is a bona fide employee within the requirements of section 3121(d)(2) of the Internal Revenue Code of 1986.

"(4) EFFECT OF ADVISORY OPINIONS.—

"(A) BINDING AS TO SECRETARY AND PARTIES INVOLVED.—Each advisory opinion issued by the Secretary shall be binding as to the Secretary and the party or parties requesting the opinion.

"(B) FAILURE TO SEEK OPINION.—The failure of a party to seek an advisory opinion may not be introduced into evidence to prove that the party intended to violate the provisions of sections 1128, 1128A, or 1128B.

"(5) REGULATIONS.—

"(A) IN GENERAL.—Not later than 180 days after the date of the enactment of this section, the Secretary shall issue regulations to carry out this section. Such regulations shall provide for—

"(i) the procedure to be followed by a party applying for an advisory opinion;

"(ii) the procedure to be followed by the Secretary in responding to a request for an advisory opinion;

"(iii) the interval in which the Secretary shall respond;

"(iv) the reasonable fee to be charged to the party requesting an advisory opinion; and

"(v) the manner in which advisory opinions will be made available to the public.

"(B) SPECIFIC CONTENTS.—Under the regulations promulgated pursuant to subparagraph (A)—

"(i) the Secretary shall be required to issue to a party requesting an advisory opinion by not later than 60 days after the request is received; and

"(ii) the fee charged to the party requesting an advisory opinion shall be equal to the costs incurred by the Secretary in responding to the request.

"(6) APPLICATION OF SUBSECTION.—This subsection shall apply to requests for advisory opinions made on or after the date which is 6 months after the date of enactment of this section and before the date which is 4 years after such date of enactment.

"(c) SPECIAL FRAUD ALERTS.—

"(1) IN GENERAL.—

"(A) REQUEST FOR SPECIAL FRAUD ALERTS.—Any person may present, at any time, a request to the Inspector General for a notice which informs the public of practices which the Inspector General considers to be suspect or of particular concern under the medicare program under title XVIII or a State health care program, as defined in section 1128(h) (in this subsection referred to as a 'special fraud alert').

"(B) ISSUANCE AND PUBLICATION OF SPECIAL FRAUD ALERTS.—Upon receipt of a request described in subparagraph (A), the Inspector General shall investigate the subject matter of the request to determine whether a special *fraud alert should be issued. If appropriate, the Inspector General shall issue a special fraud alert in response to the request. All special fraud alerts issued pursuant to this subparagraph shall be published in the Federal Register.*

"(2) CRITERIA FOR SPECIAL FRAUD ALERTS.—In determining whether to issue a special fraud alert upon a request described in paragraph (1), the Inspector General may consider—

"(A) whether and to what extent the practices that would be identified in the special fraud alert may result in any of the consequences described in subsection (a)(2); and

"(B) the volume and frequency of the conduct that would be identified in the special fraud alert.".

Subtitle B—Revisions to Current Sanctions for Fraud and Abuse

SEC. 211. MANDATORY EXCLUSION FROM PARTICIPATION IN MEDICARE AND STATE HEALTH CARE PROGRAMS.

(a) INDIVIDUAL CONVICTED OF FELONY RELATING TO HEALTH CARE FRAUD.—

(1) IN GENERAL.—Section 1128(a) (42 U.S.C. 1320a–7(a)) is amended by adding at the end the following new paragraph:

"(3) FELONY CONVICTION RELATING TO HEALTH CARE FRAUD.—Any individual or entity that has been convicted for an offense which occurred after the date of the enactment of the Health Insurance Portability and Accountability Act of 1996, under Federal or State law, in connection with the delivery of a health care item or service or with respect to any act or omission in a health care program (other than those specifically described in paragraph (1)) operated by or financed in whole or in part by any Federal, State, or local government agency, of a criminal offense consisting of a felony relating to fraud, theft, embezzlement, breach of fiduciary responsibility, or other financial misconduct.".

(2) CONFORMING AMENDMENT.—Paragraph (1) of section 1128(b) (42 U.S.C. 1320a–7(b)) is amended to read as follows:

"(1) CONVICTION RELATING TO FRAUD.—Any individual or entity that has been convicted for an offense which occurred after the date of the enactment of the Health Insurance Portability and Accountability Act of 1996, under Federal or State law—

"(A) of a criminal offense consisting of a misdemeanor relating to fraud, theft, embezzlement, breach of fiduciary responsibility, or other financial misconduct—

"(i) in connection with the delivery of a health care item or service, or

"(ii) with respect to any act or omission in a health care program (other than those specifically described in subsection (a)(1)) operated by or financed in whole or in part by any Federal, State, or local government agency; or

"(B) of a criminal offense relating to fraud, theft, embezzlement, breach of fiduciary responsibility, or other fi-

nancial misconduct with respect to any act or omission in a program (other than a health care program) operated by or financed in whole or in part by any Federal, State, or local government agency.".

(b) INDIVIDUAL CONVICTED OF FELONY RELATING TO CONTROLLED SUBSTANCE.—

(1) IN GENERAL.—Section 1128(a) (42 U.S.C. 1320a–7(a)), as amended by subsection (a), is amended by adding at the end the following new paragraph:

"(4) FELONY CONVICTION RELATING TO CONTROLLED SUBSTANCE.—Any individual or entity that has been convicted for an offense which occurred after the date of the enactment of the Health Insurance Portability and Accountability Act of 1996, under Federal or State law, of a criminal offense consisting of a felony relating to the unlawful manufacture, distribution, prescription, or dispensing of a controlled substance.".

(2) CONFORMING AMENDMENT.—Section 1128(b)(3) (42 U.S.C. 1320a–7(b)(3)) is amended—

(A) in the heading, by striking "CONVICTION" and inserting "MISDEMEANOR CONVICTION"; and

(B) by striking "criminal offense" and inserting "criminal offense consisting of a misdemeanor".

SEC. 212. ESTABLISHMENT OF MINIMUM PERIOD OF EXCLUSION FOR CERTAIN INDIVIDUALS AND ENTITIES SUBJECT TO PERMISSIVE EXCLUSION FROM MEDICARE AND STATE HEALTH CARE PROGRAMS.

Section 1128(c)(3) (42 U.S.C. 1320a–7(c)(3)) is amended by adding at the end the following new subparagraphs:

"(D) In the case of an exclusion of an individual or entity under paragraph (1), (2), or (3) of subsection (b), the period of the exclusion shall be 3 years, unless the Secretary determines in accordance with published regulations that a shorter period is appropriate because of mitigating circumstances or that a longer period is appropriate because of aggravating circumstances.

"(E) In the case of an exclusion of an individual or entity under subsection (b)(4) or (b)(5), the period of the exclusion shall not be less than the period during which the individual's or entity's license to provide health care is revoked, suspended, or surrendered, or the individual or the entity is excluded or suspended from a Federal or State health care program.

"(F) In the case of an exclusion of an individual or entity under subsection (b)(6)(B), the period of the exclusion shall be not less than 1 year.".

SEC. 213. PERMISSIVE EXCLUSION OF INDIVIDUALS WITH OWNERSHIP OR CONTROL INTEREST IN SANCTIONED ENTITIES.

Section 1128(b) (42 U.S.C. 1320a–7(b)) is amended by adding at the end the following new paragraph:

"(15) INDIVIDUALS CONTROLLING A SANCTIONED ENTITY.—

(A) Any individual—

"(i) who has a direct or indirect ownership or control interest in a sanctioned entity and who knows or should know (as defined in section 1128A(i)(6)) of the action constituting the basis for the conviction or exclusion described in subparagraph (B); or

"(ii) who is an officer or managing employee (as defined in section 1126(b)) of such an entity.

"(B) For purposes of subparagraph (A), the term 'sanctioned entity' means an entity—

"(i) that has been convicted of any offense described in subsection (a) or in paragraph (1), (2), or (3) of this subsection; or

"(ii) that has been excluded from participation under a program under title XVIII or under a State health care program.".

SEC. 214. SANCTIONS AGAINST PRACTITIONERS AND PERSONS FOR FAILURE TO COMPLY WITH STATUTORY OBLIGATIONS.

(a) MINIMUM PERIOD OF EXCLUSION FOR PRACTITIONERS AND PERSONS FAILING TO MEET STATUTORY OBLIGATIONS.—

(1) IN GENERAL.—The second sentence of section 1156(b)(1) (42 U.S.C. 1320c–5(b)(1)) is amended by striking "may prescribe)" and inserting "may prescribe, except that such period may not be less than 1 year)".

(2) CONFORMING AMENDMENT.—Section 1156(b)(2) (42 U.S.C. 1320c–5(b)(2)) is amended by striking "shall remain" and inserting "shall (subject to the minimum period specified in the second sentence of paragraph (1)) remain".

(b) REPEAL OF "UNWILLING OR UNABLE" CONDITION FOR IMPOSITION OF SANCTION.—Section 1156(b)(1) (42 U.S.C. 1320c–5(b)(1)) is amended—

(1) in the second sentence, by striking "and determines" and all that follows through "such obligations,"; and

(2) by striking the third sentence.

SEC. 215. INTERMEDIATE SANCTIONS FOR MEDICARE HEALTH MAINTENANCE ORGANIZATIONS.

(a) APPLICATION OF INTERMEDIATE SANCTIONS FOR ANY PROGRAM VIOLATIONS.—

(1) IN GENERAL.—Section 1876(i)(1) (42 U.S.C. 1395mm(i)(1)) is amended by striking "the Secretary may terminate" and all that follows and inserting "in accordance with procedures established under paragraph (9), the Secretary may at any time terminate any such contract or may impose the intermediate sanctions described in paragraph (6)(B) or (6)(C) (whichever is applicable) on the eligible organization if the Secretary determines that the organization—

"(A) has failed substantially to carry out the contract;

"(B) is carrying out the contract in a manner substantially inconsistent with the efficient and effective administration of this section; or

"(C) no longer substantially meets the applicable conditions of subsections (b), (c), (e), and (f).".

(2) OTHER INTERMEDIATE SANCTIONS FOR MISCELLANEOUS PROGRAM VIOLATIONS.—Section 1876(i)(6) (42 U.S.C. 1395mm(i)(6)) is amended by adding at the end the following new subparagraph:

"(C) In the case of an eligible organization for which the Secretary makes a determination under paragraph (1), the basis of which is not described in subparagraph (A), the Secretary may apply the following intermediate sanctions:

"(i) Civil money penalties of not more than $25,000 for each determination under paragraph (1) if the deficiency that is the basis of the determination has directly adversely affected (or has the substantial likelihood of adversely affecting) an individual covered under the organization's contract.

"(ii) Civil money penalties of not more than $10,000 for each week beginning after the initiation of procedures by the Secretary under paragraph (9) during which the deficiency that is the basis of a determination under paragraph (1) exists.

"(iii) Suspension of enrollment of individuals under this section after the date the Secretary notifies the organization of a determination under paragraph (1) and until the Secretary is satisfied that the deficiency that is the basis for the determination has been corrected and is not likely to recur.".

(3) PROCEDURES FOR IMPOSING SANCTIONS.—Section 1876(i) (42 U.S.C. 1395mm(i)) is amended by adding at the end the following new paragraph:

"(9) The Secretary may terminate a contract with an eligible organization under this section or may impose the intermediate sanctions described in paragraph (6) on the organization in accordance with formal investigation and compliance procedures established by the Secretary under which—

"(A) the Secretary first provides the organization with the reasonable opportunity to develop and implement a corrective action plan to correct the deficiencies that were the basis of the Secretary's determination under paragraph (1) and the organization fails to develop or implement such a plan;

"(B) in deciding whether to impose sanctions, the Secretary considers aggravating factors such as whether an organization has a history of deficiencies or has not taken action to correct deficiencies the Secretary has brought to the organization's attention;

"(C) there are no unreasonable or unnecessary delays between the finding of a deficiency and the imposition of sanctions; and

"(D) the Secretary provides the organization with reasonable notice and opportunity for hearing (including the right to appeal an initial decision) before imposing any sanction or terminating the contract.".

(4) CONFORMING AMENDMENTS.—Section 1876(i)(6)(B) (42 U.S.C. 1395mm(i)(6)(B)) is amended by striking the second sentence.

(b) AGREEMENTS WITH PEER REVIEW ORGANIZATIONS.—Section 1876(i)(7)(A) (42 U.S.C. 1395mm(i)(7)(A)) is amended by striking "an agreement" and inserting "a written agreement".

(c) EFFECTIVE DATE.—The amendments made by this section shall apply with respect to contract years beginning on or after January 1, 1997.

SEC. 216. ADDITIONAL EXCEPTION TO ANTI-KICKBACK PENALTIES FOR RISK-SHARING ARRANGEMENTS.

(a) IN GENERAL.—Section 1128B(b)(3) (42 U.S.C. 1320a–7b(b)(3)) is amended—

(1) by striking "and" at the end of subparagraph (D);

(2) by striking the period at the end of subparagraph (E) and inserting "; and"; and

(3) by adding at the end the following new subparagraph:

"(F) any remuneration between an organization and an individual or entity providing items or services, or a combination thereof, pursuant to a written agreement between the organization and the individual or entity if the organization is an eligible organization under section 1876 or if the written agreement, through a risk-sharing arrangement, places the individual or entity at substantial financial risk for the cost or utilization of the items or services, or a combination thereof, which the individual or entity is obligated to provide.".

(b) NEGOTIATED RULEMAKING FOR RISK-SHARING EXCEPTION.—

(1) ESTABLISHMENT.—

(A) IN GENERAL.—The Secretary of Health and Human Services (in this subsection referred to as the "Secretary") shall establish, on an expedited basis and using a negotiated rulemaking process under subchapter 3 of chapter 5 of title 5, United States Code, standards relating to the exception for risk-sharing arrangements to the anti-kickback penalties described in section 1128B(b)(3)(F) of the Social Security Act, as added by subsection (a).

(B) FACTORS TO CONSIDER.—In establishing standards relating to the exception for risk-sharing arrangements to the anti-kickback penalties under subparagraph (A), the Secretary—

(i) shall consult with the Attorney General and representatives of the hospital, physician, other health practitioner, and health plan communities, and other interested parties; and

(ii) shall take into account—

(I) the level of risk appropriate to the size and type of arrangement;

(II) the frequency of assessment and distribution of incentives;

(III) the level of capital contribution; and

(IV) the extent to which the risk-sharing arrangement provides incentives to control the cost and quality of health care services.

(2) PUBLICATION OF NOTICE.—In carrying out the rulemaking process under this subsection, the Secretary shall publish the notice provided for under section 564(a) of title 5, United States Code, by not later than 45 days after the date of the enactment of this Act.

(3) TARGET DATE FOR PUBLICATION OF RULE.—As part of the notice under paragraph (2), and for purposes of this subsection, the 'target date for publication' (referred to in section 564(a)(5) of such title) shall be January 1, 1997.

(4) ABBREVIATED PERIOD FOR SUBMISSION OF COMMENTS.— In applying section 564(c) of such title under this subsection, '15 days' shall be substituted for '30 days'.

(5) APPOINTMENT OF NEGOTIATED RULEMAKING COMMITTEE AND FACILITATOR.—The Secretary shall provide for—

(A) the appointment of a negotiated rulemaking committee under section 565(a) of such title by not later than 30 days after the end of the comment period provided for under section 564(c) of such title (as shortened under paragraph (4)), and

(B) the nomination of a facilitator under section 566(c) of such title by not later than 10 days after the date of appointment of the committee.

(6) PRELIMINARY COMMITTEE REPORT.—The negotiated rulemaking committee appointed under paragraph (5) shall report to the Secretary, by not later than October 1, 1996, regarding the committee's progress on achieving a consensus with regard to the rulemaking proceeding and whether such consensus is likely to occur before one month before the target date for publication of the rule. If the committee reports that the committee has failed to make significant progress towards such consensus or is unlikely to reach such consensus by the target date, the Secretary may terminate such process and provide for the publication of a rule under this subsection through such other methods as the Secretary may provide.

(7) FINAL COMMITTEE REPORT.—If the committee is not terminated under paragraph (6), the rulemaking committee shall submit a report containing a proposed rule by not later than one month before the target publication date.

(8) INTERIM, FINAL EFFECT.—The Secretary shall publish a rule under this subsection in the Federal Register by not later than the target publication date. Such rule shall be effective and final immediately on an interim basis, but is subject to change and revision after public notice and opportunity for a period (of not less than 60 days) for public comment. In connection with such rule, the Secretary shall specify the process for the timely review and approval of applications of entities to be certified as provider-sponsored organizations pursuant to such rules and consistent with this subsection.

(9) PUBLICATION OF RULE AFTER PUBLIC COMMENT.—The Secretary shall provide for consideration of such comments and republication of such rule by not later than 1 year after the target publication date.

(c) EFFECTIVE DATE.—The amendments made by subsection (a) shall apply to written agreements entered into on or after January 1, 1997, without regard to whether regulations have been issued to implement such amendments.

SEC. 217. CRIMINAL PENALTY FOR FRAUDULENT DISPOSITION OF ASSETS IN ORDER TO OBTAIN MEDICAID BENEFITS.

Section 1128B(a) (42 U.S.C. 1320a–7b(a)) is amended—

(1) by striking "or" at the end of paragraph (4);

(2) by adding "or" at the end of paragraph (5); and

(3) by inserting after paragraph (5) the following new paragraph:

"(6) knowingly and willfully disposes of assets (including by any transfer in trust) in order for an individual to become eligible for medical assistance under a State plan under title XIX, if disposing of the assets results in the imposition of a period of ineligibility for such assistance under section 1917(c),".

SEC. 218. EFFECTIVE DATE.

Except as otherwise provided, the amendments made by this subtitle shall take effect January 1, 1997.

Subtitle C—Data Collection

SEC. 221. ESTABLISHMENT OF THE HEALTH CARE FRAUD AND ABUSE DATA COLLECTION PROGRAM.

(a) IN GENERAL.—Title XI (42 U.S.C. 1301 et seq.), as amended by sections 201 and 205, is amended by inserting after section 1128D the following new section:

"HEALTH CARE FRAUD AND ABUSE DATA COLLECTION PROGRAM

"SEC. 1128E. (a) GENERAL PURPOSE.—Not later than January 1, 1997, the Secretary shall establish a national health care fraud and abuse data collection program for the reporting of final adverse actions (not including settlements in which no findings of liability have been made) against health care providers, suppliers, or practitioners as required by subsection (b), with access as set forth in subsection (c), and shall maintain a database of the information collected under this section.

"(b) REPORTING OF INFORMATION.—

"(1) IN GENERAL.—Each Government agency and health plan shall report any final adverse action (not including settlements in which no findings of liability have been made) taken against a health care provider, supplier, or practitioner.

"(2) INFORMATION TO BE REPORTED.—The information to be reported under paragraph (1) includes:

"(A) The name and TIN (as defined in section 7701(a)(41) of the Internal Revenue Code of 1986) of any health care provider, supplier, or practitioner who is the subject of a final adverse action.

"(B) The name (if known) of any health care entity with which a health care provider, supplier, or practitioner, who is the subject of a final adverse action, is affiliated or associated.

"(C) The nature of the final adverse action and whether such action is on appeal.

"(D) A description of the acts or omissions and injuries upon which the final adverse action was based, and such other information as the Secretary determines by regulation is required for appropriate interpretation of information reported under this section.

"(3) CONFIDENTIALITY.—In determining what information is required, the Secretary shall include procedures to assure that the privacy of individuals receiving health care services is appropriately protected.

"(4) TIMING AND FORM OF REPORTING.—The information required to be reported under this subsection shall be reported regularly (but not less often than monthly) and in such form and manner as the Secretary prescribes. Such information shall first be required to be reported on a date specified by the Secretary.

"(5) TO WHOM REPORTED.—The information required to be reported under this subsection shall be reported to the Secretary.

"(c) DISCLOSURE AND CORRECTION OF INFORMATION.—

"(1) DISCLOSURE.—With respect to the information about final adverse actions (not including settlements in which no findings of liability have been made) reported to the Secretary under this section with respect to a health care provider, supplier, or practitioner, the Secretary shall, by regulation, provide for—

"(A) disclosure of the information, upon request, to the health care provider, supplier, or licensed practitioner, and

"(B) procedures in the case of disputed accuracy of the information.

"(2) CORRECTIONS.—Each Government agency and health plan shall report corrections of information already reported about any final adverse action taken against a health care provider, supplier, or practitioner, in such form and manner that the Secretary prescribes by regulation.

"(d) ACCESS TO REPORTED INFORMATION.—

"(1) AVAILABILITY.—The information in the database maintained under this section shall be available to Federal and State government agencies and health plans pursuant to procedures that the Secretary shall provide by regulation.

"(2) FEES FOR DISCLOSURE.—The Secretary may establish or approve reasonable fees for the disclosure of information in such database (other than with respect to requests by Federal agencies). The amount of such a fee shall be sufficient to recover the full costs of operating the database. Such fees shall be available to the Secretary or, in the Secretary's discretion to the agency designated under this section to cover such costs.

"(e) PROTECTION FROM LIABILITY FOR REPORTING.—No person or entity, including the agency designated by the Secretary in subsection (b)(5) shall be held liable in any civil action with respect to any report made as required by this section, without knowledge of the falsity of the information contained in the report.

"(f) COORDINATION WITH NATIONAL PRACTITIONER DATA BANK.—The Secretary shall implement this section in such a manner as to avoid duplication with the reporting requirements established for the National Practitioner Data Bank under the Health Care Quality Improvement Act of 1986 (42 U.S.C. 11101 et seq.).

"(g) DEFINITIONS AND SPECIAL RULES.—For purposes of this section:

"(1) FINAL ADVERSE ACTION.—

"(A) IN GENERAL.—The term 'final adverse action' includes:

"(i) Civil judgments against a health care provider, supplier, or practitioner in Federal or State court related to the delivery of a health care item or service.

"(ii) Federal or State criminal convictions related to the delivery of a health care item or service.

"(iii) Actions by Federal or State agencies responsible for the licensing and certification of health care

providers, suppliers, and licensed health care practitioners, including—

> *"(I) formal or official actions, such as revocation or suspension of a license (and the length of any such suspension), reprimand, censure or probation,*
>
> *"(II) any other loss of license or the right to apply for, or renew, a license of the provider, supplier, or practitioner, whether by operation of law, voluntary surrender, non-renewability, or otherwise, or*
>
> *"(III) any other negative action or finding by such Federal or State agency that is publicly available information.*
>
> *"(iv) Exclusion from participation in Federal or State health care programs (as defined in sections 1128B(f) and 1128(h), respectively).*
>
> *"(v) Any other adjudicated actions or decisions that the Secretary shall establish by regulation.*

"(B) EXCEPTION.—The term does not include any action with respect to a malpractice claim.

"(2) PRACTITIONER.—The terms 'licensed health care practitioner', 'licensed practitioner', and 'practitioner' mean, with respect to a State, an individual who is licensed or otherwise authorized by the State to provide health care services (or any individual who, without authority holds himself or herself out to be so licensed or authorized).

"(3) GOVERNMENT AGENCY.—The term 'Government agency' shall include:

> *"(A) The Department of Justice.*
>
> *"(B) The Department of Health and Human Services.*
>
> *"(C) Any other Federal agency that either administers or provides payment for the delivery of health care services, including, but not limited to the Department of Defense and the Veterans' Administration.*
>
> *"(D) State law enforcement agencies.*
>
> *"(E) State medicaid fraud control units.*
>
> *"(F) Federal or State agencies responsible for the licensing and certification of health care providers and licensed health care practitioners.*

"(4) HEALTH PLAN.—The term 'health plan' has the meaning given such term by section 1128C(c).

"(5) DETERMINATION OF CONVICTION.—For purposes of paragraph (1), the existence of a conviction shall be determined under paragraph (4) of section 1128(i).".

(b) IMPROVED PREVENTION IN ISSUANCE OF MEDICARE PROVIDER NUMBERS.—Section 1842(r) (42 U.S.C. 1395u(r)) is amended by adding at the end the following new sentence: "Under such system, the Secretary may impose appropriate fees on such physicians to cover the costs of investigation and recertification activities with respect to the issuance of the identifiers.".

Subtitle D—Civil Monetary Penalties

SEC. 231. SOCIAL SECURITY ACT CIVIL MONETARY PENALTIES.

(a) GENERAL CIVIL MONETARY PENALTIES.—Section 1128A (42 U.S.C. 1320a–7a) is amended as follows:

(1) In the third sentence of subsection (a), by striking "programs under title XVIII" and inserting "Federal health care programs (as defined in section 1128B(f)(1))".

(2) In subsection (f)—

(A) by redesignating paragraph (3) as paragraph (4); and

(B) by inserting after paragraph (2) the following new paragraph:

"(3) With respect to amounts recovered arising out of a claim under a Federal health care program (as defined in section 1128B(f)), the portion of such amounts as is determined to have been paid by the program shall be repaid to the program, and the portion of such amounts attributable to the amounts recovered under this section by reason of the amendments made by the Health Insurance Portability and Accountability Act of 1996 (as estimated by the Secretary) shall be deposited into the Federal Hospital Insurance Trust Fund pursuant to section 1817(k)(2)(C).".

(3) In subsection (i)—

(A) in paragraph (2), by striking "title V, XVIII, XIX, or XX of this Act" and inserting "a Federal health care program (as defined in section 1128B(f))",

(B) in paragraph (4), by striking "a health insurance or medical services program under title XVIII or XIX of this Act" and inserting "a Federal health care program (as so defined)", and

(C) in paragraph (5), by striking "title V, XVIII, XIX, or XX" and inserting "a Federal health care program (as so defined)".

(4) By adding at the end the following new subsection:

"(m)(1) For purposes of this section, with respect to a Federal health care program not contained in this Act, references to the Secretary in this section shall be deemed to be references to the Secretary or Administrator of the department or agency with jurisdiction over such program and references to the Inspector General of the Department of Health and Human Services in this section shall be deemed to be references to the Inspector General of the applicable department or agency.

"(2)(A) The Secretary and Administrator of the departments and agencies referred to in paragraph (1) may include in any action pursuant to this section, claims within the jurisdiction of other Federal departments or agencies as long as the following conditions are satisfied:

"(i) The case involves primarily claims submitted to the Federal health care programs of the department or agency initiating the action.

"(ii) The Secretary or Administrator of the department or agency initiating the action gives notice and an opportunity to

participate in the investigation to the Inspector General of the department or agency with primary jurisdiction over the Federal health care programs to which the claims were submitted.

"(B) If the conditions specified in subparagraph (A) are fulfilled, the Inspector General of the department or agency initiating the action is authorized to exercise all powers granted under the Inspector General Act of 1978 (5 U.S.C. App.) with respect to the claims submitted to the other departments or agencies to the same manner and extent as provided in that Act with respect to claims submitted to such departments or agencies.".

(b) EXCLUDED INDIVIDUAL RETAINING OWNERSHIP OR CONTROL INTEREST IN PARTICIPATING ENTITY.—Section 1128A(a) (42 U.S.C. 1320a–7a(a)) is amended—

(1) by striking "or" at the end of paragraph (1)(D);

(2) by striking ", or" at the end of paragraph (2) and inserting a semicolon;

(3) by striking the semicolon at the end of paragraph (3) and inserting "; or"; and

(4) by inserting after paragraph (3) the following new paragraph:

"(4) in the case of a person who is not an organization, agency, or other entity, is excluded from participating in a program under title XVIII or a State health care program in accordance with this subsection or under section 1128 and who, at the time of a violation of this subsection—

"(A) retains a direct or indirect ownership or control interest in an entity that is participating in a program under title XVIII or a State health care program, and who knows or should know of the action constituting the basis for the exclusion; or

"(B) is an officer or managing employee (as defined in section 1126(b)) of such an entity;".

(c) MODIFICATIONS OF AMOUNTS OF PENALTIES AND ASSESSMENTS.—Section 1128A(a) (42 U.S.C. 1320a–7a(a)), as amended by subsection (b), is amended in the matter following paragraph (4)—

(1) by striking "$2,000" and inserting "$10,000";

(2) by inserting "; in cases under paragraph (4), $10,000 for each day the prohibited relationship occurs" after "false or misleading information was given"; and

(3) by striking "twice the amount" and inserting "3 times the amount".

(d) CLARIFICATION OF LEVEL OF KNOWLEDGE REQUIRED FOR IMPOSITION OF CIVIL MONETARY PENALTIES.—

(1) IN GENERAL.—Section 1128A(a) (42 U.S.C. 1320a–7a(a)) is amended—

(A) in paragraphs (1) and (2), by inserting "knowingly" before "presents" each place it appears; and

(B) in paragraph (3), by striking "gives" and inserting "knowingly gives or causes to be given".

(2) DEFINITION OF STANDARD.—Section 1128A(i) (42 U.S.C. 1320a–7a(i)), as amended by subsection (h)(2), is amended by adding at the end the following new paragraph:

"(7) The term 'should know' means that a person, with respect to information—

"(A) acts in deliberate ignorance of the truth or falsity of the information; or

"(B) acts in reckless disregard of the truth or falsity of the information,

and no proof of specific intent to defraud is required.".

(e) CLAIM FOR ITEM OR SERVICE BASED ON INCORRECT CODING OR MEDICALLY UNNECESSARY SERVICES.—Section 1128A(a)(1) (42 U.S.C. 1320a–7a(a)(1)), as amended by subsection (b), is amended—

(1) in subparagraph (A) by striking "claimed," and inserting "claimed, including any person who engages in a pattern or practice of presenting or causing to be presented a claim for an item or service that is based on a code that the person knows or should know will result in a greater payment to the person than the code the person knows or should know is applicable to the item or service actually provided,";

(2) in subparagraph (C), by striking "or" at the end;

(3) in subparagraph (D), by striking the semicolon and inserting ", or"; and

(4) by inserting after subparagraph (D) the following new subparagraph:

"(E) is for a pattern of medical or other items or services that a person knows or should know are not medically necessary;".

(f) SANCTIONS AGAINST PRACTITIONERS AND PERSONS FOR FAILURE TO COMPLY WITH STATUTORY OBLIGATIONS.—Section 1156(b)(3) (42 U.S.C. 1320c–5(b)(3)) is amended by striking "the actual or estimated cost" and inserting "up to $10,000 for each instance".

(g) PROCEDURAL PROVISIONS.—Section 1876(i)(6) (42 U.S.C. 1395mm(i)(6)), as amended by section 215(a)(2), is amended by adding at the end the following new subparagraph:

"(D) The provisions of section 1128A (other than subsections (a) and (b)) shall apply to a civil money penalty under subparagraph (B)(i) or (C)(i) in the same manner as such provisions apply to a civil money penalty or proceeding under section 1128A(a).".

(h) PROHIBITION AGAINST OFFERING INDUCEMENTS TO INDIVIDUALS ENROLLED UNDER PROGRAMS OR PLANS.—

(1) OFFER OF REMUNERATION.—Section 1128A(a) (42 U.S.C. 1320a–7a(a)), as amended by subsection (b), is amended—

(A) by striking "or" at the end of paragraph (3);

(B) by striking the semicolon at the end of paragraph (4) and inserting "; or"; and

(D) by inserting after paragraph (4) the following new paragraph:

"(5) offers to or transfers remuneration to any individual eligible for benefits under title XVIII of this Act, or under a State health care program (as defined in section 1128(h)) that such person knows or should know is likely to influence such individual to order or receive from a particular provider, practitioner, or supplier any item or service for which payment may be made, in whole or in part, under title XVIII, or a State health care program (as so defined);".

(2) REMUNERATION DEFINED.—Section 1128A(i) (42 U.S.C. 1320a–7a(i)) is amended by adding at the end the following new paragraph:

"(6) The term 'remuneration' includes the waiver of coinsurance and deductible amounts (or any part thereof), and transfers of items or services for free or for other than fair market value. The term 'remuneration' does not include—

"(A) the waiver of coinsurance and deductible amounts by a person, if—

"(i) the waiver is not offered as part of any advertisement or solicitation;

"(ii) the person does not routinely waive coinsurance or deductible amounts; and

"(iii) the person—

"(I) waives the coinsurance and deductible amounts after determining in good faith that the individual is in financial need;

"(II) fails to collect coinsurance or deductible amounts after making reasonable collection efforts; or

"(III) provides for any permissible waiver as specified in section 1128B(b)(3) or in regulations issued by the Secretary;

"(B) differentials in coinsurance and deductible amounts as part of a benefit plan design as long as the differentials have been disclosed in writing to all beneficiaries, third party payers, and providers, to whom claims are presented and as long as the differentials meet the standards as defined in regulations promulgated by the Secretary not later than 180 days after the date of the enactment of the Health Insurance Portability and Accountability Act of 1996; or

"(C) incentives given to individuals to promote the delivery of preventive care as determined by the Secretary in regulations so promulgated.".

(i) EFFECTIVE DATE.—The amendments made by this section shall apply to acts or omissions occurring on or after January 1, 1997.

SEC. 232. PENALTY FOR FALSE CERTIFICATION FOR HOME HEALTH SERVICES.

(a) IN GENERAL.—Section 1128A(b) (42 U.S.C. 1320a–7a(b)) is amended by adding at the end the following new paragraph:

"(3)(A) Any physician who executes a document described in subparagraph (B) with respect to an individual knowing that all of the requirements referred to in such subparagraph are not met with respect to the individual shall be subject to a civil monetary penalty of not more than the greater of—

"(i) $5,000, or

"(ii) three times the amount of the payments under title XVIII for home health services which are made pursuant to such certification.

"(B) A document described in this subparagraph is any document that certifies, for purposes of title XVIII, that an individual

meets the requirements of section 1814(a)(2)(C) or 1835(a)(2)(A) in the case of home health services furnished to the individual.".

(b) EFFECTIVE DATE.—The amendment made by subsection (a) shall apply to certifications made on or after the date of the enactment of this Act.

Subtitle E—Revisions to Criminal Law

SEC. 241. DEFINITIONS RELATING TO FEDERAL HEALTH CARE OFFENSE.

(a) IN GENERAL.—Chapter 1 of title 18, United States Code, is amended by adding at the end the following:

"§ 24. Definitions relating to Federal health care offense

"(a) As used in this title, the term 'Federal health care offense' means a violation of, or a criminal conspiracy to violate—

"(1) section 669, 1035, 1347, or 1518 of this title;

"(2) section 287, 371, 664, 666, 1001, 1027, 1341, 1343, or 1954 of this title, if the violation or conspiracy relates to a health care benefit program.

"(b) As used in this title, the term 'health care benefit program' means any public or private plan or contract, affecting commerce, under which any medical benefit, item, or service is provided to any individual, and includes any individual or entity who is providing a medical benefit, item, or service for which payment may be made under the plan or contract.".

(b) CLERICAL AMENDMENT.—The table of sections at the beginning of chapter 2 of title 18, United States Code, is amended by inserting after the item relating to section 23 the following new item:

"24. Definitions relating to Federal health care offense.".

SEC. 242. HEALTH CARE FRAUD.

(a) OFFENSE.—

(1) IN GENERAL.—Chapter 63 of title 18, United States Code, is amended by adding at the end the following:

"§ 1347. Health care fraud

"Whoever knowingly and willfully executes, or attempts to execute, a scheme or artifice—

"(1) to defraud any health care benefit program; or

"(2) to obtain, by means of false or fraudulent pretenses, representations, or promises, any of the money or property owned by, or under the custody or control of, any health care benefit program,

in connection with the delivery of or payment for health care benefits, items, or services, shall be fined under this title or imprisoned not more than 10 years, or both. If the violation results in serious bodily injury (as defined in section 1365 of this title), such person shall be fined under this title or imprisoned not more than 20 years, or both; and if the violation results in death, such person shall be fined under this title, or imprisoned for any term of years or for life, or both.".

(2) CLERICAL AMENDMENT.—The table of sections at the beginning of chapter 63 of title 18, United States Code, is amended by adding at the end the following:

"1347. Health care fraud.".

(b) CRIMINAL FINES DEPOSITED IN FEDERAL HOSPITAL INSURANCE TRUST FUND.—The Secretary of the Treasury shall deposit into the Federal Hospital Insurance Trust Fund pursuant to section 1817(k)(2)(C) of the Social Security Act (42 U.S.C. 1395i) an amount equal to the criminal fines imposed under section 1347 of title 18, United States Code (relating to health care fraud).

SEC. 243. THEFT OR EMBEZZLEMENT.

(a) IN GENERAL.—Chapter 31 of title 18, United States Code, is amended by adding at the end the following:

"§ 669. Theft or embezzlement in connection with health care

"(a) Whoever knowingly and willfully embezzles, steals, or otherwise without authority converts to the use of any person other than the rightful owner, or intentionally misapplies any of the moneys, funds, securities, premiums, credits, property, or other assets of a health care benefit program, shall be fined under this title or imprisoned not more than 10 years, or both; but if the value of such property does not exceed the sum of $100 the defendant shall be fined under this title or imprisoned not more than one year, or both.

"(b) As used in this section, the term 'health care benefit program' has the meaning given such term in section 1347(b) of this title.".

(b) CLERICAL AMENDMENT.—The table of sections at the beginning of chapter 31 of title 18, United States Code, is amended by adding at the end the following:

"669. Theft or embezzlement in connection with health care.".

SEC. 244. FALSE STATEMENTS.

(a) IN GENERAL.—Chapter 47 of title 18, United States Code, is amended by adding at the end the following:

"§ 1035. False statements relating to health care matters

"(a) Whoever, in any matter involving a health care benefit program, knowingly and willfully—

"(1) falsifies, conceals, or covers up by any trick, scheme, or device a material fact; or

"(2) makes any materially false, fictitious, or fraudulent statements or representations, or makes or uses any materially false writing or document knowing the same to contain any materially false, fictitious, or fraudulent statement or entry,

in connection with the delivery of or payment for health care benefits, items, or services, shall be fined under this title or imprisoned not more than 5 years, or both.

"(b) As used in this section, the term 'health care benefit program' has the meaning given such term in section 1347(b) of this title.".

(b) CLERICAL AMENDMENT.—The table of sections at the beginning of chapter 47 of title 18, United States Code, is amended by adding at the end the following new item:

"1035. False statements relating to health care matters.".

SEC. 245. OBSTRUCTION OF CRIMINAL INVESTIGATIONS OF HEALTH CARE OFFENSES.

(a) IN GENERAL.—Chapter 73 of title 18, United States Code, is amended by adding at the end the following:

"§ 1518. Obstruction of criminal investigations of health care offenses

"(a) Whoever willfully prevents, obstructs, misleads, delays or attempts to prevent, obstruct, mislead, or delay the communication of information or records relating to a violation of a Federal health care offense to a criminal investigator shall be fined under this title or imprisoned not more than 5 years, or both.

"(b) As used in this section the term 'criminal investigator' means any individual duly authorized by a department, agency, or armed force of the United States to conduct or engage in investigations for prosecutions for violations of health care offenses.".

(b) CLERICAL AMENDMENT.—The table of sections at the beginning of chapter 73 of title 18, United States Code, is amended by adding at the end the following new item:

"1518. Obstruction of criminal investigations of health care offenses.".

SEC. 246. LAUNDERING OF MONETARY INSTRUMENTS.

Section 1956(c)(7) of title 18, United States Code, is amended by adding at the end the following:

> *"(F) Any act or activity constituting an offense involving a Federal health care offense.".*

SEC. 247. INJUNCTIVE RELIEF RELATING TO HEALTH CARE OFFENSES.

(a) IN GENERAL.—Section 1345(a)(1) of title 18, United States Code, is amended—

(1) by striking "or" at the end of subparagraph (A);

(2) by inserting "or" at the end of subparagraph (B); and

(3) by adding at the end the following:

"(C) committing or about to commit a Federal health care offense.".

(b) FREEZING OF ASSETS.—Section 1345(a)(2) of title 18, United States Code, is amended by inserting "or a Federal health care offense" after "title)".

SEC. 248. AUTHORIZED INVESTIGATIVE DEMAND PROCEDURES.

(a) IN GENERAL.—Chapter 223 of title 18, United States Code, is amended by adding after section 3485 the following:

"§ 3486. Authorized investigative demand procedures

"(a) AUTHORIZATION.—(1) In any investigation relating to any act or activity involving a Federal health care offense, the Attorney General or the Attorney General's designee may issue in writing and cause to be served a subpoena—

"(A) requiring the production of any records (including any books, papers, documents, electronic media, or other objects or tangible things), which may be relevant to an authorized law enforcement inquiry, that a person or legal entity may possess or have care, custody, or control; or

"(B) requiring a custodian of records to give testimony concerning the production and authentication of such records.

"(2) A subpoena under this subsection shall describe the objects required to be produced and prescribe a return date within a reasonable period of time within which the objects can be assembled and made available.

"(3) The production of records shall not be required under this section at any place more than 500 miles distant from the place where the subpoena for the production of such records is served.

"(4) Witnesses summoned under this section shall be paid the same fees and mileage that are paid witnesses in the courts of the United States.

"(b) SERVICE.—A subpoena issued under this section may be served by any person who is at least 18 years of age and is designated in the subpoena to serve it. Service upon a natural person may be made by personal delivery of the subpoena to him. Service may be made upon a domestic or foreign corporation or upon a partnership or other unincorporated association which is subject to suit under a common name, by delivering the subpoena to an officer, to a managing or general agent, or to any other agent authorized by appointment or by law to receive service of process. The affidavit of the person serving the subpoena entered on a true copy thereof by the person serving it shall be proof of service.

"(c) ENFORCEMENT.—In the case of contumacy by or refusal to obey a subpoena issued to any person, the Attorney General may invoke the aid of any court of the United States within the jurisdiction of which the investigation is carried on or of which the subpoenaed person is an inhabitant, or in which he carries on business or may be found, to compel compliance with the subpoena. The court may issue an order requiring the subpoenaed person to appear before the Attorney General to produce records, if so ordered, or to give testimony concerning the production and authentication of such records. Any failure to obey the order of the court may be punished by the court as a contempt thereof. All process in any such case may be served in any judicial district in which such person may be found.

"(d) IMMUNITY FROM CIVIL LIABILITY.—Notwithstanding any Federal, State, or local law, any person, including officers, agents, and employees, receiving a summons under this section, who complies in good faith with the summons and thus produces the materials sought, shall not be liable in any court of any State or the United States to any customer or other person for such production or for nondisclosure of that production to the customer.

"(e) LIMITATION ON USE.—(1) Health information about an individual that is disclosed under this section may not be used in, or disclosed to any person for use in, any administrative, civil, or criminal action or investigation directed against the individual who is the subject of the information unless the action or investigation arises out of and is directly related to receipt of health care or payment for health care or action involving a fraudulent claim related to health; or if authorized by an appropriate order of a court of competent jurisdiction, granted after application showing good cause therefor.

"(2) In assessing good cause, the court shall weigh the public interest and the need for disclosure against the injury to the patient, to the physician-patient relationship, and to the treatment services.

"(3) Upon the granting of such order, the court, in determining the extent to which any disclosure of all or any part of any record is necessary, shall impose appropriate safeguards against unauthorized disclosure.".

(b) CLERICAL AMENDMENT.—The table of sections at the beginning of chapter 223 of title 18, United States Code, is amended by inserting after the item relating to section 3485 the following new item:

"3486. Authorized investigative demand procedures.".

(c) CONFORMING AMENDMENT.—Section 1510(b)(3)(B) of title 18, United States Code, is amended by inserting "or a Department of Justice subpoena (issued under section 3486 of title 18)," after "subpoena".

SEC. 249. FORFEITURES FOR FEDERAL HEALTH CARE OFFENSES.

(a) IN GENERAL.—Section 982(a) of title 18, United States Code, is amended by adding after paragraph (5) the following new paragraph:

"(6) The court, in imposing sentence on a person convicted of a Federal health care offense, shall order the person to forfeit property, real or personal, that constitutes or is derived, directly or indirectly, from gross proceeds traceable to the commission of the offense.".

(b) CONFORMING AMENDMENT.—Section 982(b)(1)(A) of title 18, United States Code, is amended by inserting "or (a)(6)" after "(a)(1)".

(c) PROPERTY FORFEITED DEPOSITED IN FEDERAL HOSPITAL INSURANCE TRUST FUND.—

(1) IN GENERAL.—After the payment of the costs of asset forfeiture has been made and after all restoration payments (if any) have been made, and notwithstanding any other provision of law, the Secretary of the Treasury shall deposit into the Federal Hospital Insurance Trust Fund pursuant to section 1817(k)(2)(C) of the Social Security Act, as added by section 301(b), an amount equal to the net amount realized from the forfeiture of property by reason of a Federal health care offense pursuant to section 982(a)(6) of title 18, United States Code.

(2) COSTS OF ASSET FORFEITURE.—For purposes of paragraph (1), the term "payment of the costs of asset forfeiture" means—

(A) the payment, at the discretion of the Attorney General, of any expenses necessary to seize, detain, inventory, safeguard, maintain, advertise, sell, or dispose of property under seizure, detention, or forfeited, or of any other necessary expenses incident to the seizure, detention, forfeiture, or disposal of such property, including payment for—

(i) contract services;

(ii) the employment of outside contractors to operate and manage properties or provide other specialized services necessary to dispose of such properties in an effort to maximize the return from such properties; and

(iii) reimbursement of any Federal, State, or local agency for any expenditures made to perform the functions described in this subparagraph;

(B) at the discretion of the Attorney General, the payment of awards for information or assistance leading to a civil or criminal forfeiture involving any Federal agency participating in the Health Care Fraud and Abuse Control Account;

(C) the compromise and payment of valid liens and mortgages against property that has been forfeited, subject to the discretion of the Attorney General to determine the validity of any such lien or mortgage and the amount of payment to be made, and the employment of attorneys and other personnel skilled in State real estate law as necessary;

(D) payment authorized in connection with remission or mitigation procedures relating to property forfeited; and

(E) the payment of State and local property taxes on forfeited real property that accrued between the date of the violation giving rise to the forfeiture and the date of the forfeiture order.

(3) RESTORATION PAYMENT.—Notwithstanding any other provision of law, if the Federal health care offense referred to in paragraph (1) resulted in a loss to an employee welfare benefit plan within the meaning of section 3(1) of the Employee Retirement Income Security Act of 1974, the Secretary of the Treasury shall transfer to such employee welfare benefit plan, from the amount realized from the forfeiture of property referred to in paragraph (1), an amount equal to such loss. For purposes of paragraph (1), the term 'restoration payment' means the amount transferred to an employee welfare benefit plan pursuant to this paragraph.".

SEC. 250. RELATION TO ERISA AUTHORITY.

Nothing in this subtitle shall be construed as affecting the authority of the Secretary of Labor under section 506(b) of the Employee Retirement Income Security Act of 1974, including the Secretary's authority with respect to violations of title 18, United States Code (as amended by this subtitle).

Subtitle F—Administrative Simplification

SEC. 261. PURPOSE.

It is the purpose of this subtitle to improve the medicare program under title XVIII of the Social Security Act, the medicaid program under title XIX of such Act, and the efficiency and effectiveness of the health care system, by encouraging the development of a health information system through the establishment of standards and requirements for the electronic transmission of certain health information.

SEC. 262. ADMINISTRATIVE SIMPLIFICATION.

(a) IN GENERAL.—Title XI (42 U.S.C. 1301 et seq.) is amended by adding at the end the following:

"PART C—ADMINISTRATIVE SIMPLIFICATION

"DEFINITIONS

"SEC. 1171. For purposes of this part:

"(1) CODE SET.—The term 'code set' means any set of codes used for encoding data elements, such as tables of terms, medical concepts, medical diagnostic codes, or medical procedure codes.

"(2) HEALTH CARE CLEARINGHOUSE.—The term 'health care clearinghouse' means a public or private entity that processes or facilitates the processing of nonstandard data elements of health information into standard data elements.

"(3) HEALTH CARE PROVIDER.—The term 'health care provider' includes a provider of services (as defined in section 1861(u)), a provider of medical or other health services (as defined in section 1861(s)), and any other person furnishing health care services or supplies.

"(4) HEALTH INFORMATION.—The term 'health information' means any information, whether oral or recorded in any form or medium, that—

"(A) is created or received by a health care provider, health plan, public health authority, employer, life insurer, school or university, or health care clearinghouse; and

"(B) relates to the past, present, or future physical or mental health or condition of an individual, the provision of health care to an individual, or the past, present, or future payment for the provision of health care to an individual.

"(5) HEALTH PLAN.—The term 'health plan' means an individual or group plan that provides, or pays the cost of, medical care (as such term is defined in section 2791 of the Public Health Service Act). Such term includes the following, and any combination thereof:

"(A) A group health plan (as defined in section 2791(a) of the Public Health Service Act), but only if the plan—

"(i) has 50 or more participants (as defined in section 3(7) of the Employee Retirement Income Security Act of 1974); or

"(ii) is administered by an entity other than the employer who established and maintains the plan.

"(B) A health insurance issuer (as defined in section 2791(b) of the Public Health Service Act).

"(C) A health maintenance organization (as defined in section 2791(b) of the Public Health Service Act).

"(D) Part A or part B of the medicare program under title XVIII.

"(E) The medicaid program under title XIX.

"(F) A medicare supplemental policy (as defined in section 1882(g)(1)).

"(G) A long-term care policy, including a nursing home fixed indemnity policy (unless the Secretary determines that such a policy does not provide sufficiently comprehensive coverage of a benefit so that the policy should be treated as a health plan).

"(H) An employee welfare benefit plan or any other arrangement which is established or maintained for the purpose of offering or providing health benefits to the employees of 2 or more employers.

"(I) The health care program for active military personnel under title 10, United States Code.

"(J) The veterans health care program under chapter 17 of title 38, United States Code.

"(K) The Civilian Health and Medical Program of the Uniformed Services (CHAMPUS), as defined in section 1072(4) of title 10, United States Code.

"(L) The Indian health service program under the Indian Health Care Improvement Act (25 U.S.C. 1601 et seq.).

"(M) The Federal Employees Health Benefit Plan under chapter 89 of title 5, United States Code.

"(6) INDIVIDUALLY IDENTIFIABLE HEALTH INFORMATION.— The term 'individually identifiable health information' means any information, including demographic information collected from an individual, that—

"(A) is created or received by a health care provider, health plan, employer, or health care clearinghouse; and

"(B) relates to the past, present, or future physical or mental health or condition of an individual, the provision of health care to an individual, or the past, present, or future payment for the provision of health care to an individual, and—

"(i) identifies the individual; or

"(ii) with respect to which there is a reasonable basis to believe that the information can be used to identify the individual.

"(7) STANDARD.—The term 'standard', when used with reference to a data element of health information or a transaction referred to in section 1173(a)(1), means any such data element or transaction that meets each of the standards and implementation specifications adopted or established by the Secretary with respect to the data element or transaction under sections 1172 through 1174.

"(8) STANDARD SETTING ORGANIZATION.—The term 'standard setting organization' means a standard setting organization accredited by the American National Standards Institute, including the National Council for Prescription Drug Programs, that develops standards for information transactions, data elements, or any other standard that is necessary to, or will facilitate, the implementation of this part.

"GENERAL REQUIREMENTS FOR ADOPTION OF STANDARDS

"SEC. 1172. (a) APPLICABILITY.—Any standard adopted under this part shall apply, in whole or in part, to the following persons:

"(1) A health plan.

"(2) A health care clearinghouse.

"(3) A health care provider who transmits any health information in electronic form in connection with a transaction referred to in section 1173(a)(1).

"(b) REDUCTION OF COSTS.—Any standard adopted under this part shall be consistent with the objective of reducing the administrative costs of providing and paying for health care.

"(c) ROLE OF STANDARD SETTING ORGANIZATIONS.—

"(1) IN GENERAL.—Except as provided in paragraph (2), any standard adopted under this part shall be a standard that has been developed, adopted, or modified by a standard setting organization.

"(2) SPECIAL RULES.—

"(A) DIFFERENT STANDARDS.—The Secretary may adopt a standard that is different from any standard developed, adopted, or modified by a standard setting organization, if—

"(i) the different standard will substantially reduce administrative costs to health care providers and health plans compared to the alternatives; and

"(ii) the standard is promulgated in accordance with the rulemaking procedures of subchapter III of chapter 5 of title 5, United States Code.

"(B) NO STANDARD BY STANDARD SETTING ORGANIZATION.—If no standard setting organization has developed, adopted, or modified any standard relating to a standard that the Secretary is authorized or required to adopt under this part—

"(i) paragraph (1) shall not apply; and

"(ii) subsection (f) shall apply.

"(3) CONSULTATION REQUIREMENT.—

"(A) IN GENERAL.—A standard may not be adopted under this part unless—

"(i) in the case of a standard that has been developed, adopted, or modified by a standard setting organization, the organization consulted with each of the organizations described in subparagraph (B) in the course of such development, adoption, or modification; and

"(ii) in the case of any other standard, the Secretary, in complying with the requirements of subsection (f), consulted with each of the organizations described in subparagraph (B) before adopting the standard.

"(B) ORGANIZATIONS DESCRIBED.—The organizations referred to in subparagraph (A) are the following:

"(i) The National Uniform Billing Committee.

"(ii) The National Uniform Claim Committee.

"(iii) The Workgroup for Electronic Data Interchange.

"(iv) The American Dental Association.

"(d) IMPLEMENTATION SPECIFICATIONS.—The Secretary shall establish specifications for implementing each of the standards adopted under this part.

"(e) PROTECTION OF TRADE SECRETS.—Except as otherwise required by law, a standard adopted under this part shall not require disclosure of trade secrets or confidential commercial information by a person required to comply with this part.

"(f) ASSISTANCE TO THE SECRETARY.—In complying with the requirements of this part, the Secretary shall rely on the recommendations of the National Committee on Vital and Health Statistics established under section 306(k) of the Public Health Service Act (42 U.S.C. 242k(k)), and shall consult with appropriate Federal and State agencies and private organizations. The Secretary shall publish in the Federal Register any recommendation of the National Committee on Vital and Health Statistics regarding the adoption of a standard under this part.

"(g) APPLICATION TO MODIFICATIONS OF STANDARDS.—This section shall apply to a modification to a standard (including an addition to a standard) adopted under section 1174(b) in the same manner as it applies to an initial standard adopted under section 1174(a).

"STANDARDS FOR INFORMATION TRANSACTIONS AND DATA ELEMENTS

"SEC. 1173. (a) STANDARDS TO ENABLE ELECTRONIC EXCHANGE.—

"(1) IN GENERAL.—The Secretary shall adopt standards for transactions, and data elements for such transactions, to enable health information to be exchanged electronically, that are appropriate for—

"(A) the financial and administrative transactions described in paragraph (2); and

"(B) other financial and administrative transactions determined appropriate by the Secretary, consistent with the goals of improving the operation of the health care system and reducing administrative costs.

"(2) TRANSACTIONS.—The transactions referred to in paragraph (1)(A) are transactions with respect to the following:

"(A) Health claims or equivalent encounter information.

"(B) Health claims attachments.

"(C) Enrollment and disenrollment in a health plan.

"(D) Eligibility for a health plan.

"(E) Health care payment and remittance advice.

"(F) Health plan premium payments.

"(G) First report of injury.

"(H) Health claim status.

"(I) Referral certification and authorization.

"(3) ACCOMMODATION OF SPECIFIC PROVIDERS.—The standards adopted by the Secretary under paragraph (1) shall accommodate the needs of different types of health care providers.

"(b) UNIQUE HEALTH IDENTIFIERS.—

"(1) IN GENERAL.—The Secretary shall adopt standards providing for a standard unique health identifier for each individual, employer, health plan, and health care provider for use in the health care system. In carrying out the preceding sentence for each health plan and health care provider, the Secretary shall take into account multiple uses for identifiers and multiple locations and specialty classifications for health care providers.

"(2) USE OF IDENTIFIERS.—The standards adopted under paragraphs (1) shall specify the purposes for which a unique health identifier may be used.

"(c) CODE SETS.—

"(1) IN GENERAL.—The Secretary shall adopt standards that—

"(A) select code sets for appropriate data elements for the transactions referred to in subsection (a)(1) from among the code sets that have been developed by private and public entities; or

"(B) establish code sets for such data elements if no code sets for the data elements have been developed.

"(2) DISTRIBUTION.—The Secretary shall establish efficient and low-cost procedures for distribution (including electronic distribution) of code sets and modifications made to such code sets under section 1174(b).

"(d) SECURITY STANDARDS FOR HEALTH INFORMATION.—

"(1) SECURITY STANDARDS.—The Secretary shall adopt security standards that—

"(A) take into account—

"(i) the technical capabilities of record systems used to maintain health information;

"(ii) the costs of security measures;

"(iii) the need for training persons who have access to health information;

"(iv) the value of audit trails in computerized record systems; and

"(v) the needs and capabilities of small health care providers and rural health care providers (as such providers are defined by the Secretary); and

"(B) ensure that a health care clearinghouse, if it is part of a larger organization, has policies and security procedures which isolate the activities of the health care clearinghouse with respect to processing information in a manner that prevents unauthorized access to such information by such larger organization.

"(2) SAFEGUARDS.—Each person described in section 1172(a) who maintains or transmits health information shall maintain reasonable and appropriate administrative, technical, and physical safeguards—

"(A) to ensure the integrity and confidentiality of the information;

"(B) to protect against any reasonably anticipated—

"(i) threats or hazards to the security or integrity of the information; and

"(ii) unauthorized uses or disclosures of the information; and

"(C) otherwise to ensure compliance with this part by the officers and employees of such person.

"(e) ELECTRONIC SIGNATURE.—

"(1) STANDARDS.—The Secretary, in coordination with the Secretary of Commerce, shall adopt standards specifying procedures for the electronic transmission and authentication of sig-

natures with respect to the transactions referred to in subsection (a)(1).

"(2) EFFECT OF COMPLIANCE.—Compliance with the standards adopted under paragraph (1) shall be deemed to satisfy Federal and State statutory requirements for written signatures with respect to the transactions referred to in subsection (a)(1).

"(f) TRANSFER OF INFORMATION AMONG HEALTH PLANS.—The Secretary shall adopt standards for transferring among health plans appropriate standard data elements needed for the coordination of benefits, the sequential processing of claims, and other data elements for individuals who have more than one health plan.

"TIMETABLES FOR ADOPTION OF STANDARDS

"SEC. 1174. (a) INITIAL STANDARDS.—The Secretary shall carry out section 1173 not later than 18 months after the date of the enactment of the Health Insurance Portability and Accountability Act of 1996, except that standards relating to claims attachments shall be adopted not later than 30 months after such date.

"(b) ADDITIONS AND MODIFICATIONS TO STANDARDS.—

"(1) IN GENERAL.—Except as provided in paragraph (2), the Secretary shall review the standards adopted under section 1173, and shall adopt modifications to the standards (including additions to the standards), as determined appropriate, but not more frequently than once every 12 months. Any addition or modification to a standard shall be completed in a manner which minimizes the disruption and cost of compliance.

"(2) SPECIAL RULES.—

"(A) FIRST 12-MONTH PERIOD.—Except with respect to additions and modifications to code sets under subparagraph (B), the Secretary may not adopt any modification to a standard adopted under this part during the 12-month period beginning on the date the standard is initially adopted, unless the Secretary determines that the modification is necessary in order to permit compliance with the standard.

"(B) ADDITIONS AND MODIFICATIONS TO CODE SETS.—

"(i) IN GENERAL.—The Secretary shall ensure that procedures exist for the routine maintenance, testing, enhancement, and expansion of code sets.

"(ii) ADDITIONAL RULES.—If a code set is modified under this subsection, the modified code set shall include instructions on how data elements of health information that were encoded prior to the modification may be converted or translated so as to preserve the informational value of the data elements that existed before the modification. Any modification to a code set under this subsection shall be implemented in a manner that minimizes the disruption and cost of complying with such modification.

"REQUIREMENTS

"SEC. 1175. (a) CONDUCT OF TRANSACTIONS BY PLANS.—

"(1) IN GENERAL.—If a person desires to conduct a transaction referred to in section 1173(a)(1) with a health plan as a standard transaction—

"(A) the health plan may not refuse to conduct such transaction as a standard transaction;

"(B) the insurance plan may not delay such transaction, or otherwise adversely affect, or attempt to adversely affect, the person or the transaction on the ground that the transaction is a standard transaction; and

"(C) the information transmitted and received in connection with the transaction shall be in the form of standard data elements of health information.

"(2) SATISFACTION OF REQUIREMENTS.—A health plan may satisfy the requirements under paragraph (1) by—

"(A) directly transmitting and receiving standard data elements of health information; or

"(B) submitting nonstandard data elements to a health care clearinghouse for processing into standard data elements and transmission by the health care clearinghouse, and receiving standard data elements through the health care clearinghouse.

"(3) TIMETABLE FOR COMPLIANCE.—Paragraph (1) shall not be construed to require a health plan to comply with any standard, implementation specification, or modification to a standard or specification adopted or established by the Secretary under sections 1172 through 1174 at any time prior to the date on which the plan is required to comply with the standard or specification under subsection (b).

"(b) COMPLIANCE WITH STANDARDS.—

"(1) INITIAL COMPLIANCE.—

"(A) IN GENERAL.—Not later than 24 months after the date on which an initial standard or implementation specification is adopted or established under sections 1172 and 1173, each person to whom the standard or implementation specification applies shall comply with the standard or specification.

"(B) SPECIAL RULE FOR SMALL HEALTH PLANS.—In the case of a small health plan, paragraph (1) shall be applied by substituting '36 months' for '24 months'. For purposes of this subsection, the Secretary shall determine the plans that qualify as small health plans.

"(2) COMPLIANCE WITH MODIFIED STANDARDS.—If the Secretary adopts a modification to a standard or implementation specification under this part, each person to whom the standard or implementation specification applies shall comply with the modified standard or implementation specification at such time as the Secretary determines appropriate, taking into account the time needed to comply due to the nature and extent of the modification. The time determined appropriate under the preceding sentence may not be earlier than the last day of the 180-day period beginning on the date such modification is adopted. The Secretary may extend the time for compliance for small health plans, if the Secretary determines that such extension is appropriate.

"(3) CONSTRUCTION.—Nothing in this subsection shall be construed to prohibit any person from complying with a standard or specification by—

"(A) submitting nonstandard data elements to a health care clearinghouse for processing into standard data elements and transmission by the health care clearinghouse; or

"(B) receiving standard data elements through a health care clearinghouse.

"GENERAL PENALTY FOR FAILURE TO COMPLY WITH REQUIREMENTS AND STANDARDS

"SEC. 1176. (a) GENERAL PENALTY.—

"(1) IN GENERAL.—Except as provided in subsection (b), the Secretary shall impose on any person who violates a provision of this part a penalty of not more than $100 for each such violation, except that the total amount imposed on the person for all violations of an identical requirement or prohibition during a calendar year may not exceed $25,000.

"(2) PROCEDURES.—The provisions of section 1128A (other than subsections (a) and (b) and the second sentence of subsection (f)) shall apply to the imposition of a civil money penalty under this subsection in the same manner as such provisions apply to the imposition of a penalty under such section 1128A.

"(b) LIMITATIONS.—

"(1) OFFENSES OTHERWISE PUNISHABLE.—A penalty may not be imposed under subsection (a) with respect to an act if the act constitutes an offense punishable under section 1177.

"(2) NONCOMPLIANCE NOT DISCOVERED.—A penalty may not be imposed under subsection (a) with respect to a provision of this part if it is established to the satisfaction of the Secretary that the person liable for the penalty did not know, and by exercising reasonable diligence would not have known, that such person violated the provision.

"(3) FAILURES DUE TO REASONABLE CAUSE.—

"(A) IN GENERAL.—Except as provided in subparagraph (B), a penalty may not be imposed under subsection (a) if—

"(i) the failure to comply was due to reasonable cause and not to willful neglect; and

"(ii) the failure to comply is corrected during the 30-day period beginning on the first date the person liable for the penalty knew, or by exercising reasonable diligence would have known, that the failure to comply occurred.

"(B) EXTENSION OF PERIOD.—

"(i) NO PENALTY.—The period referred to in subparagraph (A)(ii) may be extended as determined appropriate by the Secretary based on the nature and extent of the failure to comply.

"(ii) ASSISTANCE.—If the Secretary determines that a person failed to comply because the person was unable to comply, the Secretary may provide technical assistance to the person during the period described in subparagraph (A)(ii). Such assistance shall be pro-

vided in any manner determined appropriate by the Secretary.

"(4) REDUCTION.—In the case of a failure to comply which is due to reasonable cause and not to willful neglect, any penalty under subsection (a) that is not entirely waived under paragraph (3) may be waived to the extent that the payment of such penalty would be excessive relative to the compliance failure involved.

"WRONGFUL DISCLOSURE OF INDIVIDUALLY IDENTIFIABLE HEALTH INFORMATION

"SEC. 1177. (a) OFFENSE.—A person who knowingly and in violation of this part—

"(1) uses or causes to be used a unique health identifier;

"(2) obtains individually identifiable health information relating to an individual; or

"(3) discloses individually identifiable health information to another person,

shall be punished as provided in subsection (b).

"(b) PENALTIES.—A person described in subsection (a) shall—

"(1) be fined not more than $50,000, imprisoned not more than 1 year, or both;

"(2) if the offense is committed under false pretenses, be fined not more than $100,000, imprisoned not more than 5 years, or both; and

"(3) if the offense is committed with intent to sell, transfer, or use individually identifiable health information for commercial advantage, personal gain, or malicious harm, fined not more than $250,000, imprisoned not more than 10 years, or both.

"EFFECT ON STATE LAW

"SEC. 1178. (a) GENERAL EFFECT.—

"(1) GENERAL RULE.—Except as provided in paragraph (2), a provision or requirement under this part, or a standard or implementation specification adopted or established under sections 1172 through 1174, shall supersede any contrary provision of State law, including a provision of State law that requires medical or health plan records (including billing information) to be maintained or transmitted in written rather than electronic form.

"(2) EXCEPTIONS.—A provision or requirement under this part, or a standard or implementation specification adopted or established under sections 1172 through 1174, shall not supersede a contrary provision of State law, if the provision of State law—

"(A) is a provision the Secretary determines—

"(i) is necessary—

"(I) to prevent fraud and abuse;

"(II) to ensure appropriate State regulation of insurance and health plans;

"(III) for State reporting on health care delivery or costs; or

"(IV) for other purposes; or

"(ii) addresses controlled substances; or

"(B) subject to section 264(c)(2) of the Health Insurance Portability and Accountability Act of 1996, relates to the privacy of individually identifiable health information.

"(b) PUBLIC HEALTH.—Nothing in this part shall be construed to invalidate or limit the authority, power, or procedures established under any law providing for the reporting of disease or injury, child abuse, birth, or death, public health surveillance, or public health investigation or intervention.

"(c) STATE REGULATORY REPORTING.—Nothing in this part shall limit the ability of a State to require a health plan to report, or to provide access to, information for management audits, financial audits, program monitoring and evaluation, facility licensure or certification, or individual licensure or certification.

"PROCESSING PAYMENT TRANSACTIONS BY FINANCIAL INSTITUTIONS

"SEC. 1179. To the extent that an entity is engaged in activities of a financial institution (as defined in section 1101 of the Right to Financial Privacy Act of 1978), or is engaged in authorizing, processing, clearing, settling, billing, transferring, reconciling, or collecting payments, for a financial institution, this part, and any standard adopted under this part, shall not apply to the entity with respect to such activities, including the following:

"(1) The use or disclosure of information by the entity for authorizing, processing, clearing, settling, billing, transferring, reconciling or collecting, a payment for, or related to, health plan premiums or health care, where such payment is made by any means, including a credit, debit, or other payment card, an account, check, or electronic funds transfer.

"(2) The request for, or the use or disclosure of, information by the entity with respect to a payment described in paragraph (1)—

"(A) for transferring receivables;

"(B) for auditing;

"(C) in connection with—

"(i) a customer dispute; or

"(ii) an inquiry from, or to, a customer;

"(D) in a communication to a customer of the entity regarding the customer's transactions, payment card, account, check, or electronic funds transfer;

"(E) for reporting to consumer reporting agencies; or

"(F) for complying with—

"(i) a civil or criminal subpoena; or

"(ii) a Federal or State law regulating the entity.".

(b) CONFORMING AMENDMENTS.—

(1) REQUIREMENT FOR MEDICARE PROVIDERS.—Section 1866(a)(1) (42 U.S.C. 1395cc(a)(1)) is amended—

(A) by striking "and" at the end of subparagraph (P);

(B) by striking the period at the end of subparagraph (Q) and inserting "; and"; and

(C) by inserting immediately after subparagraph (Q) the following new subparagraph:

"(R) to contract only with a health care clearinghouse (as defined in section 1171) that meets each standard and imple-

mentation specification adopted or established under part C of title XI on or after the date on which the health care clearinghouse is required to comply with the standard or specification.".

(2) TITLE HEADING.—Title XI (42 U.S.C. 1301 et seq.) is amended by striking the title heading and inserting the following:

"TITLE XI—GENERAL PROVISIONS, PEER REVIEW, AND ADMINISTRATIVE SIMPLIFICATION".

SEC. 263. CHANGES IN MEMBERSHIP AND DUTIES OF NATIONAL COMMITTEE ON VITAL AND HEALTH STATISTICS.

Section 306(k) of the Public Health Service Act (42 U.S.C. 242k(k)) is amended—

(1) in paragraph (1), by striking "16" and inserting "18";

(2) by amending paragraph (2) to read as follows:

"(2) The members of the Committee shall be appointed from among persons who have distinguished themselves in the fields of health statistics, electronic interchange of health care information, privacy and security of electronic information, population-based public health, purchasing or financing health care services, integrated computerized health information systems, health services research, consumer interests in health information, health data standards, epidemiology, and the provision of health services. Members of the Committee shall be appointed for terms of 4 years.";

(3) by redesignating paragraphs (3) through (5) as paragraphs (4) through (6), respectively, and inserting after paragraph (2) the following:

"(3) Of the members of the Committee—

"(A) 1 shall be appointed, not later than 60 days after the date of the enactment of the Health Insurance Portability and Accountability Act of 1996, by the Speaker of the House of Representatives after consultation with the minority leader of the House of Representatives;

"(B) 1 shall be appointed, not later than 60 days after the date of the enactment of the Health Insurance Portability and Accountability Act of 1996, by the President pro tempore of the Senate after consultation with the minority leader of the Senate; and

"(C) 16 shall be appointed by the Secretary.";

(4) by amending paragraph (5) (as so redesignated) to read as follows:

"(5) The Committee—

"(A) shall assist and advise the Secretary—

"(i) to delineate statistical problems bearing on health and health services which are of national or international interest;

"(ii) to stimulate studies of such problems by other organizations and agencies whenever possible or to make investigations of such problems through subcommittees;

"(iii) to determine, approve, and revise the terms, definitions, classifications, and guidelines for assessing health status and health services, their distribution and costs, for use (I) within the Department of Health and Human Services, (II) by all programs administered or funded by the

Secretary, including the Federal-State-local cooperative health statistics system referred to in subsection (e), and (III) to the extent possible as determined by the head of the agency involved, by the Department of Veterans Affairs, the Department of Defense, and other Federal agencies concerned with health and health services;

"(iv) with respect to the design of and approval of health statistical and health information systems concerned with the collection, processing, and tabulation of health statistics within the Department of Health and Human Services, with respect to the Cooperative Health Statistics System established under subsection (e), and with respect to the standardized means for the collection of health information and statistics to be established by the Secretary under subsection (j)(1);

"(v) to review and comment on findings and proposals developed by other organizations and agencies and to make recommendations for their adoption or implementation by local, State, national, or international agencies;

"(vi) to cooperate with national committees of other countries and with the World Health Organization and other national agencies in the studies of problems of mutual interest;

"(vii) to issue an annual report on the state of the Nation's health, its health services, their costs and distributions, and to make proposals for improvement of the Nation's health statistics and health information systems; and

"(viii) in complying with the requirements imposed on the Secretary under part C of title XI of the Social Security Act;

"(B) shall study the issues related to the adoption of uniform data standards for patient medical record information and the electronic exchange of such information;

"(C) shall report to the Secretary not later than 4 years after the date of the enactment of the Health Insurance Portability and Accountability Act of 1996 recommendations and legislative proposals for such standards and electronic exchange; and

"(D) shall be responsible generally for advising the Secretary and the Congress on the status of the implementation of part C of title XI of the Social Security Act."; and

(5) by adding at the end the following:

"(7) Not later than 1 year after the date of the enactment of the Health Insurance Portability and Accountability Act of 1996, and annually thereafter, the Committee shall submit to the Congress, and make public, a report regarding the implementation of part C of title XI of the Social Security Act. Such report shall address the following subjects, to the extent that the Committee determines appropriate:

"(A) The extent to which persons required to comply with part C of title XI of the Social Security Act are cooperating in implementing the standards adopted under such part.

"(B) The extent to which such entities are meeting the security standards adopted under such part and the types of penalties assessed for noncompliance with such standards.

"(C) Whether the Federal and State Governments are receiving information of sufficient quality to meet their responsibilities under such part.

"(D) Any problems that exist with respect to implementation of such part.

"(E) The extent to which timetables under such part are being met.".

SEC. 264. RECOMMENDATIONS WITH RESPECT TO PRIVACY OF CERTAIN HEALTH INFORMATION.

(a) IN GENERAL.—Not later than the date that is 12 months after the date of the enactment of this Act, the Secretary of Health and Human Services shall submit to the Committee on Labor and Human Resources and the Committee on Finance of the Senate and the Committee on Commerce and the Committee on Ways and Means of the House of Representatives detailed recommendations on standards with respect to the privacy of individually identifiable health information.

(b) SUBJECTS FOR RECOMMENDATIONS.—The recommendations under subsection (a) shall address at least the following:

(1) The rights that an individual who is a subject of individually identifiable health information should have.

(2) The procedures that should be established for the exercise of such rights.

(3) The uses and disclosures of such information that should be authorized or required.

(c) REGULATIONS.—

(1) IN GENERAL.—If legislation governing standards with respect to the privacy of individually identifiable health information transmitted in connection with the transactions described in section 1173(a) of the Social Security Act (as added by section 262) is not enacted by the date that is 36 months after the date of the enactment of this Act, the Secretary of Health and Human Services shall promulgate final regulations containing such standards not later than the date that is 42 months after the date of the enactment of this Act. Such regulations shall address at least the subjects described in subsection (b).

(2) PREEMPTION.—A regulation promulgated under paragraph (1) shall not supercede a contrary provision of State law, if the provision of State law imposes requirements, standards, or implementation specifications that are more stringent than the requirements, standards, or implementation specifications imposed under the regulation.

(d) CONSULTATION.—In carrying out this section, the Secretary of Health and Human Services shall consult with—

(1) the National Committee on Vital and Health Statistics established under section 306(k) of the Public Health Service Act (42 U.S.C. 242k(k)); and

(2) the Attorney General.

Subtitle G—Duplication and Coordination of Medicare-Related Plans

SEC. 271. DUPLICATION AND COORDINATION OF MEDICARE-RELATED PLANS.

(a) TREATMENT OF CERTAIN HEALTH INSURANCE POLICIES AS NONDUPLICATIVE.—Section 1882(d)(3)(A) (42 U.S.C. 1395ss(d)(3)(A)) is amended—

(1) in clause (iii), by striking "clause (i)" and inserting "clause (i)(II)"; and

(2) by adding at the end the following:

"(iv) For purposes of this subparagraph, a health insurance policy (other than a medicare supplemental policy) providing for benefits which are payable to or on behalf of an individual without regard to other health benefit coverage of such individual is not considered to 'duplicate' any health benefits under this title, under title XIX, or under a health insurance policy, and subclauses (I) and (III) of clause (i) do not apply to such a policy.

"(v) For purposes of this subparagraph, a health insurance policy (or a rider to an insurance contract which is not a health insurance policy) is not considered to 'duplicate' health benefits under this title or under another health insurance policy if it—

"(I) provides health care benefits only for long-term care, nursing home care, home health care, or community-based care, or any combination thereof,

"(II) coordinates against or excludes items and services available or paid for under this title or under another health insurance policy, and

"(III) for policies sold or issued on or after the end of the 90-day period beginning on the date of enactment of the Health Insurance Portability and Accountability Act of 1996) discloses such coordination or exclusion in the policy's outline of coverage.

For purposes of this clause, the terms 'coordinates' and 'coordination' mean, with respect to a policy in relation to health benefits under this title or under another health insurance policy, that the policy under its terms is secondary to, or excludes from payment, items and services to the extent available or paid for under this title or under another health insurance policy.

"(vi)(I) An individual entitled to benefits under part A or enrolled under part B of this title who is applying for a health insurance policy (other than a policy described in subclause (III)) shall be furnished a disclosure statement described in clause (vii) for the type of policy being applied for. Such statement shall be furnished as a part of (or together with) the application for such policy.

"(II) Whoever issues or sells a health insurance policy (other than a policy described in subclause (III)) to an individual described in subclause (I) and fails to furnish the appropriate disclosure statement as required under such subclause shall be fined under title 18, United States Code, or imprisoned not more than 5 years, or both, and, in addition to or in lieu of such a criminal penalty, is subject to a civil money penalty of not to exceed $25,000 (or

$15,000 in the case of a person other than the issuer of the policy) for each such violation.

"(III) A policy described in this subclause (to which subclauses (I) and (II) do not apply) is a medicare supplemental policy or a health insurance policy identified under 60 Federal Register 30880 (June 12, 1995) as a policy not required to have a disclosure statement.

"(IV) Any reference in this section to the revised NAIC model regulation (referred to in subsection (m)(1)(A)) is deemed a reference to such regulation as revised by section 171(m)(2) of the Social Security Act Amendments of 1994 (Public Law 103–432) and as modified by substituting, for the disclosure required under section 16D(2), disclosure under subclause (I) of an appropriate disclosure statement under clause (vii).

"(vii) The disclosure statement described in this clause for a type of policy is the statement specified under subparagraph (D) of this paragraph (as in effect before the date of the enactment of the Health Insurance Portability and Accountability Act of 1996) for that type of policy, as revised as follows:

"(I) In each statement, amend the second line to read as follows:

'THIS IS NOT MEDICARE SUPPLEMENT INSURANCE'.

"(II) In each statement, strike the third line and insert the following: '**Some health care services paid for by Medicare may also trigger the payment of benefits under this policy.**'.

"(III) In each statement not described in subclause (V), strike the boldface matter that begins '**This insurance**' and all that follows up to the next paragraph that begins '**Medicare**'.

"(IV) In each statement not described in subclause (V), insert before the boxed matter (that states '**Before You Buy This Insurance**') the following: '**This policy must pay benefits without regard to other health benefit coverage to which you may be entitled under Medicare or other insurance.**'.

"(V) In a statement relating to policies providing both nursing home and non-institutional coverage, to policies providing nursing home benefits only, or policies providing home care benefits only, amend the sentence that begins 'Federal law' to read as follows: 'Federal law requires us to inform you that in certain situations this insurance may pay for some care also covered by Medicare.'.

"(viii)(I) Subject to subclause (II), nothing in this subparagraph shall restrict or preclude a State's ability to regulate health insurance policies, including any health insurance policy that is described in clause (iv), (v), or (vi)(III).

"(II) A State may not declare or specify, in statute, regulation, or otherwise, that a health insurance policy (other than a medicare supplemental policy) or rider to an insurance contract which is not a health insurance policy, that is described in clause (iv), (v), or (vi)(III) and that is sold, issued, or renewed to an individual entitled to benefits under part A or enrolled under part B 'duplicates' health benefits under this title or under a medicare supplemental policy.".

(b) CONFORMING AMENDMENTS.—Section 1882(d)(3) (42 U.S.C. 1395ss(d)(3)) is amended—

(1) in subparagraph (C)—

(A) by striking "with respect to (i)" and inserting "with respect to", and

(B) by striking ", (ii) the sale" and all that follows up to the period at the end; and

(2) by striking subparagraph (D).

(c) TRANSITIONAL PROVISION.—

(1) NO PENALTIES.—Subject to paragraph (3), no criminal or civil money penalty may be imposed under section 1882(d)(3)(A) of the Social Security Act for any act or omission that occurred during the transition period (as defined in paragraph (4)) and that relates to any health insurance policy that is described in clause (iv) or (v) of such section (as amended by subsection (a)).

(2) LIMITATION ON LEGAL ACTION.—Subject to paragraph (3), no legal action shall be brought or continued in any Federal or State court insofar as such action—

(A) includes a cause of action which arose, or which is based on or evidenced by any act or omission which occurred, during the transition period; and

(B) relates to the application of section 1882(d)(3)(A) of the Social Security Act to any act or omission with respect to the sale, issuance, or renewal of any health insurance policy that is described in clause (iv) or (v) of such section (as amended by subsection (a)).

(3) DISCLOSURE CONDITION.—In the case of a policy described in clause (iv) of section 1882(d)(3)(A) of the Social Security Act that is sold or issued on or after the effective date of statements under section 171(d)(3)(C) of the Social Security Act Amendments of 1994 and before the end of the 30-day period beginning on the date of the enactment of this Act, paragraphs (1) and (2) shall only apply if disclosure was made in accordance with section 1882(d)(3)(C)(ii) of the Social Security Act (as in effect before the date of the enactment of this Act).

(4) TRANSITION PERIOD.—In this subsection, the term "transition period" means the period beginning on November 5, 1991, and ending on the date of the enactment of this Act.

(d) EFFECTIVE DATE.—(1) Except as provided in this subsection, the amendment made by subsection (a) shall be effective as if included in the enactment of section 4354 of the Omnibus Budget Reconciliation Act of 1990.

(2)(A) Clause (vi) of section 1882(d)(3)(A) of the Social Security Act, as added by subsection (a), shall only apply to individuals applying for—

(i) a health insurance policy described in section 1882(d)(3)(A)(iv) of such Act (as added by subsection (a)), after the date of the enactment of this Act, or

(ii) another health insurance policy after the end of the 30-day period beginning on the date of the enactment of this Act.

(B) A seller or issuer of a health insurance policy may substitute, for the disclosure statement described in clause (vii) of such section, the statement specified under section 1882(d)(3)(D) of the

Social Security Act (as in effect before the date of the enactment of this Act), without the revision specified in such clause.

Subtitle H—Patent Extension

SEC. 281. PATENT EXTENSION.

(a) IN GENERAL.—Any owner on the date of the enactment of this Act of the right to market a non-steroidal anti-inflammatory drug that—

> *(1) contains a patented active agent,*
>
> *(2) has been reviewed by the Federal Food and Drug Administration for a period of more than 96 months as a new drug application, and*
>
> *(3) was approved as safe and effective by the Federal Food and Drug Administration on January 31, 1991,*

shall be entitled, for the 2-year period beginning on February 28, 1997, to exclude others from making, using, offering for sale, selling, or importing into the United States such active agent, in accordance with section 154(a)(1) of title 35, United States Code.

(b) INFRINGEMENT.—Section 271 of title 35, United States Code, shall apply to the infringement of the entitlement provided under subsection (a) to the same extent as such section applies to infringement of a patent.

(c) NOTIFICATION.—Not later than 30 days after the date of the enactment of this Act, any owner granted an entitlement under subsection (a) shall notify the Commissioner of Patents and Trademarks and the Secretary for Health and Human Services of such entitlement. Not later than 7 days after the receipt of such notice, the Commissioner and the Secretary shall publish an appropriate notice of the receipt of such notice.

(d) OFFSET.—An owner described in subsection (a) shall pay the amount of $10,000,000 to the Secretary of Health and Human Services in each of the fiscal years 1997 and 1998 as a condition for being eligible to qualify for the entitlement under subsection (a). As a further condition for eligibility, such owner shall enter into a legally binding agreement with the Secretary of Health and Human Services which shall provide a means for ensuring that the entitlement under subsection (a) shall not create any net costs to the States under the medicaid program under title XIX of the Social Security Act.

TITLE III—TAX-RELATED HEALTH PROVISIONS

SEC. 300. AMENDMENT OF 1986 CODE.

Except as otherwise expressly provided, whenever in this title an amendment or repeal is expressed in terms of an amendment to, or repeal of, a section or other provision, the reference shall be considered to be made to a section or other provision of the Internal Revenue Code of 1986.

Subtitle A—Medical Savings Accounts

SEC. 301. MEDICAL SAVINGS ACCOUNTS.

(a) IN GENERAL.—Part VII of subchapter B of chapter 1 (relating to additional itemized deductions for individuals) is amended by redesignating section 220 as section 221 and by inserting after section 219 the following new section:

"SEC. 220. MEDICAL SAVINGS ACCOUNTS.

"(a) DEDUCTION ALLOWED.—In the case of an individual who is an eligible individual for any month during the taxable year, there shall be allowed as a deduction for the taxable year an amount equal to the aggregate amount paid in cash during such taxable year by such individual to a medical savings account of such individual.

"(b) LIMITATIONS.—

"(1) IN GENERAL.—The amount allowable as a deduction under subsection (a) to an individual for the taxable year shall not exceed the sum of the monthly limitations for months during such taxable year that the individual is an eligible individual.

"(2) MONTHLY LIMITATION.—The monthly limitation for any month is the amount equal to $1/12$ of—

"(A) in the case of an individual who has self-only coverage under the high deductible health plan as of the first day of such month, 65 percent of the annual deductible under such coverage, and

"(B) in the case of an individual who has family coverage under the high deductible health plan as of the first day of such month, 75 percent of the annual deductible under such coverage.

"(3) SPECIAL RULE FOR MARRIED INDIVIDUALS.—In the case of individuals who are married to each other, if either spouse has family coverage—

"(A) both spouses shall be treated as having only such family coverage (and if such spouses each have family coverage under different plans, as having the family coverage with the lowest annual deductible), and

"(B) the limitation under paragraph (1) (after the application of subparagraph (A) of this paragraph) shall be divided equally between them unless they agree on a different division.

"(4) DEDUCTION NOT TO EXCEED COMPENSATION.—

"(A) EMPLOYEES.—The deduction allowed under subsection (a) for contributions as an eligible individual described in subclause (I) of subsection (c)(1)(A)(iii) shall not exceed such individual's wages, salaries, tips, and other employee compensation which are attributable to such individual's employment by the employer referred to in such subclause.

"(B) SELF-EMPLOYED INDIVIDUALS.—The deduction allowed under subsection (a) for contributions as an eligible individual described in subclause (II) of subsection (c)(1)(A)(iii) shall not exceed such individual's earned in-

come (as defined in section 401(c)(1)) derived by the taxpayer from the trade or business with respect to which the high deductible health plan is established.

"(C) COMMUNITY PROPERTY LAWS NOT TO APPLY.—The limitations under this paragraph shall be determined without regard to community property laws.

"(5) COORDINATION WITH EXCLUSION FOR EMPLOYER CONTRIBUTIONS.—No deduction shall be allowed under this section for any amount paid for any taxable year to a medical savings account of an individual if—

"(A) any amount is contributed to any medical savings account of such individual for such year which is excludable from gross income under section 106(b), or

"(B) if such individual's spouse is covered under the high deductible health plan covering such individual, any amount is contributed for such year to any medical savings account of such spouse which is so excludable.

"(6) DENIAL OF DEDUCTION TO DEPENDENTS.—No deduction shall be allowed under this section to any individual with respect to whom a deduction under section 151 is allowable to another taxpayer for a taxable year beginning in the calendar year in which such individual's taxable year begins.

"(c) DEFINITIONS.—For purposes of this section—

"(1) ELIGIBLE INDIVIDUAL.—

"(A) IN GENERAL.—The term 'eligible individual' means, with respect to any month, any individual if—

"(i) such individual is covered under a high deductible health plan as of the 1st day of such month,

"(ii) such individual is not, while covered under a high deductible health plan, covered under any health plan—

"(I) which is not a high deductible health plan, and

"(II) which provides coverage for any benefit which is covered under the high deductible health plan, and

"(iii)(I) the high deductible health plan covering such individual is established and maintained by the employer of such individual or of the spouse of such individual and such employer is a small employer, or

"(II) such individual is an employee (within the meaning of section 401(c)(1)) or the spouse of such an employee and the high deductible health plan covering such individual is not established or maintained by any employer of such individual or spouse.

"(B) CERTAIN COVERAGE DISREGARDED.—Subparagraph (A)(ii) shall be applied without regard to—

"(i) coverage for any benefit provided by permitted insurance, and

"(ii) coverage (whether through insurance or otherwise) for accidents, disability, dental care, vision care, or long-term care.

"(C) CONTINUED ELIGIBILITY OF EMPLOYEE AND SPOUSE ESTABLISHING MEDICAL SAVINGS ACCOUNTS.—If, while an employer is a small employer—

"(i) any amount is contributed to a medical savings account of an individual who is an employee of such employer or the spouse of such an employee, and

"(ii) such amount is excludable from gross income under section 106(b) or allowable as a deduction under this section,

such individual shall not cease to meet the requirement of subparagraph (A)(iii)(I) by reason of such employer ceasing to be a small employer so long as such employee continues to be an employee of such employer.

"(D) LIMITATIONS ON ELIGIBILITY.—

"For limitations on number of taxpayers who are eligible to have medical savings accounts, see subsection (i).

"(2) HIGH DEDUCTIBLE HEALTH PLAN.—

"(A) IN GENERAL.—The term 'high deductible health plan' means a health plan—

"(i) in the case of self-only coverage, which has an annual deductible which is not less than $1,500 and not more than $2,250,

"(ii) in the case of family coverage, which has an annual deductible which is not less than $3,000 and not more than $4,500, and

"(iii) the annual out-of-pocket expenses required to be paid under the plan (other than for premiums) for covered benefits does not exceed—

"(I) $3,000 for self-only coverage, and

"(II) $5,500 for family coverage.

"(B) SPECIAL RULES.—

"(i) EXCLUSION OF CERTAIN PLANS.—Such term does not include a health plan if substantially all of its coverage is coverage described in paragraph (1)(B).

"(ii) SAFE HARBOR FOR ABSENCE OF PREVENTIVE CARE DEDUCTIBLE.—A plan shall not fail to be treated as a high deductible health plan by reason of failing to have a deductible for preventive care if the absence of a deductible for such care is required by State law.

"(3) PERMITTED INSURANCE.—The term 'permitted insurance' means—

"(A) Medicare supplemental insurance,

"(B) insurance if substantially all of the coverage provided under such insurance relates to—

"(i) liabilities incurred under workers' compensation laws,

"(ii) tort liabilities,

"(iii) liabilities relating to ownership or use of property, or

"(iv) such other similar liabilities as the Secretary may specify by regulations,

"(C) insurance for a specified disease or illness, and

"(D) insurance paying a fixed amount per day (or other period) of hospitalization.

"(4) SMALL EMPLOYER.—

"(A) IN GENERAL.—The term 'small employer' means, with respect to any calendar year, any employer if such employer employed an average of 50 or fewer employees on business days during either of the 2 preceding calendar years. For purposes of the preceding sentence, a preceding calendar year may be taken into account only if the employer was in existence throughout such year.

"(B) EMPLOYERS NOT IN EXISTENCE IN PRECEDING YEAR.—In the case of an employer which was not in existence throughout the 1st preceding calendar year, the determination under subparagraph (A) shall be based on the average number of employees that it is reasonably expected such employer will employ on business days in the current calendar year.

"(C) CERTAIN GROWING EMPLOYERS RETAIN TREATMENT AS SMALL EMPLOYER.—The term 'small employer' includes, with respect to any calendar year, any employer if—

"(i) such employer met the requirement of subparagraph (A) (determined without regard to subparagraph (B)) for any preceding calendar year after 1996,

"(ii) any amount was contributed to the medical savings account of any employee of such employer with respect to coverage of such employee under a high deductible health plan of such employer during such preceding calendar year and such amount was excludable from gross income under section 106(b) or allowable as a deduction under this section, and

"(iii) such employer employed an average of 200 or fewer employees on business days during each preceding calendar year after 1996.

"(D) SPECIAL RULES.—

"(i) CONTROLLED GROUPS.—For purposes of this paragraph, all persons treated as a single employer under subsection (b), (c), (m), or (o) of section 414 shall be treated as 1 employer.

"(ii) PREDECESSORS.—Any reference in this paragraph to an employer shall include a reference to any predecessor of such employer.

"(5) FAMILY COVERAGE.—The term 'family coverage' means any coverage other than self-only coverage.

"(d) MEDICAL SAVINGS ACCOUNT.—For purposes of this section—

"(1) MEDICAL SAVINGS ACCOUNT.—The term 'medical savings account' means a trust created or organized in the United States exclusively for the purpose of paying the qualified medical expenses of the account holder, but only if the written governing instrument creating the trust meets the following requirements:

"(A) Except in the case of a rollover contribution described in subsection (f)(5), no contribution will be accepted—

"(i) unless it is in cash, or

"(ii) to the extent such contribution, when added to previous contributions to the trust for the calendar year, exceeds 75 percent of the highest annual limit deductible permitted under subsection (c)(2)(A)(ii) for such calendar year.

"(B) The trustee is a bank (as defined in section 408(n)), an insurance company (as defined in section 816), or another person who demonstrates to the satisfaction of the Secretary that the manner in which such person will administer the trust will be consistent with the requirements of this section.

"(C) No part of the trust assets will be invested in life insurance contracts.

"(D) The assets of the trust will not be commingled with other property except in a common trust fund or common investment fund.

"(E) The interest of an individual in the balance in his account is nonforfeitable.

"(2) QUALIFIED MEDICAL EXPENSES.—

"(A) IN GENERAL.—The term 'qualified medical expenses' means, with respect to an account holder, amounts paid by such holder for medical care (as defined in section 213(d)) for such individual, the spouse of such individual, and any dependent (as defined in section 152) of such individual, but only to the extent such amounts are not compensated for by insurance or otherwise.

"(B) HEALTH INSURANCE MAY NOT BE PURCHASED FROM ACCOUNT.—

"(i) IN GENERAL.—Subparagraph (A) shall not apply to any payment for insurance.

"(ii) EXCEPTIONS.—Clause (i) shall not apply to any expense for coverage under—

"(I) a health plan during any period of continuation coverage required under any Federal law,

"(II) a qualified long-term care insurance contract (as defined in section 7702B(b)), or

"(III) a health plan during a period in which the individual is receiving unemployment compensation under any Federal or State law.

"(C) MEDICAL EXPENSES OF INDIVIDUALS WHO ARE NOT ELIGIBLE INDIVIDUALS.—Subparagraph (A) shall apply to an amount paid by an account holder for medical care of an individual who is not an eligible individual for the month in which the expense for such care is incurred only if no amount is contributed (other than a rollover contribution) to any medical savings account of such account holder for the taxable year which includes such month. This subparagraph shall not apply to any expense for coverage described in subclause (I) or (III) of subparagraph (B)(ii).

"(3) ACCOUNT HOLDER.—The term 'account holder' means the individual on whose behalf the medical savings account was established.

"(4) CERTAIN RULES TO APPLY.—Rules similar to the following rules shall apply for purposes of this section:

"(A) Section 219(d)(2) (relating to no deduction for rollovers).

"(B) Section 219(f)(3) (relating to time when contributions deemed made).

"(C) Except as provided in section 106(b), section 219(f)(5) (relating to employer payments).

"(D) Section 408(g) (relating to community property laws).

"(E) Section 408(h) (relating to custodial accounts).

"(e) TAX TREATMENT OF ACCOUNTS.—

"(1) IN GENERAL.—A medical savings account is exempt from taxation under this subtitle unless such account has ceased to be a medical savings account. Notwithstanding the preceding sentence, any such account is subject to the taxes imposed by section 511 (relating to imposition of tax on unrelated business income of charitable, etc. organizations).

"(2) ACCOUNT TERMINATIONS.—Rules similar to the rules of paragraphs (2) and (4) of section 408(e) shall apply to medical savings accounts, and any amount treated as distributed under such rules shall be treated as not used to pay qualified medical expenses.

"(f) TAX TREATMENT OF DISTRIBUTIONS.—

"(1) AMOUNTS USED FOR QUALIFIED MEDICAL EXPENSES.—Any amount paid or distributed out of a medical savings account which is used exclusively to pay qualified medical expenses of any account holder shall not be includible in gross income.

"(2) INCLUSION OF AMOUNTS NOT USED FOR QUALIFIED MEDICAL EXPENSES.—Any amount paid or distributed out of a medical savings account which is not used exclusively to pay the qualified medical expenses of the account holder shall be included in the gross income of such holder.

"(3) EXCESS CONTRIBUTIONS RETURNED BEFORE DUE DATE OF RETURN.—

"(A) IN GENERAL.—If any excess contribution is contributed for a taxable year to any medical savings account of an individual, paragraph (2) shall not apply to distributions from the medical savings accounts of such individual (to the extent such distributions do not exceed the aggregate excess contributions to all such accounts of such individual for such year) if—

"(i) such distribution is received by the individual on or before the last day prescribed by law (including extensions of time) for filing such individual's return for such taxable year, and

"(ii) such distribution is accompanied by the amount of net income attributable to such excess contribution.

Any net income described in clause (ii) shall be included in the gross income of the individual for the taxable year in which it is received.

"(B) EXCESS CONTRIBUTION.—For purposes of subparagraph (A), the term 'excess contribution' means any contribution (other than a rollover contribution) which is neither excludable from gross income under section 106(b) nor deductible under this section.

"(4) ADDITIONAL TAX ON DISTRIBUTIONS NOT USED FOR QUALIFIED MEDICAL EXPENSES.—

"(A) IN GENERAL.—The tax imposed by this chapter on the account holder for any taxable year in which there is a payment or distribution from a medical savings account of such holder which is includible in gross income under paragraph (2) shall be increased by 15 percent of the amount which is so includible.

"(B) EXCEPTION FOR DISABILITY OR DEATH.—Subparagraph (A) shall not apply if the payment or distribution is made after the account holder becomes disabled within the meaning of section 72(m)(7) or dies.

"(C) EXCEPTION FOR DISTRIBUTIONS AFTER MEDICARE ELIGIBILITY.—Subparagraph (A) shall not apply to any payment or distribution after the date on which the account holder attains the age specified in section 1811 of the Social Security Act.

"(5) ROLLOVER CONTRIBUTION.—An amount is described in this paragraph as a rollover contribution if it meets the requirements of subparagraphs (A) and (B).

"(A) IN GENERAL.—Paragraph (2) shall not apply to any amount paid or distributed from a medical savings account to the account holder to the extent the amount received is paid into a medical savings account for the benefit of such holder not later than the 60th day after the day on which the holder receives the payment or distribution.

"(B) LIMITATION.—This paragraph shall not apply to any amount described in subparagraph (A) received by an individual from a medical savings account if, at any time during the 1-year period ending on the day of such receipt, such individual received any other amount described in subparagraph (A) from a medical savings account which was not includible in the individual's gross income because of the application of this paragraph.

"(6) COORDINATION WITH MEDICAL EXPENSE DEDUCTION.— For purposes of determining the amount of the deduction under section 213, any payment or distribution out of a medical savings account for qualified medical expenses shall not be treated as an expense paid for medical care.

"(7) TRANSFER OF ACCOUNT INCIDENT TO DIVORCE.—The transfer of an individual's interest in a medical savings account to an individual's spouse or former spouse under a divorce or separation instrument described in subparagraph (A) of section 71(b)(2) shall not be considered a taxable transfer made by such individual notwithstanding any other provision of this subtitle, and such interest shall, after such transfer, be treated as a medical savings account with respect to which such spouse is the account holder.

"(8) TREATMENT AFTER DEATH OF ACCOUNT HOLDER.—

"*(A) TREATMENT IF DESIGNATED BENEFICIARY IS SPOUSE.—If the account holder's surviving spouse acquires such holder's interest in a medical savings account by reason of being the designated beneficiary of such account at the death of the account holder, such medical savings account shall be treated as if the spouse were the account holder.*

"*(B) OTHER CASES.—*

"*(i) IN GENERAL.—If, by reason of the death of the account holder, any person acquires the account holder's interest in a medical savings account in a case to which subparagraph (A) does not apply—*

"*(I) such account shall cease to be a medical savings account as of the date of death, and*

"*(II) an amount equal to the fair market value of the assets in such account on such date shall be includible if such person is not the estate of such holder, in such person's gross income for the taxable year which includes such date, or if such person is the estate of such holder, in such holder's gross income for the last taxable year of such holder.*

"*(ii) SPECIAL RULES.—*

"*(I) REDUCTION OF INCLUSION FOR PRE-DEATH EXPENSES.—The amount includible in gross income under clause (i) by any person (other than the estate) shall be reduced by the amount of qualified medical expenses which were incurred by the decedent before the date of the decedent's death and paid by such person within 1 year after such date.*

"*(II) DEDUCTION FOR ESTATE TAXES.—An appropriate deduction shall be allowed under section 691(c) to any person (other than the decedent or the decedent's spouse) with respect to amounts included in gross income under clause (i) by such person.*

"*(g) COST-OF-LIVING ADJUSTMENT.—In the case of any taxable year beginning in a calendar year after 1998, each dollar amount in subsection (c)(2) shall be increased by an amount equal to—*

"*(1) such dollar amount, multiplied by*

"*(2) the cost-of-living adjustment determined under section 1(f)(3) for the calendar year in which such taxable year begins by substituting 'calendar year 1997' for 'calendar year 1992' in subparagraph (B) thereof.*

If any increase under the preceding sentence is not a multiple of $50, such increase shall be rounded to the nearest multiple of $50.

"*(h) REPORTS.—The Secretary may require the trustee of a medical savings account to make such reports regarding such account to the Secretary and to the account holder with respect to contributions, distributions, and such other matters as the Secretary determines appropriate. The reports required by this subsection shall be filed at such time and in such manner and furnished to such indi-*

viduals at such time and in such manner as may be required by the Secretary.

"(i) LIMITATION ON NUMBER OF TAXPAYERS HAVING MEDICAL SAVINGS ACCOUNTS.—

"(1) IN GENERAL.—Except as provided in paragraph (5), no individual shall be treated as an eligible individual for any taxable year beginning after the cut-off year unless—

"(A) such individual was an active MSA participant for any taxable year ending on or before the close of the cut-off year, or

"(B) such individual first became an active MSA participant for a taxable year ending after the cut-off year by reason of coverage under a high deductible health plan of an MSA–participating employer.

"(2) CUT-OFF YEAR.—For purposes of paragraph (1), the term 'cut-off year' means the earlier of—

"(A) calendar year 2000, or

"(B) the first calendar year before 2000 for which the Secretary determines under subsection (j) that the numerical limitation for such year has been exceeded.

"(3) ACTIVE MSA PARTICIPANT.—For purposes of this subsection—

"(A) IN GENERAL.—The term 'active MSA participant' means, with respect to any taxable year, any individual who is the account holder of any medical savings account into which any contribution was made which was excludable from gross income under section 106(b), or allowable as a deduction under this section, for such taxable year.

"(B) SPECIAL RULE FOR CUT-OFF YEARS BEFORE 2000.— In the case of a cut-off year before 2000—

"(i) an individual shall not be treated as an eligible individual for any month of such year or an active MSA participant under paragraph (1)(A) unless such individual is, on or before the cut-off date, covered under a high deductible health plan, and

"(ii) an employer shall not be treated as an MSA-participating employer unless the employer, on or before the cut-off date, offered coverage under a high deductible health plan to any employee.

"(C) CUT-OFF DATE.—For purposes of subparagraph (B)—

"(i) IN GENERAL.—Except as otherwise provided in this subparagraph, the cut-off date is October 1 of the cut-off year.

"(ii) EMPLOYEES WITH ENROLLMENT PERIODS AFTER OCTOBER 1.—In the case of an individual described in subclause (I) of subsection (c)(1)(A)(iii), if the regularly scheduled enrollment period for health plans of the individual's employer occurs during the last 3 months of the cut-off year, the cut-off date is December 31 of the cut-off year.

"(iii) SELF-EMPLOYED INDIVIDUALS.—In the case of an individual described in subclause (II) of subsection

(c)(1)(A)(iii), the cut-off date is November 1 of the cut-off year.

"(iv) SPECIAL RULES FOR 1997.—If 1997 is a cut-off year by reason of subsection (j)(1)(A)—

"(I) each of the cut-off dates under clauses (i) and (iii) shall be 1 month earlier than the date determined without regard to this clause, and

"(II) clause (ii) shall be applied by substituting '4 months' for '3 months'.

"(4) MSA-PARTICIPATING EMPLOYER.—For purposes of this subsection, the term 'MSA-participating employer' means any small employer if—

"(A) such employer made any contribution to the medical savings account of any employee during the cut-off year or any preceding calendar year which was excludable from gross income under section 106(b), or

"(B) at least 20 percent of the employees of such employer who are eligible individuals for any month of the cut-off year by reason of coverage under a high deductible health plan of such employer each made a contribution of at least $100 to their medical savings accounts for any taxable year ending with or within the cut-off year which was allowable as a deduction under this section.

"(5) ADDITIONAL ELIGIBILITY AFTER CUT-OFF YEAR.—If the Secretary determines under subsection (j)(2)(A) that the numerical limit for the calendar year following a cut-off year described in paragraph (2)(B) has not been exceeded—

"(A) this subsection shall not apply to any otherwise eligible individual who is covered under a high deductible health plan during the first 6 months of the second calendar year following the cut-off year (and such individual shall be treated as an active MSA participant for purposes of this subsection if a contribution is made to any medical savings account with respect to such coverage), and

"(B) any employer who offers coverage under a high deductible health plan to any employee during such 6-month period shall be treated as an MSA-participating employer for purposes of this subsection if the requirements of paragraph (4) are met with respect to such coverage.

For purposes of this paragraph, subsection (j)(2)(A) shall be applied for 1998 by substituting '750,000' for '600,000'.

"(j) DETERMINATION OF WHETHER NUMERICAL LIMITS ARE EXCEEDED.—

"(1) DETERMINATION OF WHETHER LIMIT EXCEEDED FOR 1997.—The numerical limitation for 1997 is exceeded if, based on the reports required under paragraph (4), the number of medical savings accounts established as of—

"(A) April 30, 1997, exceeds 375,000, or

"(B) June 30, 1997, exceeds 525,000.

"(2) DETERMINATION OF WHETHER LIMIT EXCEEDED FOR 1998 OR 1999.—

"(A) IN GENERAL.—The numerical limitation for 1998 or 1999 is exceeded if the sum of—

"(i) the number of MSA returns filed on or before April 15 of such calendar year for taxable years ending with or within the preceding calendar year, plus

"(ii) the Secretary's estimate (determined on the basis of the returns described in clause (i)) of the number of MSA returns for such taxable years which will be filed after such date,

exceeds 600,000 (750,000 in the case of 1999). For purposes of the preceding sentence, the term 'MSA return' means any return on which any exclusion is claimed under section 106(b) or any deduction is claimed under this section.

"(B) ALTERNATIVE COMPUTATION OF LIMITATION.—The numerical limitation for 1998 or 1999 is also exceeded if the sum of—

"(i) 90 percent of the sum determined under subparagraph (A) for such calendar year, plus

"(ii) the product of 2.5 and the number of medical savings accounts established during the portion of such year preceding July 1 (based on the reports required under paragraph (4)) for taxable years beginning in such year,

exceeds 750,000.

"(3) PREVIOUSLY UNINSURED INDIVIDUALS NOT INCLUDED IN DETERMINATION.—

"(A) IN GENERAL.—The determination of whether any calendar year is a cut-off year shall be made by not counting the medical savings account of any previously uninsured individual.

"(B) PREVIOUSLY UNINSURED INDIVIDUAL.—For purposes of this subsection, the term 'previously uninsured individual' means, with respect to any medical savings account, any individual who had no health plan coverage (other than coverage referred to in subsection (c)(1)(B)) at any time during the 6-month period before the date such individual's coverage under the high deductible health plan commences.

"(4) REPORTING BY MSA TRUSTEES.—

"(A) IN GENERAL.—Not later than August 1 of 1997, 1998, and 1999, each person who is the trustee of a medical savings account established before July 1 of such calendar year shall make a report to the Secretary (in such form and manner as the Secretary shall specify) which specifies—

"(i) the number of medical savings accounts established before such July 1 (for taxable years beginning in such calendar year) of which such person is the trustee,

"(ii) the name and TIN of the account holder of each such account, and

"(iii) the number of such accounts which are accounts of previously uninsured individuals.

"(B) ADDITIONAL REPORT FOR 1997.—Not later than June 1, 1997, each person who is the trustee of a medical savings account established before May 1, 1997, shall make an additional report described in subparagraph (A) but

only with respect to accounts established before May 1, 1997.

"(C) PENALTY FOR FAILURE TO FILE REPORT.—The penalty provided in section 6693(a) shall apply to any report required by this paragraph, except that—

"(i) such section shall be applied by substituting '$25' for '$50', and

"(ii) the maximum penalty imposed on any trustee shall not exceed $5,000.

"(D) AGGREGATION OF ACCOUNTS.—To the extent practical, in determining the number of medical savings accounts on the basis of the reports under this paragraph, all medical savings accounts of an individual shall be treated as 1 account and all accounts of individuals who are married to each other shall be treated as 1 account.

"(5) DATE OF MAKING DETERMINATIONS.—Any determination under this subsection that a calendar year is a cut-off year shall be made by the Secretary and shall be published not later than October 1 of such year.

(b) DEDUCTION ALLOWED WHETHER OR NOT INDIVIDUAL ITEMIZES OTHER DEDUCTIONS.—Subsection (a) of section 62 is amended by inserting after paragraph (15) the following new paragraph:

"(16) MEDICAL SAVINGS ACCOUNTS.—The deduction allowed by section 220."

(c) EXCLUSIONS FOR EMPLOYER CONTRIBUTIONS TO MEDICAL SAVINGS ACCOUNTS.—

(1) EXCLUSION FROM INCOME TAX.—The text of section 106 (relating to contributions by employer to accident and health plans) is amended to read as follows:

"(a) GENERAL RULE.—Except as otherwise provided in this section, gross income of an employee does not include employer-provided coverage under an accident or health plan.

"(b) CONTRIBUTIONS TO MEDICAL SAVINGS ACCOUNTS.—

"(1) IN GENERAL.—In the case of an employee who is an eligible individual, amounts contributed by such employee's employer to any medical savings account of such employee shall be treated as employer-provided coverage for medical expenses under an accident or health plan to the extent such amounts do not exceed the limitation under section 220(b)(1) (determined without regard to this subsection) which is applicable to such employee for such taxable year.

"(2) NO CONSTRUCTIVE RECEIPT.—No amount shall be included in the gross income of any employee solely because the employee may choose between the contributions referred to in paragraph (1) and employer contributions to another health plan of the employer.

"(3) SPECIAL RULE FOR DEDUCTION OF EMPLOYER CONTRIBUTIONS.—Any employer contribution to a medical savings account, if otherwise allowable as a deduction under this chapter, shall be allowed only for the taxable year in which paid.

"(4) EMPLOYER MSA CONTRIBUTIONS REQUIRED TO BE SHOWN ON RETURN.—Every individual required to file a return under section 6012 for the taxable year shall include on such return the aggregate amount contributed by employers to the

medical savings accounts of such individual or such individual's spouse for such taxable year.

"(5) MSA CONTRIBUTIONS NOT PART OF COBRA COVERAGE.— Paragraph (1) shall not apply for purposes of section 4980B.

"(6) DEFINITIONS.—For purposes of this subsection, the terms 'eligible individual' and 'medical savings account' have the respective meanings given to such terms by section 220.

"(7) CROSS REFERENCE.—

"For penalty on failure by employer to make comparable contributions to the medical savings accounts of comparable employees, see section 4980E.".

(2) EXCLUSION FROM EMPLOYMENT TAXES.—

(A) RAILROAD RETIREMENT TAX.—Subsection (e) of section 3231 is amended by adding at the end the following new paragraph:

"(10) MEDICAL SAVINGS ACCOUNT CONTRIBUTIONS.—The term 'compensation' shall not include any payment made to or for the benefit of an employee if at the time of such payment it is reasonable to believe that the employee will be able to exclude such payment from income under section 106(b)."

(B) UNEMPLOYMENT TAX.—Subsection (b) of section 3306 is amended by striking "or" at the end of paragraph (15), by striking the period at the end of paragraph (16) and inserting "; or", and by inserting after paragraph (16) the following new paragraph:

"(17) any payment made to or for the benefit of an employee if at the time of such payment it is reasonable to believe that the employee will be able to exclude such payment from income under section 106(b)."

(C) WITHHOLDING TAX.—Subsection (a) of section 3401 is amended by striking "or" at the end of paragraph (19), by striking the period at the end of paragraph (20) and inserting "; or", and by inserting after paragraph (20) the following new paragraph:

"(21) any payment made to or for the benefit of an employee if at the time of such payment it is reasonable to believe that the employee will be able to exclude such payment from income under section 106(b)."

(3) EMPLOYER CONTRIBUTIONS REQUIRED TO BE SHOWN ON W-2.—Subsection (a) of section 6051 is amended by striking "and" at the end of paragraph (9), by striking the period at the end of paragraph (10) and inserting ", and", and by inserting after paragraph (10) the following new paragraph:

"(11) the amount contributed to any medical savings account (as defined in section 220(d)) of such employee or such employee's spouse."

(4) PENALTY FOR FAILURE OF EMPLOYER TO MAKE COMPARABLE MSA CONTRIBUTIONS.—

(A) IN GENERAL.—Chapter 43 is amended by adding after section 4980D the following new section:

"SEC. 4980E. FAILURE OF EMPLOYER TO MAKE COMPARABLE MEDICAL SAVINGS ACCOUNT CONTRIBUTIONS.

"(a) GENERAL RULE.—In the case of an employer who makes a contribution to the medical savings account of any employee with re-

spect to coverage under a high deductible health plan of the employer during a calendar year, there is hereby imposed a tax on the failure of such employer to meet the requirements of subsection (d) for such calendar year.

"(b) AMOUNT OF TAX.—The amount of the tax imposed by subsection (a) on any failure for any calendar year is the amount equal to 35 percent of the aggregate amount contributed by the employer to medical savings accounts of employees for taxable years of such employees ending with or within such calendar year.

"(c) WAIVER BY SECRETARY.—In the case of a failure which is due to reasonable cause and not to willful neglect, the Secretary may waive part or all of the tax imposed by subsection (a) to the extent that the payment of such tax would be excessive relative to the failure involved.

"(d) EMPLOYER REQUIRED TO MAKE COMPARABLE MSA CONTRIBUTIONS FOR ALL PARTICIPATING EMPLOYEES.—

"(1) IN GENERAL.—An employer meets the requirements of this subsection for any calendar year if the employer makes available comparable contributions to the medical savings accounts of all comparable participating employees for each coverage period during such calendar year.

"(2) COMPARABLE CONTRIBUTIONS.—

"(A) IN GENERAL.—For purposes of paragraph (1), the term 'comparable contributions' means contributions—

"(i) which are the same amount, or

"(ii) which are the same percentage of the annual deductible limit under the high deductible health plan covering the employees.

"(B) PART-YEAR EMPLOYEES.—In the case of an employee who is employed by the employer for only a portion of the calendar year, a contribution to the medical savings account of such employee shall be treated as comparable if it is an amount which bears the same ratio to the comparable amount (determined without regard to this subparagraph) as such portion bears to the entire calendar year.

"(3) COMPARABLE PARTICIPATING EMPLOYEES.—For purposes of paragraph (1), the term 'comparable participating employees' means all employees—

"(A) who are eligible individuals covered under any high deductible health plan of the employer, and

"(B) who have the same category of coverage.

For purposes of subparagraph (B), the categories of coverage are self-only and family coverage.

"(4) PART-TIME EMPLOYEES.—

"(A) IN GENERAL.—Paragraph (3) shall be applied separately with respect to part-time employees and other employees.

"(B) PART-TIME EMPLOYEE.—For purposes of subparagraph (A), the term 'part-time employee' means any employee who is customarily employed for fewer than 30 hours per week.

"(e) CONTROLLED GROUPS.—For purposes of this section, all persons treated as a single employer under subsection (b), (c), (m), or (o) of section 414 shall be treated as 1 employer.

"(f) DEFINITIONS.—Terms used in this section which are also used in section 220 have the respective meanings given such terms in section 220."

(B) CLERICAL AMENDMENT.—The table of sections for chapter 43 is amended by adding after the item relating to section 4980D the following new item:

"Sec. 4980E. Failure of employer to make comparable medical savings account contributions."

(d) MEDICAL SAVINGS ACCOUNT CONTRIBUTIONS NOT AVAILABLE UNDER CAFETERIA PLANS.—Subsection (f) of section 125 of such Code is amended by inserting "106(b)," before "117".

(e) TAX ON EXCESS CONTRIBUTIONS.—Section 4973 (relating to tax on excess contributions to individual retirement accounts, certain section 403(b) contracts, and certain individual retirement annuities) is amended—

(1) by inserting "**MEDICAL SAVINGS ACCOUNTS,**" after "**ACCOUNTS,**" in the heading of such section,

(2) by striking "or" at the end of paragraph (1) of subsection (a),

(3) by redesignating paragraph (2) of subsection (a) as paragraph (3) and by inserting after paragraph (1) the following:

"(2) a medical savings account (within the meaning of section 220(d)), or", and

(4) by adding at the end the following new subsection:

"(d) EXCESS CONTRIBUTIONS TO MEDICAL SAVINGS ACCOUNTS.—For purposes of this section, in the case of medical savings accounts (within the meaning of section 220(d)), the term 'excess contributions' means the sum of—

"(1) the aggregate amount contributed for the taxable year to the accounts (other than rollover contributions described in section 220(f)(5)) which is neither excludable from gross income under section 106(b) nor allowable as a deduction under section 220 for such year, and

"(2) the amount determined under this subsection for the preceding taxable year, reduced by the sum of—

"(A) the distributions out of the accounts which were included in gross income under section 220(f)(2), and

"(B) the excess (if any) of—

"(i) the maximum amount allowable as a deduction under section 220(b)(1) (determined without regard to section 106(b)) for the taxable year, over

"(ii) the amount contributed to the accounts for the taxable year.

For purposes of this subsection, any contribution which is distributed out of the medical savings account in a distribution to which section 220(f)(3) applies shall be treated as an amount not contributed."

(f) TAX ON PROHIBITED TRANSACTIONS.—

(1) Section 4975 (relating to tax on prohibited transactions) is amended by adding at the end of subsection (c) the following new paragraph:

"(4) SPECIAL RULE FOR MEDICAL SAVINGS ACCOUNTS.—An individual for whose benefit a medical savings account (within the meaning of section 220(d)) is established shall be exempt from the tax imposed by this section with respect to any transaction concerning such account (which would otherwise be taxable under this section) if, with respect to such transaction, the account ceases to be a medical savings account by reason of the application of section 220(e)(2) to such account."

(2) Paragraph (1) of section 4975(e) is amended to read as follows:

"(1) PLAN.—For purposes of this section, the term 'plan' means—

"(A) a trust described in section 401(a) which forms a part of a plan, or a plan described in section 403(a), which trust or plan is exempt from tax under section 501(a),

"(B) an individual retirement account described in section 408(a),

"(C) an individual retirement annuity described in section 408(b),

"(D) a medical savings account described in section 220(d), or

"(E) a trust, plan, account, or annuity which, at any time, has been determined by the Secretary to be described in any preceding subparagraph of this paragraph."

(g) FAILURE TO PROVIDE REPORTS ON MEDICAL SAVINGS ACCOUNTS.—

(1) Subsection (a) of section 6693 (relating to failure to provide reports on individual retirement accounts or annuities) is amended to read as follows:

"(a) REPORTS.—

"(1) IN GENERAL.—If a person required to file a report under a provision referred to in paragraph (2) fails to file such report at the time and in the manner required by such provision, such person shall pay a penalty of $50 for each failure unless it is shown that such failure is due to reasonable cause.

"(2) PROVISIONS.—The provisions referred to in this paragraph are—

"(A) subsections (i) and (l) of section 408 (relating to individual retirement plans), and

"(B) section 220(h) (relating to medical savings accounts)."

(h) EXCEPTION FROM CAPITALIZATION OF POLICY ACQUISITION EXPENSES.—Subparagraph (B) of section 848(e)(1) (defining specified insurance contract) is amended by striking "and" at the end of clause (ii), by striking the period at the end of clause (iii) and inserting ", and", and by adding at the end the following new clause:

"(iv) any contract which is a medical savings account (as defined in section 220(d))."

(i) CLERICAL AMENDMENT.—The table of sections for part VII of subchapter B of chapter 1 is amended by striking the last item and inserting the following:

"Sec. 220. Medical savings accounts.
"Sec. 221. Cross reference.".

(j) EFFECTIVE DATE.—The amendments made by this section shall apply to taxable years beginning after December 31, 1996.

(k) MONITORING OF PARTICIPATION IN MEDICAL SAVINGS ACCOUNTS.—The Secretary of the Treasury or his delegate shall—

(1) during 1997, 1998, 1999, and 2000, regularly evaluate the number of individuals who are maintaining medical savings accounts and the reduction in revenues to the United States by reason of such accounts, and

(2) provide such reports of such evaluations to Congress as such Secretary determines appropriate.

(l) STUDY OF EFFECTS OF MEDICAL SAVINGS ACCOUNTS ON SMALL GROUP MARKET.—The Comptroller General of the United States shall enter into a contract with an organization with expertise in health economics, health insurance markets, and actuarial science to conduct a comprehensive study regarding the effects of medical savings accounts in the small group market on—

(1) selection, including adverse selection,

(2) health costs, including any impact on premiums of individuals with comprehensive coverage,

(3) use of preventive care,

(4) consumer choice,

(5) the scope of coverage of high deductible plans purchased in conjunction with such accounts, and

(6) other relevant items.

A report on the results of the study conducted under this subsection shall be submitted to the Congress no later than January 1, 1999.

Subtitle B—Increase in Deduction for Health Insurance Costs of Self-Employed Individuals

SEC. 311. INCREASE IN DEDUCTION FOR HEALTH INSURANCE COSTS OF SELF-EMPLOYED INDIVIDUALS.

(a) IN GENERAL.—Paragraph (1) of section 162(l) is amended to read as follows:

"(1) ALLOWANCE OF DEDUCTION.—

"(A) IN GENERAL.—In the case of an individual who is an employee within the meaning of section 401(c)(1), there shall be allowed as a deduction under this section an amount equal to the applicable percentage of the amount paid during the taxable year for insurance which constitutes medical care for the taxpayer, his spouse, and dependents.

"(B) APPLICABLE PERCENTAGE.—For purposes of subparagraph (A), the applicable percentage shall be determined under the following table:

"For taxable years beginning in calendar year—	The applicable percentage is—
1997	40 percent
1998 through 2002	45 percent
2003	50 percent

124

"For taxable years beginning in calendar year—	The applicable percentage is—
2004	60 percent
2005	70 percent
2006 or thereafter	80 percent.".

(b) EXCLUSION FOR AMOUNTS RECEIVED UNDER CERTAIN SELF-INSURED PLANS.—Paragraph (3) of section 104(a) is amended by inserting "(or through an arrangement having the effect of accident or health insurance)" after "health insurance".

(c) EFFECTIVE DATE.—The amendments made by this section shall apply to taxable years beginning after December 31, 1996.

Subtitle C—Long-Term Care Services and Contracts

PART I—GENERAL PROVISIONS

SEC. 321. TREATMENT OF LONG-TERM CARE INSURANCE.

(a) GENERAL RULE.—Chapter 79 (relating to definitions) is amended by inserting after section 7702A the following new section:

"SEC. 7702B. TREATMENT OF QUALIFIED LONG-TERM CARE INSURANCE.

"(a) IN GENERAL.—For purposes of this title—

"(1) a qualified long-term care insurance contract shall be treated as an accident and health insurance contract,

"(2) amounts (other than policyholder dividends, as defined in section 808, or premium refunds) received under a qualified long-term care insurance contract shall be treated as amounts received for personal injuries and sickness and shall be treated as reimbursement for expenses actually incurred for medical care (as defined in section 213(d)),

"(3) any plan of an employer providing coverage under a qualified long-term care insurance contract shall be treated as an accident and health plan with respect to such coverage,

"(4) except as provided in subsection (e)(3), amounts paid for a qualified long-term care insurance contract providing the benefits described in subsection (b)(2)(A) shall be treated as payments made for insurance for purposes of section 213(d)(1)(D), and

"(5) a qualified long-term care insurance contract shall be treated as a guaranteed renewable contract subject to the rules of section 816(e).

"(b) QUALIFIED LONG-TERM CARE INSURANCE CONTRACT.—For purposes of this title—

"(1) IN GENERAL.—The term 'qualified long-term care insurance contract' means any insurance contract if—

"(A) the only insurance protection provided under such contract is coverage of qualified long-term care services,

"(B) such contract does not pay or reimburse expenses incurred for services or items to the extent that such expenses are reimbursable under title XVIII of the Social Security Act or would be so reimbursable but for the application of a deductible or coinsurance amount,

---

"(C) such contract is guaranteed renewable,

"(D) such contract does not provide for a cash surrender value or other money that can be—

　"(i) paid, assigned, or pledged as collateral for a loan, or

　"(ii) borrowed,

other than as provided in subparagraph (E) or paragraph (2)(C),

"(E) all refunds of premiums, and all policyholder dividends or similar amounts, under such contract are to be applied as a reduction in future premiums or to increase future benefits, and

"(F) such contract meets the requirements of subsection (g).

"(2) SPECIAL RULES.—

"(A) PER DIEM, ETC. PAYMENTS PERMITTED.—A contract shall not fail to be described in subparagraph (A) or (B) of paragraph (1) by reason of payments being made on a per diem or other periodic basis without regard to the expenses incurred during the period to which the payments relate.

"(B) SPECIAL RULES RELATING TO MEDICARE.—

　"(i) Paragraph (1)(B) shall not apply to expenses which are reimbursable under title XVIII of the Social Security Act only as a secondary payor.

　"(ii) No provision of law shall be construed or applied so as to prohibit the offering of a qualified long-term care insurance contract on the basis that the contract coordinates its benefits with those provided under such title.

"(C) REFUNDS OF PREMIUMS.—Paragraph (1)(E) shall not apply to any refund on the death of the insured, or on a complete surrender or cancellation of the contract, which cannot exceed the aggregate premiums paid under the contract. Any refund on a complete surrender or cancellation of the contract shall be includible in gross income to the extent that any deduction or exclusion was allowable with respect to the premiums.

"(c) QUALIFIED LONG-TERM CARE SERVICES.—For purposes of this section—

"(1) IN GENERAL.—The term 'qualified long-term care services' means necessary diagnostic, preventive, therapeutic, curing, treating, mitigating, and rehabilitative services, and maintenance or personal care services, which—

"(A) are required by a chronically ill individual, and

"(B) are provided pursuant to a plan of care prescribed by a licensed health care practitioner.

"(2) CHRONICALLY ILL INDIVIDUAL.—

"(A) IN GENERAL.—The term 'chronically ill individual' means any individual who has been certified by a licensed health care practitioner as—

　"(i) being unable to perform (without substantial assistance from another individual) at least 2 activities of daily living for a period of at least 90 days due to a loss of functional capacity,

"(ii) having a level of disability similar (as deter-mined under regulations prescribed by the Secretary in consultation with the Secretary of Health and Human Services) to the level of disability described in clause (i), or

"(iii) requiring substantial supervision to protect such individual from threats to health and safety due to severe cognitive impairment.

Such term shall not include any individual otherwise meet-ing the requirements of the preceding sentence unless with-in the preceding 12-month period a licensed health care practitioner has certified that such individual meets such requirements.

"(B) ACTIVITIES OF DAILY LIVING.—For purposes of sub-paragraph (A), each of the following is an activity of daily living:

"(i) Eating.

"(ii) Toileting.

"(iii) Transferring.

"(iv) Bathing.

"(v) Dressing.

"(vi) Continence.

A contract shall not be treated as a qualified long-term care insurance contract unless the determination of whether an individual is a chronically ill individual takes into account at least 5 of such activities.

"(3) MAINTENANCE OR PERSONAL CARE SERVICES.—The term 'maintenance or personal care services' means any care the primary purpose of which is the provision of needed assistance with any of the disabilities as a result of which the individual is a chronically ill individual (including the protection from threats to health and safety due to severe cognitive impairment).

"(4) LICENSED HEALTH CARE PRACTITIONER.—The term 'li-censed health care practitioner' means any physician (as de-fined in section 1861(r)(1) of the Social Security Act) and any registered professional nurse, licensed social worker, or other individual who meets such requirements as may be prescribed by the Secretary.

"(d) AGGREGATE PAYMENTS IN EXCESS OF LIMITS.—

"(1) IN GENERAL.—If the aggregate of—

"(A) the periodic payments received for any period under all qualified long-term care insurance contracts which are treated as made for qualified long-term care services for an insured, and

"(B) the periodic payments received for such period which are treated under section 101(g) as paid by reason of the death of such insured,

exceeds the per diem limitation for such period, such excess shall be includible in gross income without regard to section 72. A payment shall not be taken into account under subparagraph (B) if the insured is a terminally ill individual (as defined in section 101(g)) at the time the payment is received.

"(2) PER DIEM LIMITATION.—For purposes of paragraph (1), the per diem limitation for any period is an amount equal to the excess (if any) of—

"(A) the greater of—

"(i) the dollar amount in effect for such period under paragraph (4), or

"(ii) the costs incurred for qualified long-term care services provided for the insured for such period, over

"(B) the aggregate payments received as reimbursements (through insurance or otherwise) for qualified long-term care services provided for the insured during such period.

"(3) AGGREGATION RULES.—For purposes of this subsection—

"(A) all persons receiving periodic payments described in paragraph (1) with respect to the same insured shall be treated as 1 person, and

"(B) the per diem limitation determined under paragraph (2) shall be allocated first to the insured and any remaining limitation shall be allocated among the other such persons in such manner as the Secretary shall prescribe.

"(4) DOLLAR AMOUNT.—The dollar amount in effect under this subsection shall be $175 per day (or the equivalent amount in the case of payments on another periodic basis).

"(5) INFLATION ADJUSTMENT.—In the case of a calendar year after 1997, the dollar amount contained in paragraph (4) shall be increased at the same time and in the same manner as amounts are increased pursuant to section 213(d)(10).

"(6) PERIODIC PAYMENTS.—For purposes of this subsection, the term 'periodic payment' means any payment (whether on a periodic basis or otherwise) made without regard to the extent of the costs incurred by the payee for qualified long-term care services.

"(e) TREATMENT OF COVERAGE PROVIDED AS PART OF A LIFE INSURANCE CONTRACT.—Except as otherwise provided in regulations prescribed by the Secretary, in the case of any long-term care insurance coverage (whether or not qualified) provided by a rider on or as part of a life insurance contract—

"(1) IN GENERAL.—This section shall apply as if the portion of the contract providing such coverage is a separate contract.

"(2) APPLICATION OF 7702.—Section 7702(c)(2) (relating to the guideline premium limitation) shall be applied by increasing the guideline premium limitation with respect to a life insurance contract, as of any date—

"(A) by the sum of any charges (but not premium payments) against the life insurance contract's cash surrender value (within the meaning of section 7702(f)(2)(A)) for such coverage made to that date under the contract, less

"(B) any such charges the imposition of which reduces the premiums paid for the contract (within the meaning of section 7702(f)(1)).

"(3) APPLICATION OF SECTION 213.—No deduction shall be allowed under section 213(a) for charges against the life insurance contract's cash surrender value described in paragraph

(2), unless such charges are includible in income as a result of the application of section 72(e)(10) and the rider is a qualified long-term care insurance contract under subsection (b).

"(4) PORTION DEFINED.—For purposes of this subsection, the term 'portion' means only the terms and benefits under a life insurance contract that are in addition to the terms and benefits under the contract without regard to long-term care insurance coverage.

"(f) TREATMENT OF CERTAIN STATE-MAINTAINED PLANS.—

"(1) IN GENERAL.—If—

"(A) an individual receives coverage for qualified long-term care services under a State long-term care plan, and

"(B) the terms of such plan would satisfy the requirements of subsection (b) were such plan an insurance contract,

such plan shall be treated as a qualified long-term care insurance contract for purposes of this title.

"(2) STATE LONG-TERM CARE PLAN.—For purposes of paragraph (1), the term 'State long-term care plan' means any plan—

"(A) which is established and maintained by a State or an instrumentality of a State,

"(B) which provides coverage only for qualified long-term care services, and

"(C) under which such coverage is provided only to—

"(i) employees and former employees of a State (or any political subdivision or instrumentality of a State),

"(ii) the spouses of such employees, and

"(iii) individuals bearing a relationship to such employees or spouses which is described in any of paragraphs (1) through (8) of section 152(a)."

(b) RESERVE METHOD.—Clause (iii) of section 807(d)(3)(A) is amended by inserting "(other than a qualified long-term care insurance contract, as defined in section 7702B(b))" after "insurance contract".

(c) LONG-TERM CARE INSURANCE NOT PERMITTED UNDER CAFETERIA PLANS OR FLEXIBLE SPENDING ARRANGEMENTS.—

(1) CAFETERIA PLANS.—Section 125(f) is amended by adding at the end the following new sentence: "Such term shall not include any product which is advertised, marketed, or offered as long-term care insurance."

(2) FLEXIBLE SPENDING ARRANGEMENTS.—Section 106 (relating to contributions by employer to accident and health plans), as amended by section 301(c), is amended by adding at the end the following new subsection:

"(c) INCLUSION OF LONG-TERM CARE BENEFITS PROVIDED THROUGH FLEXIBLE SPENDING ARRANGEMENTS.—

"(1) IN GENERAL.—Effective on and after January 1, 1997, gross income of an employee shall include employer-provided coverage for qualified long-term care services (as defined in section 7702B(c)) to the extent that such coverage is provided through a flexible spending or similar arrangement.

"(2) FLEXIBLE SPENDING ARRANGEMENT.—For purposes of this subsection, a flexible spending arrangement is a benefit

program which provides employees with coverage under which—

"(A) specified incurred expenses may be reimbursed (subject to reimbursement maximums and other reasonable conditions), and

"(B) the maximum amount of reimbursement which is reasonably available to a participant for such coverage is less than 500 percent of the value of such coverage.

In the case of an insured plan, the maximum amount reasonably available shall be determined on the basis of the underlying coverage."

(d) CONTINUATION COVERAGE RULES NOT TO APPLY.—

(1) Paragraph (2) of section 4980B(g) is amended by adding at the end the following new sentence: "Such term shall not include any plan substantially all of the coverage under which is for qualified long-term care services (as defined in section 7702B(c))."

(2) Paragraph (1) of section 607 of the Employee Retirement Income Security Act of 1974 is amended by adding at the end the following new sentence: "Such term shall not include any plan substantially all of the coverage under which is for qualified long-term care services (as defined in section 7702B(c) of such Code)."

(3) Paragraph (1) of section 2208 of the Public Health Service Act is amended by adding at the end the following new sentence: "Such term shall not include any plan substantially all of the coverage under which is for qualified long-term care services (as defined in section 7702B(c) of such Code)."

(e) CLERICAL AMENDMENT.—The table of sections for chapter 79 is amended by inserting after the item relating to section 7702A the following new item:

"Sec. 7702B. Treatment of qualified long-term care insurance.".

(f) EFFECTIVE DATES.—

(1) GENERAL EFFECTIVE DATE.—

(A) IN GENERAL.—Except as provided in subparagraph (B), the amendments made by this section shall apply to contracts issued after December 31, 1996.

(B) RESERVE METHOD.—The amendment made by subsection (b) shall apply to contracts issued after December 31, 1997.

(2) CONTINUATION OF EXISTING POLICIES.—In the case of any contract issued before January 1, 1997, which met the long-term care insurance requirements of the State in which the contract was sitused at the time the contract was issued—

(A) such contract shall be treated for purposes of the Internal Revenue Code of 1986 as a qualified long-term care insurance contract (as defined in section 7702B(b) of such Code), and

(B) services provided under, or reimbursed by, such contract shall be treated for such purposes as qualified long-term care services (as defined in section 7702B(c) of such Code).

In the case of an individual who is covered on December 31, 1996, under a State long-term care plan (as defined in section

7702B(f)(2) of such Code), the terms of such plan on such date shall be treated for purposes of the preceding sentence as a contract issued on such date which met the long-term care insurance requirements of such State.

(3) EXCHANGES OF EXISTING POLICIES.—If, after the date of enactment of this Act and before January 1, 1998, a contract providing for long-term care insurance coverage is exchanged solely for a qualified long-term care insurance contract (as defined in section 7702B(b) of such Code), no gain or loss shall be recognized on the exchange. If, in addition to a qualified long-term care insurance contract, money or other property is received in the exchange, then any gain shall be recognized to the extent of the sum of the money and the fair market value of the other property received. For purposes of this paragraph, the cancellation of a contract providing for long-term care insurance coverage and reinvestment of the cancellation proceeds in a qualified long-term care insurance contract within 60 days thereafter shall be treated as an exchange.

(4) ISSUANCE OF CERTAIN RIDERS PERMITTED.—For purposes of applying sections 101(f), 7702, and 7702A of the Internal Revenue Code of 1986 to any contract—

> *(A) the issuance of a rider which is treated as a qualified long-term care insurance contract under section 7702B, and*

> *(B) the addition of any provision required to conform any other long-term care rider to be so treated,*

shall not be treated as a modification or material change of such contract.

(5) APPLICATION OF PER DIEM LIMITATION TO EXISTING CONTRACTS.—The amount of per diem payments made under a contract issued on or before July 31, 1996, with respect to an insured which are excludable from gross income by reason of section 7702B of the Internal Revenue Code of 1986 (as added by this section) shall not be reduced under subsection (d)(2)(B) thereof by reason of reimbursements received under a contract issued on or before such date. The preceding sentence shall cease to apply as of the date (after July 31, 1996) such contract is exchanged or there is any contract modification which results in an increase in the amount of such per diem payments or the amount of such reimbursements.

(g) LONG-TERM CARE STUDY REQUEST.—The Chairman of the Committee on Ways and Means of the House of Representatives and the Chairman of the Committee on Finance of the Senate shall jointly request the National Association of Insurance Commissioners, in consultation with representatives of the insurance industry and consumer organizations, to formulate, develop, and conduct a study to determine the marketing and other effects of per diem limits on certain types of long-term care policies. If the National Association of Insurance Commissioners agrees to the study request, the National Association of Insurance Commissioners shall report the results of its study to such committees not later than 2 years after accepting the request.

SEC. 322. QUALIFIED LONG-TERM CARE SERVICES TREATED AS MEDI-CAL CARE.

(a) GENERAL RULE.—Paragraph (1) of section 213(d) (defining medical care) is amended by striking "or" at the end of subparagraph (B), by redesignating subparagraph (C) as subparagraph (D), and by inserting after subparagraph (B) the following new subparagraph:

"(C) for qualified long-term care services (as defined in section 7702B(c)), or".

(b) TECHNICAL AMENDMENTS.—

(1) Subparagraph (D) of section 213(d)(1) (as redesignated by subsection (a)) is amended by inserting before the period "or for any qualified long-term care insurance contract (as defined in section 7702B(b))".

(2)(A) Paragraph (1) of section 213(d) is amended by adding at the end the following new flush sentence:

"In the case of a qualified long-term care insurance contract (as defined in section 7702B(b)), only eligible long-term care premiums (as defined in paragraph (10)) shall be taken into account under subparagraph (D)."

(B) Paragraph (2) of section 162(l) is amended by adding at the end the following new subparagraph:

"(C) LONG-TERM CARE PREMIUMS.—In the case of a qualified long-term care insurance contract (as defined in section 7702B(b)), only eligible long-term care premiums (as defined in section 213(d)(10)) shall be taken into account under paragraph (1)."

(C) Subsection (d) of section 213 is amended by adding at the end the following new paragraphs:

"(10) ELIGIBLE LONG-TERM CARE PREMIUMS.—

"(A) IN GENERAL.—For purposes of this section, the term 'eligible long-term care premiums' means the amount paid during a taxable year for any qualified long-term care insurance contract (as defined in section 7702B(b)) covering an individual, to the extent such amount does not exceed the limitation determined under the following table:

"In the case of an individual with an attained age before the close of the taxable year of:	The limitation is:
40 or less	$200
More than 40 but not more than 50	375
More than 50 but not more than 60	750
More than 60 but not more than 70	2,000
More than 70	2,500.

"(B) INDEXING.—

"(i) IN GENERAL.—In the case of any taxable year beginning in a calendar year after 1997, each dollar amount contained in subparagraph (A) shall be increased by the medical care cost adjustment of such amount for such calendar year. If any increase determined under the preceding sentence is not a multiple of $10, such increase shall be rounded to the nearest multiple of $10.

"(ii) MEDICAL CARE COST ADJUSTMENT.—For purposes of clause (i), the medical care cost adjustment for any calendar year is the percentage (if any) by which—

"(I) the medical care component of the Consumer Price Index (as defined in section 1(f)(5)) for August of the preceding calendar year, exceeds

"(II) such component for August of 1996.

The Secretary shall, in consultation with the Secretary of Health and Human Services, prescribe an adjustment which the Secretary determines is more appropriate for purposes of this paragraph than the adjustment described in the preceding sentence, and the adjustment so prescribed shall apply in lieu of the adjustment described in the preceding sentence.

"(11) CERTAIN PAYMENTS TO RELATIVES TREATED AS NOT PAID FOR MEDICAL CARE.—An amount paid for a qualified long-term care service (as defined in section 7702B(c)) provided to an individual shall be treated as not paid for medical care if such service is provided—

"(A) by the spouse of the individual or by a relative (directly or through a partnership, corporation, or other entity) unless the service is provided by a licensed professional with respect to such service, or

"(B) by a corporation or partnership which is related (within the meaning of section 267(b) or 707(b)) to the individual.

For purposes of this paragraph, the term 'relative' means an individual bearing a relationship to the individual which is described in any of paragraphs (1) through (8) of section 152(a). This paragraph shall not apply for purposes of section 105(b) with respect to reimbursements through insurance." .

(3) Paragraph (6) of section 213(d) is amended—

(A) by striking "subparagraphs (A) and (B)" and inserting "subparagraphs (A), (B), and (C)", and

(B) by striking "paragraph (1)(C)" in subparagraph (A) and inserting "paragraph (1)(D)".

(4) Paragraph (7) of section 213(d) is amended by striking "subparagraphs (A) and (B)" and inserting "subparagraphs (A), (B), and (C)".

(c) EFFECTIVE DATE.—The amendments made by this section shall apply to taxable years beginning after December 31, 1996.

SEC. 323. REPORTING REQUIREMENTS.

(a) IN GENERAL.—Subpart B of part III of subchapter A of chapter 61 is amended by adding at the end the following new section:

"SEC. 6050Q. CERTAIN LONG-TERM CARE BENEFITS.

"(a) REQUIREMENT OF REPORTING.—Any person who pays long-term care benefits shall make a return, according to the forms or regulations prescribed by the Secretary, setting forth—

"(1) the aggregate amount of such benefits paid by such person to any individual during any calendar year,

"(2) whether or not such benefits are paid in whole or in part on a per diem or other periodic basis without regard to the expenses incurred during the period to which the payments relate,

"(3) the name, address, and TIN of such individual, and

"(4) the name, address, and TIN of the chronically ill or terminally ill individual on account of whose condition such benefits are paid.

"(b) STATEMENTS TO BE FURNISHED TO PERSONS WITH RE-SPECT TO WHOM INFORMATION IS REQUIRED.—Every person required to make a return under subsection (a) shall furnish to each individual whose name is required to be set forth in such return a written statement showing—

"(1) the name of the person making the payments, and

"(2) the aggregate amount of long-term care benefits paid to the individual which are required to be shown on such return. The written statement required under the preceding sentence shall be furnished to the individual on or before January 31 of the year following the calendar year for which the return under subsection (a) was required to be made.

"(c) LONG-TERM CARE BENEFITS.—For purposes of this section, the term 'long-term care benefit' means—

"(1) any payment under a product which is advertised, marketed, or offered as long-term care insurance, and

"(2) any payment which is excludable from gross income by reason of section 101(g).".

(b) PENALTIES.—

(1) Subparagraph (B) of section 6724(d)(1) is amended by redesignating clauses (ix) through (xiv) as clauses (x) through (xv), respectively, and by inserting after clause (viii) the following new clause:

"(ix) section 6050Q (relating to certain long-term care benefits),".

(2) Paragraph (2) of section 6724(d) is amended by redesignating subparagraphs (Q) through (T) as subparagraphs (R) through (U), respectively, and by inserting after subparagraph (P) the following new subparagraph:

"(Q) section 6050Q(b) (relating to certain long-term care benefits),".

(c) CLERICAL AMENDMENT.—The table of sections for subpart B of part III of subchapter A of chapter 61 is amended by adding at the end the following new item:

"Sec. 6050Q. Certain long-term care benefits.".

(d) EFFECTIVE DATE.—The amendments made by this section shall apply to benefits paid after December 31, 1996.

PART II—CONSUMER PROTECTION PROVISIONS

SEC. 325. POLICY REQUIREMENTS.

Section 7702B (as added by section 321) is amended by adding at the end the following new subsection:

"(g) CONSUMER PROTECTION PROVISIONS.—

"(1) IN GENERAL.—The requirements of this subsection are met with respect to any contract if the contract meets—

"(A) the requirements of the model regulation and model Act described in paragraph (2),

"(B) the disclosure requirement of paragraph (3), and

"(C) the requirements relating to nonforfeitability under paragraph (4).

"(2) REQUIREMENTS OF MODEL REGULATION AND ACT.—

"(A) IN GENERAL.—The requirements of this paragraph are met with respect to any contract if such contract meets—

"(i) MODEL REGULATION.—The following requirements of the model regulation:

"(I) Section 7A (relating to guaranteed renewal or noncancellability), and the requirements of section 6B of the model Act relating to such section 7A.

"(II) Section 7B (relating to prohibitions on limitations and exclusions).

"(III) Section 7C (relating to extension of benefits).

"(IV) Section 7D (relating to continuation or conversion of coverage).

"(V) Section 7E (relating to discontinuance and replacement of policies).

"(VI) Section 8 (relating to unintentional lapse).

"(VII) Section 9 (relating to disclosure), other than section 9F thereof.

"(VIII) Section 10 (relating to prohibitions against post-claims underwriting).

"(IX) Section 11 (relating to minimum standards).

"(X) Section 12 (relating to requirement to offer inflation protection), except that any requirement for a signature on a rejection of inflation protection shall permit the signature to be on an application or on a separate form.

"(XI) Section 23 (relating to prohibition against preexisting conditions and probationary periods in replacement policies or certificates).

"(ii) MODEL ACT.—The following requirements of the model Act:

"(I) Section 6C (relating to preexisting conditions).

"(II) Section 6D (relating to prior hospitalization).

"(B) DEFINITIONS.—For purposes of this paragraph—

"(i) MODEL PROVISIONS.—The terms 'model regulation' and 'model Act' mean the long-term care insurance model regulation, and the long-term care insurance model Act, respectively, promulgated by the National Association of Insurance Commissioners (as adopted as of January 1993).

"(ii) COORDINATION.—Any provision of the model regulation or model Act listed under clause (i) or (ii) of subparagraph (A) shall be treated as including any other provision of such regulation or Act necessary to implement the provision.

"*(iii) DETERMINATION.—For purposes of this section and section 4980C, the determination of whether any requirement of a model regulation or the model Act has been met shall be made by the Secretary.*

"*(3) DISCLOSURE REQUIREMENT.—The requirement of this paragraph is met with respect to any contract if such contract meets the requirements of section 4980C(d).*

"*(4) NONFORFEITURE REQUIREMENTS.—*

"*(A) IN GENERAL.—The requirements of this paragraph are met with respect to any level premium contract, if the issuer of such contract offers to the policyholder, including any group policyholder, a nonforfeiture provision meeting the requirements of subparagraph (B).*

"*(B) REQUIREMENTS OF PROVISION.—The nonforfeiture provision required under subparagraph (A) shall meet the following requirements:*

"*(i) The nonforfeiture provision shall be appropriately captioned.*

"*(ii) The nonforfeiture provision shall provide for a benefit available in the event of a default in the payment of any premiums and the amount of the benefit may be adjusted subsequent to being initially granted only as necessary to reflect changes in claims, persistency, and interest as reflected in changes in rates for premium paying contracts approved by the Secretary for the same contract form.*

"*(iii) The nonforfeiture provision shall provide at least one of the following:*

"*(I) Reduced paid-up insurance.*

"*(II) Extended term insurance.*

"*(III) Shortened benefit period.*

"*(IV) Other similar offerings approved by the Secretary.*

"*(5) CROSS REFERENCE.—*

"**For coordination of the requirements of this subsection with State requirements, see section 4980C(f).**"

SEC. 326. REQUIREMENTS FOR ISSUERS OF QUALIFIED LONG-TERM CARE INSURANCE CONTRACTS.

(a) IN GENERAL.—Chapter 43 is amended by adding at the end the following new section:

"SEC. 4980C. REQUIREMENTS FOR ISSUERS OF QUALIFIED LONG-TERM CARE INSURANCE CONTRACTS.

"*(a) GENERAL RULE.—There is hereby imposed on any person failing to meet the requirements of subsection (c) or (d) a tax in the amount determined under subsection (b).*

"*(b) AMOUNT.—*

"*(1) IN GENERAL.—The amount of the tax imposed by subsection (a) shall be $100 per insured for each day any requirement of subsection (c) or (d) is not met with respect to each qualified long-term care insurance contract.*

"*(2) WAIVER.—In the case of a failure which is due to reasonable cause and not to willful neglect, the Secretary may waive part or all of the tax imposed by subsection (a) to the ex-*

tent that payment of the tax would be excessive relative to the failure involved.

"(c) RESPONSIBILITIES.—The requirements of this subsection are as follows:

 "(1) REQUIREMENTS OF MODEL PROVISIONS.—

  "(A) MODEL REGULATION.—The following requirements of the model regulation must be met:

   "(i) Section 13 (relating to application forms and replacement coverage).

   "(ii) Section 14 (relating to reporting requirements), except that the issuer shall also report at least annually the number of claims denied during the reporting period for each class of business (expressed as a percentage of claims denied), other than claims denied for failure to meet the waiting period or because of any applicable preexisting condition.

   "(iii) Section 20 (relating to filing requirements for marketing).

   "(iv) Section 21 (relating to standards for marketing), including inaccurate completion of medical histories, other than sections 21C(1) and 21C(6) thereof, except that—

    "(I) in addition to such requirements, no person shall, in selling or offering to sell a qualified long-term care insurance contract, misrepresent a material fact; and

    "(II) no such requirements shall include a requirement to inquire or identify whether a prospective applicant or enrollee for long-term care insurance has accident and sickness insurance.

   "(v) Section 22 (relating to appropriateness of recommended purchase).

   "(vi) Section 24 (relating to standard format outline of coverage).

   "(vii) Section 25 (relating to requirement to deliver shopper's guide).

  "(B) MODEL ACT.—The following requirements of the model Act must be met:

   "(i) Section 6F (relating to right to return), except that such section shall also apply to denials of applications and any refund shall be made within 30 days of the return or denial.

   "(ii) Section 6G (relating to outline of coverage).

   "(iii) Section 6H (relating to requirements for certificates under group plans).

   "(iv) Section 6I (relating to policy summary).

   "(v) Section 6J (relating to monthly reports on accelerated death benefits).

   "(vi) Section 7 (relating to incontestability period).

  "(C) DEFINITIONS.—For purposes of this paragraph, the terms 'model regulation' and 'model Act' have the meanings given such terms by section 7702B(g)(2)(B).

 "(2) DELIVERY OF POLICY.—If an application for a qualified long-term care insurance contract (or for a certificate under

such a contract for a group) is approved, the issuer shall deliver to the applicant (or policyholder or certificateholder) the contract (or certificate) of insurance not later than 30 days after the date of the approval.

"(3) INFORMATION ON DENIALS OF CLAIMS.—If a claim under a qualified long-term care insurance contract is denied, the issuer shall, within 60 days of the date of a written request by the policyholder or certificateholder (or representative)—

"(A) provide a written explanation of the reasons for the denial, and

"(B) make available all information directly relating to such denial.

"(d) DISCLOSURE.—The requirements of this subsection are met if the issuer of a long-term care insurance policy discloses in such policy and in the outline of coverage required under subsection (c)(1)(B)(ii) that the policy is intended to be a qualified long-term care insurance contract under section 7702B(b).

"(e) QUALIFIED LONG-TERM CARE INSURANCE CONTRACT DEFINED.—For purposes of this section, the term 'qualified long-term care insurance contract' has the meaning given such term by section 7702B.

"(f) COORDINATION WITH STATE REQUIREMENTS.—If a State imposes any requirement which is more stringent than the analogous requirement imposed by this section or section 7702B(g), the requirement imposed by this section or section 7702B(g) shall be treated as met if the more stringent State requirement is met.".

(b) CONFORMING AMENDMENT.—The table of sections for chapter 43 is amended by adding at the end the following new item:

"Sec. 4980C. Requirements for issuers of qualified long-term care insurance contracts."

SEC. 327. EFFECTIVE DATES.

(a) IN GENERAL.—The provisions of, and amendments made by, this part shall apply to contracts issued after December 31, 1996. The provisions of section 321(f) (relating to transition rule) shall apply to such contracts.

(b) ISSUERS.—The amendments made by section 326 shall apply to actions taken after December 31, 1996.

Subtitle D—Treatment of Accelerated Death Benefits

SEC. 331. TREATMENT OF ACCELERATED DEATH BENEFITS BY RECIPIENT.

(a) IN GENERAL.—Section 101 (relating to certain death benefits) is amended by adding at the end the following new subsection:

"(g) TREATMENT OF CERTAIN ACCELERATED DEATH BENEFITS.—

"(1) IN GENERAL.—For purposes of this section, the following amounts shall be treated as an amount paid by reason of the death of an insured:

"(A) Any amount received under a life insurance contract on the life of an insured who is a terminally ill individual.

"(B) Any amount received under a life insurance contract on the life of an insured who is a chronically ill individual.

"(2) TREATMENT OF VIATICAL SETTLEMENTS.—

"(A) IN GENERAL.—If any portion of the death benefit under a life insurance contract on the life of an insured described in paragraph (1) is sold or assigned to a viatical settlement provider, the amount paid for the sale or assignment of such portion shall be treated as an amount paid under the life insurance contract by reason of the death of such insured.

"(B) VIATICAL SETTLEMENT PROVIDER.—

"(i) IN GENERAL.—The term 'viatical settlement provider' means any person regularly engaged in the trade or business of purchasing, or taking assignments of, life insurance contracts on the lives of insureds described in paragraph (1) if—

"(I) such person is licensed for such purposes (with respect to insureds described in the same subparagraph of paragraph (1) as the insured) in the State in which the insured resides, or

"(II) in the case of an insured who resides in a State not requiring the licensing of such persons for such purposes with respect to such insured, such person meets the requirements of clause (ii) or (iii), whichever applies to such insured.

"(ii) TERMINALLY ILL INSUREDS.—A person meets the requirements of this clause with respect to an insured who is a terminally ill individual if such person—

"(I) meets the requirements of sections 8 and 9 of the Viatical Settlements Model Act of the National Association of Insurance Commissioners, and

"(II) meets the requirements of the Model Regulations of the National Association of Insurance Commissioners (relating to standards for evaluation of reasonable payments) in determining amounts paid by such person in connection with such purchases or assignments.

"(iii) CHRONICALLY ILL INSUREDS.—A person meets the requirements of this clause with respect to an insured who is a chronically ill individual if such person—

"(I) meets requirements similar to the requirements referred to in clause (ii)(I), and

"(II) meets the standards (if any) of the National Association of Insurance Commissioners for evaluating the reasonableness of amounts paid by such person in connection with such purchases or assignments with respect to chronically ill individuals.

"(3) SPECIAL RULES FOR CHRONICALLY ILL INSUREDS.—In the case of an insured who is a chronically ill individual—

"(A) IN GENERAL.—*Paragraphs (1) and (2) shall not apply to any payment received for any period unless—*

"*(i) such payment is for costs incurred by the payee (not compensated for by insurance or otherwise) for qualified long-term care services provided for the insured for such period, and*

"*(ii) the terms of the contract giving rise to such payment satisfy—*

"*(I) the requirements of section 7702B(b)(1)(B), and*

"*(II) the requirements (if any) applicable under subparagraph (B).*

For purposes of the preceding sentence, the rule of section 7702B(b)(2)(B) shall apply.

"(B) OTHER REQUIREMENTS.—*The requirements applicable under this subparagraph are—*

"*(i) those requirements of section 7702B(g) and section 4980C which the Secretary specifies as applying to such a purchase, assignment, or other arrangement,*

"*(ii) standards adopted by the National Association of Insurance Commissioners which specifically apply to chronically ill individuals (and, if such standards are adopted, the analogous requirements specified under clause (i) shall cease to apply), and*

"*(iii) standards adopted by the State in which the policyholder resides (and if such standards are adopted, the analogous requirements specified under clause (i) and (subject to section 4980C(f)) standards under clause (ii), shall cease to apply).*

"(C) PER DIEM PAYMENTS.—*A payment shall not fail to be described in subparagraph (A) by reason of being made on a per diem or other periodic basis without regard to the expenses incurred during the period to which the payment relates.*

"(D) LIMITATION ON EXCLUSION FOR PERIODIC PAYMENTS.—

"**For limitation on amount of periodic payments which are treated as described in paragraph (1), see section 7702B(d).**"

"(4) DEFINITIONS.—*For purposes of this subsection—*

"(A) TERMINALLY ILL INDIVIDUAL.—*The term 'terminally ill individual' means an individual who has been certified by a physician as having an illness or physical condition which can reasonably be expected to result in death in 24 months or less after the date of the certification.*

"(B) CHRONICALLY ILL INDIVIDUAL.—*The term 'chronically ill individual' has the meaning given such term by section 7702B(c)(2); except that such term shall not include a terminally ill individual.*

"(C) QUALIFIED LONG-TERM CARE SERVICES.—*The term 'qualified long-term care services' has the meaning given such term by section 7702B(c).*

"(D) PHYSICIAN.—*The term 'physician' has the meaning given to such term by section 1861(r)(1) of the Social Security Act (42 U.S.C. 1395x(r)(1)).*

"(5) EXCEPTION FOR BUSINESS-RELATED POLICIES.—This subsection shall not apply in the case of any amount paid to any taxpayer other than the insured if such taxpayer has an insurable interest with respect to the life of the insured by reason of the insured being a director, officer, or employee of the taxpayer or by reason of the insured being financially interested in any trade or business carried on by the taxpayer.".

(b) EFFECTIVE DATE.—The amendment made by subsection (a) shall apply to amounts received after December 31, 1996.

SEC. 332. TAX TREATMENT OF COMPANIES ISSUING QUALIFIED ACCELERATED DEATH BENEFIT RIDERS.

(a) QUALIFIED ACCELERATED DEATH BENEFIT RIDERS TREATED AS LIFE INSURANCE.—Section 818 (relating to other definitions and special rules) is amended by adding at the end the following new subsection:

"(g) QUALIFIED ACCELERATED DEATH BENEFIT RIDERS TREATED AS LIFE INSURANCE.—For purposes of this part—

"(1) IN GENERAL.—Any reference to a life insurance contract shall be treated as including a reference to a qualified accelerated death benefit rider on such contract.

"(2) QUALIFIED ACCELERATED DEATH BENEFIT RIDERS.—For purposes of this subsection, the term 'qualified accelerated death benefit rider' means any rider on a life insurance contract if the only payments under the rider are payments meeting the requirements of section 101(g).

"(3) EXCEPTION FOR LONG-TERM CARE RIDERS.—Paragraph (1) shall not apply to any rider which is treated as a long-term care insurance contract under section 7702B.".

(b) EFFECTIVE DATE.—

(1) IN GENERAL.—The amendment made by this section shall take effect on January 1, 1997.

(2) ISSUANCE OF RIDER NOT TREATED AS MATERIAL CHANGE.—For purposes of applying sections 101(f), 7702, and 7702A of the Internal Revenue Code of 1986 to any contract—

(A) the issuance of a qualified accelerated death benefit rider (as defined in section 818(g) of such Code (as added by this Act)), and

(B) the addition of any provision required to conform an accelerated death benefit rider to the requirements of such section 818(g),

shall not be treated as a modification or material change of such contract.

Subtitle E—State Insurance Pools

SEC. 341. EXEMPTION FROM INCOME TAX FOR STATE-SPONSORED ORGANIZATIONS PROVIDING HEALTH COVERAGE FOR HIGH-RISK INDIVIDUALS.

(a) IN GENERAL.—Subsection (c) of section 501 (relating to list of exempt organizations) is amended by adding at the end the following new paragraph:

"(26) Any membership organization if—

"(A) such organization is established by a State exclusively to provide coverage for medical care (as defined in

section 213(d)) on a not-for-profit basis to individuals described in subparagraph (B) through—

"(i) insurance issued by the organization, or

"(ii) a health maintenance organization under an arrangement with the organization,

"(B) the only individuals receiving such coverage through the organization are individuals—

"(i) who are residents of such State, and

"(ii) who, by reason of the existence or history of a medical condition—

"(I) are unable to acquire medical care coverage for such condition through insurance or from a health maintenance organization, or

"(II) are able to acquire such coverage only at a rate which is substantially in excess of the rate for such coverage through the membership organization,

"(C) the composition of the membership in such organization is specified by such State, and

"(D) no part of the net earnings of the organization inures to the benefit of any private shareholder or individual.".

(b) EFFECTIVE DATE.—The amendment made by this section shall apply to taxable years beginning after December 31, 1996.

SEC. 342. EXEMPTION FROM INCOME TAX FOR STATE-SPONSORED WORKMEN'S COMPENSATION REINSURANCE ORGANIZATIONS.

(a) IN GENERAL.—Subsection (c) of section 501 (relating to list of exempt organizations), as amended by section 341, is amended by adding at the end the following new paragraph:

"(27) Any membership organization if—

"(A) such organization is established before June 1, 1996, by a State exclusively to reimburse its members for losses arising under workmen's compensation acts,

"(B) such State requires that the membership of such organization consist of—

"(i) all persons who issue insurance covering workmen's compensation losses in such State, and

"(ii) all persons and governmental entities who self-insure against such losses, and

"(C) such organization operates as a non-profit organization by—

"(i) returning surplus income to its members or workmen's compensation policyholders on a periodic basis, and

"(ii) reducing initial premiums in anticipation of investment income."

(b) EFFECTIVE DATE.—The amendment made by this section shall apply to taxable years ending after the date of the enactment of this Act.

Subtitle F—Organizations Subject to Section 833

SEC. 351. ORGANIZATIONS SUBJECT TO SECTION 833.

(a) IN GENERAL.—Section 833(c) (relating to organization to which section applies) is amended by adding at the end the following new paragraph:

"(4) TREATMENT AS EXISTING BLUE CROSS OR BLUE SHIELD ORGANIZATION.—

"(A) IN GENERAL.—Paragraph (2) shall be applied to an organization described in subparagraph (B) as if it were a Blue Cross or Blue Shield organization.

"(B) APPLICABLE ORGANIZATION.—An organization is described in this subparagraph if it—

"(i) is organized under, and governed by, State laws which are specifically and exclusively applicable to not-for-profit health insurance or health service type organizations, and

"(ii) is not a Blue Cross or Blue Shield organization or health maintenance organization.".

(b) EFFECTIVE DATE.—The amendment made by this section shall apply to taxable years ending after December 31, 1996.

Subtitle G—IRA Distributions to the Unemployed

SEC. 361. DISTRIBUTIONS FROM CERTAIN PLANS MAY BE USED WITHOUT ADDITIONAL TAX TO PAY FINANCIALLY DEVASTATING MEDICAL EXPENSES.

(a) IN GENERAL.—Section 72(t)(3)(A) is amended by striking "(B),".

(b) DISTRIBUTIONS FOR PAYMENT OF HEALTH INSURANCE PREMIUMS OF CERTAIN UNEMPLOYED INDIVIDUALS.—Paragraph (2) of section 72(t) is amended by adding at the end the following new subparagraph:

"(D) DISTRIBUTIONS TO UNEMPLOYED INDIVIDUALS FOR HEALTH INSURANCE PREMIUMS.—

"(i) IN GENERAL.—Distributions from an individual retirement plan to an individual after separation from employment—

"(I) if such individual has received unemployment compensation for 12 consecutive weeks under any Federal or State unemployment compensation law by reason of such separation,

"(II) if such distributions are made during any taxable year during which such unemployment compensation is paid or the succeeding taxable year, and

"(III) to the extent such distributions do not exceed the amount paid during the taxable year for insurance described in section 213(d)(1)(D) with *respect to the individual and the individual's spouse and dependents (as defined in section 152).*

"(ii) DISTRIBUTIONS AFTER REEMPLOYMENT.— Clause (i) shall not apply to any distribution made after the individual has been employed for at least 60 days after the separation from employment to which clause (i) applies.

"(iii) SELF-EMPLOYED INDIVIDUALS.—To the extent provided in regulations, a self-employed individual shall be treated as meeting the requirements of clause (i)(I) if, under Federal or State law, the individual would have received unemployment compensation but for the fact the individual was self-employed.".

(c) CONFORMING AMENDMENT.—Subparagraph (B) of section 72(t)(2) is amended by striking "or (C)" and inserting ", (C), or (D)".

(d) EFFECTIVE DATE.—The amendments made by this section shall apply to distributions after December 31, 1996.

Subtitle H—Organ and Tissue Donation Information Included With Income Tax Refund Payments

SEC. 371. ORGAN AND TISSUE DONATION INFORMATION INCLUDED WITH INCOME TAX REFUND PAYMENTS.

(a) IN GENERAL.—The Secretary of the Treasury shall, to the extent practicable, include with the mailing of any payment of a refund of individual income tax made during the period beginning on February 1, 1997, and ending on June 30, 1997, a copy of the document described in subsection (b).

(b) TEXT OF DOCUMENT.—The Secretary of the Treasury shall, after consultation with the Secretary of Health and Human Services and organizations promoting organ and tissue (including eye) donation, prepare a document suitable for inclusion with individual income tax refund payments which—

(1) encourages organ and tissue donation;

(2) includes a detachable organ and tissue donor card; and

(3) urges recipients to—

(A) sign the organ and tissue donor card;

(B) discuss organ and tissue donation with family members and tell family members about the recipient's desire to be an organ and tissue donor if the occasion arises; and

(C) encourage family members to request or authorize organ and tissue donation if the occasion arises.

TITLE IV—APPLICATION AND ENFORCE-MENT OF GROUP HEALTH PLAN REQUIREMENTS

Subtitle A—Application and Enforcement of Group Health Plan Requirements

SEC. 401. GROUP HEALTH PLAN PORTABILITY, ACCESS, AND RENEWABILITY REQUIREMENTS.

(a) IN GENERAL.—The Internal Revenue Code of 1986 is amended by adding at the end the following new subtitle:

"Subtitle K—Group Health Plan Portability, Access, and Renewability Requirements

"*Chapter 100. Group health plan portability, access, and renewability requirements.*

"CHAPTER 100—GROUP HEALTH PLAN PORTABILITY, ACCESS, AND RENEWABILITY REQUIREMENTS

"*Sec. 9801. Increased portability through limitation on preexisting condition exclusions.*
"*Sec. 9802. Prohibiting discrimination against individual participants and beneficiaries based on health status.*
"*Sec. 9803. Guaranteed renewability in multiemployer plans and certain multiple employer welfare arrangements.*
"*Sec. 9804. General exceptions.*
"*Sec. 9805. Definitions.*
"*Sec. 9806. Regulations.*

"SEC. 9801. INCREASED PORTABILITY THROUGH LIMITATION ON PRE-EXISTING CONDITION EXCLUSIONS.

"(a) LIMITATION ON PREEXISTING CONDITION EXCLUSION PERIOD; CREDITING FOR PERIODS OF PREVIOUS COVERAGE.—Subject to subsection (d), a group health plan may, with respect to a participant or beneficiary, impose a preexisting condition exclusion only if—

"(1) such exclusion relates to a condition (whether physical or mental), regardless of the cause of the condition, for which medical advice, diagnosis, care, or treatment was recommended or received within the 6-month period ending on the enrollment date;

"(2) such exclusion extends for a period of not more than 12 months (or 18 months in the case of a late enrollee) after the enrollment date; and

"(3) the period of any such preexisting condition exclusion is reduced by the length of the aggregate of the periods of creditable coverage (if any) applicable to the participant or beneficiary as of the enrollment date.

"(b) DEFINITIONS.—For purposes of this section—

"(1) PREEXISTING CONDITION EXCLUSION.—

"(A) IN GENERAL.—The term 'preexisting condition exclusion' means, with respect to coverage, a limitation or exclusion of benefits relating to a condition based on the fact that the condition was present before the date of enrollment for such coverage, whether or not any medical advice, diagnosis, care, or treatment was recommended or received before such date.

"(B) TREATMENT OF GENETIC INFORMATION.—For purposes of this section, genetic information shall not be treated as a condition described in subsection (a)(1) in the absence of a diagnosis of the condition related to such information.

"(2) ENROLLMENT DATE.—The term 'enrollment date' means, with respect to an individual covered under a group health plan, the date of enrollment of the individual in the plan or, if earlier, the first day of the waiting period for such enrollment.

"(3) LATE ENROLLEE.—The term 'late enrollee' means, with respect to coverage under a group health plan, a participant or beneficiary who enrolls under the plan other than during—

"(A) the first period in which the individual is eligible to enroll under the plan, or

"(B) a special enrollment period under subsection (f).

"(4) WAITING PERIOD.—The term 'waiting period' means, with respect to a group health plan and an individual who is a potential participant or beneficiary in the plan, the period that must pass with respect to the individual before the individual is eligible to be covered for benefits under the terms of the plan.

"(c) RULES RELATING TO CREDITING PREVIOUS COVERAGE.—

"(1) CREDITABLE COVERAGE DEFINED.—For purposes of this part, the term 'creditable coverage' means, with respect to an individual, coverage of the individual under any of the following:

"(A) A group health plan.

"(B) Health insurance coverage.

"(C) Part A or part B of title XVIII of the Social Security Act.

"(D) Title XIX of the Social Security Act, other than coverage consisting solely of benefits under section 1928.

"(E) Chapter 55 of title 10, United States Code.

"(F) A medical care program of the Indian Health Service or of a tribal organization.

"(G) A State health benefits risk pool.

"(H) A health plan offered under chapter 89 of title 5, United States Code.

"(I) A public health plan (as defined in regulations).

"(J) A health benefit plan under section 5(e) of the Peace Corps Act (22 U.S.C. 2504(e).

Such term does not include coverage consisting solely of coverage of excepted benefits (as defined in section 9805(c)).

"(2) NOT COUNTING PERIODS BEFORE SIGNIFICANT BREAKS IN COVERAGE.—

"(A) IN GENERAL.—A period of creditable coverage shall not be counted, with respect to enrollment of an individual

under a group health plan, if, after such period and before the enrollment date, there was a 63-day period during all of which the individual was not covered under any creditable coverage.

"(B) WAITING PERIOD NOT TREATED AS A BREAK IN COVERAGE.—For purposes of subparagraph (A) and subsection (d)(4), any period that an individual is in a waiting period for any coverage under a group health plan or is in an affiliation period shall not be taken into account in determining the continuous period under subparagraph (A).

"(C) AFFILIATION PERIOD.—

"(i) IN GENERAL.—For purposes of this section, the term 'affiliation period' means a period which, under the terms of the health insurance coverage offered by the health maintenance organization, must expire before the health insurance coverage becomes effective. During such an affiliation period, the organization is not required to provide health care services or benefits and no premium shall be charged to the participant or beneficiary.

"(ii) BEGINNING.—Such period shall begin on the enrollment date.

"(iii) RUNS CONCURRENTLY WITH WAITING PERIODS.—Any such affiliation period shall run concurrently with any waiting period under the plan.

"(3) METHOD OF CREDITING COVERAGE.—

"(A) STANDARD METHOD.—Except as otherwise provided under subparagraph (B), for purposes of applying subsection (a)(3), a group health plan shall count a period of creditable coverage without regard to the specific benefits for which coverage is offered during the period.

"(B) ELECTION OF ALTERNATIVE METHOD.—A group health plan may elect to apply subsection (a)(3) based on coverage of any benefits within each of several classes or categories of benefits specified in regulations rather than as provided under subparagraph (A). Such election shall be made on a uniform basis for all participants and beneficiaries. Under such election a group health plan shall count a period of creditable coverage with respect to any class or category of benefits if any level of benefits is covered within such class or category.

"(C) PLAN NOTICE.—In the case of an election with respect to a group health plan under subparagraph (B), the plan shall—

"(i) prominently state in any disclosure statements concerning the plan, and state to each enrollee at the time of enrollment under the plan, that the plan has made such election, and

"(ii) include in such statements a description of the effect of this election.

"(4) ESTABLISHMENT OF PERIOD.—Periods of creditable coverage with respect to an individual shall be established through presentation of certifications described in subsection (e) or in such other manner as may be specified in regulations.

"(d) EXCEPTIONS.—

"(1) EXCLUSION NOT APPLICABLE TO CERTAIN NEWBORNS.— Subject to paragraph (4), a group health plan may not impose any preexisting condition exclusion in the case of an individual who, as of the last day of the 30-day period beginning with the date of birth, is covered under creditable coverage.

"(2) EXCLUSION NOT APPLICABLE TO CERTAIN ADOPTED CHILDREN.—Subject to paragraph (4), a group health plan may not impose any preexisting condition exclusion in the case of a child who is adopted or placed for adoption before attaining 18 years of age and who, as of the last day of the 30-day period beginning on the date of the adoption or placement for adoption, is covered under creditable coverage. The previous sentence shall not apply to coverage before the date of such adoption or placement for adoption.

"(3) EXCLUSION NOT APPLICABLE TO PREGNANCY.—For purposes of this section, a group health plan may not impose any preexisting condition exclusion relating to pregnancy as a preexisting condition.

"(4) LOSS IF BREAK IN COVERAGE.—Paragraphs (1) and (2) shall no longer apply to an individual after the end of the first 63-day period during all of which the individual was not covered under any creditable coverage.

"(e) CERTIFICATIONS AND DISCLOSURE OF COVERAGE.—

"(1) REQUIREMENT FOR CERTIFICATION OF PERIOD OF CREDITABLE COVERAGE.—

"(A) IN GENERAL.—A group health plan shall provide the certification described in subparagraph (B)—

"(i) at the time an individual ceases to be covered under the plan or otherwise becomes covered under a COBRA continuation provision,

"(ii) in the case of an individual becoming covered under such a provision, at the time the individual ceases to be covered under such provision, and

"(iii) on the request on behalf of an individual made not later than 24 months after the date of cessation of the coverage described in clause (i) or (ii), whichever is later.

The certification under clause (i) may be provided, to the extent practicable, at a time consistent with notices required under any applicable COBRA continuation provision.

"(B) CERTIFICATION.—The certification described in this subparagraph is a written certification of—

"(i) the period of creditable coverage of the individual under such plan and the coverage under such COBRA continuation provision, and

"(ii) the waiting period (if any) (and affiliation period, if applicable) imposed with respect to the individual for any coverage under such plan.

"(C) ISSUER COMPLIANCE.—To the extent that medical care under a group health plan consists of health insurance coverage offered in connection with the plan, the plan is deemed to have satisfied the certification requirement

under this paragraph if the issuer provides for such certification in accordance with this paragraph.

"(2) DISCLOSURE OF INFORMATION ON PREVIOUS BENEFITS.—

> *"(A) IN GENERAL.—In the case of an election described in subsection (c)(3)(B) by a group health plan, if the plan enrolls an individual for coverage under the plan and the individual provides a certification of coverage of the individual under paragraph (1)—*

>> *"(i) upon request of such plan, the entity which issued the certification provided by the individual shall promptly disclose to such requesting plan information on coverage of classes and categories of health benefits available under such entity's plan, and*

>> *"(ii) such entity may charge the requesting plan or issuer for the reasonable cost of disclosing such information.*

"(3) REGULATIONS.—The Secretary shall establish rules to prevent an entity's failure to provide information under paragraph (1) or (2) with respect to previous coverage of an individual from adversely affecting any subsequent coverage of the individual under another group health plan or health insurance coverage.

"(f) SPECIAL ENROLLMENT PERIODS.—

"(1) INDIVIDUALS LOSING OTHER COVERAGE.—A group health plan shall permit an employee who is eligible, but not enrolled, for coverage under the terms of the plan (or a dependent of such an employee if the dependent is eligible, but not enrolled, for coverage under such terms) to enroll for coverage under the terms of the plan if each of the following conditions is met:

> *"(A) The employee or dependent was covered under a group health plan or had health insurance coverage at the time coverage was previously offered to the employee or individual.*

> *"(B) The employee stated in writing at such time that coverage under a group health plan or health insurance coverage was the reason for declining enrollment, but only if the plan sponsor (or the health insurance issuer offering health insurance coverage in connection with the plan) required such a statement at such time and provided the employee with notice of such requirement (and the consequences of such requirement) at such time.*

> *"(C) The employee's or dependent's coverage described in subparagraph (A)—*

>> *"(i) was under a COBRA continuation provision and the coverage under such provision was exhausted; or*

>> *"(ii) was not under such a provision and either the coverage was terminated as a result of loss of eligibility for the coverage (including as a result of legal separation, divorce, death, termination of employment, or reduction in the number of hours of employment) or em-*

ployer contributions towards such coverage were terminated.

"(D) Under the terms of the plan, the employee requests such enrollment not later than 30 days after the date of exhaustion of coverage described in subparagraph (C)(i) or termination of coverage or employer contribution described in subparagraph (C)(ii).

"(2) FOR DEPENDENT BENEFICIARIES.—

"(A) IN GENERAL.—If—

"(i) a group health plan makes coverage available with respect to a dependent of an individual,

"(ii) the individual is a participant under the plan (or has met any waiting period applicable to becoming a participant under the plan and is eligible to be enrolled under the plan but for a failure to enroll during a previous enrollment period), and

"(iii) a person becomes such a dependent of the individual through marriage, birth, or adoption or placement for adoption,

the group health plan shall provide for a dependent special enrollment period described in subparagraph (B) during which the person (or, if not otherwise enrolled, the individual) may be enrolled under the plan as a dependent of the individual, and in the case of the birth or adoption of a child, the spouse of the individual may be enrolled as a dependent of the individual if such spouse is otherwise eligible for coverage.

"(B) DEPENDENT SPECIAL ENROLLMENT PERIOD.—The dependent special enrollment period under this subparagraph shall be a period of not less than 30 days and shall begin on the later of—

"(i) the date dependent coverage is made available, or

"(ii) the date of the marriage, birth, or adoption or placement for adoption (as the case may be) described in subparagraph (A)(iii).

"(C) NO WAITING PERIOD.—If an individual seeks coverage of a dependent during the first 30 days of such a dependent special enrollment period, the coverage of the dependent shall become effective—

"(i) in the case of marriage, not later than the first day of the first month beginning after the date the completed request for enrollment is received;

"(ii) in the case of a dependent's birth, as of the date of such birth; or

"(iii) in the case of a dependent's adoption or placement for adoption, the date of such adoption or placement for adoption.

"SEC. 9802. PROHIBITING DISCRIMINATION AGAINST INDIVIDUAL PARTICIPANTS AND BENEFICIARIES BASED ON HEALTH STATUS.

"(a) IN ELIGIBILITY TO ENROLL.—

"(1) IN GENERAL.—Subject to paragraph (2), a group health plan may not establish rules for eligibility (including continued

eligibility) of any individual to enroll under the terms of the plan based on any of the following factors in relation to the individual or a dependent of the individual:

> *"(A) Health status.*
>
> *"(B) Medical condition (including both physical and mental illnesses).*
>
> *"(C) Claims experience.*
>
> *"(D) Receipt of health care.*
>
> *"(E) Medical history.*
>
> *"(F) Genetic information.*
>
> *"(G) Evidence of insurability (including conditions arising out of acts of domestic violence).*
>
> *"(H) Disability.*

"(2) NO APPLICATION TO BENEFITS OR EXCLUSIONS.—To the extent consistent with section 9801, paragraph (1) shall not be construed—

> *"(A) to require a group health plan to provide particular benefits (or benefits with respect to a specific procedure, treatment, or service) other than those provided under the terms of such plan; or*
>
> *"(B) to prevent such a plan from establishing limitations or restrictions on the amount, level, extent, or nature of the benefits or coverage for similarly situated individuals enrolled in the plan or coverage.*

"(3) CONSTRUCTION.—For purposes of paragraph (1), rules for eligibility to enroll under a plan include rules defining any applicable waiting periods for such enrollment.

"(b) IN PREMIUM CONTRIBUTIONS.—

"(1) IN GENERAL.—A group health plan may not require any individual (as a condition of enrollment or continued enrollment under the plan) to pay a premium or contribution which is greater than such premium or contribution for a similarly situated individual enrolled in the plan on the basis of any factor described in subsection (a)(1) in relation to the individual or to an individual enrolled under the plan as a dependent of the individual.

"(2) CONSTRUCTION.—Nothing in paragraph (1) shall be construed—

> *"(A) to restrict the amount that an employer may be charged for coverage under a group health plan; or*
>
> *"(B) to prevent a group health plan from establishing premium discounts or rebates or modifying otherwise applicable copayments or deductibles in return for adherence to programs of health promotion and disease prevention.*

"SEC. 9803. GUARANTEED RENEWABILITY IN MULTIEMPLOYER PLANS AND CERTAIN MULTIPLE EMPLOYER WELFARE ARRANGEMENTS.

"(a) IN GENERAL.—A group health plan which is a multiemployer plan (as defined in section 414(f)) or which is a multiple employer welfare arrangement may not deny an employer continued access to the same or different coverage under such plan, other than—

> *"(1) for nonpayment of contributions;*

"(2) for fraud or other intentional misrepresentation of material fact by the employer;

"(3) for noncompliance with material plan provisions;

"(4) because the plan is ceasing to offer any coverage in a geographic area;

"(5) in the case of a plan that offers benefits through a network plan, because there is no longer any individual enrolled through the employer who lives, resides, or works in the service area of the network plan and the plan applies this paragraph uniformly without regard to the claims experience of employers or a factor described in section 9802(a)(1) in relation to such individuals or their dependents; or

"(6) for failure to meet the terms of an applicable collective bargaining agreement, to renew a collective bargaining or other agreement requiring or authorizing contributions to the plan, or to employ employees covered by such an agreement.

"(b) MULTIPLE EMPLOYER WELFARE ARRANGEMENT.—For purposes of subsection (a), the term 'multiple employer welfare arrangement' has the meaning given such term by section 3(40) of the Employee Retirement Income Security Act of 1974, as in effect on the date of the enactment of this section.

"SEC. 9804. GENERAL EXCEPTIONS.

"(a) EXCEPTION FOR CERTAIN PLANS.—The requirements of this chapter shall not apply to—

"(1) any governmental plan, and

"(2) any group health plan for any plan year if, on the first day of such plan year, such plan has less than 2 participants who are current employees.

"(b) EXCEPTION FOR CERTAIN BENEFITS.—The requirements of this chapter shall not apply to any group health plan in relation to its provision of excepted benefits described in section 9805(c)(1).

"(c) EXCEPTION FOR CERTAIN BENEFITS IF CERTAIN CONDITIONS MET.—

"(1) LIMITED, EXCEPTED BENEFITS.—The requirements of this chapter shall not apply to any group health plan in relation to its provision of excepted benefits described in section 9805(c)(2) if the benefits—

"(A) are provided under a separate policy, certificate, or contract of insurance; or

"(B) are otherwise not an integral part of the plan.

"(2) NONCOORDINATED, EXCEPTED BENEFITS.—The requirements of this chapter shall not apply to any group health plan in relation to its provision of excepted benefits described in section 9805(c)(3) if all of the following conditions are met:

"(A) The benefits are provided under a separate policy, certificate, or contract of insurance.

"(B) There is no coordination between the provision of such benefits and any exclusion of benefits under any group health plan maintained by the same plan sponsor.

"(C) Such benefits are paid with respect to an event without regard to whether benefits are provided with respect to such an event under any group health plan maintained by the same plan sponsor.

"(3) SUPPLEMENTAL EXCEPTED BENEFITS.—The requirements of this chapter shall not apply to any group health plan in relation to its provision of excepted benefits described in section 9805(c)(4) if the benefits are provided under a separate policy, certificate, or contract of insurance.

"SEC. 9805. DEFINITIONS.

"(a) GROUP HEALTH PLAN.—For purposes of this chapter, the term 'group health plan' has the meaning given to such term by section 5000(b)(1).

"(b) DEFINITIONS RELATING TO HEALTH INSURANCE.—For purposes of this chapter—

"(1) HEALTH INSURANCE COVERAGE.—

"(A) IN GENERAL.—Except as provided in subparagraph (B), the term 'health insurance coverage' means benefits consisting of medical care (provided directly, through insurance or reimbursement, or otherwise) under any hospital or medical service policy or certificate, hospital or medical service plan contract, or health maintenance organization contract offered by a health insurance issuer.

"(B) NO APPLICATION TO CERTAIN EXCEPTED BENEFITS.—In applying subparagraph (A), excepted benefits described in subsection (c)(1) shall not be treated as benefits consisting of medical care.

"(2) HEALTH INSURANCE ISSUER.—The term 'health insurance issuer' means an insurance company, insurance service, or insurance organization (including a health maintenance organization, as defined in paragraph (3)) which is licensed to engage in the business of insurance in a State and which is subject to State law which regulates insurance (within the meaning of section 514(b)(2) of the Employee Retirement Income Security Act of 1974, as in effect on the date of the enactment of this section). Such term does not include a group health plan.

"(3) HEALTH MAINTENANCE ORGANIZATION.—The term 'health maintenance organization' means—

"(A) a Federally qualified health maintenance organization (as defined in section 1301(a) of the Public Health Service Act (42 U.S.C. 300e(a))),

"(B) an organization recognized under State law as a health maintenance organization, or

"(C) a similar organization regulated under State law for solvency in the same manner and to the same extent as such a health maintenance organization.

"(c) EXCEPTED BENEFITS.—For purposes of this chapter, the term 'excepted benefits' means benefits under one or more (or any combination thereof) of the following:

"(1) BENEFITS NOT SUBJECT TO REQUIREMENTS.—

"(A) Coverage only for accident, or disability income insurance, or any combination thereof.

"(B) Coverage issued as a supplement to liability insurance.

"(C) Liability insurance, including general liability insurance and automobile liability insurance.

"(D) Workers' compensation or similar insurance.

"(E) Automobile medical payment insurance.

"(F) Credit-only insurance.

"(G) Coverage for on-site medical clinics.

"(H) Other similar insurance coverage, specified in regulations, under which benefits for medical care are secondary or incidental to other insurance benefits.

"(2) BENEFITS NOT SUBJECT TO REQUIREMENTS IF OFFERED SEPARATELY.—

"(A) Limited scope dental or vision benefits.

"(B) Benefits for long-term care, nursing home care, home health care, community-based care, or any combination thereof.

"(C) Such other similar, limited benefits as are specified in regulations.

"(3) BENEFITS NOT SUBJECT TO REQUIREMENTS IF OFFERED AS INDEPENDENT, NONCOORDINATED BENEFITS.—

"(A) Coverage only for a specified disease or illness.

"(B) Hospital indemnity or other fixed indemnity insurance.

"(4) BENEFITS NOT SUBJECT TO REQUIREMENTS IF OFFERED AS SEPARATE INSURANCE POLICY.—Medicare supplemental health insurance (as defined under section 1882(g)(1) of the Social Security Act), coverage supplemental to the coverage provided under chapter 55 of title 10, United States Code, and similar supplemental coverage provided to coverage under a group health plan.

"(d) OTHER DEFINITIONS.—For purposes of this chapter—

"(1) COBRA CONTINUATION PROVISION.—The term 'COBRA continuation provision' means any of the following:

"(A) Section 4980B, other than subsection (f)(1) thereof insofar as it relates to pediatric vaccines.

"(B) Part 6 of subtitle B of title I of the Employee Retirement Income Security Act of 1974 (29 U.S.C. 1161 et seq.), other than section 609 of such Act.

"(C) Title XXII of the Public Health Service Act.

"(2) GOVERNMENTAL PLAN.—The term 'governmental plan' has the meaning given such term by section 414(d).

"(3) MEDICAL CARE.—The term 'medical care' has the meaning given such term by section 213(d) determined without regard to—

"(A) paragraph (1)(C) thereof, and

"(B) so much of paragraph (1)(D) thereof as relates to qualified long-term care insurance.

"(4) NETWORK PLAN.—The term 'network plan' means health insurance coverage of a health insurance issuer under which the financing and delivery of medical care are provided, in whole or in part, through a defined set of providers under contract with the issuer.

"(5) PLACED FOR ADOPTION DEFINED.—The term 'placement', or being 'placed', for adoption, in connection with any placement for adoption of a child with any person, means the assumption and retention by such person of a legal obligation for total or partial support of such child in anticipation of adoption of such child. The child's placement with such person terminates upon the termination of such legal obligation.

"SEC. 9806. REGULATIONS.

"The Secretary, consistent with section 104 of the Health Care Portability and Accountability Act of 1996, may promulgate such regulations as may be necessary or appropriate to carry out the provisions of this chapter. The Secretary may promulgate any interim final rules as the Secretary determines are appropriate to carry out this chapter."

(b) CLERICAL AMENDMENT.—The table of subtitles of such Code is amended by adding at the end the following new item:

> *"Subtitle K. Group health plan portability, access, and renewability requirements."*

(c) EFFECTIVE DATE.—

(1) IN GENERAL.—The amendments made by this section shall apply to plan years beginning after June 30, 1997.

(2) DETERMINATION OF CREDITABLE COVERAGE.—

(A) PERIOD OF COVERAGE.—

(i) IN GENERAL.—Subject to clause (ii), no period before July 1, 1996, shall be taken into account under chapter 100 of the Internal Revenue Code of 1986 (as added by this section) in determining creditable coverage.

(ii) SPECIAL RULE FOR CERTAIN PERIODS.—The Secretary of the Treasury, consistent with section 104, shall provide for a process whereby individuals who need to establish creditable coverage for periods before July 1, 1996, and who would have such coverage credited but for clause (i) may be given credit for creditable coverage for such periods through the presentation of documents or other means.

(B) CERTIFICATIONS, ETC.—

(i) IN GENERAL.—Subject to clauses (ii) and (iii), subsection (e) of section 9801 of the Internal Revenue Code of 1986 (as added by this section) shall apply to events occurring after June 30, 1996.

(ii) NO CERTIFICATION REQUIRED TO BE PROVIDED BEFORE JUNE 1, 1997.—In no case is a certification required to be provided under such subsection before June 1, 1997.

(iii) CERTIFICATION ONLY ON WRITTEN REQUEST FOR EVENTS OCCURRING BEFORE OCTOBER 1, 1996.—In the case of an event occurring after June 30, 1996, and before October 1, 1996, a certification is not required to be provided under such subsection unless an individual (with respect to whom the certification is otherwise required to be made) requests such certification in writing.

(C) TRANSITIONAL RULE.—In the case of an individual who seeks to establish creditable coverage for any period for which certification is not required because it relates to an event occurring before June 30, 1996—

(i) the individual may present other credible evidence of such coverage in order to establish the period of creditable coverage; and

(ii) a group health plan and a health insurance issuer shall not be subject to any penalty or enforcement

action with respect to the plan's or issuer's crediting (or not crediting) such coverage if the plan or issuer has sought to comply in good faith with the applicable requirements under the amendments made by this section.

(3) SPECIAL RULE FOR COLLECTIVE BARGAINING AGREEMENTS.—Except as provided in paragraph (2), in the case of a group health plan maintained pursuant to 1 or more collective bargaining agreements between employee representatives and one or more employers ratified before the date of the enactment of this Act, the amendments made by this section shall not apply to plan years beginning before the later of—

(A) the date on which the last of the collective bargaining agreements relating to the plan terminates (determined without regard to any extension thereof agreed to after the date of the enactment of this Act), or

(B) July 1, 1997.

For purposes of subparagraph (A), any plan amendment made pursuant to a collective bargaining agreement relating to the plan which amends the plan solely to conform to any requirement added by this section shall not be treated as a termination of such collective bargaining agreement.

(4) TIMELY REGULATIONS.—The Secretary of the Treasury, consistent with section 104, shall first issue by not later than April 1, 1997, such regulations as may be necessary to carry out the amendments made by this section.

(5) LIMITATION ON ACTIONS.—No enforcement action shall be taken, pursuant to the amendments made by this section, against a group health plan or health insurance issuer with respect to a violation of a requirement imposed by such amendments before January 1, 1998, or, if later, the date of issuance of regulations referred to in paragraph (4), if the plan or issuer has sought to comply in good faith with such requirements.

SEC. 402. PENALTY ON FAILURE TO MEET CERTAIN GROUP HEALTH PLAN REQUIREMENTS.

(a) IN GENERAL.—Chapter 43 of the Internal Revenue Code of 1986 (relating to qualified pension, etc., plans) is amended by adding after section 4980C the following new section:

"SEC. 4980D. FAILURE TO MEET CERTAIN GROUP HEALTH PLAN REQUIREMENTS.

"(a) GENERAL RULE.—There is hereby imposed a tax on any failure of a group health plan to meet the requirements of chapter 100 (relating to group health plan portability, access, and renewability requirements).

"(b) AMOUNT OF TAX.—

"(1) IN GENERAL.—The amount of the tax imposed by subsection (a) on any failure shall be $100 for each day in the noncompliance period with respect to each individual to whom such failure relates.

"(2) NONCOMPLIANCE PERIOD.—For purposes of this section, the term 'noncompliance period' means, with respect to any failure, the period—

"(A) beginning on the date such failure first occurs, and

"(B) ending on the date such failure is corrected.

"(3) MINIMUM TAX FOR NONCOMPLIANCE PERIOD WHERE FAILURE DISCOVERED AFTER NOTICE OF EXAMINATION.—Notwithstanding paragraphs (1) and (2) of subsection (c)—

"(A) IN GENERAL.—In the case of 1 or more failures with respect to an individual—

"(i) which are not corrected before the date a notice of examination of income tax liability is sent to the employer, and

"(ii) which occurred or continued during the period under examination,

the amount of tax imposed by subsection (a) by reason of such failures with respect to such individual shall not be less than the lesser of $2,500 or the amount of tax which would be imposed by subsection (a) without regard to such paragraphs.

"(B) HIGHER MINIMUM TAX WHERE VIOLATIONS ARE MORE THAN DE MINIMIS.—To the extent violations for which any person is liable under subsection (e) for any year are more than de minimis, subparagraph (A) shall be applied by substituting '$15,000' for '$2,500' with respect to such person.

"(C) EXCEPTION FOR CHURCH PLANS.—This paragraph shall not apply to any failure under a church plan (as defined in section 414(e)).

"(c) LIMITATIONS ON AMOUNT OF TAX.—

"(1) TAX NOT TO APPLY WHERE FAILURE NOT DISCOVERED EXERCISING REASONABLE DILIGENCE.—No tax shall be imposed by subsection (a) on any failure during any period for which it is established to the satisfaction of the Secretary that the person otherwise liable for such tax did not know, and exercising reasonable diligence would not have known, that such failure existed.

"(2) TAX NOT TO APPLY TO FAILURES CORRECTED WITHIN CERTAIN PERIODS.—No tax shall be imposed by subsection (a) on any failure if—

"(A) such failure was due to reasonable cause and not to willful neglect, and

"(B)(i) in the case of a plan other than a church plan (as defined in section 414(e)), such failure is corrected during the 30-day period beginning on the 1st date the person otherwise liable for such tax knew, or exercising reasonable diligence would have known, that such failure existed, and

"(ii) in the case of a church plan (as so defined), such failure is corrected before the close of the correction period (determined under the rules of section 414(e)(4)(C)).

"(3) OVERALL LIMITATION FOR UNINTENTIONAL FAILURES.—In the case of failures which are due to reasonable cause and not to willful neglect—

"(A) SINGLE EMPLOYER PLANS.—

"(i) IN GENERAL.—In the case of failures with respect to plans other than specified multiple employer health plans, the tax imposed by subsection (a) for failures during the taxable year of the employer shall not exceed the amount equal to the lesser of—

"(I) 10 percent of the aggregate amount paid or incurred by the employer (or predecessor employer) during the preceding taxable year for group health plans, or

"(II) $500,000.

"(ii) TAXABLE YEARS IN THE CASE OF CERTAIN CONTROLLED GROUPS.—For purposes of this subparagraph, if not all persons who are treated as a single employer for purposes of this section have the same taxable year, the taxable years taken into account shall be determined under principles similar to the principles of section 1561.

"(B) SPECIFIED MULTIPLE EMPLOYER HEALTH PLANS.—

"(i) IN GENERAL.—In the case of failures with respect to a specified multiple employer health plan, the tax imposed by subsection (a) for failures during the taxable year of the trust forming part of such plan shall not exceed the amount equal to the lesser of—

"(I) 10 percent of the amount paid or incurred by such trust during such taxable year to provide medical care (as defined in section 9805(d)(3)) directly or through insurance, reimbursement, or otherwise, or

"(II) $500,000.

For purposes of the preceding sentence, all plans of which the same trust forms a part shall be treated as 1 plan.

"(ii) SPECIAL RULE FOR EMPLOYERS REQUIRED TO PAY TAX.—If an employer is assessed a tax imposed by subsection (a) by reason of a failure with respect to a specified multiple employer health plan, the limit shall be determined under subparagraph (A) (and not under this subparagraph) and as if such plan were not a specified multiple employer health plan.

"(4) WAIVER BY SECRETARY.—In the case of a failure which is due to reasonable cause and not to willful neglect, the Secretary may waive part or all of the tax imposed by subsection (a) to the extent that the payment of such tax would be excessive relative to the failure involved.

"(d) TAX NOT TO APPLY TO CERTAIN INSURED SMALL EMPLOYER PLANS.—

"(1) IN GENERAL.—In the case of a group health plan of a small employer which provides health insurance coverage solely through a contract with a health insurance issuer, no tax shall be imposed by this section on the employer on any failure which is solely because of the health insurance coverage offered by such issuer.

"(2) SMALL EMPLOYER.—

"(A) IN GENERAL.—For purposes of paragraph (1), the term 'small employer' means, with respect to a calendar year and a plan year, an employer who employed an average of at least 2 but not more than 50 employees on busi-

ness days during the preceding calendar year and who employs at least 2 employees on the first day of the plan year. For purposes of the preceding sentence, all persons treated as a single employer under subsection (b), (c), (m), or (o) of section 414 shall be treated as 1 employer.

"(B) EMPLOYERS NOT IN EXISTENCE IN PRECEDING YEAR.—In the case of an employer which was not in existence throughout the preceding calendar year, the determination of whether such employer is a small employer shall be based on the average number of employees that it is reasonably expected such employer will employ on business days in the current calendar year.

"(C) PREDECESSORS.—Any reference in this paragraph to an employer shall include a reference to any predecessor of such employer.

"(3) HEALTH INSURANCE COVERAGE; HEALTH INSURANCE ISSUER.—For purposes of paragraph (1), the terms 'health insurance coverage' and 'health insurance issuer' have the respective meanings given such terms by section 9805.

"(e) LIABILITY FOR TAX.—The following shall be liable for the tax imposed by subsection (a) on a failure:

"(1) Except as otherwise provided in this subsection, the employer.

"(2) In the case of a multiemployer plan, the plan.

"(3) In the case of a failure under section 9803 (relating to guaranteed renewability) with respect to a plan described in subsection (f)(2)(B), the plan.

"(f) DEFINITIONS.—For purposes of this section—

"(1) GROUP HEALTH PLAN.—The term 'group health plan' has the meaning given such term by section 9805(a).

"(2) SPECIFIED MULTIPLE EMPLOYER HEALTH PLAN.—The term 'specified multiple employer health plan' means a group health plan which is—

"(A) any multiemployer plan, or

"(B) any multiple employer welfare arrangement (as defined in section 3(40) of the Employee Retirement Income Security Act of 1974, as in effect on the date of the enactment of this section).

"(3) CORRECTION.—A failure of a group health plan shall be treated as corrected if—

"(A) such failure is retroactively undone to the extent possible, and

"(B) the person to whom the failure relates is placed in a financial position which is as good as such person would have been in had such failure not occurred."

(b) CLERICAL AMENDMENT.—The table of sections for chapter 43 of such Code is amended by adding after the item relating to section 4980C the following new item:

"Sec. 4980D. Failure to meet certain group health plan requirements."

(c) EFFECTIVE DATE.—The amendments made by this section shall apply to failures under chapter 100 of the Internal Revenue Code of 1986 (as added by section 401 of this Act).

Subtitle B—Clarification of Certain Continuation Coverage Requirements

SEC. 421. COBRA CLARIFICATIONS.

(a) PUBLIC HEALTH SERVICE ACT.—

(1) PERIOD OF COVERAGE.—Section 2202(2) of the Public Health Service Act (42 U.S.C. 300bb–2(2)) is amended—

(A) in subparagraph (A)—

(i) by transferring the sentence immediately preceding clause (iv) so as to appear immediately following such clause (iv); and

(ii) in the last sentence (as so transferred)—

(I) by striking "an individual" and inserting "a qualified beneficiary";

(II) by striking "at the time of a qualifying event described in section 2203(2)" and inserting "at any time during the first 60 days of continuation coverage under this title";

(III) by striking "with respect to such event,"; and

(IV) by inserting "(with respect to all qualified beneficiaries)" after "29 months";

(B) in subparagraph (D)(i), by inserting before ", or" the following: "(other than such an exclusion or limitation which does not apply to (or is satisfied by) such beneficiary by reason of chapter 100 of the Internal Revenue Code of 1986, part 7 of subtitle B of title I of the Employee Retirement Income Security Act of 1974, or title XXVII of this Act)"; and

(C) in subparagraph (E), by striking "at the time of a qualifying event described in section 2203(2)" and inserting "at any time during the first 60 days of continuation coverage under this title".

(2) NOTICES.—Section 2206(3) of the Public Health Service Act (42 U.S.C. 300bb–6(3)) is amended by striking "at the time of a qualifying event described in section 2203(2)" and inserting "at any time during the first 60 days of continuation coverage under this title".

(3) BIRTH OR ADOPTION OF A CHILD.—Section 2208(3)(A) of the Public Health Service Act (42 U.S.C. 300bb–8(3)(A)) is amended by adding at the end thereof the following new flush sentence:

"Such term shall also include a child who is born to or placed for adoption with the covered employee during the period of continuation coverage under this title.".

(b) EMPLOYEE RETIREMENT INCOME SECURITY ACT OF 1974.—

(1) PERIOD OF COVERAGE.—Section 602(2) of the Employee Retirement Income Security Act of 1974 (29 U.S.C. 1162(2)) is amended—

(A) in the last sentence of subparagraph (A)—

(i) by striking "an individual" and inserting "a qualified beneficiary";

(ii) by striking "at the time of a qualifying event described in section 603(2)" and inserting "at any time during the first 60 days of continuation coverage under this part";

(iii) by striking "with respect to such event"; and

(iv) by inserting "(with respect to all qualified beneficiaries)" after "29 months";

(B) in subparagraph (D)(i), by inserting before ", or" the following: "(other than such an exclusion or limitation which does not apply to (or is satisfied by) such beneficiary by reason of chapter 100 of the Internal Revenue Code of 1986, part 7 of this subtitle, or title XXVII of the Public Health Service Act)"; and

(C) in subparagraph (E), by striking "at the time of a qualifying event described in section 603(2)" and inserting "at any time during the first 60 days of continuation coverage under this part".

(2) NOTICES.—Section 606(a)(3) of the Employee Retirement Income Security Act of 1974 (29 U.S.C. 1166(a)(3)) is amended by striking "at the time of a qualifying event described in section 603(2)" and inserting "at any time during the first 60 days of continuation coverage under this part".

(3) BIRTH OR ADOPTION OF A CHILD.—Section 607(3)(A) of the Employee Retirement Income Security Act of 1974 (29 U.S.C. 1167(3)) is amended by adding at the end thereof the following new flush sentence:

"Such term shall also include a child who is born to or placed for adoption with the covered employee during the period of continuation coverage under this part.".

(c) INTERNAL REVENUE CODE OF 1986.—

(1) PERIOD OF COVERAGE.—Section 4980B(f)(2)(B) of the Internal Revenue Code of 1986 is amended—

(A) in the last sentence of clause (i)—

(i) by striking "at the time of a qualifying event described in paragraph (3)(B)" and inserting "at any time during the first 60 days of continuation coverage under this section";

(ii) by striking "with respect to such event"; and

(iii) by inserting "(with respect to all qualified beneficiaries)" after "29 months";

(B) in clause (iv)(I), by inserting before ", or" the following: "(other than such an exclusion or limitation which does not apply to (or is satisfied by) such beneficiary by reason of chapter 100 of this title, part 7 of subtitle B of title I of the Employee Retirement Income Security Act of 1974, or title XXVII of the Public Health Service Act)"; and

(C) in clause (v), by striking "at the time of a qualifying event described in paragraph (3)(B)" and inserting "at any time during the first 60 days of continuation coverage under this section".

(2) NOTICES.—Section 4980B(f)(6)(C) of the Internal Revenue Code of 1986 is amended by striking "at the time of a qualifying event described in paragraph (3)(B)" and inserting

"*at any time during the first 60 days of continuation coverage under this section*".

    (3) BIRTH OR ADOPTION OF A CHILD.—Section 4980B(g)(1)(A) of the Internal Revenue Code of 1986 is amended by adding at the end thereof the following new flush sentence:

        "*Such term shall also include a child who is born to or placed for adoption with the covered employee during the period of continuation coverage under this section.*".

    (d) EFFECTIVE DATE.—The amendments made by this section shall become effective on January 1, 1997, regardless of whether the qualifying event occurred before, on, or after such date.

    (e) NOTIFICATION OF CHANGES.—Not later than November 1, 1996, each group health plan (covered under title XXII of the Public Health Service Act, part 6 of subtitle B of title I of the Employee Retirement Income Security Act of 1974, and section 4980B(f) of the Internal Revenue Code of 1986) shall notify each qualified beneficiary who has elected continuation coverage under such title, part or section of the amendments made by this section.

TITLE V—REVENUE OFFSETS

SEC. 500. AMENDMENT OF 1986 CODE.

    Except as otherwise expressly provided, whenever in this title an amendment or repeal is expressed in terms of an amendment to, or repeal of, a section or other provision, the reference shall be considered to be made to a section or other provision of the Internal Revenue Code of 1986.

Subtitle A—Company-Owned Life Insurance

SEC. 501. DENIAL OF DEDUCTION FOR INTEREST ON LOANS WITH RESPECT TO COMPANY-OWNED LIFE INSURANCE.

    (a) IN GENERAL.—Paragraph (4) of section 264(a) is amended—

    (1) by inserting ", or any endowment or annuity contracts owned by the taxpayer covering any individual," after "the life of any individual", and

    (2) by striking all that follows "carried on by the taxpayer" and inserting a period.

    (b) EXCEPTION FOR CONTRACTS RELATING TO KEY PERSONS; PERMISSIBLE INTEREST RATES.—Section 264 is amended—

    (1) by striking "Any" in subsection (a)(4) and inserting "Except as provided in subsection (d), any", and

    (2) by adding at the end the following new subsection:

    "*(d) SPECIAL RULES FOR APPLICATION OF SUBSECTION (a)(4).—*

        "*(1) EXCEPTION FOR KEY PERSONS.—Subsection (a)(4) shall not apply to any interest paid or accrued on any indebtedness with respect to policies or contracts covering an individual who is a key person to the extent that the aggregate amount of such indebtedness with respect to policies and contracts covering such individual does not exceed $50,000.*

"(2) INTEREST RATE CAP ON KEY PERSONS AND PRE-1986 CONTRACTS.—

"(A) IN GENERAL.—No deduction shall be allowed by reason of paragraph (1) or the last sentence of subsection (a) with respect to interest paid or accrued for any month beginning after December 31, 1995, to the extent the amount of such interest exceeds the amount which would have been determined if the applicable rate of interest were used for such month.

"(B) APPLICABLE RATE OF INTEREST.—For purposes of subparagraph (A)—

"(i) IN GENERAL.—The applicable rate of interest for any month is the rate of interest described as Moody's Corporate Bond Yield Average-Monthly Average Corporates as published by Moody's Investors Service, Inc., or any successor thereto, for such month.

"(ii) PRE-1986 CONTRACTS.—In the case of indebtedness on a contract purchased on or before June 20, 1986—

"(I) which is a contract providing a fixed rate of interest, the applicable rate of interest for any month shall be the Moody's rate described in clause (i) for the month in which the contract was purchased, or

"(II) which is a contract providing a variable rate of interest, the applicable rate of interest for any month in an applicable period shall be such Moody's rate for the third month preceding the first month in such period.

For purposes of subclause (II), the taxpayer shall elect an applicable period for such contract on its return of tax imposed by this chapter for its first taxable year ending on or after October 13, 1995. Such applicable period shall be for any number of months (not greater than 12) specified in the election and may not be changed by the taxpayer without the consent of the Secretary.

"(3) KEY PERSON.—For purposes of paragraph (1), the term 'key person' means an officer or 20-percent owner, except that the number of individuals who may be treated as key persons with respect to any taxpayer shall not exceed the greater of—

"(A) 5 individuals, or

"(B) the lesser of 5 percent of the total officers and employees of the taxpayer or 20 individuals.

"(4) 20-PERCENT OWNER.—For purposes of this subsection, the term '20-percent owner' means—

"(A) if the taxpayer is a corporation, any person who owns directly 20 percent or more of the outstanding stock of the corporation or stock possessing 20 percent or more of the total combined voting power of all stock of the corporation, or

"(B) if the taxpayer is not a corporation, any person who owns 20 percent or more of the capital or profits interest in the employer.

"(5) AGGREGATION RULES.—

"(A) IN GENERAL.—For purposes of paragraph (4)(A) and applying the $50,000 limitation in paragraph (1)—

"(i) all members of a controlled group shall be treated as 1 taxpayer, and

"(ii) such limitation shall be allocated among the members of such group in such manner as the Secretary may prescribe.

"(B) CONTROLLED GROUP.—For purposes of this paragraph, all persons treated as a single employer under subsection (a) or (b) of section 52 or subsection (m) or (o) of section 414 shall be treated as members of a controlled group.".

(c) EFFECTIVE DATES.—

(1) IN GENERAL.—The amendments made by this section shall apply to interest paid or accrued after October 13, 1995.

(2) TRANSITION RULE FOR EXISTING INDEBTEDNESS.—

(A) IN GENERAL.—In the case of—

(i) indebtedness incurred before January 1, 1996, or

(ii) indebtedness incurred before January 1, 1997 with respect to any contract or policy entered into in 1994 or 1995,

the amendments made by this section shall not apply to qualified interest paid or accrued on such indebtedness after October 13, 1995, and before January 1, 1999.

(B) QUALIFIED INTEREST.—For purposes of subparagraph (A), the qualified interest with respect to any indebtedness for any month is the amount of interest (otherwise deductible) which would be paid or accrued for such month on such indebtedness if—

(i) in the case of any interest paid or accrued after December 31, 1995, indebtedness with respect to no more than 20,000 insured individuals were taken into account, and

(ii) the lesser of the following rates of interest were used for such month:

(I) The rate of interest specified under the terms of the indebtedness as in effect on October 13, 1995 (and without regard to modification of such terms after such date).

(II) The applicable percentage of the rate of interest described as Moody's Corporate Bond Yield Average-Monthly Average Corporates as published by Moody's Investors Service, Inc., or any successor thereto, for such month.

For purposes of clause (i), all persons treated as a single employer under subsection (a) or (b) of section 52 of the Internal Revenue Code of 1986 or subsection (m) or (o) of section 414 of such Code shall be treated as 1 person. Subclause (II) of clause (ii) shall not apply to any month before January 1, 1996.

(C) APPLICABLE PERCENTAGE.—For purposes of subparagraph (B), the applicable percentage is as follows:

For calendar year:	The percentage is:
1996	100 percent
1997	90 percent
1998	80 percent.

(3) SPECIAL RULE FOR GRANDFATHERED CONTRACTS.—This section shall not apply to any contract purchased on or before June 20, 1986, except that section 264(d)(2) of the Internal Revenue Code of 1986 shall apply to interest paid or accrued after October 13, 1995.

(d) SPREAD OF INCOME INCLUSION ON SURRENDER, ETC. OF CONTRACTS.—

(1) IN GENERAL.—If any amount is received under any life insurance policy or endowment or annuity contract described in paragraph (4) of section 264(a) of the Internal Revenue Code of 1986—

(A) on the complete surrender, redemption, or maturity of such policy or contract during calendar year 1996, 1997, or 1998, or

(B) in full discharge during any such calendar year of the obligation under the policy or contract which is in the nature of a refund of the consideration paid for the policy or contract,

then (in lieu of any other inclusion in gross income) such amount shall be includible in gross income ratably over the 4-taxable year period beginning with the taxable year such amount would (but for this paragraph) be includible. The preceding sentence shall only apply to the extent the amount is includible in gross income for the taxable year in which the event described in subparagraph (A) or (B) occurs.

(2) SPECIAL RULES FOR APPLYING SECTION 264.—A contract shall not be treated as—

(A) failing to meet the requirement of section 264(c)(1) of the Internal Revenue Code of 1986, or

(B) a single premium contract under section 264(b)(1) of such Code,

solely by reason of an occurrence described in subparagraph (A) or (B) of paragraph (1) of this subsection or solely by reason of no additional premiums being received under the contract by reason of a lapse occurring after October 13, 1995.

(3) SPECIAL RULE FOR DEFERRED ACQUISITION COSTS.—In the case of the occurrence of any event described in subparagraph (A) or (B) of paragraph (1) of this subsection with respect to any policy or contract—

(A) section 848 of the Internal Revenue Code of 1986 shall not apply to the unamortized balance (if any) of the specified policy acquisition expenses attributable to such policy or contract immediately before the insurance company's taxable year in which such event occurs, and

(B) there shall be allowed as a deduction to such company for such taxable year under chapter 1 of such Code an amount equal to such unamortized balance.

Subtitle B—Treatment of Individuals Who Lose United States Citizenship

SEC. 511. REVISION OF INCOME, ESTATE, AND GIFT TAXES ON INDIVIDUALS WHO LOSE UNITED STATES CITIZENSHIP.

(a) IN GENERAL.—Subsection (a) of section 877 is amended to read as follows:

"(a) TREATMENT OF EXPATRIATES.—

"(1) IN GENERAL.—Every nonresident alien individual who, within the 10-year period immediately preceding the close of the taxable year, lost United States citizenship, unless such loss did not have for 1 of its principal purposes the avoidance of taxes under this subtitle or subtitle B, shall be taxable for such taxable year in the manner provided in subsection (b) if the tax imposed pursuant to such subsection exceeds the tax which, without regard to this section, is imposed pursuant to section 871.

"(2) CERTAIN INDIVIDUALS TREATED AS HAVING TAX AVOIDANCE PURPOSE.—For purposes of paragraph (1), an individual shall be treated as having a principal purpose to avoid such taxes if—

"(A) the average annual net income tax (as defined in section 38(c)(1)) of such individual for the period of 5 taxable years ending before the date of the loss of United States citizenship is greater than $100,000, or

"(B) the net worth of the individual as of such date is $500,000 or more.

In the case of the loss of United States citizenship in any calendar year after 1996, such $100,000 and $500,000 amounts shall be increased by an amount equal to such dollar amount multiplied by the cost-of-living adjustment determined under section 1(f)(3) for such calendar year by substituting '1994' for '1992' in subparagraph (B) thereof. Any increase under the preceding sentence shall be rounded to the nearest multiple of $1,000.".

(b) EXCEPTIONS.—

(1) IN GENERAL.—Section 877 is amended by striking subsection (d), by redesignating subsection (c) as subsection (d), and by inserting after subsection (b) the following new subsection:

"(c) TAX AVOIDANCE NOT PRESUMED IN CERTAIN CASES.—

"(1) IN GENERAL.—Subsection (a)(2) shall not apply to an individual if—

"(A) such individual is described in a subparagraph of paragraph (2) of this subsection, and

"(B) within the 1-year period beginning on the date of the loss of United States citizenship, such individual submits a ruling request for the Secretary's determination as to whether such loss has for 1 of its principal purposes the avoidance of taxes under this subtitle or subtitle B.

"(2) INDIVIDUALS DESCRIBED.—

"(A) DUAL CITIZENSHIP, ETC.—An individual is described in this subparagraph if—

"(i) the individual became at birth a citizen of the United States and a citizen of another country and continues to be a citizen of such other country, or

"(ii) the individual becomes (not later than the close of a reasonable period after loss of United States citizenship) a citizen of the country in which—

"(I) such individual was born,

"(II) if such individual is married, such individual's spouse was born, or

"(III) either of such individual's parents were born.

"(B) LONG-TERM FOREIGN RESIDENTS.—An individual is described in this subparagraph if, for each year in the 10-year period ending on the date of loss of United States citizenship, the individual was present in the United States for 30 days or less. The rule of section 7701(b)(3)(D)(ii) shall apply for purposes of this subparagraph.

"(C) RENUNCIATION UPON REACHING AGE OF MAJORITY.—An individual is described in this subparagraph if the individual's loss of United States citizenship occurs before such individual attains age 18½.

"(D) INDIVIDUALS SPECIFIED IN REGULATIONS.—An individual is described in this subparagraph if the individual is described in a category of individuals prescribed by regulation by the Secretary."

(2) TECHNICAL AMENDMENT.—Paragraph (1) of section 877(b) of such Code is amended by striking "subsection (c)" and inserting "subsection (d)".

(c) TREATMENT OF PROPERTY DISPOSED OF IN NONRECOGNITION TRANSACTIONS; TREATMENT OF DISTRIBUTIONS FROM CERTAIN CONTROLLED FOREIGN CORPORATIONS.—Subsection (d) of section 877, as redesignated by subsection (b), is amended to read as follows:

"(d) SPECIAL RULES FOR SOURCE, ETC.—For purposes of subsection (b)—

"(1) SOURCE RULES.—The following items of gross income shall be treated as income from sources within the United States:

"(A) SALE OF PROPERTY.—Gains on the sale or exchange of property (other than stock or debt obligations) located in the United States.

"(B) STOCK OR DEBT OBLIGATIONS.—Gains on the sale or exchange of stock issued by a domestic corporation or debt obligations of United States persons or of the United States, a State or political subdivision thereof, or the District of Columbia.

"(C) INCOME OR GAIN DERIVED FROM CONTROLLED FOREIGN CORPORATION.—Any income or gain derived from stock in a foreign corporation but only—

"(i) if the individual losing United States citizenship owned (within the meaning of section 958(a)), or is considered as owning (by applying the ownership rules of section 958(b)), at any time during the 2-year period ending on the date of the loss of United States citizenship, more than 50 percent of—

"(I) the total combined voting power of all classes of stock entitled to vote of such corporation, or

"(II) the total value of the stock of such corporation, and

"(ii) to the extent such income or gain does not exceed the earnings and profits attributable to such stock which were earned or accumulated before the loss of citizenship and during periods that the ownership requirements of clause (i) are met.

"(2) GAIN RECOGNITION ON CERTAIN EXCHANGES.—

"(A) IN GENERAL.—In the case of any exchange of property to which this paragraph applies, notwithstanding any other provision of this title, such property shall be treated as sold for its fair market value on the date of such exchange, and any gain shall be recognized for the taxable year which includes such date.

"(B) EXCHANGES TO WHICH PARAGRAPH APPLIES.—This paragraph shall apply to any exchange during the 10-year period described in subsection (a) if—

"(i) gain would not (but for this paragraph) be recognized on such exchange in whole or in part for purposes of this subtitle,

"(ii) income derived from such property was from sources within the United States (or, if no income was so derived, would have been from such sources), and

"(iii) income derived from the property acquired in the exchange would be from sources outside the United States.

"(C) EXCEPTION.—Subparagraph (A) shall not apply if the individual enters into an agreement with the Secretary which specifies that any income or gain derived from the property acquired in the exchange (or any other property which has a basis determined in whole or part by reference to such property) during such 10-year period shall be treated as from sources within the United States. If the property transferred in the exchange is disposed of by the person acquiring such property, such agreement shall terminate and any gain which was not recognized by reason of such agreement shall be recognized as of the date of such disposition.

"(D) SECRETARY MAY EXTEND PERIOD.—To the extent provided in regulations prescribed by the Secretary, subparagraph (B) shall be applied by substituting the 15-year period beginning 5 years before the loss of United States citizenship for the 10-year period referred to therein.

"(E) SECRETARY MAY REQUIRE RECOGNITION OF GAIN IN CERTAIN CASES.—To the extent provided in regulations prescribed by the Secretary—

"(i) the removal of appreciated tangible personal property from the United States, and

"(ii) any other occurrence which (without recognition of gain) results in a change in the source of the income or gain from property from sources within the United States to sources outside the United States,

shall be treated as an exchange to which this paragraph applies.

"(3) SUBSTANTIAL DIMINISHING OF RISKS OF OWNERSHIP.— For purposes of determining whether this section applies to any gain on the sale or exchange of any property, the running of the 10-year period described in subsection (a) shall be suspended for any period during which the individual's risk of loss with respect to the property is substantially diminished by—

"(A) the holding of a put with respect to such property (or similar property),

"(B) the holding by another person of a right to acquire the property, or

"(C) a short sale or any other transaction.

"(4) TREATMENT OF PROPERTY CONTRIBUTED TO CONTROLLED FOREIGN CORPORATIONS.—

"(A) IN GENERAL.—If—

"(i) an individual losing United States citizenship contributes property to any corporation which, at the time of the contribution, is described in subparagraph (B), and

"(ii) income derived from such property was from sources within the United States (or, if no income was so derived, would have been from such sources),

during the 10-year period referred to in subsection (a), any income or gain on such property (or any other property which has a basis determined in whole or part by reference to such property) received or accrued by the corporation shall be treated as received or accrued directly by such individual and not by such corporation. The preceding sentence shall not apply to the extent the property has been treated under subparagraph (C) as having been sold by such corporation.

"(B) CORPORATION DESCRIBED.—A corporation is described in this subparagraph with respect to an individual if, were such individual a United States citizen—

"(i) such corporation would be a controlled foreign corporation (as defined in 957), and

"(ii) such individual would be a United States shareholder (as defined in section 951(b)) with respect to such corporation.

"(C) DISPOSITION OF STOCK IN CORPORATION.—If stock in the corporation referred to in subparagraph (A) (or any other stock which has a basis determined in whole or part by reference to such stock) is disposed of during the 10-year period referred to in subsection (a) and while the property referred to in subparagraph (A) is held by such corporation, a pro rata share of such property (determined on the basis of the value of such stock) shall be treated as sold by the corporation immediately before such disposition.

"(D) ANTI-ABUSE RULES.—The Secretary shall prescribe such regulations as may be necessary to prevent the avoidance of the purposes of this paragraph, including where—

"(i) the property is sold to the corporation, and

"(ii) the property taken into account under subparagraph (A) is sold by the corporation.

"(E) INFORMATION REPORTING.—The Secretary shall require such information reporting as is necessary to carry out the purposes of this paragraph."

(d) CREDIT FOR FOREIGN TAXES IMPOSED ON UNITED STATES SOURCE INCOME.—

(1) Subsection (b) of section 877 is amended by adding at the end the following new sentence: "The tax imposed solely by reason of this section shall be reduced (but not below zero) by the amount of any income, war profits, and excess profits taxes (within the meaning of section 903) paid to any foreign country or possession of the United States on any income of the taxpayer on which tax is imposed solely by reason of this section."

(2) Subsection (a) of section 877, as amended by subsection (a), is amended by inserting "(after any reduction in such tax under the last sentence of such subsection)" after "such subsection".

(e) COMPARABLE ESTATE AND GIFT TAX TREATMENT.—

(1) ESTATE TAX.—

(A) IN GENERAL.—Subsection (a) of section 2107 is amended to read as follows:

"(a) TREATMENT OF EXPATRIATES.—

"(1) RATE OF TAX.—A tax computed in accordance with the table contained in section 2001 is hereby imposed on the transfer of the taxable estate, determined as provided in section 2106, of every decedent nonresident not a citizen of the United States if, within the 10-year period ending with the date of death, such decedent lost United States citizenship, unless such loss did not have for 1 of its principal purposes the avoidance of taxes under this subtitle or subtitle A.

"(2) CERTAIN INDIVIDUALS TREATED AS HAVING TAX AVOIDANCE PURPOSE.—

"(A) IN GENERAL.—For purposes of paragraph (1), an individual shall be treated as having a principal purpose to avoid such taxes if such individual is so treated under section 877(a)(2).

"(B) EXCEPTION.—Subparagraph (A) shall not apply to a decedent meeting the requirements of section 877(c)(1).".

(B) CREDIT FOR FOREIGN DEATH TAXES.—Subsection (c) of section 2107 is amended by redesignating paragraph (2) as paragraph (3) and by inserting after paragraph (1) the following new paragraph:

"(2) CREDIT FOR FOREIGN DEATH TAXES.—

"(A) IN GENERAL.—The tax imposed by subsection (a) shall be credited with the amount of any estate, inheritance, legacy, or succession taxes actually paid to any foreign country in respect of any property which is included in the gross estate solely by reason of subsection (b).

"(B) LIMITATION ON CREDIT.—The credit allowed by subparagraph (A) for such taxes paid to a foreign country shall not exceed the lesser of—

"(i) the amount which bears the same ratio to the amount of such taxes actually paid to such foreign *country in respect of property included in the gross estate as the value of the property included in the gross estate solely by reason of subsection (b) bears to the value of all property subjected to such taxes by such foreign country, or*

"(ii) such property's proportionate share of the excess of—

"(I) the tax imposed by subsection (a), over

"(II) the tax which would be imposed by section 2101 but for this section.

"(C) PROPORTIONATE SHARE.—For purposes of subparagraph (B), a property's proportionate share is the percentage of the value of the property which is included in the gross estate solely by reason of subsection (b) bears to the total value of the gross estate.".

(C) EXPANSION OF INCLUSION IN GROSS ESTATE OF STOCK OF FOREIGN CORPORATIONS.—Paragraph (2) of section 2107(b) is amended by striking "more than 50 percent of" and all that follows and inserting "more than 50 percent of—

"(A) the total combined voting power of all classes of stock entitled to vote of such corporation, or

"(B) the total value of the stock of such corporation,".

(2) GIFT TAX.—

(A) IN GENERAL.—Paragraph (3) of section 2501(a) is amended to read as follows:

"(3) EXCEPTION.—

"(A) CERTAIN INDIVIDUALS.—Paragraph (2) shall not apply in the case of a donor who, within the 10-year period ending with the date of transfer, lost United States citizenship, unless such loss did not have for 1 of its principal purposes the avoidance of taxes under this subtitle or subtitle A.

"(B) CERTAIN INDIVIDUALS TREATED AS HAVING TAX AVOIDANCE PURPOSE.—For purposes of subparagraph (A), an individual shall be treated as having a principal purpose to avoid such taxes if such individual is so treated under section 877(a)(2).

"(C) EXCEPTION FOR CERTAIN INDIVIDUALS.—Subparagraph (B) shall not apply to a decedent meeting the requirements of section 877(c)(1).

"(D) CREDIT FOR FOREIGN GIFT TAXES.—The tax imposed by this section solely by reason of this paragraph shall be credited with the amount of any gift tax actually paid to any foreign country in respect of any gift which is taxable under this section solely by reason of this paragraph.".

(f) COMPARABLE TREATMENT OF LAWFUL PERMANENT RESIDENTS WHO CEASE TO BE TAXED AS RESIDENTS.—

(1) IN GENERAL.—Section 877 is amended by redesignating subsection (e) as subsection (f) and by inserting after subsection (d) the following new subsection:

"(e) COMPARABLE TREATMENT OF LAWFUL PERMANENT RESIDENTS WHO CEASE TO BE TAXED AS RESIDENTS.—

"(1) IN GENERAL.—Any long-term resident of the United States who—

"(A) ceases to be a lawful permanent resident of the United States (within the meaning of section 7701(b)(6)), or

"(B) commences to be treated as a resident of a foreign country under the provisions of a tax treaty between the United States and the foreign country and who does not waive the benefits of such treaty applicable to residents of the foreign country,

shall be treated for purposes of this section and sections 2107, 2501, and 6039F in the same manner as if such resident were a citizen of the United States who lost United States citizenship on the date of such cessation or commencement.

"(2) LONG-TERM RESIDENT.—For purposes of this subsection, the term 'long-term resident' means any individual (other than a citizen of the United States) who is a lawful permanent resident of the United States in at least 8 taxable years during the period of 15 taxable years ending with the taxable year during which the event described in subparagraph (A) or (B) of paragraph (1) occurs. For purposes of the preceding sentence, an individual shall not be treated as a lawful permanent resident for any taxable year if such individual is treated as a resident of a foreign country for the taxable year under the provisions of a tax treaty between the United States and the foreign country and does not waive the benefits of such treaty applicable to residents of the foreign country.

"(3) SPECIAL RULES.—

"(A) EXCEPTIONS NOT TO APPLY.—Subsection (c) shall not apply to an individual who is treated as provided in paragraph (1).

"(B) STEP-UP IN BASIS.—Solely for purposes of determining any tax imposed by reason of this subsection, property which was held by the long-term resident on the date the individual first became a resident of the United States shall be treated as having a basis on such date of not less than the fair market value of such property on such date. The preceding sentence shall not apply if the individual elects not to have such sentence apply. Such an election, once made, shall be irrevocable.

"(4) AUTHORITY TO EXEMPT INDIVIDUALS.—This subsection shall not apply to an individual who is described in a category of individuals prescribed by regulation by the Secretary.

"(5) REGULATIONS.—The Secretary shall prescribe such regulations as may be appropriate to carry out this subsection, including regulations providing for the application of this subsection in cases where an alien individual becomes a resident of the United States during the 10-year period after being treated as provided in paragraph (1).".

(2) CONFORMING AMENDMENTS.—

(A) Section 2107 is amended by striking subsection (d), by redesignating subsection (e) as subsection (d), and by inserting after subsection (d) (as so redesignated) the following new subsection:

"(e) CROSS REFERENCE.—

"For comparable treatment of long-term lawful permanent residents who ceased to be taxed as residents, see section 877(e).".

(B) Paragraph (3) of section 2501(a) (as amended by subsection (e)) is amended by adding at the end the following new subparagraph:

"(E) CROSS REFERENCE.—

"For comparable treatment of long-term lawful permanent residents who ceased to be taxed as residents, see section 877(e).".

(g) EFFECTIVE DATE.—

(1) IN GENERAL.—The amendments made by this section shall apply to—

(A) individuals losing United States citizenship (within the meaning of section 877 of the Internal Revenue Code of 1986) on or after February 6, 1995, and

(B) long-term residents of the United States with respect to whom an event described in subparagraph (A) or (B) of section 877(e)(1) of such Code occurs on or after February 6, 1995.

(2) RULING REQUESTS.—In no event shall the 1-year period referred to in section 877(c)(1)(B) of such Code, as amended by this section, expire before the date which is 90 days after the date of the enactment of this Act.

(3) SPECIAL RULE.—

(A) IN GENERAL.—In the case of an individual who performed an act of expatriation specified in paragraph (1), (2), (3), or (4) of section 349(a) of the Immigration and Nationality Act (8 U.S.C. 1481(a)(1)–(4)) before February 6, 1995, but who did not, on or before such date, furnish to the United States Department of State a signed statement of voluntary relinquishment of United States nationality confirming the performance of such act, the amendments made by this section and section 512 shall apply to such individual except that the 10-year period described in section 877(a) of such Code shall not expire before the end of the 10-year period beginning on the date such statement is so furnished.

(B) EXCEPTION.—Subparagraph (A) shall not apply if the individual establishes to the satisfaction of the Secretary of the Treasury that such loss of United States citizenship occurred before February 6, 1994.

SEC. 512. INFORMATION ON INDIVIDUALS LOSING UNITED STATES CITIZENSHIP.

(a) IN GENERAL.—Subpart A of part III of subchapter A of chapter 61 is amended by inserting after section 6039E the following new section:

"SEC. 6039F. INFORMATION ON INDIVIDUALS LOSING UNITED STATES CITIZENSHIP.

"(a) IN GENERAL.—Notwithstanding any other provision of law, any individual who loses United States citizenship (within the meaning of section 877(a)) shall provide a statement which includes the information described in subsection (b). Such statement shall be—

"(1) provided not later than the earliest date of any act referred to in subsection (c), and

"(2) provided to the person or court referred to in subsection (c) with respect to such act.

"(b) INFORMATION TO BE PROVIDED.—Information required under subsection (a) shall include—

"(1) the taxpayer's TIN,

"(2) the mailing address of such individual's principal foreign residence,

"(3) the foreign country in which such individual is residing,

"(4) the foreign country of which such individual is a citizen,

"(5) in the case of an individual having a net worth of at least the dollar amount applicable under section 877(a)(2)(B), information detailing the assets and liabilities of such individual, and

"(6) such other information as the Secretary may prescribe.

"(c) ACTS DESCRIBED.—For purposes of this section, the acts referred to in this subsection are—

"(1) the individual's renunciation of his United States nationality before a diplomatic or consular officer of the United States pursuant to paragraph (5) of section 349(a) of the Immigration and Nationality Act (8 U.S.C. 1481(a)(5)),

"(2) the individual's furnishing to the United States Department of State a signed statement of voluntary relinquishment of United States nationality confirming the performance of an act of expatriation specified in paragraph (1), (2), (3), or (4) of section 349(a) of the Immigration and Nationality Act (8 U.S.C. 1481(a)(1)–(4)),

"(3) the issuance by the United States Department of State of a certificate of loss of nationality to the individual, or

"(4) the cancellation by a court of the United States of a naturalized citizen's certificate of naturalization.

"(d) PENALTY.—Any individual failing to provide a statement required under subsection (a) shall be subject to a penalty for each year (of the 10-year period beginning on the date of loss of United States citizenship) during any portion of which such failure continues in an amount equal to the greater of—

"(1) 5 percent of the tax required to be paid under section 877 for the taxable year ending during such year, or

"(2) $1,000,

unless it is shown that such failure is due to reasonable cause and not to willful neglect.

"(e) INFORMATION TO BE PROVIDED TO SECRETARY.—Notwithstanding any other provision of law—

"(1) any Federal agency or court which collects (or is required to collect) the statement under subsection (a) shall provide to the Secretary—

"(A) a copy of any such statement, and

"(B) the name (and any other identifying information) of any individual refusing to comply with the provisions of subsection (a),

"(2) the Secretary of State shall provide to the Secretary a copy of each certificate as to the loss of American nationality

under section 358 of the Immigration and Nationality Act which is approved by the Secretary of State, and

"(3) the Federal agency primarily responsible for administering the immigration laws shall provide to the Secretary the name of each lawful permanent resident of the United States (within the meaning of section 7701(b)(6)) whose status as such has been revoked or has been administratively or judicially determined to have been abandoned.

Notwithstanding any other provision of law, not later than 30 days after the close of each calendar quarter, the Secretary shall publish in the Federal Register the name of each individual losing United States citizenship (within the meaning of section 877(a)) with respect to whom the Secretary receives information under the preceding sentence during such quarter.

"(f) REPORTING BY LONG-TERM LAWFUL PERMANENT RESIDENTS WHO CEASE TO BE TAXED AS RESIDENTS.—In lieu of applying the last sentence of subsection (a), any individual who is required to provide a statement under this section by reason of section 877(e)(1) shall provide such statement with the return of tax imposed by chapter 1 for the taxable year during which the event described in such section occurs.

"(g) EXEMPTION.—The Secretary may by regulations exempt any class of individuals from the requirements of this section if he determines that applying this section to such individuals is not necessary to carry out the purposes of this section.".

(b) CLERICAL AMENDMENT.—The table of sections for such subpart A is amended by inserting after the item relating to section 6039E the following new item:

> *"Sec. 6039F. Information on individuals losing United States citizenship.".*

(c) EFFECTIVE DATE.—The amendments made by this section shall apply to—

(1) individuals losing United States citizenship (within the meaning of section 877 of the Internal Revenue Code of 1986) on or after February 6, 1995, and

(2) long-term residents of the United States with respect to whom an event described in subparagraph (A) or (B) of section 877(e)(1) of such Code occurs on or after such date.

In no event shall any statement required by such amendments be due before the 90th day after the date of the enactment of this Act.

SEC. 513. REPORT ON TAX COMPLIANCE BY UNITED STATES CITIZENS AND RESIDENTS LIVING ABROAD.

Not later than 90 days after the date of the enactment of this Act, the Secretary of the Treasury shall prepare and submit to the Committee on Ways and Means of the House of Representatives and the Committee on Finance of the Senate a report—

(1) describing the compliance with subtitle A of the Internal Revenue Code of 1986 by citizens and lawful permanent residents of the United States (within the meaning of section 7701(b)(6) of such Code) residing outside the United States, and

(2) recommending measures to improve such compliance (including improved coordination between executive branch agencies).

Subtitle C—Repeal of Financial Institution Transition Rule to Interest Allocation Rules

SEC. 521. REPEAL OF FINANCIAL INSTITUTION TRANSITION RULE TO INTEREST ALLOCATION RULES.

(a) IN GENERAL.—Paragraph (5) of section 1215(c) of the Tax Reform Act of 1986 (Public Law 99–514, 100 Stat. 2548) is hereby repealed.

(b) EFFECTIVE DATE.—

(1) IN GENERAL.—The amendment made by this section shall apply to taxable years beginning after December 31, 1995.

(2) SPECIAL RULE.—In the case of the first taxable year beginning after December 31, 1995, the pre-effective date portion of the interest expense of the corporation referred to in such paragraph (5) of such section 1215(c) for such taxable year shall be allocated and apportioned without regard to such amendment. For purposes of the preceding sentence, the pre-effective date portion is the amount which bears the same ratio to the interest expense for such taxable year as the number of days during such taxable year before the date of the enactment of this Act bears to 366.

And the Senate agree to the same.

BILL ARCHER,
BILL THOMAS,
TOM BLILEY,
MICHAEL BILIRAKIS,
WILLIAM F. GOODLING,
H.W. FAWELL,
HENRY HYDE,
BILL MCCOLLUM,
J. DENNIS HASTERT,
Managers on the Part of the House.

BILL ROTH,
NANCY LANDON KASSEBAUM,
TRENT LOTT,
TED KENNEDY,
Managers on the Part of the Senate.

JOINT EXPLANATORY STATEMENT OF THE COMMITTEE OF CONFERENCE

The managers on the part of the House and the Senate at the conference on the disagreeing votes of the two Houses on the amendment of the Senate to the bill (H.R. 3103) to amend the Internal Revenue Code of 1986 to improve portability and continuity of health insurance coverage in the group and individual markets, to combat waste, fraud, and abuse in health insurance and health care delivery, to promote the use of medical savings accounts, to improve access to long-term care services and coverage, to simplify the administration of health insurance, and for other purposes, submit the following joint statement to the House and the Senate in explanation of the effect of the action agreed upon by the managers and recommended in the accompanying conference report:

The Senate amendment struck all of the House bill after the enacting clause and inserted a substitute text.

The House recedes from its disagreement to the amendment of the Senate with an amendment that is a substitute for the House bill and the Senate amendment. The differences between the House bill, the Senate amendment, and the substitute agreed to in conference are noted below, except for clerical corrections, conforming changes made necessary by agreements reached by the conferees, and minor drafting and clerical changes.

TITLE I.—HEALTH CARE ACCESS, PORTABILITY, AND RENEWABILITY

I. STRUCTURE

House bill

The House bill would amend the Internal Revenue Code (IRC) and the Employee Retirement Income Security Act of 1974 (ERISA), and includes free-standing provisions.

Senate amendment

The Senate amendment includes free-standing provisions.

Conference agreement

The conference agreement adds new provisions to the Employee Retirement Income Security Act of 1974 (ERISA), the Public Health Services (PHS) Act, and the Internal Revenue Code (IRC).

II. AVAILABILITY AND PORTABILITY OF GROUP HEALTH PLANS

Current law

Current federal law does not impose any requirements on employers to provide or contribute toward the health insurance coverage of their employees or their employees' dependents. However, specific federal requirements do apply to existing employer-sponsored health plans (e.g., fiduciary, notification and disclosure requirements under ERISA and COBRA continuation coverage, nondiscrimination requirements under ERISA and the Internal Revenue Code.)

House bill

The House bill would provide for federal requirements on group health plans (and insurers and health maintenance organizations (HMOs) selling to such plans) relating to portability, the use of preexisting medical condition, and discrimination based on health status.

Senate amendment

The Senate amendment would provide for federal requirements on group health plans, health plan issuers (entities licensed by the state to offer a group or individual health plan) and employee health benefit plans, relating to portability, the use of preexisting medical conditions, and discrimination based on health status.

Conference agreement

The conference agreement provides for federal requirements on group health plans and health insurance issuers offering group health insurance coverage relating to portability, access, and renewability.

A. DEFINITIONS

(Also see item IX below.)

Current law

Section 5000(b)(1) of the Internal Revenue Code (IRC) defines a group health plan as a plan (including a self-insured plan) of, or contributed to by, an employer (including a self-employed person) or employee organization to provide health care (directly or otherwise) to the employees, former employees, the employer, others associated or formerly associated with the employer in a business relationship, or their families.

Section 607(1) of ERISA defines a group health plan as an employee welfare benefit plan providing medical care to participants or beneficiaries directly or through insurance, reimbursement, or otherwise.

Church plans are excluded from federal requirements on existing employer plans such as ERISA's requirements on employee health benefit plans and COBRA continuation coverage requirements under the IRC and ERISA.

House bill

Group health plan means an employee welfare benefit plan to the extent that the plan provides medical care employees and their dependents directly or through insurance, reimbursement, or otherwise, and includes a group health plan within the meaning of section 5000(b)(1) of the IRC.

The provisions of this subtitle (other than those relating to individual coverage) apply to group health plans with 2 or more participants as current employees on the first day of the plan year.

The requirements would not apply to church plans unless such plans met the exemption for multiple employer health plans under subtitle c (see item V). For purposes of applying the provisions related to qualified prior coverage (II(B) below), a group health plan could elect to disregard periods of coverage of an individual under a church plan that is not subject to this subtitle.

Governmental plans could elect not to be a group health plan covered under the subtitle. For purposes of applying the provisions related to qualified prior coverage, a group health plan could elect not to include coverage under a governmental plan that elected to be excluded from this subtitle's requirements.

Senate amendment

Employee health benefit plan means any employee welfare benefit plan, governmental plan, or church plan, or any health benefit plan under section 5(e) of the Peace Corps Act, that provides or pays for health benefit for participants or beneficiaries whether directly, through a group health plan offered by a health plan issuer (see item III(A) below), or otherwise.

Conference agreement

The conference agreement defines a group health plan as an employee welfare benefit plan to the extent that the plan provides medical care to employees or their dependents directly or through insurance, reimbursement, or otherwise. Both governmental and church plans are included, but certain plans with limited coverage are excluded.

The portability and guaranteed availability provisions (other than those relating to individual coverage) apply to group health plans with 2 or more participants who are active employees on the first day of the plan year. These provisions would apply to nonfederal governmental plans, unless they elected to be excluded as described below, and to church and governmental plans. (See section III(B)(3) below for exceptions from availability, renewability, and portability requirements for group health plans and group health insurance coverage for certain benefits.)

Nonfederal governmental plans could elect not to be a group health plan covered under the amendments to the PHS. An election would apply for a single specified plan year, or, in the case of a plan provided pursuant to a collective bargaining agreement, for the term of such agreement. If a nonfederal governmental plan makes this election, it must notify enrollees of the fact and consequences of the election. The plan must still provide certification and disclosure of creditable coverage under the plan to enrollees who leave the plan, for purposes of portability.

Upon request, Medicare, Medicaid, a program of the Indian Health Service or a tribal organization, and military-sponsored health care programs must also provide notice of previous creditable coverage to individuals who leave such coverage.

B. PORTABILITY OF COVERAGE FOR PREVIOUSLY COVERED INDIVIDUALS

Current law

No provision.

House bill

The House bill would provide that in general, a group health plan and an insurer or HMO offering health insurance coverage in connection with a group health plan would have to reduce any pre-existing condition limitation period by the length of the aggregate period of prior coverage. Prior coverage would not qualify under this provision if there was more than a 60-day break in coverage under a group health plan. (Waiting periods would not be considered a break in coverage.) Qualified coverage would include coverage of the individual under a group health plan, health insurance coverage, Medicare, Medicaid, Tricare, a program of the Indian Health Service, and State health insurance coverage or risk pool, and coverage under the Federal Employees Health Benefit Program (FEHBP).

Senate amendment

The Senate Amendment is similar. An employee benefit plan or a health plan issuer offering a group health plan would have to reduce any preexisting condition limitation period by 1 month for each month for which the person was in a period of previous qualifying coverage. This provision would not apply if there was a break of more than 30 days. (Waiting periods would not be considered a break in coverage.) Previous qualifying coverage includes enrollment under an employee health benefit plan, group health plan, individual health plan, or under a public or private health plan established under federal or state law.

Conference agreement

The conference agreement provides that in general, group health plans, and health insurance issuers offering group health insurance coverage, would have to reduce any preexisting condition limitation period by the length of the aggregate period of prior creditable coverage. Prior coverage would not qualify under this provision if there was a break in coverage under a group health plan that was longer than a 63-day period. (Waiting periods and affiliation periods would not be considered a break in coverage.) Creditable coverage includes coverage of the individual under a group health plan (including a governmental or church plan), health insurance coverage (either group or individual insurance), Medicare, Medicaid, military-sponsored health care, a program of the Indian Health Service, a State health benefits risk pool, the FEHBP, a public health plan as defined in regulations, and any health benefit plan under section 5(e) of the Peace Corps Act. An individual would establish a creditable coverage period through presentation of certifications describing previous coverage, or through other procedures specified in regulations to carry out this provision. The conferees intend that creditable coverage includes short-term, limited coverage.

1. *Method for establishing qualified coverage periods*

Current law

No provision.

House bill

The House bill would provide that a group health plan or insurer or HMO offering health insurance coverage in connection with a group health plan could determine qualified coverage periods without regard to the specific benefits offered, referred to as the standard method. Alternatively, it could make such determination on a benefit-specific basis and not include as a qualified coverage period a specific benefit that had not been included at the end of the most recent period of coverage. If this alternative method were to be used, the group plan or insurer would be required to state prominently in any disclosure statements and to each enrollee at the time of enrollment that such a method of determining qualifying coverage was being used, and include a description of the effect of this method. The plan, insurer, or HMO would request a certification from prior plan administrators, insurers, or HMOs which discloses the plan statement related to health benefits under the plan or other detailed benefit information on the benefits available under the previous plan or coverage. The entity providing the certification could charge the reasonable cost for providing the benefit information to the requesting plan or insurer.

Senate bill

The Senate Amendment would provide that an employee health benefit plan or health plan issuer offering a group plan could impose a limitation or exclusion of benefits relating to the treatment of a preexisting condition only to the extent that such service or benefit was not previously covered under the plan in which the participant or beneficiary was enrolled immediately prior to enrollment in the plan involved.

Conference agreement

The conference agreement provides that a group health plan, and issuer offering group health insurance coverage, could determine creditable coverage periods without regard to the specific benefits covered during the period. Alternatively, it could make such determination based on several classes or categories of benefits, as specified in regulations. A group health plan and issuer would be required to count a period of creditable coverage with respect to any class or category of benefits if any level of benefits is provided. This alternative would have to be used uniformly for all participants and beneficiaries.

It is the intent of the conferees that the alternate method be available to account for significant differences in benefits. For example, the inclusion versus exclusion of a category of benefits such as pharmaceuticals could be considered a difference in classes of benefits. Similarly, significant differentials in deductibles could be considered differences in classes of benefits, but the alternative method would not apply to small differences in deductibles, such as

182

$250 versus $200. The alternative method would not apply for differences in specific services or treatments.

If the alternate method were to be used, the group health plan and issuer would be required to state prominently in any disclosure statements that such a method of determining qualifying coverage was being used, and would be required to include a description of the effect of this election. A group health plan using the alternate method would be required to notify each enrollee at the time of enrollment that the plan had made such an election, and describe the effect. An issuer would be required to notify each employer at the time of offer or sale of the coverage.

2. Certification of prior coverage

Current law

No provision.

House bill

The House bill would require the plan administrator of a group health plan, or the insurer or HMO offering health insurance coverage to a group plan, on request made on behalf of an individual covered or previously covered within the past 18 months under the plan or coverage, to provide for a certification of the period of coverage of the individual under the plan and of the waiting period (if any) imposed.

Senate amendment

The Senate Amendment would require an employee health plan to provide documentation of coverage to participants and beneficiaries whose coverage was terminated under the plan. As specified by regulation, the duty of an employee health benefit plan to verify previous qualifying coverage would be discharged when such plan provided documentation to the participant or beneficiary including the following information: (1) the dates that the person was covered under the plan; and (2) the benefits and cost-sharing arrangement available to the person under the plan.

Conference agreement

The conference agreement requires the group health plan, and health insurance issuer offering group health insurance coverage, to provide a certification of the period of creditable coverage under the plan, the coverage under any applicable COBRA continuation provision, and waiting period (if any) (and affiliation period if applicable) imposed on the individual. This certification would have to be provided when the individual ceases to be covered under the plan or otherwise becomes covered under a COBRA continuation provision, after any COBRA continuation coverage ceases, and on the request of an individual not later than 24 months after coverage ceased. The certification may be provided, to the extent practicable, at a time consistent with notices required under any applicable COBRA continuation provision. A group health plan offering medical care through health insurance coverage would not be required to provide certification if the health insurance issuer provides certification.

If a group health plan or health insurance issuer elects the alternative method of crediting coverage, the plan or issuer would request, from prior entities providing coverage, information on coverage of classes and categories of benefits available under the previous plan or coverage. The entity providing the certification could charge the reasonable cost for providing such information to the requesting plan or insurer. The Secretary is required to establish rules to prevent an entity's failure to provide information on health benefits under previous coverage from adversely affecting any subsequent coverage under another group health plan or health insurance coverage.

C. RESTRICTIONS ON USE OF PRE-EXISTING CONDITION LIMITATION PERIOD

Current law

No provision.

House bill

The House bill would restrict the use of preexisting condition limitation periods in group health plans and in plans offered by insurers and HMOs to group health plans.

Senate amendment

The Senate Amendment is similar but would apply to employee health benefit plans and group plans offered by health plan issuers.

Conference agreement

The conference agreement restricts the use of preexisting condition limitation exclusions by group health plans and health insurance issuers offering group health insurance coverage.

1. Definition of preexisting condition

Current law

No provision.

House bill

The House bill would define a preexisting condition to be a condition, regardless of the cause of condition, for which medical advice, diagnosis, care, or treatment was recommended or received within the 6-months ending on the day before the effective date of the coverage or the earliest date upon which such coverage would have been effective if no waiting period was applicable, whichever was earlier. Genetic information would not be considered a preexisting condition, so long as the treatment of the condition to which the information was applicable had not been sought in the 6-month period just described.

Senate amendment

The Senate Amendment provides a similar definition of preexisting condition. It does not include the genetic information language.

Conference agreement

The conference agreement defines a preexisting condition exclusion to be a limitation or exclusion of benefits relating to a condition, whether physical or mental, based on the fact that the condition was present before the enrollment date, whether or not any medical advice, diagnosis, care, or treatment was recommended or received before that date. Genetic information would not be considered a condition in the absence of a diagnosis of the condition related to such information.

2. Restrictions on limitation period

Current law

No provision.

House bill

The House bill would prohibit a group health plan, and an insurer or HMO offering health insurance coverage in connection with a group health plan from imposing a preexisting condition limitation period in excess of 12 months, or 18 months in the event of a late enrollment. A preexisting condition limitation period could not be applied to a newborn, adopted child, or child placed for adoption, so long as the individual became covered within 30 days of birth or adoption or placement for adoption. Preexisting condition limitation periods would not apply to pregnancies. An HMO could impose an eligibility period as an alternative to a preexisting condition limitation period but only if it did not exceed 60 days for timely enrollment and 90 days for late enrollment. An HMO could use alternative methods to address adverse selection as approved by state regulators.

Senate amendment

The Senate Amendment includes a similar provision, but with respect to affiliation periods of an HMO, would specify that during such a period the plan could not be required to provide health care services or benefits and no premium could be charged to the participant or beneficiary.

Conference agreement

The conference agreement permits a group health plan and health insurance issuers to impose a preexisting condition exclusion if the exclusion relates to a condition (whether physical or mental), regardless of the cause of condition, for which medical advice, diagnosis, care, or treatment was recommended or received within the 6-month period ending on the enrollment date. The exclusion could extend to not more than 12 months (18 months for late enrollees) after the enrollment date. The exclusion would be reduced by the aggregate of the periods of creditable coverage. Enrollment date is defined as the date of enrollment in the plan or coverage or, if earlier, the first day of the waiting period for such enrollment.

Any waiting period or affiliation period would run concurrently with any preexisting condition exclusion period. A preexisting condition limitation period could not be applied to a newborn, an adopted child or child placed for adoption under age 18, so long as the individual becomes covered under creditable coverage within 30 days of birth or adoption or placement for adoption. These exceptions for newborns and certain adopted children would not apply if the individual had a break in coverage longer than a 63-day period. Preexisting condition exclusions could not apply to pregnancies.

A group health plan offering health insurance coverage through an HMO, or an HMO which offers health insurance coverage in connection with a group health plan, may impose an affiliation period only if no preexisting condition exclusion is imposed, the period is imposed uniformly without regard to health status, and does not exceed 2 months for timely enrollment and 3 months for late enrollment. It is the intent of the conferees that any affiliation period would apply to all new enrollees and beneficiaries. During the affiliation period, the HMO could not be required to provide health care services or benefits and no premium could be charged to the participant or beneficiary. The affiliation period would begin on the enrollment date and would run concurrently with any other applicable waiting period under the plan. An HMO could use alternative methods to address adverse selection as approved by state regulators.

D. PROHIBITING EXCLUSIONS BASED ON HEALTH STATUS (ACCESS)

Current law

Under section 510 of ERISA, an employee benefit plan may not discriminate against a particular beneficiary for exercising any right to which he or she is entitled under the provisions of an employee benefit plan. Section 105(h) of the IRC prohibits discrimination in favor of highly compensated individuals by self-insured employer health plans.

House bill

Except as specified below, a group health plan, and an insurer or HMO offering coverage in connection with a plan, cannot exclude an employee or his or her beneficiary from being (or continuing to be enrolled) as a participant or beneficiary under the plan based on health status. Health status includes, with respect to an individual, medical condition, claims experience, receipt of health care, medical history, genetic information, evidence of insurability (including conditions arising out of domestic violence), or disability. A group health plan and an insurer or HMO offering coverage in connection with a group health plan cannot require a premium or contribution which is greater than such premium or contribution for a similarly situated participant or beneficiary solely on the basis of health status. It can, however, vary the premium or contribution based on factors that are not directly related to health status (such as scope of benefits, geographic area of resident, or wage levels).

The House bill provides that nothing is intended to affect the premium rates an insurer or HMO could charge an employer for health insurance coverage provided in connection with a group health plan.

A group health plan (or insurer or HMO providing coverage in connection to a group plan) could establish premium discounts or modify otherwise applicable copayments or deductibles in return for adherence to programs of health promotion and disease prevention.

Senate amendment

Except as specified below, a health plan issuer offering a group health plan may not decline to offer whole group coverage to a group purchaser desiring to purchase the coverage. An employee health benefit plan or a health plan issuer offering a group health plan could not condition eligibility, enrollment, or premium contribution requirements based on health status, medical condition, claims experience, receipt of health care, medical history, evidence of insurability (including conditions arising out of domestic violence), genetic information, or disability.

The bill does not include a specific rule of construction relating to premium rates charged to group health plans other than a prohibition of premium contribution requirements based on health status.

A group health plan (or insurer of HMO providing coverage in connection to a group plan) could establish premium discounts or modify otherwise applicable copayments or deductibles in return for adherence to programs of health promotion and disease prevention.

Conference agreement

Except as specified below, a group health plan, and a health insurance issuer offering group health insurance coverage, cannot establish rules for eligibility (including continued eligibility) of an individual to enroll under the terms of the plan based on any of the following health-related factors in relation to the individual or a dependent of the individual: health status, medical condition (including both physical and mental illness), claims experience, receipt of health care, medical history, genetic information, evidence of insurability (including conditions arising out of domestic violence), or disability.

The inclusion of evidence of insurability in the definition of health status is intended to ensure, among other things, that individuals are not excluded from health care coverage due to their participation in activities such as motorcycling, snowmobiling, all-terrain vehicle riding, horseback riding, skiing and other similar activities.

It is the intent of the conferees that a plan cannot knowingly be designed to exclude individuals and their dependents on the basis of health status. However, generally applicable terms of the plan may have a disparate impact on individual enrollees. For example, a plan may exclude all coverage of a specific condition, or may include a lifetime cap on all benefits, or a lifetime cap on specific benefits. Although individuals with the specific condition would be adversely affected by an exclusion of coverage for that condition, and individuals with serious illnesses may be adversely affected by a lifetime cap on all or specific benefits, such plan characteristics would be permitted as long as they are not directed at individual sick employees or dependents.

The Conference agreement does not require a group health plan or health insurance coverage to provide particular benefits other than those provided under the terms of the plan or coverage. Nor does it prevent any plan or coverage from establishing limitations or restrictions on the amount, level, extent, or nature of the benefits or coverage for similarly situated individuals enrolled in the plan or coverage. Rules defining any applicable waiting periods for enrollment may not be established based on health status related factors.

It is the intent of the conferees that a plan or coverage cannot single out an individual based on the health status or health status related factors of that individual for denial of a benefit otherwise provided other individuals covered under the plan or coverage. For example, the plan or coverage may not deny coverage for prescription drugs to a particular beneficiary or dependent if such coverage is available to other similarly situated individual covered under the plan or coverage. However, the plan or coverage could deny coverage for prescription drugs to all beneficiaries and dependents. The term "similarly situated" means that a plan or coverage would be permitted to vary benefits available to different groups of employees, such as full-time versus part-time employees or employees in different geographic locations. In addition, a plan or coverage could have different benefit schedules for different collective bargaining units.

The conference agreement provides that a group health plan and an issuer offering group coverage cannot require a premium or contribution which is greater than such premium or contribution for a similarly situated individual enrolled in the plan on the basis of any health status-related factor relating to the individual or to any individual enrolled under the plan as a dependent of the individual. It does not restrict the amount that an employer may be charged for coverage under a group health plan. The group health plan and health insurance issuer may establish premium discounts or rebates, or modify otherwise applicable copayments or deductibles in return for adherence to programs of health promotion and disease prevention.

The conferees intend that these provisions preclude insurance companies from denying coverage to employers based on health status and related factors that they have traditionally used. In addition, this provision is meant to prohibit insurers or employers from excluding employees in a group from coverage or charging them higher premiums based on their health status and other related factors that could lead to higher health costs. This does not mean that an entire group cannot be charged more. But it does preclude health plans from singling out individuals in the group for higher premiums or dropping them from coverage altogether.

1. Exceptions to the non-discrimination requirement

Current law

No provision.

House bill

No provision for group health plans (i.e., the plans of the employer). See item III(B) below on requirements on insurers and HMOs.

Senate amendment

Exceptions are provided to health plan issuers with respect to enrollment in the event that: (1) the health plan ceases to offer coverage to any additional group purchasers; or (2) the issuer can demonstrate to the state insurance regulator that to enroll new people would impair its financial or provider capacity. See item III–B(3) below.

Conference agreement

See item III(B) below on requirements for health plan issuers offering group health insurance coverage.

E. ENROLLMENT OF ELIGIBLE INDIVIDUALS WHO LOSE OTHER COVERAGE

Current law

No provision.

House bill

The House bill would require group health plans to permit an uncovered employee (or uncovered dependent) otherwise eligible for coverage to enroll under at least one benefit option if certain conditions are met: (1) the person was already covered when the plan was previously offered; (2) the person stated in writing at such time that another source of coverage was the reason for declining enrollment; (3) the person lost coverage as a result of a loss of eligibility or termination from or reduction in hours of employment; and (4) the person requested enrollment within 30 days after the date of the coverage's termination.

If a group health plan offered dependent coverage, it could not require, as a condition of coverage as a dependent, a waiting period applicable to: (1) a newborn, (2) adopted child or child placed for adoption, or (3) a spouse, at the time of marriage if the person had met any applicable waiting period.

Enrollment of a participant's beneficiary would be considered to be timely if a request for enrollment were made within 30 days of the date family coverage was first made available or, in the case of a newborn or adoption or placement for adoption, within 30 days of that event; and in the case of marriage, within 30 days of the date of the marriage, if family coverage was available.

Senate amendment

The Senate Amendment would require employee health benefit plans to provide for special enrollment periods extending for a reasonable time after certain qualifying events to permit the participant to change individual or family basis of coverage or to enroll in the plan if coverage would have otherwise been available. The qualifying events would be: (1) changes in family status affecting eligibility under a plan including marriage, separation, divorce, death, birth, or placement of a child for adoption; (2) changes in employment status that would otherwise cause the loss of eligibility for coverage (other than COBRA continuation coverage); or (3) changes in employment status of a family member that results in a loss of eligibility under a group, individual, or employee health benefit plan.

The special enrollment period would have to ensure that a child born or placed for adoption was deemed covered as of the date of birth or placement so long as the child was enrolled within 30 days.

Conference agreement

The conference agreement requires special enrollment periods for certain individuals losing other coverage and for certain dependent beneficiaries. It requires group health plans, and health insurance issuers offering group health insurance coverage, to permit eligible employees or dependents who lose other coverage to enroll under the terms of the plan if each of the following conditions is met: (1) the employee or dependent was already covered when the plan was previously offered; (2) the employee stated in writing at such time that another source of coverage was the reason for declining enrollment, but only if the plan sponsor or issuer required such a statement and provided the employee with notice of this requirement; (3) the person was covered under COBRA continuation coverage which was exhausted, or coverage was not under a COBRA continuation provision and was terminated as a result of a loss of eligibility for the coverage (including as a result of legal separation, divorce, death, termination of employment, or reduction in hours of employment) or termination of employer contributions towards such coverage; and (4) the person requested enrollment not later than 30 days after the loss of other coverage.

If a group health plan offers dependent coverage, it must offer a dependent special enrollment period for persons becoming a dependent through marriage, birth, or adoption or placement for adoption. The dependent special enrollment period must last for not less than 30 days. The dependent may be enrolled as a dependent of the individual. If the individual is eligible for enrollment, but not enrolled, the individual may also enroll at this time. Moreover, in the case of the birth or adoption of a child, the spouse of the individual also may be enrolled as a dependent of the individual if the spouse is otherwise eligible for coverage but not already enrolled. If an individual seeks to enroll a dependent during the first 30 days of a dependent special enrollment period, the coverage would become effective as of the date of birth, of adoption or placement for adoption, or, in the case of marriage, not later than the first day of the first month beginning after the date the completed request for enrollment was received.

F. APPLICABILITY OF RENEWAL REQUIREMENTS TO MULTIPLE EMPLOYER ARRANGEMENTS

Current law

Under section 3(37) of ERISA, a multiemployer plan is one in which more than one employer contributes and which is established through a collective bargaining agreement. (Such plans are commonly found in unionized sectors of the building and construction, publishing, and entertainment trades, and the lumber, maritime, retail, food, hotel, and restaurant industries.) Under section 3(40) of ERISA, a multiple employer welfare arrangement (MEWA) is an employee welfare benefit plan or any other arrangement which offers or provides health benefits and meets additional criteria, (e.g., it must offer such benefits to the employees of 2 or more employers). There is no provision or definition under current law for "multiple employer health plans."

House bill

Such plans could not deny an employer who employees are covered under the plan or arrangement continued access to the same or different coverage except: (1) for cause (e.g., nonpayment of premiums, fraud, and noncompliance with plan provisions); (2) because the plan is not offering coverage in a geographic area; or (3) due to a failure to meet the terms of an applicable collective bargaining agreement. Certain collectively bargained arrangements and "multiple employer health plans" (MEHPs) would be required to meet specific requirements relating to the nondiscrimination requirements. (MEHPs are established under this bill (see item V below) and are generally non-fully-insured MEWAs that meet certain requirements excepting them from state regulation.)

Senate amendment

No provision. (Note that the rules regarding group and individual health plans (e.g., guaranteed renewal, nondiscrimination, and portability) or state laws not preempted by the Senate amendment also apply to health plans offered by health plan issuers to a purchasing cooperative. See item VIII below).

Conference agreement

The conference agreement provides that a group health plan which is a multiemployer plan or a multiple employer welfare arrangement may not deny an employer continued access to the same or different coverage under the terms of such plan except: (1) for nonpayment of contributions; (2) for fraud; (3) for noncompliance with plan provisions; (4) because the plan is ceasing to offer any coverage in a geographic area; (5) in the case of a network plan, there is no longer any individual enrolled through the employer who lives, resides, or works in the service area of the network plan, and the plan applies this provision uniformly without regard to claims experience or health status-related factors; or (6) due to a failure to meet the terms of an applicable collective bargaining agreement, to renew a collective bargaining agreement or other agreement requiring or authorizing contributions to the plan, or to employ employees covered by such an agreement.

G. ENFORCEMENT OF GROUP HEALTH PLAN REQUIREMENTS

Current law

Federal requirements on existing group health plans are enforced through various laws, including ERISA, the Public Health Service (PHS) Act, the IRC, and Medicare.

House bill

The House bill would provide for enforcement of the federal group health plan availability and portability requirements through the IRC, ERISA, and through civil monetary penalties imposed through the Secretary of Health and Human Services

Senate amendment

The Senate Amendment would provide for enforcement of the federal group health plan availability and portability requirements through the Secretary of Labor, in consultation with the Secretary of Health and Human Services using ERISA civil enforcement provisions.

Conference agreement

The conference agreement provides for enforcement of the federal group health plan availability and portability requirements through the IRC, ERISA, and through civil monetary penalties imposed through the Secretary of Health and Human Services (HHS).

1. Enforcement through COBRA provisions of IRC

Current law

Plans that fail to comply with the IRC COBRA provision are subject to an excise tax of $100 per day per violation. The tax is not applied where the failure was determined to be unintentional or if the failure was corrected within 30 days. An overall limitation on the tax applies in the event of an unintentional failure.

House bill

The House bill would provide that noncomplying plans and insurers and HMOs selling to group health plans would be subject to an excise tax of $100 per day per violation enforced through the COBRA provisions of the IRC. Penalties would not be assessed if the failure was determined to be unintentional or a correction was made within 30 days. No tax could be imposed on a noncomplying insurer or HMO subject to state insurance regulation if the Secretary of Health and Human Services (HHS) determined that the state had an effective enforcement mechanism. In the case of a group health plan of a small employer that provided coverage solely through a contract with an insurer or HMO, no tax would be imposed upon the employer if the failure was solely because of the product offered by the insurer or HMO. No tax penalty would be assessed for a failure under this provision if a sanction had been imposed under ERISA or by the Secretary of HHS.

Senate amendment

No provision.

Conference agreement

See Title IV.

2. Enforcement through ERISA

Current law

Under section 502 of ERISA, employee benefit plans that fail to comply with applicable requirements can be sued for relief and be subject to civil money penalties, and can be sued to recover any benefits due under the plan. Section 504 of ERISA provides the Secretary of Labor with investigative authority to determine whether any person is out of compliance with the law's requirements. Section 506 provides for coordination and responsibility of agencies in enforcement. Section 510 prohibits a health plan from discriminating against a participant or beneficiary for exercising any right under the plan.

House bill

The House bill would provide that ERISA sanctions apply to group health plans by deeming the provisions of subtitle A and subtitle D (insofar as it is applicable to this subtitle) to be provisions of title I of ERISA. Such sanctions also would apply to an insurer or HMO that was subject to state law in the event that the Secretary of Labor determined that the state had not provided for enforcement of the above provisions of this Act. Sanctions would not apply in the event that the Secretary of Labor established that none of the persons against whom the liability would be imposed knew, or exercising reasonable diligence, would have known that a failure existed, or if the noncomplying entity acted within 30 days to correct the failure. In no case would a civil money penalty be imposed under ERISA for a violation for which an excise tax under the COBRA enforcement provisions was imposed or for which a civil money penalty was imposed by the Secretary of HHS.

Senate amendment

The Senate Amendment would provide that for employee health benefit plans, the Secretary would be required to enforce the reform standards established by the bill in the same manner as provided under sections 502, 504, 506, and 510 of ERISA. (See item IV(I) below for enforcement provisions relating to health plan issuers and group health plans sold to employers and others.)

Conference agreement

The conference agreement provides that provisions with respect to group health plans would be enforced under Title I of ERISA as under current law. The Secretary of Labor would not enforce the provisions of Title I applicable to health insurance issuers. However, private right of action under part V of ERISA would apply to such issuers. Enforcement of provisions with respect to health insurance issuers generally would be limited to civil remedies established under the PHS Act amendments (as described in the following subsection).

The conference agreement provides that a state may enter into an agreement with the Secretary for delegation to the state of some or all of the Secretary's authority under sections 502 and 504 of ERISA to enforce the requirements of this part in connection with MEWAs providing medical care which are not group health plans.

3. Enforcement through civil money penalties

Current law

No provision.

House bill

The House bill would provide that a group health plan, insurer, or HMO that failed to meet the above requirements would be subject to a civil money penalty. Rules similar to those imposed under the COBRA penalties would apply. The maximum amount of penalty would be $100 for each day for each individual with respect to which a failure occurred. In determining the penalty amount, the Secretary of HHS would have to take into account the previous record of compliance of the person being assessed with the applicable requirements of this subtitle, the gravity of the violation, and the overall limitations for unintentional failures provided under the IRC COBRA provisions. No penalty could be assessed if the failure was not intentional or if the failure was corrected within 30 days. A procedure would be available for administrative and judicial review of a penalty assessment. Collected penalties would be paid to the Secretary of HHS and would be available for the purpose of enforcing the provisions with respect to which the penalty was imposed.

The authority for the Secretary of HHS to impose civil money penalties would not apply to enforcement with respect to any entity which offered health insurance coverage and which was an insurer or HMO subject to state regulation by an applicable state authority if the Secretary of HHS determined that the state had established an effective enforcement plan. In no case would a civil money penalty be imposed under this provision for a violation for which an excise tax under COBRA or civil money penalty under ERISA was assessed.

Senate amendment

No provision.

Conference agreement

The conference agreement provides that each state may require that health insurance issuers that issue, sell, renew, or offer health insurance coverage in the state in the small or large group markets meet the Act's requirements. In the case of a determination by the Secretary of HHS that a state has failed to substantially enforce a provision or provisions of part A with respect to health insurance issuers in the state, the Secretary would enforce such provision or provisions insofar as they relate to the issuance, sale, renewal, and offering of health insurance coverage in connection with group health plans in the state. Secretarial enforcement would apply only in the absence of state enforcement and with respect to group health plans that are nonfederal governmental plans.

In the case of a failure by a health insurance issuer, the issuer is liable for any penalty. In the case of failure by a group health plan that is a nonfederal governmental plan, the plan is liable if it is sponsored by 2 or more employers; otherwise the employer is liable. Rules similar to those imposed under the COBRA penalties would apply. The maximum amount of penalty for noncompliance would be $100 per day per individual. In determining the penalty amount, the Secretary of HHS would have to take into account the previous record of compliance and the gravity of the violation. No penalty could be assessed if the failure was not intentional or if the failure was corrected within 30 days. A procedure would be available for administrative and judicial review of a penalty assessment. Collected penalties would be paid to the Secretary of HHS and would be available for the purpose of enforcing the provisions with respect to which the penalty was imposed.

4. Coordination in administration

Current law

Section 506 of ERISA provides for coordination of other federal agencies (e.g., the Internal Revenue Service) with the Department of Labor in enforcing ERISA.

House bill

The House bill would require the Secretaries of Treasury, Labor, and HHS to issue regulations that are not duplicative to carry out this subtitle. The bill would require these regulations to be issued in a manner that assures coordination and nonduplication in their activities under this subtitle.

Senate amendment

No provision.

Conference agreement

The conference agreement provides that the Secretaries of Treasury, Labor, and HHS would ensure, through execution of an interagency memorandum of understanding, that regulations, rulings, and interpretations are administered so as to have the same effect at all times. It requires the Secretaries to coordinate enforcement policies for the same requirements to avoid duplication of enforcement efforts and assign priorities in enforcement.

It is the intent of the conferees that the committees of jurisdiction should work together to assure the coordination of policies under this Act. Such coordination is considered necessary to maintain consistency in the IRC, ERISA, and the PHS Act.

III. AVAILABILITY, PORTABILITY, AND RENEWABILITY REQUIREMENTS ON INSURERS, HMOS, AND ISSUERS OF HEALTH PLANS IN THE GROUP MARKET

Current law

The McCarran Ferguson Act of 1945 (P.L. 79–15) exempts the business of insurance from federal antitrust regulation to the extent that it is regulated by the states and indicates that no federal law should be interpreted as overriding state insurance regulation unless it does so explicitly. Section 514(b)(2)(A) of ERISA leaves to the states the regulation of insurance. (Employee benefit plans are not insurance and are regulated by the federal government.)

House bill

The House bill would establish federal requirements on insurers and HMOs selling in the group market to provide for guaranteed availability of health insurance coverage.

Senate amendment

The Senate Amendment is similar but would apply requirements to health plan issuers offering plans in the group market.

Conference agreement

The conference agreement establishes federal requirements on health insurance issuers offering group health insurance coverage to provide for guaranteed availability of health insurance coverage.

A. DEFINITIONS

Current law

No provision.

House bill

The House bill would define insurer to mean an insurance company, insurance service, or insurance organization which is licensed to engage in the business of insurance in a state and which (except for the purposes of individual health insurance availability provisions of this subtitle) is subject to state law which regulates insurance within the meaning of section 514(b)(2)(A) of ERISA.

The House bill would define a health maintenance organization to mean (a) a federally qualified HMO, (b) an organization recognized under state law as an HMO, or (c) a similar organization regulated under state law for solvency in the same manner and extent as an HMO, if (other than for the purposes of individual health insurance availability provisions of the bill) it is subject to state law which regulates insurance within the meaning of section 514(b)(2) of ERISA.

Under the House bill, a bona fide association would be defined as an association which (a) has been actively in existence for at least 5 years; (b) has been formed and maintained in good faith for purposes other than obtaining insurance; (c) does not condition membership in the association on health status; (d) makes health insurance coverage offered through the association available to any individual who is a member (or dependent of a member) of the association at the time the coverage is initially issued; (e) does not make health insurance coverage offered through the association available to any member who is not a member (or dependent of a member) of the association at the time coverage is initially issued; (f) does not impose preexisting condition exclusions consistent with the requirements of this bill relating to group health plans; and (g) provides for renewal and continuation of coverage consistent with the requirements of this bill.

Senate amendment

The Senate Amendment would define health plan issuer as any entity that is licensed (prior to or after the date of enactment of this Act) by a state to offer a group health plan or an individual health plan.

The Senate Amendment does not use the terms health maintenance organization, or bona fide association.

Conference agreement

The conference agreement defines a health insurance issuer as an insurance company, insurance service, or insurance organization, including an HMO, which is licensed to engage in the business of insurance in a state and which is subject to state law which regulates insurance within the meaning of section 514(b)(2) of ERISA. A group health plan is not a health insurance issuer.

An HMO is: (a) a federally qualified HMO, (b) an organization recognized under state law as an HMO, or (c) a similar organization regulated under state law for solvency in the same manner and extent as an HMO.

A bona fide association is an association which: (a) has been actively in existence for at least 5 years; (b) has been formed and maintained in good faith for purposes other than obtaining insurance; (c) does not condition membership in the association on any health status-related factor; (d) makes health insurance coverage offered through the association available to any member, or individuals eligible for coverage through such member, regardless of any health status-related factor; (e) does not make health insurance coverage offered through the association available other than in connection with a member of the association; and (f) meets additional requirements as may be imposed under state law.

B. GUARANTEED AVAILABILITY OF COVERAGE

Current law

No provision.

House bill

The House bill would require each insurer or HMO offering health insurance coverage in the small group market to accept every small employer in the state that applied for coverage and to accept for enrollment under such coverage every eligible individual who applied for enrollment during the initial enrollment period in which the individual first became eligible for the group coverage. No restriction could be imposed on an eligible individual based on his or her health status. An eligible individual is determined in accordance with the terms of the plan consistent with all applicable state laws.

Senate amendment

The Senate Amendment would require a health plan issuer offering a group health plan to accept the whole group desiring to purchase the coverage. A health plan issuer offering a group health plan could not condition eligibility, continuation of eligibility, enrollment, or premium contribution requirements based on health status. (Health status is defined the same as under the House bill.)

Conference agreement

The conference agreement requires each health insurance issuer that offers health insurance coverage in the small group market in a state to accept every small employer in the state that applies for coverage, and to accept for enrollment under such coverage every eligible individual who applies for enrollment during the period in which the individual first became eligible to enroll under the terms of the group health plan. The health plan issuer may not impose restrictions on any eligible individual being a participant or beneficiary based on his or her health status, or the health status of dependents. An eligible individual is determined in accordance with the terms of the plan, as provided by the health insurance issuer under the rules of the issuer which are uniformly applicable in a state to small employers in the small group market, and consistent with all applicable state laws governing the issuer and market.

1. Scope of requirement

Current law

No provision.

House bill

The House bill provides that the guaranteed availability requirement apply to the small group market only. Small groups are those with 2 to 50 employees.

Senate amendment

The Senate Amendment provides that the guaranteed availability requirement apply to all health plan issuers and group health plans.

Conference agreement

The conference agreement provides that the guaranteed availability requirement applies to the small group market only. Small groups are those with 2 to 50 employees on a typical business day.

To assure access in the large group market, the conference agreement provides that the Secretary of HHS request that the chief executive officer of each state submit a report on the access of large employers to health insurance coverage and the circumstances for lack of access to coverage, if any, of large employers, and classes of employers. The Secretary shall request the reports not later than December 31, 2000 and every 3 years thereafter. Based on the state reports and other information, the Secretary would be required to prepare a report for Congress, every 3 years, describing the access to health insurance for large employers, and classes of employers in each state. The Secretary may include recommendations to assure access.

In addition, the Comptroller General will submit to Congress not later than 18 months after the date of enactment of this Act, a report on access of classes of large employers to health insurance coverage in the different states, and the circumstances for lack of access, if any.

2. Restrictions on preexisting condition limitation periods

Current law

No provision.

House bill

The House bill would provide for the same restrictions on the use of preexisting condition limitations by each insurer and HMO that offers health insurance coverage in connection with a group health plan as those described in above item II–(C).

Senate amendment

The Senate amendment would provide for the same restrictions on the use of preexisting condition limitations by health plan issuers as described in above item II–(C).

Conference agreement

The conference agreement provides us for the same restrictions on the use of preexisting condition limitations by each health insurance issuer that offers group health insurance coverage as those described in above item II–(C).

3. Exceptions to guaranteed availability

Current law

No provision.

House bill

The House bill would provide that an HMO or an insurer offering coverage in the small group market through a network plan could: (1) limit employers for such coverage to those with eligible individuals whose place of employment or residence was in the plan's or HMO's service area; (2) limit the individuals who might be enrolled to those whose place of residence or employment was within the service area; (3) within the service area, deny coverage if the plan or HMO demonstrated lack of capacity to deliver services adequately, but only if it was applying the capacity limit to all employers without regard to the group's claims experience or the health status of its participants and beneficiaries. Those denying coverage on the basis of capacity could not offer small groups coverage in the service area for 180 days. Similar exceptions would apply in the event of financial capacity limits.

Senate amendment

The Senate amendment would provide that a health plan issuer offering a group health plan could cease offering coverage to group purchasers if (1) the plan ceased to offer coverage to any additional group purchasers, and (2) the issuer could demonstrate to the applicable certifying authority that its financial or provider capacity would be impaired if the issuer were required to offer coverage to additional group purchasers. Such an issuer would be prohibited from offering coverage for 6 months or until the issuer could demonstrate that the capacity was adequate, whichever was later. An issuer would only be eligible for this exception if it offered coverage on a first-come-first-served basis or other basis established by a state to ensure a fair opportunity to enroll and avoid risk selection.

Conference agreement

The conference agreement provides that a health insurance issuer offering coverage in the small group market through a network plan could: (1) limit employers for such coverage to those with eligible individuals who live, work, or reside in the service area for the network plan; (2) within the service area, deny coverage to small employers if the issuer has demonstrated, if required, to the applicable state authority, the lack of capacity to deliver services adequately to additional groups, but only if it was applying the capacity limit to all employers uniformly without regard to claims experience or any health status-related factor. An issuer denying coverage on the basis of capacity could not offer coverage in the small group market in the service area for 180 days.

A health insurance issuer may deny coverage in the small group market if the issuer has demonstrated, if required, to the applicable state authority, that it does not have the financial reserves necessary to underwrite additional coverage. The issuer would be required to apply the financial capacity limit to all employers in the small group market in the state, consistent with applicable state law, and without regard to claims experience or health status-related factors. An issuer denying coverage on the basis of financial capacity could not offer coverage in the small group market in the service area for 180 days or until the issuer has demonstrated, if required, to the applicable state authority, that it has adequate capacity, whichever is later. A State may provide for determination of adequate capacity on a service-area-specific basis. It is the intent of the conferees that an issuer denying coverage on the basis of capacity limitations may demonstrate compliance if enrollment is provided on a first-come first-serve basis, or other state approved method.

The conference agreement imposes requirements for renewal and continuation on issuers offering health insurance plans to bona fide associations, but does not require these issuers to guarantee issue of the coverage offered to bona fide associations. The conferees do not intend the provision to mean that issuers of coverage to an association have to offer a particular association plan to any other employer. Thus issuers offering coverage to associations are not required to guarantee issue the association's plan to other small employers. Nondiscrimination rules would apply to these association plans, and no employee or dependent could be excluded from coverage on the basis of any health status-related factor.

The conference agreement provides exceptions to the availability, renewability and portability requirements for group health plans and group health insurance coverage for certain benefits, sometimes under certain conditions. First, these requirements would not apply to provision of certain excepted benefits including: coverage only for accident, or disability insurance, or any combination thereof; coverage issued as a supplement to liability insurance; liability insurance; workers' compensation or similar insurance; automobile medical payment insurance; credit-only insurance; coverage for on-site medical clinics; and, other similar coverage, as specified in regulations, under which benefits for medical care are secondary or incidental to other insurance benefits.

Second, if the following benefits are (a) provided under a separate policy, certificate, or contract or insurance, or (b) if the benefits are otherwise not an integral part of the plan, the requirements would not apply to: limited scope dental or vision benefits; benefits for long-term care, nursing home care, home health care, community-based care, or any combination thereof; or, similar limited benefits as specified in regulations.

Third, if the following benefits: (a) are provided under a separate policy, certificate, or contract of insurance; (b) there is no coordination between the provision of these benefits and any exclusion of benefits under any group health plan maintained by the same plan sponsor; and (c) such benefits are paid with respect to an event without regard to whether benefits are provided for that event under any group health plan maintained by the same plan sponsor, the requirements would not apply to: coverage only for a specified disease or illness, or hospital indemnity or other fixed indemnity insurance.

Fourth, if the following benefits are provided under a separate policy, certificate, or contract of insurance, the requirements would not apply to: Medicare supplemental health insurance; coverage supplemental to coverage provided under military health care; and, similar supplemental coverage provided to coverage under a group health plan.

4. Exceptions for failure to meet participation or contribution rules

Current law

No provision.

House bill

The House bill would provide that an exception to the guaranteed availability requirement would apply in the case of any group health plan which failed to meet the participation or contribution rules of the insurer or HMO. Such participation and contribution rules would have to be uniformly applicable and in accordance with state law.

Senate amendment

No provision.

Conference agreement

The conference agreement provides that an exception to the guaranteed availability requirement would apply in the case of any group health plan which failed to meet the participation or contribution rules of the health insurance issuer. Such participation and contribution rules would have to be in accordance with state law.

C. GUARANTEED RENEWABILITY

Current law

No provision.

House bill

The House bill would provide that regardless of the size of the group, insurers and HMOs would be required to renew or continue in force coverage at the option of the covered employer with certain exceptions.

Senate amendment

The Senate provision is similar but at the option of the group purchaser.

Conference agreement

The conference agreement provides that a health insurance issuer offering group health insurance coverage in the small or large group market would be required to renew or continue in force coverage at the option of the plan sponsor of the plan.

1. Exceptions to guaranteed renewability of group coverage

Current law

No provision.

House bill

The House bill would provide exceptions to the guaranteed renewability requirement for: nonpayment of premiums, fraud, violation of participation and contribution rules, termination of the plan in a state or geographic area, or the employer moved outside the service area (but only if this last provision was applied uniformly without regard to health status). Exceptions to guaranteed renewability would also apply in the event that the insurer or plan no longer offered a particular type of coverage but only if prior notice was provided, the employer was given the chance to buy another plan offered by the insurer or HMO, and the termination was applied uniformly without regard to health status or insurability. An exception would also apply in the event of discontinuance of all coverage, but only if certain conditions were met. In this instance, the insurer or HMO could not market small and/or large group coverage for 5 years.

Senate amendment

The Senate Amendment is similar. It would include as exceptions to the guaranteed renewability requirement the loss of eligibility of COBRA continuation coverage, and failure of a participant or beneficiary to meet requirements for eligibility for coverage under the group health plan that are not prohibited by this subtitle.

A network plan could deny continued participation under the plan to participant or beneficiaries who did not live, reside, or work in an area in which the plan was offered, but only if the denial was applied uniformly, without regard to health status or insurability.

The provisions relating to discontinuation of a plan or of coverage in general are similar to the House bill.

Conference agreement

The conference agreement provides exceptions to the guaranteed renewability requirement for one or more of the following: (1) nonpayment of premiums; (2) fraud; (3) violation of participation or contribution rules; (4) termination of coverage in the market in accordance with applicable state law, as outlined below; (5) for network plans, no enrollees connected to the plan live, reside, or work in the service area of the issuer, or area for which the issuer is authorized to do business, and, in the case of the small group market only if the issuer would deny enrollment to the plan under regulations governing guaranteed availability of coverage; (6) for coverage made available to bona fide associations, if membership in the association ceases, but only if coverage is terminated uniformly without regard to any health status-related factor relating to any covered individual.

Exceptions to guaranteed renewability would also apply if the issuer or plan no longer offered a particular type of group coverage in the small or large group market so long as the issuer, in accordance with applicable state law: (1) provided prior notice to each plan sponsor and participants and beneficiaries; (2) gave the plan sponsor the chance to purchase all (or, in the case of the large group market, any) other plans offered by the issuer in such market; and (3) applied the termination uniformly without regard to the claims experience of the sponsors or any health status-related factor to any participants or beneficiaries covered or new participants or beneficiaries who may become eligible for such coverage.

An exception would also apply in the event of discontinuance of all coverage, but only if certain conditions were met. In this instance, the issuer could not offer coverage in the market and state involved for 5 years.

Issuers would be permitted to modify the health insurance coverage for a product offered to a group health plan in the large group market, and in the small group market if the modification was effective on a uniform basis among group health plans with that product.

For example, the conferees intend that issuers could uniformly modify the terms of treatment for particular conditions among group health plans within a type of coverage. An exception would apply to coverage available in the small group market only through 1 or more bona fide associations. Issuers could modify a product offered to a group plan in the large group market.

See section B(3) above for exceptions from availability, renewability, and portability requirements for certain benefits.

D. DISCLOSURE OF INFORMATION BY HEALTH PLAN ISSUERS

Current law

Section 101 of ERISA requires covered plans to furnish summary plan descriptions and other information and notices to plan participants and the Secretary of Labor. Section 104 of ERISA requires covered plans to file certain information with the Secretary of Labor and to furnish certain information to plan participants.

House bill

The House bill does not include a provision.

Senate amendment

The Senate Amendment would require that in connection with the offering of any group health plan to a small employer (defined under state law or, if not so defined, one with not more than 50 employees), that a health plan issuer make a reasonable disclosure as part of its solicitation and sales materials of certain information, such as the provisions of the plan concerning the right of the issuer to change premium rates and the factors that could affect such changes, the provisions of the plan relating to renewability and any preexisting condition provisions, and descriptive information about the plan's benefits and premiums. The information would have to be understandable by the average small employer and sufficiently accurate and comprehensive to reasonably inform employers, participants, and beneficiaries of their rights and obligations under the plan. These requirements would not apply to proprietary and trade secret information under applicable law and do not preempt state reporting and disclosure requirements.

The Senate Amendment would amend section 104(b)(1) of ERISA relating to the summary plan description to provide that if there is a modification or change described in the summary plan description that is a material reduction in covered services or benefits provided, a summary of such changes would have to be furnished to participants within 60 days after the date of its adoption. Alternatively, plans sponsors could provide such a description at regular intervals of not more than 90 days. The bill requires the Secretary of Labor to issue regulations providing alternative mechanisms to delivering by mail through which employee benefit plans may notify participants of material reductions in covered services. It further amends the summary plan description provisions of ERISA to require the inclusion of certain information.

Conference agreement

The conference agreement requires a health plan issuer offering any health insurance coverage to a small employer to make a reasonable disclosure of the availability of information as part of its solicitation and sales materials. At the small employer's request, the issuer must provide the provisions of the plan concerning the right of the issuer to change premium rates and the factors that could affect such changes, the provisions of the plan relating to renewability and any preexisting condition provisions, and the benefits and premiums under all health insurance coverage for which the employer is qualified. The information would have to be understandable by the average small employer and sufficient to reasonably inform small employers of their rights and obligations under the health insurance coverage. These requirements would not apply to proprietary and trade secret information under applicable law.

The conference agreement would amend section 104(b)(1) of ERISA relating to the summary plan description to provide that if there is a material reduction in covered services or benefits, a summary of such changes would have to be furnished to participants within 60 days after the date of its adoption. Alternatively, plan sponsors could provide a description at regular intervals of not more than 90 days. The conference agreement requires the Secretary of Labor to issue regulations within 180 days of enactment of this Act which would provide for alternative mechanisms, besides delivery by mail, through which employee benefit plans may notify participants of material reductions in covered services. It further amends the summary plan description provisions of ERISA to require the inclusion of certain information.

The conference agreement would amend section 101 of ERISA to permit the Secretary, in accordance with regulations prescribed by the Secretary, to require MEWAs that provide medical care benefits, but are not group health plans, to report, not more frequently than annually, in such form and manner as the Secretary may require to determine the extent to which the requirements of this part are being carried out.

E. STATE FLEXIBILITY

Current law

The McCarran Ferguson Act of 1945 (P.L. 79–15) exempts the business of insurance from federal antitrust regulation to the extent that it is regulated by the states and indicates that no federal law should be interpreted as overriding state insurance regulation unless it does so explicitly. Section 514 of ERISA leaves to the states the regulation of insurance. (Employee benefit plans are not insurance and are regulated by the federal government.)

House bill

The House bill would provide that unless preempted by section 514 of ERISA, state laws would not be preempted that (1) related to matters not specifically addressed in subtitles A and B, or (2) that required insurers or HMOs to: (a) impose a limitation or exclusion of benefits relating to the treatment of a preexisting condition for periods shorter than specified in the bill, (b) allowed persons to be considered to be in a period of previous qualifying coverage if they experienced a lapse in coverage greater than 60 days, or (c) had a look-back provision shorter than 6 months.

Senate amendment

The Senate Amendment does not include "related to matters not specifically addressed in subtitles A and B." The Senate Amendment would provide that unless preempted by section 514 of ERISA, state laws would not be preempted that (1) required health plan issuers to impose a limitation or exclusion of benefits relating to the treatment of a preexisting condition for periods that are shorter than specified in the bill; (2) allowed individuals, participants, and beneficiaries to be considered in a period of previous qualifying coverage if such person experienced a lapse in coverage that was greater than the 30-days provided under this bill; or (3) required issuers to have a lookback period shorter than provided for under this subtitle.

Conference agreement

The conference agreement provides that any provision of state law which establishes, implements, or continues in effect any standard or requirement solely relating to health insurance issuers in connection with health insurance coverage would not be superseded unless the state standard or requirement prevents the application of a federal requirement of this part. Nothing in this part of the Act would affect or modify the provisions of section 514 of ERISA with respect to group health plans.

The conferees intend the narrowest preemption. State laws which are broader than federal requirements would not prevent the application of federal requirements. For example, states may require guaranteed availability of coverage for groups of more than 50 employees, or for groups of 1.

The conference agreement provides special rules in the case of portability requirements. State laws applicable to a preexisting condition exclusion which differ from the standards or requirements specified in this part would be superseded except if they: (1) shorten the lookback period in determination of a preexisting condition limitation (from 6 months to any shorter period of time); (2) shorter the length of a preexisting condition limitation exclusion (from 12 months, or 18 months for late enrollees, to any shorter period); (3) lengthen the break in coverage time from 63 days to any greater number; (4) lengthen the time for enrollment of newborns, or certain children adopted or placed for adoption, from 30 days to any greater number; (5) prohibit the imposition of any preexisting condition exclusions in cases not described, or expand the exclusions described; (6) require additional special enrollment periods; (7) reduce the maximum period permitted in an affiliation period.

A group health plan or health insurance coverage is not required to provide specific benefits other than those provided under the terms of such plan or coverage.

IV. INDIVIDUAL MARKET RULES

Current law

The individual health insurance market is currently regulated by the states. As of December, 1995, 11 states required that individual insurers write policies on a guaranteed issue basis; 16 states required guaranteed renewal; and 22 states limited the use of preexisting condition limitation periods.

House bill

The House bill would provide for federal requirements to guarantee availability of individual health insurance coverage to certain qualified individuals with prior group coverage, without limitation or exclusion of benefits, and to guarantee renewability of individual health insurance coverage.

Senate amendment

Similar.

Conference agreement

The conference agreement provides for federal requirements to guarantee availability of individual health insurance coverage to certain qualified individuals with prior group coverage, without limitation or exclusion of benefits, and to guarantee renewability of individual health insurance coverage.

A. GUARANTEED AVAILABILITY OF INDIVIDUAL HEALTH INSURANCE COVERAGE

Current law

No provision.

House bill

The House bill would include goals that any qualifying individual would be able to obtain qualifying coverage and that qualifying individuals would receive credit for prior coverage toward the new coverage's preexisting condition exclusion period, if any. If states fail to implement programs meeting these goals, a federal fall back requirement would take effect requiring that each individual insurer enroll all eligible individuals and that such persons receive credit for their prior coverage toward any preexisting condition limitation period. (See item IV(D) below on exceptions for network plans and HMOs.)

The House bill would require that any preexisting condition exclusion period be reduced by the length of the aggregate period of qualified prior coverage. To determine qualified coverage, the plan could choose one of two alternatives: (1) it could disregard specific benefits covered and include all periods of coverage from qualified sources; or (2) it could examine prior coverage on a benefit-specific basis, and exclude from qualified coverage any specific benefits not covered under the most recent prior plan. If the second method were chosen, plans would be required to disclose this procedure at the time of enrollment or sale of the plan.

Senate amendment

The Senate Amendment would provide that all health plan issuers that issue or renew individual health plans must enroll all eligible individuals except if the insurer demonstrates that it would have financial problems, or, that its ability to service individuals already enrolled in the plan would diminish if new enrollees were allowed to join the plan. In these cases, the insurer would be prohibited from enrolling new individuals for a period of 6 months, or, if later, when the insurer could demonstrate that they could properly service new entrants. An insurer would have to enroll individuals on a first-come-first-served basis, or other basis determined by the state, to be eligible for this limitation. States implementing guaranteed availability programs meeting certain requirements would be excepted from the federal requirements.

The Senate amendment would provide that a health plan issuer may not impose a limitation or exclusion of benefits on benefits that were covered under prior health plans.

Conference agreement

The conference agreement provides that each health insurance issuer that offers health insurance coverage in the individual market in a state may not decline to offer coverage to, or deny enrollment of an eligible individual and may not impose any preexisting condition exclusions with respect to such coverage. This requirement will not apply in States with acceptable alternative mechanisms as described in section IV(E) below. In addition, in States without an acceptable alternative mechanism, a health insurance issuer may limit the coverage offered as described in section IV(C).

B. QUALIFYING/ELIGIBLE INDIVIDUALS

Current law

No provision.

House bill

The House bill would provide that qualifying individuals are individuals: with 18 or more months of qualified coverage periods; with most recent prior coverage from a group health plan, governmental plan, or church plan; ineligible for group health coverage, Medicare Parts A or B, Medicaid, and without individual coverage; not terminated from most recent prior coverage for nonpayment of premiums or fraud; who, if eligible for continuation coverage under COBRA or similar state program, elected and exhausted this coverage; and who applied for individual coverage not more than 60 days after the last day of coverage under a group plan, or the termination date of COBRA benefits.

Senate amendment

Similar, but individual would have to apply for individual coverage not more than 30 days after the last day of coverage under a group plan.

Conference agreement

The conference agreement defines eligible individuals as individuals: with 18 or more months of aggregate creditable coverage; with most recent prior coverage from a group health plan, governmental plan, or church plan (or health insurance coverage offered in connection with any such plan); ineligible for group health coverage, Medicare Parts A or B, Medicaid (or any successor program), and without any other health insurance coverage; not terminated from their most recent prior coverage for nonpayment of premiums or fraud; and who, if eligible for continuation coverage under COBRA or a similar state program, elected and exhausted this coverage.

C. QUALIFYING COVERAGE

Current law

No provision.

House bill

The House bill would require coverage with an actuarial value of benefits not less than the weighted average actuarial value of the benefits provided by all the individual health insurance coverage (excluding coverage issued under this section) during the previous year, issued by: (1) the insurer or HMO in the state; or (2) all insurers and HMOs in the state. Requires that the actuarial value of benefits be calculated based on a standardized population and a set of standardized utilization and cost factors.

Senate amendment

No provision.

Conference agreement

The conference agreement requires individual health insurance issuers to offer coverage to eligible individuals under all policy forms with exceptions. First, a health insurance issuer may not offer coverage under all policy forms if the state is implementing an acceptable alternative mechanism (see section IV(E) below). If a state is not implementing an acceptable alternative mechanism, the health insurance issuer may elect to limit the policy forms offered to eligible individuals so long as it offers at least two different policy forms of health insurance coverage both of which are designed for, made generally available and actively marketed to, and enroll both eligible and other individuals by the issuer. In addition, the 2 policy forms must meet one of the following: (1) the 2 policy forms have the largest and next to the largest premium volume; or (2) the 2 policy forms are representative of individual health insurance coverage by the issuer. An issuer must apply the election uniformly to all eligible individuals in the state for that issuer, and the election will be effective for policies offered for not less than 2 years.

The 2 representative policy forms would include a lower and higher-level of coverage, each of which has benefits substantially similar to other individual health insurance coverage offered by the issuer in the state. The lower-level policy form would have benefits with an actuarial value at least 85 percent, but not greater than 100 percent of a weighted average benefit. The higher-level policy form would have benefits with an actuarial value: (1) at least 15 percent greater than the actuarial value of the lower-level policy form; and (2) between 100 and 120 percent of the weighted average benefit. Both products must include benefits substantially similar to other individual health insurance coverage offered by the issuer in the state. The weighted average may be either: (1) the average actuarial value of the benefits from individual coverage provided by the issuer; or (2) the average actuarial value of the benefits from individual coverage provided by all issuers in the state. The weighted average will be based on coverage provided during the previous year and exclude coverage of eligible individuals. Actuarial values will be calculated based on a standardized population and a set of standardized utilization and cost factors.

Network plans may limit coverage to those who live, reside, or work within the service area for the network plan. Within the service area for the plan, the issuer may deny coverage to individuals if the issuer has demonstrated, if required, to the applicable state authority that it will not have the capacity to deliver services adequately to additional individual enrollees. Denial must be made uniformly to individuals without regard to any health status-related factor and without regard to whether the individuals are eligible individuals. Upon denial, the issuer may not offer coverage in the individual market within the service area for 180 days. Similar rules apply for financial capacity limits.

D. GUARANTEED RENEWAL

Current law

No provision.

House bill

The House bill would require that individual coverage is renewable at the option of the individual except for: nonpayment; fraud; termination of all individual coverage by the insurer or HMO, or termination of coverage in a geographic area in the case of network or HMO plans; movement of the individual outside the insurer's service area; termination of the particular type of coverage by the insurer or HMO, after the insurer has provided 90 day notice, offered the option to purchase any other coverage, and acted without regard to health status or insurability; discontinuation of all individual coverage by the insurer or HMO, after 180 days notice; uniform modification of all health plans within the individual's type of coverage.

Senate amendment

The Senate Amendment would require that individual coverage is renewable at the option of the individual except for: nonpayment; fraud; termination of the particular type of coverage by the insurer or HMO, which has provided 90 day notice, offered the option to purchase any other coverage, and acted without regard to health status or insurability; termination of all individual coverage by the insurer or HMO, after 180 days notice, and prohibition against market re-entry for 5 years; change such that the individual lives or works outside the insurer's service area but only if denial of coverage is applied uniformly without regard to the health status or insurability of the individual.

Conference agreement

The conference agreement provides that a health insurance issuer that provides individual health insurance coverage to an individual must renew or continue in force such coverage at the option of the individual. It provides exceptions to the guaranteed renewability requirement for one or more of the following: (1) nonpayment of premiums or untimely payment; (2) fraud; (3) termination of coverage in the market (as outlined below) in accordance with applicable state law; (4) for network plans, the individual no longer lives, resides, or works in the service area of the issuer, or area for which the issuer is authorized to do business but only if coverage is terminated uniformly without regard to any health status-related factor; (5) for coverage made available to bona fide associations, if membership in the association ceases, but only if the coverage is terminated uniformly without regard to any health status-related factor.

An issuer may discontinue a particular type of coverage in the individual market only if the issuer: (1) provides prior notice to each covered individual; (2) offers each individual the option to purchase any other individual health insurance coverage offered by the issuer for individuals; and (3) acts uniformly without regard to any health status-related factor of enrolled individuals or individuals who may become eligible for such coverage. An issuer may elect to discontinue offering all health insurance coverage in the individual market in a state only if certain conditions are met. In this case, the issuer could not issue coverage in the market and state involved for 5 years. Issuers could modify the health insurance coverage for a policy form offered to individuals in the individual market so long as the modification was consistent with state law and was effective on a uniform basis among all individuals with that policy form.

In the case of health insurance coverage that is made available by a health insurance issuer in the individual market to individuals only through one or more associations, the issuer would be required to meet the Act's requirements related to individuals.

Health insurance issuers in the individual market must provide certifications of coverage in the same manner as health insurance issuers in the small group market.

E. OPTIONAL STATE PROGRAMS/STATE FLEXIBILITY

1. In general

Current law

No provision.

House bill.

The House bill would provide that a state may establish public or private mechanisms to meet the goals of guaranteed availability of coverage. The chief executive officer of the state must notify the Secretary of HHS if the state elects to use state mechanisms. Under a state mechanism, a state may define qualified coverage as coverage with benefits not less than the weighted average actuarial value of the benefits provided by all the individual health insurance coverage (excluding coverage issued under this section) during the previous year, issued by: the insurer or HMO in the state; or all insurers and HMOs in the state. The state may elect to establish qualified coverage for all insurers and HMOs in the state after it has established qualified coverage for each insurer or HMO.

State mechanisms could include one or more, or a combination of: health insurance coverage pools or programs authorized or established by the state; mandatory group conversion policies; guaranteed issue of one or more plans; or open enrollment by one or more insurers or HMOs. This list is not exclusive.

A state with a health insurance coverage pool or risk pool in effect on March 12, 1996, which offers qualified coverage, would automatically be considered to have met the Federal access objectives.

In general, states would have until July 1, 1997 to implement a state program. States without a regular legislative session between January 1, 1997 and June 30, 1997 would have a deadline of July 1, 1998.

Senate amendment

Similar. The Senate Amendment would provide that a state may adopt alternative public or private mechanisms to provide access to affordable health benefits for eligible individuals. The Governor of the state must notify the Secretary of Health and Human Services that the state has adopted an alternative mechanism which achieves the goals of portability and renewability, and that the state intends to implement this mechanism.

State mechanisms could include guaranteed issue, open enrollment by one or more health plan issuers, high-risk pools, mandatory conversion policies, or any combination of these mechanisms. A state high risk pool would meet the portability and renewability requirements if it is: (a) open to eligible individuals; (b) limits preexisting condition waiting periods; and (c) is consistent with premium rates and covered benefits in the National Association of Insurance Commissioners (NAIC) Model Health Plan for Uninsurable Individuals Act. States which adopt a NAIC model act, including group to individual market portability provisions that meet the Federal portability and renewability goals, would not be subject to federal rules.

A state may notify the Secretary, within 6 months after enactment of this Act, that state alternate mechanism(s) would meet portability and renewability goals. The Secretary would not determine if the state mechanism meets the goals until 12 months after the initial state notification, or January 1, 1998, whichever is later. The Secretary would not make a determination until January 1, 1999 for states without legislative sessions within the 12 months after enactment of this Act.

Conference agreement

The conference agreement provides that a state may implement an acceptable alternative mechanism that is designed to provide access to health benefits for individuals. This mechanism must: (1) provide a choice of health insurance coverage to all eligible individuals; (2) not impose any preexisting condition exclusions; and (3) include at least one policy form of coverage that is comparable to either comprehensive health insurance coverage offered in the individual market in the state or a standard option of coverage available under the group or individual health insurance laws in the state. If a state elects to implement the following mechanisms, the state must also meet the preceding requirements. These mechanisms are: (1) the NAIC Small Employer and Individual Health Insurance Availability Model Act (as it applies to individual health insurance coverage) or the Individual Health Insurance Portability Model Act; (2) a qualified high risk pool that meets certain specified requirements; or (3) other mechanisms that provide for risk adjustment, risk spreading, or a risk spreading mechanism (by an issuer or among issuers or policies of an issuer), or otherwise provide some financial subsidies for participating insurers or eligible individuals, or, alternatively, a mechanism under which each eligible individual is provided a choice of all individual health insurance coverage otherwise available.

Examples of potential alternative mechanisms include health insurance coverage pools or programs, mandatory group conversion policies, guaranteed issue of one or more plans of individual health insurance coverage, or open enrollment by one or more health insurance issuers, or a combination of such mechanisms.

A state is presumed to be implementing an acceptable alternative mechanism as of January 1, 1998, by not later than July 1, 1997, the chief executive officer of the state notifies the Secretary that the state has enacted any necessary legislation as of January 1, 1998 and provides the Secretary with information needed to review the mechanism and its implementation, or proposed implementation. The state must provide this information to the Secretary every 3 years to continue to be presumed to have an acceptable alternative mechanism. If a state submits notice and information after July 1, 1997, and the Secretary makes no determination within 90 days, the mechanism will be considered acceptable after 90 days.

F. CONSTRUCTION/PREEMPTION

Current law

No provision.

House bill

The House bill would provide that states are not prevented from: (1) implementing guaranteed availability mechanisms before the deadline; (2) continuing state mechanisms that were in effect before the enactment of this Act; (3) offering guaranteed availability of coverage that is not qualifying coverage; or (4) offering guaranteed availability of coverage to individuals who are not qualifying individuals

Senate amendment

The Senate Amendment would provide that states are not required to replace or dissolve high risk pools or other similar state mechanisms which are designed to provide individuals in those states with access to health benefits.

Conference agreement

The conference agreement provides that nothing in this part would prevent a state from establishing, implementing, or continuing in effect standards and requirements unless they prevent the application of a requirement in this part. Nothing in this part would affect or modify the provisions of section 514 of ERISA.

G. FEDERAL RULES (FALLBACK OR IN ABSENCE OF STATE ALTERNATIVE)

Current law

No provision.

House bill

The House bill would provide that the Secretary of HHS notify a state that federal rules would apply if: (1) the state has not elected to use a state mechanism; or (2) if the Secretary finds, after consultation with state officials, that the state mechanism would not meet the federal availability goals, and the state has had reasonable opportunity to change or implement a state mechanism to meet the goals.

Federal rules would provide that each insurer or HMO which issues individual health insurance coverage in the state would have to offer qualifying coverage to qualifying individuals, and credit prior coverage toward any preexisting condition exclusion periods. In addition, no individual could be refused coverage based on health status. Network plans or HMOs could refuse coverage to individuals who did not reside or work in the plan's service area, or if network or financial capacity limits would be exceeded. Federal rules would cease to apply if the state implements a mechanism designed to meet the federal goals of availability.

Senate amendment

The Senate Amendment would provide that Federal standards would apply if the state does not notify the Secretary of HHS of its intent to implement state mechanisms, or if the Secretary finds that the state mechanism fails to: (1) offer coverage to eligible individuals; (2) prohibit preexisting condition limitations or exclusions for benefits covered under previous health plans; (3) offer eligible individuals a choice of individual health plans, including at least one comprehensive plan, or a plan comparable to a standard option plan available under the group or individual health insurance laws of the state; or (4) implement a risk spreading mechanism, cross subsidy mechanism, risk adjustment mechanism, rating limitation or other mechanism designed to reduce the variation in costs of coverage for eligible individuals and other plans offered by the carrier or available in the state.

The bill would waive the requirement for a risk spreading mechanism if all individual health plans available in the market are also available to eligible individuals.

It would provide that if the Secretary determines that the state alternative mechanism fails to meet the above criteria, or if the state mechanism is no longer being implemented, the Secretary would have to notify the Governor of the failure to meet the goals of portability and renewability, and permit the state to come into compliance. Federal individual health plan portability rules would apply if the state still does not meet these criteria. Under these rules, a plan issuer could not, with respect to an eligible individual, decline to offer coverage to or deny enrollment of the individual or impose a limitation or exclusion of benefits, otherwise available under the plan, for which coverage was available under the group health plan or employee health benefit plan in which the person was previously enrolled. (This would not prevent a health plan issuer from establishing premium discounts or modifying otherwise applicable copayments or deductibles in return for adherence to programs of health promotion or disease prevention.)

Future adoptions of a state mechanism would be subject to the same procedures of: (1) notification of the Secretary; and (2) determination of satisfaction of criteria for compliance, except in the cases of adoption of the NAIC model or high risk pool.

Conference agreement

The conference agreement provides that if the Secretary finds that the state mechanism is not acceptable or is no longer being implemented, the Secretary must notify the state of the preliminary determination and consequences of failure to implement an acceptable mechanism. The state will have a reasonable opportunity to modify the mechanism, or adopt a new mechanism. If the Secretary finds that the state mechanism is not acceptable, or is not being implemented, the Secretary must notify the state of the effective date of federal requirements for guaranteed availability. Each issuer would then be required to guarantee issue health insurance coverage to any individual, but could limit coverage to 2 policy forms as outlined in section IV(C) above. Secretarial authority would be limited to determinations based only on whether a state mechanism is not an acceptable alternative mechanism or is not being implemented. It is the intent of Congress that the risk adjustment, risk spreading, risk spreading mechanism and financial subsidization standards provide meaningful financial protection and assistance for eligible individuals, both in the case of a state alternative system and alternative coverage provided under section 2741(c).

H. CONSTRUCTION (PREMIUMS, MARKET REQUIREMENTS, ASSOCIATION COVERAGE AND MARKETING)

Current law

No provision.

House bill

The House bill would provide that insurers or HMOs are free to determine the premiums for individual health insurance coverage under applicable state law. Insurers or HMOs which only insure groups or associations would not be required to offer individual health insurance coverage. Insurers or HMOs that offer conversion policies in connection with a group health plan would not be required to offer individual coverage. Insurers or HMOs that offer coverage only in connection with a group health plan or in connection with individuals based on affiliation with one or more bona fide associations would not be considered to be offering individual coverage.

A state could require that insurers or HMOs offering individual coverage actively market this coverage.

Senate bill

The Senate Amendment is similar but did not include a provision relating to associations.

215

Conference agreement

Premiums that an issuer may charge an individual for individual health insurance coverage are not restricted by the conference agreement, but must comply with state law. The health insurance issuer may establish premium discounts or rebates, or modify otherwise applicable copayments or deductibles in return for adherence to programs of health promotion and disease prevention.

Under the conference agreement, health insurance issuers offering health insurance coverage in connection with group health plans, or through one or more bona fide associations, or both, are not required to offer health insurance coverage in the individual market. A health insurance issuer offering group health coverage is not considered to be a health insurance issuer offering individual health insurance coverage solely because the issuer offers a conversion policy.

I. ENFORCEMENT OF REQUIREMENTS ON INDIVIDUAL INSURERS, HMO'S, AND HEALTH PLAN ISSUERS

Current law

Under section 502 of ERISA, employee benefit plans that fail to comply with applicable requirements can be sued for relief and be subject to civil money penalties, and can be sued to recover any benefits due under the plan. Section 504 of ERISA provides the Secretary of Labor with investigative authority to determine whether any person is out of compliance with the law's requirements. Section 506 provides for coordination and responsibility of agencies in enforcement. Section 510 prohibits a health plan from discriminating against a participant or beneficiary for exercising any right under the plan.

House bill

Noncomplying insurers and HMOs would be subject to enforcement through federal civil money penalties (in the same manner as imposed above (see item II(G)) but only in the event that the Secretary of HHS has determined that the state in which the insurer or HMO is selling coverage is not providing for enforcement.

Senate amendment

Noncomplying individual health plans offered by a health plan issuer would be subject to state enforcement. Each state would require each individual health plan issued, sold, renewed, or offered for sale or operated in the state by a health plan issuer to meet the Act's standards pursuant to an enforcement plan filed with the Secretary of Labor. The state would be required to submit such information as required by the Secretary demonstrating effective implementation of the enforcement plan. In the event that the state failed to substantially enforce the Act's standards and requirements, the Secretary of Labor, in consultation with the Secretary of HHS, would implement an enforcement plan. Issuers would then be subject to civil enforcement as provided under sections 502, 504, 506 and 510 of ERISA. The Secretary of Labor could issue such regulations as needed to carry out this Act.

Conference agreement

Each state may require health insurance issuers that issue, sell, renew, or offer health insurance coverage in the individual market to meet the requirements under this part with respect to such issuers. If a state fails to substantially enforce the federal requirements, the Secretary will provide enforcement in the same manner as in the small group market (see section II(G) above).

V. Multiple Employer Pooling Arrangements

A. Clarification of Duty of the Secretary of Labor to Implement Current Law Providing for Exemptions from State Regulation of Multiple Employer Health Plans (MEHPS)

Current law

Section 3(40) of ERISA defines a multiple employer welfare benefit plan, or any other arrangement which offers or provides health benefits and meets additional criteria, (e.g., it must offer such benefits to the employees of 2 or more employers and cannot be a plan established under a collective bargaining agreement, a rural electric cooperative, or rural telephone cooperative association). Two or more trades or businesses, whether or not incorporated, are deemed a single employer and thus not a MEWA if such trades or businesses are within the same control group.

Section 514 of ERISA treats fully-insured MEWAs differently from those that are not fully-insured (i.e., that are partly or fully-self-insured). With respect to a fully-insured MEWA, a state may apply and enforce its insurance laws (section 514(b)(6)(A)(i)). With respect to a not-fully-insured MEWA, a state may apply and enforce its insurance laws so long as such laws or regulations are not inconsistent with ERISA (section 514(b)(6)(A)(ii). Section 514(b)(6)(B) provides that the Department of Labor (DOL) may issue an exemption from state law with respect to non-fully-insured MEWAs. (No such exemptions have been issued.)

House bill

The House bill would add a new Part 7 (Rules Governing State Regulation of Multiple Employer Health Plans) to Title I of ERISA.

It would define the following terms: insurer, fully-insured, HMO, participating employer, sponsor, and state insurance commissioner. The House bill would define a multiple employer health plan as a MEWA which provides medical care and which is or has been exempt under section 514(b)(6)(B) of ERISA.

The bill clarifies the conditions under which multiple employer health plans (MEHPs)—non-fully-insured multiple employer arrangements providing medical care—may apply for an exemption from certain state laws. It provides that only certain legitimate association health plans and other arrangements (described below) which are not fully insured are eligible for an exemption. This is accomplished by clarifying the duty of the Secretary of Labor to implement the provisions of current law section 514(b)(6)(B) to provide exemption from state law for MEHPS.

The bill would establish criteria which a not fully-insured arrangement must meet to qualify for an exemption and thus become a MEHP. The Secretary could grant an exemption to an arrangement only if: (1) a complete application has been filed, accompanied by the filing fee of $5,000; (2) the application demonstrates compliance with requirements established in new sections 703 and 704 described below; (3) the Secretary finds that the exemption is administratively feasible, not adverse to the interests of the individuals covered under it, and protective of the rights and benefits of the individuals covered under the arrangement, and (4) all other terms of the exemption are met (including financial, actuarial, reporting, participation, and such other requirements as may be specified as a condition of the exemption). The application must include: (1) identifying information about the arrangement and the states in which it will operate; (2) evidence that ERISA's bonding requirements will be met; (3) copies of all plan documents and agreements with service providers; (4) a funding report indicating that the reserve requirements of new section 705 will be met, that contribution rates will be adequate to cover obligations, and that a qualified actuary (a member in good standing of the American Academy of Actuaries or an actuary meeting such other standards the Secretary considers adequate) has issued an opinion with respect to the arrangement's assets, liabilities, and projected costs; and (5) any other information prescribed by the Secretary. Exempt arrangements must notify the Secretary of any material changes in this information at any time, must file annual reports with the Secretary, and must engage a qualified actuary.

In addition, the bill would provide for a *class exemption* from section 514(b)(6)(B)(ii) of ERISA for large MEHPs that have been in operation for at least five years on the date of enactment. An arrangement would qualify for this class exemption if, in addition to all other requirements: (1) at the time of application for exemption; the arrangement covers at least 1,000 participants and beneficiaries, or has at least 2,000 employees of eligible participating employers ; (2) a complete application has been filed and is pending; and (3) the application meets requirements established by the Secretary with respect to class exemptions. Class exemptions would be treated as having been granted with respect to the arrangement unless the Secretary provide appropriate notice that the exemption has been denied.

1. Requirements relating to MEHP sponsors, board of trustees, plan operations, and covered persons

The House bill would establish eligibility requirements for MEHPs. Applications must comply with requirements established by the Secretary. They must demonstrate that the arrangement's sponsor has been in existence for a continuous period of at least 5 years and is organized and maintained in good faith, with a constitution and by laws specifically starting its purpose and providing for at least annual meetings, as a trade association, an industry association, a professional association, or a chamber of commerce (or similar business group, including a corporation or similar organization that operates on a cooperative basis within the meaning of section 1381 of the IRC) for purposes other than that of obtaining or providing medical care. Also, the applicant must demonstrate that the sponsor is established as a permanent entity, has the active support of its members, and collects dues from its members without conditioning such on the basis of the health status or claims experience of plan participants or beneficiaries or on the basis of the member's participation in the MEHP.

The bill would require that the arrangement be operated, pursuant to a trust agreement, by a "board of trustees" which has complete fiscal control and which is responsible for all operations of the arrangement. The board of trustees must develop rules of operation and financial control based on a three-year plan of operation which is adequate to carry out the terms of the arrangement and to meet all applicable requirements of the exemption and Title I of ERISA.

With respect to covered persons, the bill would require that all employers who are association members be eligible for participation under the terms of the plan. Eligible individuals of such participating employers cannot be excluded from enrolling in the plan because of health status (as required under section 103 of the Act as described in item I-(B) above). The rules also stipulate that premium rates established under the plan with respect to any particular participating employer cannot be based on the claims experience of the particular employer.

2. Additional entities eligible to be MEHPs

In addition to the associations described above, certain other entities would be provided eligibility to seek an exemption as MEHPs under section 514(b)(6)(B). These include (1) franchise networks (section 703(b)), (2) certain existing collectively bargained arrangements which fail to meet the statutory exemption criteria (section 703(c)), and (3) certain arrangements not meeting the statutory exemption criteria for single employer plans (section 703(d)). (Section 709 of ERISA, added by section 166 of this subtitle, also makes eligible certain church plans electing to seek an exemption.)

3. Other requirements for exemption

The House bill would require a MEHP to meet the following additional requirements: (1) its governing instruments must provide that the board of trustees serves as the named fiduciary and plan administrator, that the sponsor serves as plan sponsor, and that the reserve requirements of new section 705 are met; (2) the contribution rates must be adequate, and (3) any other requirements set out in regulations by the Secretary of Labor must be met.

4. Maintenance of reserves

The House bill would require that MEHPs establish and maintain reserves sufficient for unearned contributions, benefit liabilities incurred but not yet satisfied, and for which risk of loss has not been transferred, expected administrative costs, and any other obligations and margin for error recommended by the qualified actuary. The minimum reserves must be no less than 25% of expected incurred claims and expenses for the year or $400,000, whichever is greater. The Secretary may provide additional requirements relating to reserves and excess/stop loss coverage and may provide adjustments to the levels of reserves otherwise required to take into account excess/stop loss coverage or other financial arrangements. The bill provides for an alternative means of compliance in which the Secretary could permit an arrangement to substitute, for all or part of the requirements of this section, such security, guarantee, hold-harmless arrangement, or other financial arrangement as the Secretary of Labor determined to be adequate to enable the arrangement to fully meet its financial obligations on a timely basis.

5. Notice requirements for voluntary termination

The House bill would provide that, except as permitted in new section 707 below, a MEHP may terminate only if the board of trustees provides 60 days advance written notice to participants and beneficiaries and submits to the Secretary a plan providing for timely payment of all benefit obligations.

6. Corrective actions and mandatory termination

The House bill would require a MEHP to continue to meet the reserve requirements even if its exemption is no longer in effect. The board of trustees must quarterly determine whether the reserve requirements of new section 705 (as described above) are being met and, if they are not, must, in consultation with the qualified actuary, develop a plan to ensure compliance and report such information to the Secretary. In any case where a MEHP notifies the Secretary that it has failed to meet the reserve requirements and corrective action has not restored compliance, and the Secretary of Labor determines that the failure will result in a continuing failure to pay benefit obligations, the Secretary may direct the board to terminate the arrangement and take action needed to ensure that the arrangement's affairs are resolved in a manner which will result in timely provision of all benefits for which the arrangement is obligated.

7. Temporary application of state laws

a. Provides for exclusion of arrangements from the small group market in any state upon the state's certification of guaranteed access to health insurance coverage in such state (i.e, state opt-out). Provides that a state which certifies to the Secretary that it provides guaranteed access to health coverage may deny a MEHP the right to offer coverage in the small group market (or otherwise regulate such MEHP with respect to such coverage), except as described below. The certification triggering the state opt-out could be in effect no longer than 3 years.

A state is considered to provide such guaranteed access, if (1) the state certifies that at least 90% of all state residents are covered by a group health plan or otherwise have health insurance coverage, or (2) the state has, in the small group market, provided for guaranteed issue of at least one standard benefits package and for rating reforms designed to make health insurance coverage more affordable. In states without such guaranteed access, MEHPs could offer coverage in the small group market in the state as long as they met the standards set forth in Part 7 (as established by this subtitle).

b. Provides for exceptions to the exclusion of MEHPs from state small group markets. Provides a limited exception to the state opt out for certain large, multi-state arrangements. The State opt out would not apply to new and existing MEHPs that meet the following criteria: (1) the sponsor operates in a majority of the 50 states and in at least 2 of the regions of the country; (2) the arrangement covers or will cover at least 7,500 participants and beneficiaries; and (30 at the time the application to become a MEHP is filed, the arrangement does not have pending against it any enforcement action by the state. In addition, the state opt out would not apply in a state in which an arrangement meeting the MEHP standards operates on March 6, 1996, to the extent a state enforcement action is not pending against such an entity at the time an application for an exemption is made.

The above two exceptions do not apply to any state which, as of January 1, 1996, either (1) has enacted a law providing for guaranteed issue of fully community rated individual health insurance coverage offered by insurers and HMOs, or (2) requires insurers offering group health coverage to reimburse insurers offering individual coverage for losses resulting from their offering individual coverage on an open enrollment basis. Regulations may also provide for an exemption to the application of state law for certain single industry plans.

c. Premium tax assessment authority with respect to new arrangements. Provides that a state could assess new association-based MEHPs (formed after March 6, 1996) nondiscriminatory state premium taxes set at a rate no greater than that applicable to any insurer or health maintenance organization offering health insurance coverage in the state. MEHPs existing as of March 6, 1996 would remain exempt from state premium taxes. However, if they expanded into a new state, the state could apply the above rule.

Senate amendment

No provision.

Conference agreement

The conference agreement does not include the House provision.

VI. State Authority Over Non-Exempt MEWAs

Current law

Under section 514(6)(A) of ERISA, a state may apply and enforce state insurance laws with respect to a MEWA so long as the law or regulation is not inconsistent with ERISA.

House bill

The House bill would provide that states have the authority under ERISA to regulate without limitation non-fully-insured MEWAs which are not provided an exemption under new Part 7 of ERISA (see item V above). In other words, states can continue to regulate MEWAs that are not MEHPs.

Senate amendment

No provision.

Conference agreement

The conference agreement does not include the House provision.

VII. ADDITIONAL MEWA AND RELATED PROVISIONS

A. CLARIFICATION OF TREATMENT OF SINGLE-EMPLOYER ARRANGEMENTS

Current law

Section 3(40) of ERISA defines a MEWA and specifies the conditions under which two or more trades or businesses shall be deemed a single employer, if such trades or businesses are within the same control group. Common control could not be based on an interest of less than 25%.

House bill

The House bill would modify the treatment of certain single employer arrangements under section 3(40) of ERISA. The treatment of a single employer plan as being excluded from the definition of a MEWA (and thus from state law) is clarified by defining the minimum interest required for two or more entities to be in "common control" as a percentage which cannot be required to be greater than 25%. Also a plan would be considered a single employer plan if less than 25% of the covered employees are employed by other participating employers.

Senate amendment

No provision.

Conference agreement

The conference agreement does not include the House provision.

B. CLARIFICATION OF TREATMENT OF CERTAIN COLLECTIVELY-BARGAINED ARRANGEMENTS

Current law

Under section 3(40) of ERISA, a MEWA is defined not to include any plan or arrangement which is established or maintained under or pursuant to one or more agreements which the Secretary finds to be collective bargaining agreements, or by a rural electric cooperative. (No such Secretarial finding has ever been issued).

House bill

The House bill would establish the conditions under which multiemployer and other collectively-bargained arrangements are exempted from the MEWA definition, and thus exempt from state law. Amends the definition of a MEWA to exclude a plan or arrangement which is established or maintained under or pursuant to a collective bargaining arrangement (as described in the National Labor Relations Act, the Railway Labor Act, and similar state public employee relations laws). It then specifies additional conditions which must be met for such a plan to be a statutorily excluded collectively bargained arrangement and thus not a MEWA.

These conditions include: (1) The plan cannot utilize the services of any licensed insurance agent or broker to solicit or enroll employers or pay a commission or other form of compensation to certain persons that is related to the volume or number of employers or individuals solicited or enrolled in the plan; (2) a maximum 15 percent rule applies to the number of covered individuals in the plan who are not employees (or their beneficiaries) within a bargaining unit covered by any of the collective bargaining agreements with a participating employer or who are not present or former employees (or their beneficiaries) of sponsoring employee organizations or employers who are or were a party to any of the collective bargaining agreements (provides for a higher maximum in the case of certain plans or arrangements in existence as of the date of enactment); and (3) the employee organization or other entity sponsoring the plan or arrangement must certify annually to the Secretary the plan has met the previous requirements.

If the plan or arrangement is not fully insured, it must be a multiemployer plan meeting specific requirements of the Labor Management Relations Act (i.e., the requirement for joint labor-management trusteeship under section 302(c)(5)(B)).

If the plan or arrangement is not in effect as of the date of enactment, the employee organization or other entity sponsoring the plan or arrangement must have existed for at least 3 years or have been affiliated with another employee organization in existence for at least 3 years, or demonstrates to the Secretary that certain of the above requirements have been met.

Senate amendment

No provision.

Conference agreement

The conference agreement does not include the House provision.

C. TREATMENT OF CHURCH PLANS

Current law

Section 4(b)(2) of ERISA exempts from its requirements church plans that do not elect to participate in qualified pension plans under the IRC.

House bill

The House bill would add a new section 709 to ERISA treating certain church plans (including a church, convention or association of churches or similar organization) as a MEWA and permitting such plans to voluntarily elect to apply to the Department of Labor for an exemption from state laws that would otherwise apply to a MEWA under section 514(b)(6)(B) and in accordance with new ERISA Part 7. An exempted church plan would, with certain exceptions, have to comply with the provisions of ERISA Title I in order to receive an exception from state law. The election to be covered by ERISA would be irrevocable. A church plan is covered under this section if the plan provides benefits which include medical care and some or all of the benefits are not fully insured. (Certain provisions of ERISA, such as its COBRA continuation coverage requirements, would not apply to the church plans described herein.)

Senate amendment

No provision.

Conference agreement

The conference agreement does not include the House provision.

D. ENFORCEMENT PROVISIONS RELATING TO MEWAS

Current law

MEWAs are subject to ERISA's enforcement and other provisions of title I.

House bill

The House bill would amend ERISA to establish enforcement provisions relating to the multiple employer elements of the bill: (1) a civil penalty would apply for failure of MEWAs to file registration statements; (2) state enforcement would be authorized through Federal courts with respect to violations by multiple employer health plans, subject to the existence of enforcement agreements between the states and the federal government; (3) willful misrepresentation that an entity is an exempted MEWA or collectively-bargained arrangement could result in criminal penalties; (4) cease activity orders could be issued for arrangements found to be neither licensed, registered, or otherwise approved under State insurance law, or operating in accordance with the terms of an exemption granted by the Secretary under new part 7; and (5) provides that each MEHP require its fiduciary or board of trustees to comply with the required claims procedure under ERISA.

Senate amendment

No provision.

Conference agreement

The conference agreement does not include the House provision.

E. COOPERATION BETWEEN FEDERAL AND STATE AUTHORITIES

Current law

Section 506 of ERISA provides for coordination between the Department of Labor and other federal agencies in the enforcement of ERISA. The Secretary is authorized to use the facilities or services of the states, with the consent of the affected departments, agencies, or establishments in enforcing ERISA.

House bill

The House bill would amend section 506 of ERISA to specify State responsibility with respect to self-insured MEHPs and voluntary health insurance associations (VHIAs). A State could enter into an agreement with the Secretary for delegation to the State of some or all of the Secretary's authority to enforce provisions of ERISA applicable to exempted MEHPs or to VHIAs. The Secretary would be required to enter into the agreement if the Secretary determined that delegation to the State would not result in a lower level or quality of enforcement. However, if the Secretary delegated authority to a State, the Secretary could continue to exercise such authority concurrently with the State. The Secretary would be required to provide enforcement assistance to the States with respect to MEWAs.

Senate amendment

No provision.

Conference agreement

The conference agreement does not include the House provision.

F. FILING AND DISCLOSURE REQUIREMENTS FOR MEWAs OFFERING HEALTH BENEFITS

Current law

ERISA provides for certain reporting and disclosure requirements.

House bill

The reporting and disclosure requirements of ERISA would be amended to require MEWAs offering health benefits to file with the Secretary a registration statement within 60 days before beginning operations (for those starting on or after January 1, 1997) and no later than February 15 of each year. In addition, MEWAs providing medical care would be required to issue to participating employers certain information including summary plan descriptions, contribution rates, and the status of the arrangement (whether fully-insured or an exempted self-insured plan).

Senate amendment

No provision.

Conference agreement

The conference agreement does not include the House provision.

G. SINGLE ANNUAL FILING FOR ALL PARTICIPATING EMPLOYERS

Current law

Section 110 of ERISA provides for alternative methods of compliance with reporting and disclosure requirements to those specified in previous sections of the law.

House bill

This section would amend ERISA's section 110 to provide for a single annual filing for all participating employers of fully insured MEWAs.

Senate amendment

No provision.

Conference agreement

The conference agreement does not include the House provision.

H. EFFECTIVE DATES/TRANSITION RULES

Current law

No provision.

House bill

The House bill would provide that in general, the amendments made by this title would be effective January 1, 1998. In addition, the Secretary would be required to issue all regulations needed to carry out the amendments before January 1, 1998.

The bill would provide for transition rules for self-insured MEWAs which meet the requirements of Part 7 and which are in operation as of the effective date so that those applying to the Secretary for an exemption from State regulation are deemed to be excluded for a period not to exceed 18 months unless the Secretary denies the exemption or finds the MEWAs application deficient, provided that the arrangement does not have pending against it an enforcement action by a state. The Secretary could revoke the exemption at any time if it would be detrimental to the interests of individuals covered under the Act.

Senate amendment

No provision.

Conference agreement

The conference agreement does not include the House provision.

VIII. VOLUNTARY HEALTH INSURANCE ASSOCIATIONS/HEALTH PLAN PURCHASING COOPERATIVES (HPPCs)

Current law

While the states regulate insurance sold to purchasing cooperatives, a purchasing cooperative that is also a MEWA is also regulated under ERISA. Under ERISA, a state may apply and enforce its insurance laws with respect to fully-insured MEWAs.

As of December 1995, 15 states had enacted laws relating to voluntary purchasing alliances/cooperatives.

House bill

The House bill would add a new subsection (d) to section 514 of ERISA defining under ERISA voluntary health insurance associations and establishing federal requirements for such associations. Associations meeting these requirements would be exempt from specific state laws.

Senate amendment

The Senate Amendment would provide for limited exemptions from state laws for health insurance purchasing cooperatives that meet the requirements established by this section.

Conference agreement

The conference agreement does not include the House or Senate provision.

A. DEFINITIONS/NATURE OF ORGANIZATION

Current law

No provision.

House bill

The House bill would define a voluntary health insurance association as a multiple employer welfare arrangement, maintained by a qualified association, under which all medical benefits are fully-insured, under which no employer is excluded as a participating employer (subject to minimum participation requirements of an insurer), under which the enrollment requirements of section 103 of the Act apply (see item II above), under which all health insurance coverage options are aggressively marketed, and under which the health insurance coverage is provided by an insurer or HMO to which the laws of the state in which it operates apply.

A qualified association would be an association in which the sponsor of the association is, and has been (together with its immediate predecessor, if any) for a continuous period of not less than 5 years, organized and maintained in good faith, with a constitution and bylaws specifically stating its purpose, as a trade association, an industry association, a professional association, or a chamber of commerce (or similar business group), for substantial purposes other than that of obtaining or providing medical care, is established as a permanent entity which receives the active support of its members and meets at least annually, and collects dues without conditioning such dues on the basis of the health status or claims experience of plan participants or beneficiaries or on the basis of participation in a VHIA.

A "small employer" would be defined as one who employs at least 2 but fewer than 51 employees on a typical business day in the year.

Senate amendment

The Senate Amendment would define a "health plan purchasing cooperative" or HPPC to mean a group of employees or a group of individuals and employers that, on a voluntary basis and in accordance with this section, form a cooperative for the purpose of purchasing an individual health plan or group health plans offered by health plan issuers.

An HPPC could not: (a) perform any activity relating to the licensing of health plan issuers; (b) assume financial risk directly or indirectly (that is, it would have to be fully-insured); (c) establish eligibility, enrollment, or premium contribution requirements for individual participants or beneficiaries based on health status, medical condition, claims experience, receipt of health care, medical history, evidence of insurability, genetic information, or disability; (d) operate on a for-profit or other basis where the legal structure of the cooperative permits profits to be made and not returned to the members of the cooperative, or (e) perform any other activities that conflict or are inconsistent with the performance of its duties under this Act. A for-profit cooperative could be formed by a non-profit organization or organizations in which: (1) membership in such organization is not based on health status, medical condition, claims experience, receipt of health care, medical history, evidence of insurability, genetic information, or disability and (2) that accepts as members all employers or individuals on a first-come, first-serve basis, subject to any established limit on the maximum size of an employer that may become a member.

Conference agreement

The conference agreement does not include the House or Senate provision.

B. CERTIFICATION

Current law

No provision.

House bill

No provision.

Senate agreement

The Senate Amendment would provide that a state certify a group as a HPPC if it appropriately notifies the state and the Secretary of Labor that it wants to form a HPPC under the requirements of this section. The state would be required to determine in a timely fashion whether the group is in compliance with the section's requirements and to oversee the operations of the HPPC to ensure continued compliance with the requirements. Each certified HPPC would have to register with the Secretary of Labor.

If a state failed to implement a HPPC certification program in accordance with this Act's standards, the Secretary of Labor would certify and oversee the HPPCs in that state.

However, the Secretary would not certify a HPPC if, upon submission of an application of the state to the Secretary, the Secretary determined that a state law was in effect on the date of enactment of this Act providing that all small employers in the state had a means readily available that ensured: (a) that individuals and employees had a choice of multiple, unaffiliated health plan issuers; (b) that health plan coverage was subject to state premium rating requirements that were not based on the health and other risk factors described above and that contained a mandatory minimum loss ratio; (c) that comparative health plan materials were disseminated (including information about cost, quality, benefits, and other information); and that (d) the state program otherwise met the objectives of this Act.

A HPPC operating in more than one state would be certified by the state in which the cooperative was domiciled. States could enter into cooperative agreements for the purpose of overseeing a HPPC's operation. A HPPC would be considered to be domiciled in the state in which most of the members of the HPPC reside.

Conference agreement

The conference agreement does not include the Senate provision.

C. STRUCTURE AND RESPONSIBILITIES OF ORGANIZATION

Current law

No provision.

House bill

The House bill would provide that VHIAs and qualified associations meet certain conditions (described in items VIII(A) and VIII(D)) to qualify as a VHIA and therefore for exemption from state insurance laws.

Senate amendment

The Senate Amendment would provide for the following requirements for HPPCs:

I. Board of Directors.—Requires each HPPC to be governed by a board of directors that would be responsible for ensuring the performance of the HPPC. The board would have to be composed of a cross-section of representatives of employers, employees, and individuals participating in the HPPC. The board members could not be compensated but could receive reimbursement for reasonable and necessary expenses incurred in performing their HPPC responsibilities.

2. Membership and marketing area.—Permits a HPPC to establish limits on the maximum size of employers who could become members and to determine whether to allow individuals to be members. Once membership limits were established, the HPPC would be required to accept all employers (or individuals) residing within the area served by the HPPC who met the membership requirements on a first-come, first-served basis, or on another basis established by the state to ensure equitable access to the HPPC.

3. Duties and responsibilities.—Requires a HPPC to: (a) objectively evaluate potential health plan issuers and enter into agreements with multiple, unaffiliated ones, except that this requirement would not apply in regions, such as remote or frontier areas, where compliance was not possible; (b) enter into agreements with employers and individuals who become members; (c) participate in any program of risk-adjustment or reinsurance, or any similar program established by the state; (d) prepare and disseminate comparative health plan materials concerning the plans offered through the HPPC; (e) broadly solicit and actively market to all eli-

gible employers and individuals residing within the service area; and (f) act as an ombudsman for enrollees.

4. Permissible activities.—Permits a HPPC to perform other functions as needed to further the purposes of this Act, such as: (a) collecting and distributing premiums and performing other administrative functions; (b) collecting and analyzing surveys of satisfaction; (c) charging fees for membership and participation fees to issuers; (d) cooperating with (or accepting as members) employers who provide health benefits directly but only for the purpose of negotiating with providers; and (5) negotiating with health care providers and health plan issuers.

5. Limitation on cooperative activities.—see item VIII(A) above.

6. Conflict of interest.—Prohibits any individual, partnership, or corporation from serving on the HPPC board, being employed by or receiving compensation from the HPPC, or initiating or financing a HPPC if such individual, partnership, or corporation (a) fails to discharge the duties and responsibilities in a manner that is solely in the interest of the members; or (b) derives personal benefit from the sale of, or financial interest in, health plans, services, or products sold through the HPPC. However, a HPPC could contract with third parties to provide administrative, marketing, consultive, or other services.

Conference agreement

The conference agreement does not include the House or Senate provision.

D. PREEMPTION OF STATE LAWS

Current law

Section 514(a) of ERISA preempts state laws relating to employee benefit plans. Section 514(b)(2) of ERISA provides that state laws apply in the case of the regulation of insurance.

House bill

The House bill would amend section 514 of ERISA to preempt the following state laws: (1) laws that preclude an insurer or HMO from offering health insurance coverage under VHIAs; (2) laws that preclude an insurer or HMO from setting premium rates under a VHIA based on the claims experience of the VHIA (except the VHIA's premium rates could not vary on the basis of any particular employer's claims experience); (3) laws that require coverage in connection with a VHIA to include specific items or services of medical care or that require an insurer or HMO offering coverage in connection with a VHIA to include specific item or services consisting of medical care, except to the extent that such state laws prohibit an exclusion for a specific disease in such coverage. This preemption of mandated benefits would apply only with respect to those items and services specified in a list which would be prescribed in regulations by the Secretary of Labor.

In general, states would be able to apply their laws if they had in place guaranteed access measures meeting certain conditions. A state which certified to the Secretary that it provided "guaranteed access" to health coverage could deny a VHIA the right to offer coverage in the small group market (or otherwise regulate such VHIA with respect to such coverage), except as described below. (The certification could not be in effect for more than 3 years.)

A state would be considered to provide such guaranteed access, if (1) it certified that at least 90% of all state residents were covered by a group health plan or otherwise had health insurance coverage, or (2) that it had, in the small group market, provided for guaranteed issue of at least one option of coverage and for small group rating reforms designed to make health insurance coverage more affordable. However, an exception to this provision would apply for certain large, multi-state arrangements that demonstrated to the Secretary that it met the following criteria. In other words, state laws would not apply if: (1) the VHIA sponsor operates in a majority of the 50 states and in at least 2 of the regions of the country; (2) the arrangement covers or will cover (in the case of new VHIAs) at least 7,500 participants and beneficiaries; and (3) under the terms of the arrangement, either the qualified association does not exclude from membership any small employer in the state, or the arrangement accepts every small employer in the state that applies for coverage. In addition, state laws would not apply in a state in which a VHIA operated on March 6, 1996 and under the terms of the arrangement, either the qualified association does not exclude from membership any small employer in the state, or the arrangement accepts every small employer in the state that applies for coverage.

The exemption from state laws for multistate plans and existing plans would not apply to any state which, as of January 1, 1996, either (1) had enacted a law providing for guaranteed issue of fully community rated individual health insurance coverage offered by insurers and HMOs, or (2) required insurers offering group health coverage to reimburse insurers offering individual coverage for losses resulting from their offering individual coverage on an open enrollment basis. In other words, such states could apply their insurance laws.

Senate amendment

The Senate Amendment would provide that HPPCs that meet the requirements of this Act would be exempt from state fictitious group laws.

A health plan issuer offering a group or individual health plan through a HPPC meeting the requirements of this Act would be required to comply with all otherwise applicable state rating requirements if the plan were to be offered outside the cooperative except a state would be required to permit an issuer to reduce its premiums negotiated with a HPPC to reflect savings derived from administrative costs, marketing costs, profit margins, economies of scale, or other factors. However, such premium reductions could not be based on the health status, demographic factors, industry type, duration, or other indicators of risk of HPPC members.

Health plan issuers offering coverage through the HPPC would be required to comply with state mandated benefit laws. However, in states that have enacted laws authorizing alternative benefit plans for small employers, such issuers could offer such small employer plan through a HPPC.

Conference agreement

The conference agreement does not include the House or Senate provision.

E. RULES OF CONSTRUCTION

Current law

No provision.

House bill

No provision.

Senate amendment

The Senate Amendment would provide that nothing in this section should be construed to: (1) require that a state organize, operate, or create HPPCs; (2) otherwise establish HPPCs; (3) require individuals, plan sponsors, or employers to purchase coverage through a HPPC; (4) preempt a state from requiring licensure for individuals who are involved in directly supplying advice or selling health plans on behalf of a HPPC; (5) require that a HPPC be the only type of purchasing arrangement permitted to operate in a state; (6) confer authority upon a state that the state would not otherwise have to regulate health plan issuers or employee health benefit plans; (7) confer authority upon a state (or the federal government) that it would not otherwise have to regulate group purchasing arrangements, coalitions, association plans, or similar entities that do not desire to become a HPPC; or (8) except as specifically provided for above, prevent the application of state laws and regulations otherwise to health plan issuers offering coverage through a HPPC.

Conference agreement

The conference agreement does not include the Senate provision.

F. ENFORCEMENT THROUGH ERISA

Current law

Part 4 of subtitle B of title I of ERISA provides for fiduciary responsibilities, including the fiduciary duties of a plan sponsor and prohibited transactions; part 5 provides for administration and enforcement, including criminal and civil penalties.

House bill

The House bill contains no specific provision (but as MEWAs, VHIAs would be subject to ERISA requirements including those related to fiduciary responsibilities and administration and enforcement, including enforcement of the new VHIA rules as added by this subtitle.)

Senate amendment

The Senate Amendment would provide that for enforcement purposes only, that parts 4 and 5 of subtitle B of title I of ERISA apply to a HPPC as if such plan were an employee benefit plan.

Conference agreement

The conference agreement does not include the Senate provision.

IX. ADDITIONAL DEFINITIONS/OTHER PROVISIONS

Current law

Section 3 of ERISA defines numerous terms relating to pension and employee welfare benefit plans.

House bill

The House bill:

A. Defines the following terms: group health plan, including treatment of governmental and church plans, and defines Medicaid, medicare, and the Indian Health Service programs as group health plans.

B. Incorporates specific ERISA definitions such as beneficiary, participant, employee, and employer.

C. Provides additional definitions including applicable state authority, bona fide association, COBRA continuation provision, health insurance coverage, health maintenance organization, health status, individual health insurance coverage, insurer, medical care network plan, and waiting period.

D. Provides for the treatment of partnerships.

E. Provides definitions related to markets and small employers, including individual market, large group market, small employer and small group market.

Senate bill

The Senate Amendment:

A. Defines an employee health benefit plan to include a governmental or church plan. An employee health benefit plan is not a group health plan, individual plan, or a health plan. Provides different definition for group health plan.

B. Similarly incorporates many ERISA definitions such as that for beneficiary, participant, employee, and employer.

C. Defines group purchaser and health plan issuer.

Conference agreement

The conference agreement:

A. Defines under ERISA the following terms relating to health insurance: health insurance coverage, health insurance issuer, health maintenance organization, group health insurance coverage, and excepted benefits. Also defines placed for adoption.

B. Defines under PHS Act the following terms relating to health insurance: health insurance coverage, health insurance issuer, health maintenance organization, group health insurance coverage, and excepted benefits.

C. Defines under the PHS Act: state, applicable state authority, state law, beneficiary, and bona fide association. Also, provides definitions under the PHS Act relating to markets and small employers for: large group market, small employer, and small group market.

D. Provides definitions under ERISA and the PHS Act relating to portability for: preexisting condition exclusion, enrollment date, late enrollee, waiting period, creditable coverage, and affiliation period.

E. Defines under ERISA and the PHS Act group health plan, medical care, COBRA continuation provision, and health status-related factor.

The definition of medical care is intended to parallel that of the IRC using current law, and is intended to be broad enough to encompass the services of Christian Science practitioners, nurses, and sanatoriums and nursing facilities.

F. Amends ERISA to provide for the treatment of partnerships.

G. Incorporates in the PHS Act specific ERISA definitions such as employee, employer, beneficiary, church plan, governmental plan, participant, plan sponsor.

H. Provides definitions under the PHS Act for federal governmental plan, nonfederal governmental plan, and placed for adoption.

X. Effective Dates

Current law

No provision.

House bill

The House bill, except as otherwise provided, would apply with respect to (a) group health plans, and health insurance coverage offered in connection with group health plans, for plan years beginning on or after January 1, 1998; (b) individual health insurance coverage issued, renewed, in effect, or operated on or after July 1, 1998. The bill would require the Secretaries of HHS, Treasury, and Labor to jointly establish rules regarding the treatment of certain coverage periods before the applicable effective dates, and would require the 3 Secretaries to issue such regulations on a timely basis.

Senate amendment

The Senate Amendment, except as otherwise provided, (a) with respect to group health plans, would apply to plans offered, sold, issued, renewed, in effect, or operated on or after January 1, 1997; (b) with respect to individual health plans, would apply to plans offered, sold, issued, renewed, in effect, or operated on or after the date that is 6 months after enactment or January 1, 1997, whichever is later; and (c) with respect to employee health benefit plans, would apply on the first day of the first plan year beginning on or after January 1, 1997, whichever is later.

Conference agreement

The conference agreement, except as otherwise provided, would apply with respect to (a) group health plans, and health insurance coverage offered in connection with group health plans, for plan years beginning after July 1, 1997; (b) individual health insurance coverage offered, sold, issued, renewed, in effect, or operated after July 1, 1997. In general, group health plans and health plan issuers would be required to issue certifications of coverage for periods of coverage after July 1, 1996; actual certifications need not be issued before October 1, 1996. A special rule directs the Secretaries to provide for a process whereby individuals who need to establish creditable coverage for periods before July 1, 1996 may be given credit through the presentation of documents or other means. A special rule would apply to collective bargaining agreements.

A good faith compliance provision is provided with respect to a transition period.

XI. HEALTH COVERAGE AVAILABILITY STUDIES

Current law

No provision.

House bill

No provision.

Senate amendment

The Senate Amendment would require the Secretary of HHS, in consultation with the Secretary of Labor, representatives of state officials, consumers, and other representatives of individuals and entities that have expertise in health insurance and employee benefits, to conduct a three-part study and prepare and submit reports. (A) By January 1, 1998, the Secretary would be required to prepare and submit to Congress an evaluation of the various mechanisms used to ensure the availability of reasonably priced health coverage and whether standards that limit premium variations would further the purposes of this Act. (B) No later than January 1, 1999, the Secretary would be required to prepare and submit to Congress a report concerning the effectiveness of provisions of the Act and various state laws in ensuring the availability of reasonably priced health coverage. (C) No later than January 1, 1998, the Secretary would be required to prepare and submit to Congress a report (1) evaluating the extent to which patients have direct access to, and choice of, health care providers, as well as the opportunity to utilize providers outside of the network, under the various types of coverage offered under the provisions of this Act; (2) evaluating the cost to the insurer of providing out-of-network access to providers and the feasibility of offering out-of-network access under all plans offered under this Act; and (3) evaluating the percent of premium used for medical care administration of the various types of coverage offered.

Conference agreement

The conference agreement requires the Secretary of HHS, in consultation with the Secretary of Labor, representatives of state officials, consumers, and other representatives of individuals and entities that have expertise in health insurance and employee benefits, to conduct two studies by January 1, 2000. The first study, on the effectiveness of federal and state reforms, would examine the availability of reasonably priced health coverage to employers purchasing group coverage and individuals purchasing coverage on a non-group basis. The second study, on access and choice, would examine the extent to which patients have direct access to, and choice of, health care providers, including specialty providers, within a network plan, as well as the opportunity to use providers outside of the network plan, under the various types of coverage offered under the provisions of this title. This study will also examine the cost and cost-effectiveness to health insurance issuers of providing access to out-of-network providers, and the potential impact of providing such access on the cost and quality of health insurance coverage offered under provisions of this title.

XII. REIMBURSEMENT OF TELEMEDICINE

Current law

No provision.

House bill

No provision.

Senate amendment

The Senate amendment would direct the Health Care Financing Administration (HCFA) to complete its ongoing study of reimbursement of all telemedicine services and submit a report to Congress with a proposal for reimbursement of fee-for-service medicine by March 1, 1997. The report would be required to use data compiled from the current demonstration projects already under review and gather data from other ongoing telemedicine networks, and include an analysis of the cost of services provided via telemedicine.

Conference agreement

The conference agreement directs the HCFA to complete its ongoing study of Medicare reimbursement of all telemedicine services and submit a report to Congress on reimbursement of telemedicine services by March 1, 1997. The report would be required to use data compiled from the current demonstration projects already under review and gather data from other ongoing telemedicine networks, include an analysis of the cost of services provided via telemedicine, and include a proposal for Medicare reimbursement of telemedicine services.

XIII. HMOS AND MEDICAL SAVINGS ACCOUNTS (MSAS)

Current law

Under the Public Health Service Act, federally qualified HMOs may require enrollees to pay only nominal copayments and a reasonable deductible if services are obtained from an out-of-network provider.

House bill

No provision, but see Title III, Subtitle A on Medical Savings Accounts.

Senate amendment

The PHS Act would be amended to allow federally-qualified HMOs, at the request of the HMO member, to charge a deductible to the HMO member if he or she has an MSA.

Provides that it is the sense of the Committee on Labor and Human Resources that the establishment of MSAs should be encouraged as part of any health insurance reform legislation passed by the Senate through the use of tax incentives relating to contributions to, the income growth of, and the qualified use of, such accounts.

Provides that it is the sense of the Senate that Congress should take measures to further the purposes of this Act, including any necessary changes to the Internal Revenue Code to encourage groups and individuals to obtain health coverage, and to promote access, equity, portability, affordability, and security of health benefits.

Conference agreement

The conference agreement amends the PHS Act to allow federally qualified HMOs to offer a high-deductible health plan as defined in the IRC. All other requirements of the federal HMO Act remain in effect.

XIV. VOLUNTEER SERVICES PROVIDED BY HEALTH PROFESSIONALS AT FREE CLINICS

See report language for Title II.

XV. FINDINGS; SEVERABILITY

Current law

No provision.

House bill

The House bill would provide that Congress finds: (1) that group health plans and health insurance coverage that impose pre-existing conditions impact the ability of employees to seek employment in interstate commerce and thereby impedes such commerce; (2) that health insurance coverage is commercial in nature and is in and affects interstate commerce; (3) that it is a necessary and proper exercise of congressional authority to impose requirements on group health plans and health insurance coverage to promote commerce among states; and (4) that Congress intends however to defer to the states to the maximum extent practicable in carrying out requirements with respect to insurers and HMOs that are subject to state regulation, consistent with ERISA.

Senate amendment

The Senate Amendment would provide that if any provision of the Act or application of a provision of the Act to any person or circumstance is held to be unconstitutional, the remainder of the Act and the application of the provisions of such to any person or circumstances would not be affected.

Conference agreement

The conference agreement provides that Congress finds: (1) that group health plans and health insurance coverage that impose preexisting conditions impact the ability of employees to seek employment in interstate commerce and thereby impedes such commerce; (2) that health insurance coverage is commercial in nature and is in and affects interstate commerce; (3) that it is a necessary and proper exercise of congressional authority to impose requirements under this title on group health plans and health insurance coverage, including coverage offered to individuals previously covered under group health plans, to promote commerce among states; and (4) that Congress intends to defer to the states, to the maximum extent practicable, in carrying out such requirements with respect to insurers and HMOs that are subject to state regulation, consistent with ERISA.

The conference agreement provides that if any provision of this title or application of such provision to any person or circumstance is held to be unconstitutional, the remainder of this title and the application of the provisions of such to any person or circumstances would not be affected.

XVI. COBRA Clarifications

Current law

Title X of the Consolidated Omnibus Budget Reconciliation Act of 1985 (COBRA, P.L. 99–272) amends the Internal Revenue Code (IRC), ERISA, and the Public Health Service Act to require employers who provide group health plans with 20 or more employees to offer continuation coverage to employees and their dependents who experience specific qualifying events, including changes in job or family status. In general, when a covered employee experiences termination or reductions in hours of employment, the continued coverage of the employee and any qualified beneficiaries is for 18 months. For other qualifying events (e.g., death, divorce, legal separation, and child turns age of majority under the plan), the duration of coverage is 3 years. The Omnibus Budget Reconciliation Act of 1989 (P.L. 10–239) provides that if a covered employee is determined to be disabled under the Social Security Act at the time in which he or she terminates or reduces hours of employment, then the employee is eligible for 29 months of continued coverage.

House bill

No provision.

Senate amendment

The Senate Amendment would amend the PHS Act, ERISA, and the IRC to provide for clarifications of COBRA continuation requirements. Provides that individuals who have disabled family members or who become disabled at any time during their coverage under an initial COBRA period (the first 18 months) be able to extend their coverage for the additional 11 month period currently available only to workers who are disabled at the time they lose their coverage.

Provides that newborns and children who are placed for adoption may be covered immediately under a parent's COBRA policy.

Conference agreement

See Title IV, Subtitle B.

XVII. Sense of the Committee Regarding Medicare

Current law

No provision.

House bill

No provision.

Senate amendment

The Committee on Labor and Human Resources notes that the Medicare trustees concluded in their 1995 report that: (i) the Medicare program is unsustainable in its present form; (ii) that the hospital insurance trust fund will only be able to pay for benefits for about 7 years and is severely out of financial balance in the long run; and (iii) the Public Trustees recommended that the problems be urgently addressed on a comprehensive basis including a review of the program's financing methods, benefit provisions, and delivery mechanisms. The provision expresses the sense of the Committee that the Senate should take up measures necessary to reform the Medicare program, to provide increased choice for seniors, and to respond to the findings of the Public Trustees by protecting the short term solvency and long-term sustainability of the Medicare program.

Conference agreement

The conference agreement does not include the Senate provision.

XVIII. Parity for Mental Health Services

Current law

No provision.

House bill

No provision.

Senate amendment

The Senate Amendment would prohibit an employee health benefit plan, or a health plan issuer offering a group health plan or individual health plan from imposing treatment limitations or financial requirements on the coverage of mental health services if similar requirements are not imposed on coverage for services for other conditions.

It would provide for a rule of construction that the preceding should not be construed as prohibiting an employee health benefit plan or a health plan issuer offering a group or individual health plan from requiring preadmission screening prior to the authorization of services covered under the plan or from applying other limitations that restrict coverage for mental health services to those services that are medically necessary.

Conference agreement

The conference agreement does not include the Senate provision.

XIX. Waiver of Foreign Country Residence With Respect to International Medical Graduates

Current law

The Immigration and Nationality Technical Corrections Act of 1994 provides for a waiver of the requirement that nonimmigrant international medical graduates entering as J exchange visitors return to their country of nationality for two years before being eligible to return to the U.S. The provision applies to aliens admitted to the U.S. before June 1, 1996.

House bill

No provision.

Senate bill

The Senate Amendment would extend waivers for the requirement that nonimmigrant international medical graduates entering as J exchange visitors return to their country of nationality for two years before being eligible to return to the U.S. through June 1, 2002.

It would amend provisions related to federally requested waivers requested by an interested U.S. agency on behalf of certain aliens.

Conference agreement

The conference agreement does not include the Senate provision.

XX. Organ and Tissue Donation Information Included With Income Tax Refund Payments

Current law

No provision.

House bill

No provision.

Senate bill

The Senate Amendment would require the Secretary of Treasury to include with any payment of a refund of individual income tax made during the period beginning on February 1, 1997 through June 30, 1997, a copy of the document developed in consultation with the Secretary of HHS and organizations promoting organ and tissue donation which encourages organ and tissue donation. The document would also include a detachable organ and tissue donor card, and would urge recipients to sign the card, discuss organ and tissue donations with family members, and encourage family members to request or authorize organ and tissue donation if the occasion arises.

Conference agreement

The conference agreement does not include the Senate provision.

XXI. Sense of the Senate Regarding Adequate Health Care Coverage for all Children and Pregnant Women

Current law

No provision.

House bill

No provision.

Senate amendment

The Senate Amendment provides that the Senate finds that the health care coverage of mothers and children in the United States is unacceptable, with more than 9.3 million children and 500,000 expectant mothers having no health insurance, in addition to there being high levels of infant and maternal mortality and other enumerated indicators of inadequate access to care.

The Senate Amendment provides that it is the sense of the Senate that the issue of adequate health care for our mothers and children is important to the future of the United States, and in consideration of the importance of such issue, the Senate should pass health care legislation that will ensure health care coverage for all of the United States' pregnant women and children.

Conference agreement

The conference agreement does not include the Senate provision.

XXII. Sense of the Senate Regarding Available Treatments

Current law

No provision.

House bill

No provision.

Senate amendment

The Senate Amendment provides that it is the sense of the Senate that patients deserve to know the full range of treatments available to them and Congress should thoughtfully examine these issues to ensure that all patients get the care they deserve.

Conference agreement

The conference agreement does not include the Senate provision.

XXIII. Rule of Construction

Current law

No provision.

House bill

The House bill would provide that nothing in this title or any amendment made by it may be construed to require (or to authorize any regulation that requires) the coverage of any specific procedure, treatment, or service under a group health plan or health insurance coverage.

Senate amendment

No provision.

Conference agreement

The conference agreement does not include the House provision, but see section III(E).

TITLE II—PREVENTING HEALTH CARE FRAUD AND ABUSE: ADMINISTRATIVE SIMPLIFICATION; MEDICAL LIABILITY REFORM

1. Fraud and abuse control program

(Subtitle A of title II of the House bill; title V of the Senate amendment.)

I. IN GENERAL

A. FRAUD AND ABUSE CONTROL PROGRAM

(Section 201 of the House bill; section 501 of the Senate amendment.)

Current law

Currently, the investigation and prosecution of fraud related to Federal health programs is the responsibility of the Department of Health and Human Services (DHHS), the FBI and the Department of Justice. The DHHS Office of Inspector General investigates Federal cases of fraud regarding Medicare, Medicaid, and the Maternal and Child Health Block Grant programs and is authorized by the Secretary to impose civil monetary penalties and program exclusions on fraudulent providers. The FBI can investigate both Federal and private payer cases of fraud but cannot impose sanctions. Both the Office of Inspector General and the FBI refer investigative findings to the Department of Justice which may prosecute persons for violations of federal criminal laws. State Medicaid fraud control units are responsible for the investigation, prosecution, or referral for prosecution, of fraudulent activities associated with State Medicaid programs.

House bill

The Secretary of the Department of Health and Human Services (acting through the Office of the Inspector General) and the Attorney General would be required to jointly establish a national health care fraud and abuse control program to coordinate Federal, State and local law enforcement to combat fraud with respect to health plans. To facilitate the enforcement of this fraud and abuse control program the Secretary and Attorney General would be authorized to conduct investigations, audits, evaluations and inspections relating to the delivery of and payment for health care, and would be required to arrange for the sharing of data with representatives of public and private third party payers. This program, implemented by guidelines issued by the Secretary and the Attorney General, would also facilitate the enforcement of applicable Federal statutes relating to health care fraud and abuse, and would provide for the provision of guidance to health care providers through the issuance of safe harbors, advisory opinions and special fraud alerts.

The Secretary and Attorney General would consult with and share data with representatives of health plans. Guidelines issued by the Secretary and Attorney General would ensure the confidentiality of information furnished by health plans, providers and others, as well as the privacy of individuals receiving health care services. The Inspector General would retain all current authorities.

For purposes of this section the term "health plan" means a plan or program that provides health benefits through insurance or otherwise. Such plans include health insurance policies, contracts of service benefit organizations, and membership agreements with health maintenance organizations or other prepaid health plans.

The Health Care Fraud and Abuse Control Account would be established as an expenditure account within the Federal Hospital Insurance (HI) Trust Fund. Amounts equal to monies derived from the coordinated health care anti-fraud and abuse programs from the imposition of civil money penalties, fines, forfeitures and damages assessed in criminal, civil or administrative health care cases, along with any gifts or bequests would be transferred into the Medicare HI trust fund from the U.S. Treasury. There are appropriated from the HI trust fund to the Account such sums as the Secretary and the Attorney General certify are necessary to carry out certain functions, subject to specified limits for each fiscal year beginning with 1997.

There would be appropriated from the general fund of the U.S. Treasury to the Fraud and Abuse Account for transfer to the FBI certain funds, subject to fiscal year limitations, for specified functions. These functions include prosecuting health care matters, investigations, audits of health care programs and operations, inspections and other evaluations, and provider and consumer education regarding compliance with fraud and abuse provisions. Specified amounts in the Account would also be available to carry out the Medicare Integrity Program. The Secretary and the Attorney General would be required to submit a joint annual report to Congress on the revenues and expenditures, and the justification for such disbursements from the Health Care Fraud and Abuse Control Account.

Senate amendment

Similar.

Conference agreement

The conference agreement includes the House provision with an amendment adding a requirement that the Comptroller General submit to Congress a report for certain fiscal years regarding amounts deposited in the Hospital Insurance Trust Fund under this section. The conference agreement also includes a provision regarding the availability of recoveries and forfeitures for purposes of certain provisions of the Employee Retirement Income Security Act of 1974.

B. MEDICARE INTEGRITY PROGRAM

(Section 202 of the House bill; section 502 of the Senate amendment.)

Current law

Currently Medicare's program integrity functions are subsumed under Medicare's general administrative budget. These functions are performed, along with general claims processing functions, by insurance companies under contract with the Health Care Financing Administration.

House bill

Establishes a Medicare Integrity Program under which the Secretary would promote the integrity of the Medicare program by entering into contracts with eligible private entities to carry out certain activities. These activities would include the following: (1) review of activities of providers of services or other individuals and entities furnishing items and services for which payment may be made under the Medicare program, including medical and utilization review and fraud review, (2) audit of cost reports, (3) determinations as to whether payment should not be, or should not have been, made by reason of Medicare as secondary payor provisions and recovery of payments that should not have been made, (4) education of providers of services, beneficiaries and other persons with respect to payment integrity and benefit quality assurance issues, and (5) developing and updating a list of durable medical equipment pursuant to section 1834(a)(15) of the Social Security Act. An entity is eligible to enter into a contract under this program if it meets certain requirements, including demonstrating to the Secretary that the entity's financial holdings, interests, or relationships will not interfere with its ability to perform the required functions.

Senate amendment

Similar except for differences in applicable conflict of interest requirements with regard to entities eligible to enter into contracts under this program.

Conference agreement

The conference agreement includes the House provision with a modification of the applicable conflict of interest requirements for eligible entities and assurance that current contractors meeting applicable requirements may compete for contracts on new program integrity activities.

C. BENEFICIARY INCENTIVE PROGRAMS

(Section 203 of the House bill; section 503 of the Senate amendment.)

Current law

No provision.

House bill

The Secretary would be required to provide an explanation of Medicare benefits with respect to each item or service for which payment may be made, without regard to whether a deductible or coinsurance may be imposed with respect to the item or service.

This provision would require the Secretary, within three months after enactment of this bill, to establish a program to encourage individuals to report to the Secretary information on individuals and entities who are engaging or who have engaged in acts or omissions that constitute grounds for sanctions under sections 1128, 1128A, or 1128B of the Social Security Act, or who have otherwise engaged in fraud and abuse against the Medicare program. If an individual reports information to the Secretary under this program that serves as a basis for the collection by the Secretary or the Attorney General of any amount of at least $100 (other than amounts paid as a penalty under section 1128B), the Secretary may pay a portion of the amount collected to the individual, under procedures similar to those applicable under section 7623 of the Internal Revenue Code of 1986.

The Secretary would be required, within three months after enactment of this bill, to establish a program to encourage individuals to submit to the Secretary suggestions on methods to improve the efficiency of the Medicare program. If the Secretary adopts a suggestion and savings to the program result, the Secretary would make a payment to the individual of an amount the Secretary considers appropriate.

Senate amendment

Identical.

Conference agreement

The conference agreement includes the House provision.

D. APPLICATION OF CERTAIN HEALTH ANTI-FRAUD AND ABUSE SANCTIONS TO FRAUD AND ABUSE AGAINST FEDERAL HEALTH CARE PROGRAMS

(Section 204 of the House bill; section 504 of the Senate amendment.)

Current law

Section 1128B provides for certain criminal penalties for convictions of Medicare and Medicaid (and certain other state health care programs) program-related fraud.

House bill

This provision would extend certain criminal penalties for fraud and abuse violations under the Medicare and Medicaid programs to similar violations in Federal health care programs generally. The term "Federal health care program" would mean any plan or program that provides health benefits, whether directly, through insurance, or otherwise which is funded directly, in whole or in part by the United States Government (other than the Federal Employee Health Benefit Program, Chapter 89 of Title 5 of the

United States Code). The term also would include any state health care program, which under section 1128(h), includes Medicaid, the Maternal and Child Health Services Block Grant Program and the Social Services Block Grant Program.

Senate amendment

Identical.

Conference agreement

The conference agreement includes the House provision.

E. GUIDANCE REGARDING APPLICATION OF HEALTH CARE FRAUD AND ABUSE SANCTIONS

(Section 205 of House bill, section 505 of Senate amendment.)

Current law

The 1987 Medicare and Medicaid Patient and Program Protection Act specified various payment practices which, although potentially capable of including referrals of business under Medicare or State health care programs, are protected from criminal prosecution or civil sanction under the anti-kickback provisions of the law. The 1987 law also established authority for the Secretary to promulgate regulations specifying additional payment practices, known as "safe harbors," which will not be subject to sanctions under the fraud and abuse provisions.

House bill

The Secretary would publish an annual notice in the Federal Register soliciting proposals for modifications to existing safe harbors and new safe harbors. After considering such proposals the Secretary, in consultation with the Attorney General, would issue final rules modifying existing safe harbors and establishing new safe harbors, as appropriate. The Inspector General would submit an annual report to Congress describing the proposals received, as well as the action taken regarding the proposals. The Secretary, in considering proposals, may consider a number of factors including the extent to which the proposals would affect access to health care services, quality of care services, patient freedom of choice among health care providers, competition among health care providers, ability of health care facilities to provide services in medically underserved areas or to medically underserved populations, and the like.

The Secretary of Health and Human Services would publish the first notice in the Federal Register soliciting proposals for new or modified safe harbors no later than January 1, 1997.

The Secretary would issue written advisory opinions regarding what constitutes prohibited remuneration under section 1128B(b), whether an arrangement or proposed arrangement satisfies the criteria for activities which do not result in prohibited remuneration, what constitutes an inducement to reduce or limit services to individuals entitled to benefits, and, whether an activity constitutes grounds for the imposition of civil or criminal sanctions under sections 1128, 1128A or 1128B. Advisory opinions would be binding as to the Secretary and the party requesting the opinion.

Any person would be able to request the Inspector General to issue a special fraud alert informing the public of practices which the Inspector General considers to be suspect or of particular concern under the Medicare program or a State health care program, as defined in section 1128(h) of the Social Security Act. After investigation of the subject matter of the request, and, if appropriate, the Inspector General would issue a special fraud alert in response to the request, published in the Federal Register.

Senate amendment

Identical to the House bill provisions regarding the issuance of safe harbors and special fraud alerts. However, provides for the issuance of "interpretative rulings" instead of "advisory opinions" by the Secretary.

Conference agreement

The conference agreement includes the House provision with modifications to the advisory opinion provisions. The Secretary will be required to issue to a party requesting an advisory opinion within 60 days and the advisory opinion provisions will apply to requests made for opinions on or after the date which is 6 months after the date of enactment of this section and before the date which is 4 years after such date of enactment.

II. REVISION TO CURRENT SANCTIONS FOR FRAUD AND ABUSE

(Subtitle B of the House bill; subtitle B of the Senate amendment.)

A. MANDATORY EXCLUSION FROM PARTICIPATION IN MEDICARE AND STATE HEALTH CARE PROGRAMS

(Section 211 of the House bill; section 511 of the Senate amendment.)

Current law

Section 1128 of the Social Security Act authorizes the Secretary to impose mandatory and permissive exclusions of individuals and entities from participation in the Medicare program, Medicaid program and programs receiving funds under the Maternal and Child Health Service Block Grant, or the Social Services Block Grant. Mandatory exclusions are authorized for convictions of criminal offenses related to the delivery of health care services under Medicare and State health care programs, as well as for convictions relating to patient abuse in connection with the delivery of a health care item or service. In the case of an exclusion under the mandatory exclusion authority the minimum period of exclusion could be no less than 5 years, with certain exceptions. Permissive exclusions are authorized for a number of offenses relating to fraud, kickbacks, obstruction of an investigation, and controlled substances, and activities relating to license revocations or suspensions, claims for excessive charges or unnecessary services, and the like. There are no specified minimum periods of exclusion under the permissive exclusion authority.

Under Section 1128A of the Social Security Act civil monetary penalties may be imposed for false and fraudulent claims for reimbursement under the Medicare and State health care programs.

Under section 1128B, upon conviction of a program-related felony, an individual may be fined not more than $25,000 or imprisoned for not more than five years, or both.

House bill

The provision would require the Secretary to exclude individuals and entities from Medicare and State health care programs who have been convicted of felony offenses relating to health care fraud for a minimum five year period. The Secretary would also retain the discretionary authority to exclude individuals from Medicare and State health care programs who have been convicted of misdemeanor criminal health care fraud offenses, or who have been convicted of a criminal offense relating to fraud, theft, embezzlement, breach of fiduciary responsibility, or other financial misconduct in programs (other than health care programs) funded in whole or part by any Federal, State or local agency.

The Secretary would also be required to exclude individuals and entities from Medicare and State health care programs who have been convicted of felony offenses relating to controlled substances for a minimum five year period. The Secretary would retain the discretionary authority to exclude individuals from Medicare and State health care programs who have been convicted of misdemeanor offenses relating to controlled substances.

Senate amendment

Identical.

Conference agreement

The conference agreement includes the House provision.

B. ESTABLISHMENT OF MINIMUM PERIOD OF EXCLUSION FOR CERTAIN INDIVIDUALS AND ENTITIES SUBJECT TO PERMISSIVE EXCLUSION FROM MEDICARE

(Section 212 of the House bill; section 512 of the Senate amendment.)

Current law

See above.

House bill

This section would establish a minimum period of exclusion for certain permissive exclusions from participation in Medicare and State health care programs.

For convictions of misdemeanor criminal health care fraud offenses, criminal offenses relating to fraud in non-health care Federal or State programs, convictions relating to obstruction of an investigation of health care fraud offenses, and convictions of misdemeanor offenses relating to controlled substances, the minimum period of exclusion would be three years, unless the Secretary determines that a longer or shorter period is appropriate, due to aggravating or mitigating circumstances.

For permissive exclusions from Medicare or State health care programs due to the revocation or suspension of a health care license of an individual or entity, the minimum period of exclusion would not be less than the period during which the individual's or entity's license was revoked or suspended.

For permissive exclusions from Medicare or State health care programs due to exclusion from any Federal health care program or State health care program for reasons bearing on an individual's or entity's professional competence of financial integrity, the minimum period of exclusion would not be less than the period the individual or entity is excluded or suspended from a Federal or State health care program.

For permissive exclusions from Medicare or State health care programs due to a determination by the Secretary that an individual or entity has furnished items or services to patients substantially in excess of the needs of such patients or of a quality which fails to meet professionally recognized standards of health care, the period of exclusion would be not less than one year.

Senate amendment

Identical.

Conference agreement

The conference agreement includes the House provision.

C. PERMISSIVE EXCLUSION OF INDIVIDUALS WITH OWNERSHIP OR CONTROL INTEREST IN SANCTIONED ENTITIES

(Section 213 of the House bill; section 513 of the Senate amendment.)

Current law

See above.

House bill

Under this provision an individual who has a direct or indirect ownership or control interest in a sanctioned entity and who knows or should know of the action constituting the basis for the conviction or exclusion, or who is an officer or managing employee of such an entity, may also be excluded from participation in Medicare and State health care programs by the Secretary if the entity has been convicted of an offense listed in section 1129(a) or (b)(1), (2) or (3) or otherwise excluded from program participation. Under this provision, the culpable individual would also be subject to program exclusion, even if not initially convicted or excluded.

Senate amendment

Identical.

Conference agreement

The conference agreement includes the House provision.

D. SANCTIONS AGAINST PRACTITIONERS AND PERSONS FOR FAILURE TO COMPLY WITH STATUTORY OBLIGATIONS

(Section 214 of the House bill; section 514 of the Senate amendment.)

Current law

See above.

House bill

Under this provision the Secretary may exclude a practitioner or person who has failed to comply with certain statutory obligations relating to quality of health care for such period as the Secretary may prescribe, except that such period shall be not less than one year.

The Secretary, in making his determination that a practitioner or person should be sanctioned for failure to comply with certain statutory obligations relating to quality of health care, will no longer be required to prove that the individual was either unwilling or unable to comply with such obligations.

Senate amendment

Identical.

Conference agreement

The conference agreement includes the House provision.

E. INTERMEDIATE SANCTIONS FOR MEDICARE HEALTH MAINTENANCE ORGANIZATIONS

(Section 215 of the House bill; section 515 of the Senate amendment.)

Current law

A contract between the Secretary and a Medicare Health Maintenance Organization (HMO) is generally for a 1 year term, with an option for automatic renewal. However, the Secretary may terminate any such contract at any time, after reasonable notice and an opportunity for a hearing, if the Medicare HMO has failed substantially to carry out the contract, or is carrying out the contract in a manner inconsistent with the efficient and effective administration of the requirements of section 1876 of the Social Security Act, or if the Medicare HMO no longer substantially meets the statutory requirements contained in Section 1876(b), (c), (e) and (f).

House bill

Under this section the Secretary may terminate a contract with a Medicare Health Maintenance Organization (HMO) or may impose certain intermediate sanctions on the organization if the Secretary determines that the Medicare HMO has failed substantially to carry out the contract; is carrying out the contract in a manner substantially inconsistent with the efficient and effective administration of this section; or, if the Medicare HMO no longer substantially meets the statutory requirements contained in Section 1876(b), (c), (e) and (f) of the Social Security Act.

If the basis for the determination by the Secretary that intermediate sanctions should be imposed on an eligible organization is other than that the organization has failed substantially to carry out its contract with the Secretary, then the Secretary may apply intermediate sanctions as follows: civil money penalties of not more than $25,000 for each determination if the deficiency that is the basis of the determination has directly adversely affected (or has the substantial likelihood of adversely affecting) an individual covered under the organization's contract; civil money penalties or not more than $10,000 for each week of a continuing violation; and suspension of enrollment of individuals until the Secretary is satisfied that the deficiency has been corrected and is not likely to recur.

Whenever the Secretary seeks to either terminate a Medicare HMO contract or impose intermediate sanctions on such an organization, the Secretary must do so pursuant to a formal investigation and under compliance procedures which provide the organization with a reasonable opportunity to develop and implement a corrective action plan to correct the deficiencies that were the basis of the Secretary's adverse determination. In making a decision whether to impose sanctions the Secretary is required to consider aggravating factors such as whether an entity has a history of deficiencies or has not taken action to correct deficiencies the Secretary has brought to their attention. The Secretary's compliance procedures must also include notice and opportunity for a hearing (including the right to appeal an initial decision) before the Secretary imposes any sanction or terminates the contract of a Medicare HMO, and there must not be any unreasonable or unnecessary delay between the finding of a deficiency and the imposition of sanctions.

Under this section each risk-sharing contract with a Medicare HMO must provide that the organization will maintain a written agreement with a utilization and quality control peer review organization or similar organization for quality review functions.

The amendments made by this section would apply to contract years beginning on or after January 1, 1996.

Senate amendment

Same as the House bill provision except specifies a different effective date, i.e., January 1, 1997.

Conference agreement

The conference agreement includes the House provision, but with an effective date of January 1, 1997.

F. ADDITIONAL EXCEPTION TO ANTI-KICKBACK PENALTIES FOR RISK-SHARING ARRANGEMENTS

(Section 216 of the House bill; section 516 of the Senate amendment)

Current law

The anti-kickback provision in section 1128B(b) contains several exceptions. These exceptions include discounts or other reductions in price obtained by a provider of services or other entity under Medicare or a State health care program if the reduction in price is properly disclosed and appropriately reflected in the costs claimed or charges made by the provider or entity under Medicare or a State health care program; any amount paid by an employer to an employee for employment in the provision of covered items or services; any amount paid by a vendor of goods or services to a person authorized to act as a purchasing agent for a group of individuals or entities under specified conditions; a waiver of any coinsurance under Part B of Medicare by a Federally qualified health care center with respect to an individual who qualifies for subsidized services under a provision of the Public Health Service Act; and any payment practice specified by the Secretary as a safe harbor exception.

House bill

This section would add a new exception to the anti-kickback provisions allowing remuneration between an eligible organization under section 1876 and an individual or entity providing items or services pursuant to a written agreement between an eligible organization under section 1876 and the individual or entity. Remuneration would also be allowed between an organization and an individual or entity if a written agreement places the individual or entity at substantial financial risk for the cost or utilization of the items or services which the individual or entity is obligated to provide. The risk arrangement may be provided through a withhold, capitation, incentive pool, per diem payment or other similar risk arrangement. This amendment would apply to acts of omissions occurring after January 1, 1997.

Senate amendment

Similar. However, the House provision specifically lists two permissible risk arrangements, i.e., incentive pools, and per diem payments, which are not listed in the Senate provision, and the Senate provision provides for the issuance of regulations by the Secretary, in consultation with the Attorney General, to define substantial financial risk as necessary to protect program or patient abuse.

Conference agreement

The conference agreement includes the House provision with modifications to the definition of allowable remuneration. In addition, the conference agreement adds a provision setting forth a negotiated rulemaking process for standards relating to the new exception to the anti-kickback penalties added by this section.

G. CRIMINAL PENALTY FOR FRAUDULENT DISPOSITION OF ASSETS IN ORDER TO OBTAIN MEDICAID BENEFITS

(Section 217 of the House bill.)

Current law

Under section 1128B, upon conviction of a program-related felony, an individual may be fined not more than $25,000 or imprisoned for not more than five years or both.

House bill

This provision would add a new crime to the list of prohibited activities under section 1128B of the Social Security Act for cases where a person knowingly and willfully disposes of assets by transferring assets in order to become eligible for benefits under the Medicaid program, if disposing of the assets results in the imposition of a period of ineligibility.

Senate amendment

No provision.

Conference agreement

The conference agreement includes the House provision.

III. DATA COLLECTION

(Subtitle C of the House bill; subtitle C of the Senate amendment.)

A. ESTABLISHMENT OF THE HEALTH CARE FRAUD AND ABUSE DATA COLLECTION PROGRAM

(Section 221 of the House bill; section 521 of the Senate amendment.)

Current law

No provision.

House bill

The Secretary of Health and Human Services would be required to establish a national health care fraud and abuse data collection program for reporting final adverse actions (not including settlements in which no findings of liability have been made) against health care providers, suppliers, or practitioners.

Each government agency and health plan would, on a monthly basis, report any final adverse action taken against a health care provider, supplier, or practitioner. Certain information would be included in the report, including a description of the acts or omissions and injuries upon which the final adverse action was taken. The Secretary would, however, protect the privacy of individuals receiving health care services.

The Secretary would, by regulation, provide for disclosure of the information about adverse actions, upon request, to the health care provider, supplier, or licensed practitioner and provide procedures in the case of disputed accuracy of the information. Each government agency and health plan is required to report corrections of information already reported about any final adverse action taken against a health care provider, supplier, or practitioner in such form and manner that the Secretary prescribes by regulation.

The information in the database would be available to Federal and State government agencies and health plans. The Secretary may approve reasonable fees for the disclosure of information in the data base (other than with respect to requests by Federal agencies). The amount of such a fee shall be sufficient to recover the full costs of operating the data base.

No person or entity would be held liable in any civil action with respect to any report made as required by this section, unless the person or entity knows the information is false.

The Secretary may impose appropriate fees on physicians to cover the costs of investigation and recertification activities with respect to the issuance of identifiers for physicians who furnish services for which Medicare payments are made.

Senate amendment

Similar with one additional provision requiring that the Secretary implement this section in such a manner as to avoid duplication with the reporting requirements established for the National Practitioner Data Bank.

Conference agreement

The conference agreement includes the House provision with a modification directing the Secretary to implement this section so as to avoid duplication with the reporting requirements of the National Practitioner Data Bank under the Health Care Quality Improvement Act of 1986.

IV. CIVIL MONETARY PENALTIES

(Subtitle D of the House bill; subtitle D of the Senate amendment.)

A. SOCIAL SECURITY ACT CIVIL MONETARY PENALTIES

(Section 231 of the House bill; section 531 of the Senate amendment.)

Current law

Under Section 1128A of the Social Security Act civil monetary penalties may be imposed for false and fraudulent claims for reimbursement under the Medicare and State health care programs.

House bill

The Medicare and Medicaid program provisions providing for civil monetary penalties for specified fraud and abuse violations would apply to similar violations involving other Federal health care programs. Federal health care programs would include any health insurance plans or programs funded, in whole or part, by the Federal government, such as CHAMPUS. Civil monetary penalties and assessments received by the Secretary would be deposited into the Health Care Fraud and Abuse Control Account established under this Act.

Any person who has been excluded from participating in Medicare or a State health care program and who retains a direct or indirect ownership or control interest in an entity that is participating in a program under Medicare or a State health care program, and who knows or should know of the action constituting the basis for the exclusion, or who is an officer or managing employee of such an entity, would be subject to a civil monetary penalty of not more than $10,000 for each day the prohibited relationship occurs.

Amends the civil monetary penalty provisions of Section 1128A(a) by increasing the amount of a civil money penalty from $2,000 to $10,000 for each item or service involved. Also increases the assessment which a person may be subject to from "not more than twice the amount" to "not more than three times the amount" claimed for each such item or service in lieu of damages sustained by the United States or a State agency because of such claim.

Adds two practices to the list of prohibited practices for which civil money penalties may be assessed. The first occurs when a person engages in a pattern or practice of presenting a claim for an item or service based on a code that the person knows or should know will result in greater payments than appropriate. The second is the practice whereby a person submits a claim or claims that the person knows or should know is for a medical item or service which is not medically necessary.

The sanction against practitioners and persons who fail to comply with certain statutory obligations is changed from an amount equal to "the actual or estimated cost" of the medically improper or unnecessary services provided, to "up to $10,000 for each instance of medically improper or unnecessary services provided.

The procedural provisions outlined in Section 1128A, such as notice, hearings, and judicial review rights, would apply to civil monetary penalties assessed against Medicare Health Maintenance Organizations in the same manner as they apply to civil monetary penalties assessed against health care providers generally.

This provision also adds a new practice to the list of prohibited practices for which civil monetary penalties could be assessed. Any person who offers remuneration to an individual eligible for benefits under Medicare or a State health care program that such individual knows or should know is likely to influence such individual to order or received from a particular provider, practitioner or supplier any item or service reimbursable under Medicare or a State health care program would be subject to the various civil monetary penalties, assessments and exclusion provisions of section 1128A of the Social Security Act.

The term "remuneration" is defined to include the waiver of part or all of coinsurance and deductible amounts, as well as transfers of items or services for free, or for other than fair market value. There would be exceptions to this definition. The waiver of part or all of coinsurance and deductible amounts would not be considered remuneration under this section if the waiver is not offered as part of any advertisement or solicitation, the person does not routinely waive coinsurence or deductible amounts, and the person either waives the coinsurance and deductible amounts because the individual is in financial need, or fails to collect the amounts after reasonable collection efforts, or provides for a permissible waiver under regulations issued by the Secretary. In addition, the term remuneration would not include differentials in coinsurance and deductible amounts as part of a benefit plan design if the differentials have been disclosed in writing to all beneficiaries, third party payors, and providers, and if the differentials meeting the standards defined in the Secretary's regulations. Remuneration would also not include incentives given to individuals to promote the delivery of preventive care under the Secretary's regulations.

The effective date of these provisions is January 1, 1997.

Senate amendment

Identical.

Conference agreement

The conference agreement includes the House provision. The conferees do not intend that the language of section 231(d) create any new standard for coverage of a claim. The intent is to assure that a proper evaluation by a practitioner is completed and evidence of treatment need is established before services are delivered for which claims are submitted. The conferees recognize that under current law the reasonableness of a service provided by a non-medical practitioner, including a practitioner of alternative medicine, is judged by the application of principles particular to such non-medical health care professions. For example, the provision and reasonableness of chiropractic services under Medicare is judged by the application of chiropractic principles.

There is significant concern regarding the impact of the anti-fraud provisions on the practice of complementary or alternative medicine and health care. The practice of complementary or alternative medical or health care practice itself would not constitute fraud.

The conferees do not intend to penalize the exercise of medical judgment of health care treatment choices made in good faith and which are supported by significant evidence or held by a respectable minority of those providers who customarily provide similar methods of treatment. The Act is not intended to penalize providers simply because of a professional difference of opinion regarding diagnosis or treatment.

A sanction is not intended for providers who submit claims they know will not be considered reimbursable as medically necessary services, but who are required to submit the claims because their patients need to document that Medicare will not reimburse the service. In submitting such claims, providers shall notify carriers that a claim is being submitted solely for purpose of seeking reimbursement from secondary payers.

Moreover, the conferees intend that a penalty will be imposed on presentation of a claim that is false or fraudulent. No sanction is intended for providers who simply inform beneficiaries that a particular service is not covered by Medicare. Moreover, nothing in this section is intended to supersede the limitation on liability provisions established under Section 1879 of the Social Security Act.

In addition, the conferees intend, with respect to allowable remuneration, that this provision not preclude the provision of items and services of nominal value, including, for example, refreshments, medical literature, complimentary local transportation services, or participation in free health fairs.

B. CLARIFICATION OF LEVEL OF INTENT REQUIRED FOR IMPOSITION OF SANCTIONS

(Section 232 of the House bill.)

Current law

Civil monetary penalties may be imposed for seeking reimbursement under the Medicare and Medicaid programs for items of services not provided or for services provided by someone who is not a licensed physician, whose license was obtained through misrepresentation, or who misrepresented his or her qualification as a specialist, or where the claim is otherwise fraudulent. Civil penalties may also be sought for presenting a claim due for payments which are in violation of (1) contracts limiting payment due to assignment of a patient, (2) agreements with state agencies limiting permitted charges, (3) agreements with participating physicians or suppliers, and (4) agreements with providers of services. Civil monetary penalties may also be sought against persons who provide false or misleading information that could reasonably be expected to influence a decision to discharge a person from a hospital. A person is subject to these provisions if he or she presented a claim and he or she "knows or should have known" that the claim fell into one of the categories listed above.

House bill

This provision adds a requirement, similar to the False Claims Act, that a person is subject to this provision when the person "knowingly" presents a claim that the person "knows or should know" falls into one of the prohibited categories. Thus, an assessment under this provision would only be made where a person had actual knowledge that he or she had submitted a claim or had provided false or misleading information, and where the person had actual knowledge of the fraudulent nature of the claim, acted in deliberate ignorance, or acted in reckless disregard of the truth or falsity of the information. The requirement that a person "knowingly" present a claim or "knowingly" make a false or misleading statement which influences discharge would prevent charging persons who inadvertently perform these acts.

Senate amendment

No provision.

Conference agreement

The conference agreement includes the House provision, but this provision has been added to the section of this bill entitled "Social Security Act Civil Monetary Penalties", above.

C. PENALTY FOR FALSE CERTIFICATION FOR HOME HEALTH SERVICES

(Section 233 of the House bill.)

Current law

No provision.

House bill

This provision would add an additional civil monetary penalty of not more than three times the amount of the payments, or $5,000, whichever is greater, for a physician who certifies that an individual meets all of Medicare's requirements to receive home health care while knowing that the individual does not meet all such requirements. This provision would apply to certifications made on or after the date of enactment of this Act.

Senate amendment

No provision.

Conference agreement

The conference agreement includes the House provision.

V. REVISIONS TO CRIMINAL LAW

(Subtitle E of the House bill; subtitle E of the Senate amendment.)

A. DEFINITIONS RELATING TO FEDERAL HEALTH CARE OFFENSE

(Section 241 of the House bill; section 542 of the Senate amendment.)

Current law

No provision.

House bill

This provision defines the term "Federal health care offense" to include violations of, or criminal conspiracies to violate, section 669, 1035, 1347 or 1518 of Title 18 of the United States Code, or section 287, 371, 664, 666, 1001, 1027, 1341, 1343, or 1954 of this title, if the violation or conspiracy relates to a health care benefit program. A "health care benefit program" is any public or private plan affecting commerce under which any medical benefit, item or service is provided to any individual, and includes any individual or entity providing such a medical benefit, item or service for which payment may be made under the plan.

Senate amendment

The Senate amendment defines "Federal health care offense" as a violation of, or a criminal conspiracy to violate section 1128B of the Social Security Act, section 1347 of this title, and sections 287, 371, 664, 666, 669, 1001, 1027, 1341, 1343, or 1954 of this title if the violation or conspiracy relates to health care fraud.

Conference agreement

The conference agreement includes the House provision.

B. HEALTH CARE FRAUD

(Section 242 of the House bill; section 541 of the Senate amendment.)

Current law

Depending on the facts of a particular case, criminal penalties may be imposed on persons engaged in health care fraud under federal mail and wire fraud statutes, the False Claims Act, false statement statues, money laundering statutes, racketeering, and other related laws.

House bill

Under this provision criminal penalties would be imposed for knowingly executing or attempting to execute a scheme or artifice (1) to defraud any health care benefit program; or (2) to obtain, by means of false or fraudulent pretenses, money or property owned by, or under the custody or control of, any health care benefit program. Penalties include fines and up to 10 years imprisonment. If the violation results in serious bodily injury, the person may be imprisoned up to 20 years. If the violation results in death, the person may be imprisoned for life.

Senate amendment

Similar. However, the Senate provision provides that the crime be committed "willfully" as well as knowingly, and the penalties are listed as "any term of years" if the violation results in serious bodily injury. The Senate provision also provides that criminal fines imposed under this section be deposited into the Federal Hospital Insurance Trust Fund.

Conference agreement

The conference agreement includes the House provision with a modification specifying that the standard of intent will be "knowingly and willfully".

There has been significant concern regarding the impact of the anti-fraud provisions on the practice of complementary and alternative medicine and health care. The practice of complementary, alternative, innovative, experimental or investigational medical or health care itself would not constitute fraud. The conferees intend that this proposal not be interpreted as a prohibition of the practice of these types of medical or health care. The Act is not intended to penalize a person who exercises a health care treatment choice or makes a medical or health care judgment in good faith simply because there is a difference of opinion regarding the form of diagnosis or treatment. Nor does this provision in general prohibit plans from covering specific types of treatment. Whether certain complementary and alternative practices will be covered is and should be a decision left to health care plan administrators.

C. THEFT OR EMBEZZLEMENT

Section 243 of the House bill; section 546 of the Senate amendment)

Current law

No provision.

House bill

Criminal penalties would be imposed for embezzling, stealing, or otherwise without authority knowingly converting or intentionally misapplying any of the moneys, funds, securities, premiums, credits, property, or other assets of a health care benefit program. A person convicted under this provision would be subject to a fine under Title 18 of the United States Code, or imprisoned not more than 10 years, or both. If the value of property does not exceed $100, the defendant would be fined or imprisoned not more than one year, or both.

Senate amendment

Requires that this crime be committed "willfully", and the person convicted is subject to a fine under this title or imprisonment of not more than 10 years, or both.

Conference agreement

The conference agreement includes the House provision with a modification specifying that the standard of intent will be "knowingly and willfully".

D. FALSE STATEMENTS

(Section 244 of the House bill; section 544 of the Senate amendment.)

Current law

The Federal false statements provision at 18 U.S.C. § 1001 generally prohibits false statements with regard to any matter within the jurisdiction of a Federal department or agency.

House bill

Criminal penalties would be imposed for knowingly falsifying, concealing, or covering up by any trick, scheme, or device a material fact, or making false, fictitious, or fraudulent statements or representations, or making or using any falsewriting or document knowing the same to contain any false, fictitious, or fraudulent statement or entry in any matter involving a health care benefit program. A person convicted under this provision may be punished by the imposition of fines under title 18 of the United States Code, or by imprisonment of not more than 5 years, or both.

Senate amendment

Contains additional elements of the crime of false statements, including the words "willfully" and "materially". The House bill language specifying that the false statements be "in connection with the delivery of or payment for health care benefits, items, or services" does not appear in the Senate amendment provision.

Conference agreement

The conference agreement includes the House provision with a modification specifying that the standard of intent will be "knowingly and willfully".

E. OBSTRUCTION OF CRIMINAL INVESTIGATIONS OF HEALTH CARE OFFENSES

(Section 245 of the House bill; section 545 of the Senate amendment.)

Current law

Under current law, criminal penalties are imposed for obstructing, delaying or preventing the communication of information to law enforcement officials regarding the violation of criminal statues by using bribery, intimidation, threats, corrupt persuasion, or harassment.

House bill

Criminal penalties would be imposed for willfully preventing, obstructing, misleading, delaying or attempting to prevent, obstruct, mislead or delay the communication of information or records relating to a Federal health care offense to a criminal investigator. A person convicted under this provision could be punished by the imposition of fines under title 18 of the United States Code or by imprisonment of not more than 5 years, or both. Criminal investigator would mean any individual duly authorized by a department, agency, or armed force of the United States to conduct or engage investigations for prosecution for violations of health care offenses.

Senate amendment

Similar, with only minor drafting differences.

Conference agreement

The conference agreement includes the House provision.

F. LAUNDERING OF MONETARY INSTRUMENTS

(Section 246 of the House bill; section 547 of the Senate amendment.)

Current law

The current Federal money laundering provision is found at 18 U.S.C. § 1956(c)(7), but does not include money laundering as related to health care fraud.

House bill

An act or activity constituting a Federal health care offense would be considered a "specified unlawful activity" for purposes of the prohibition on money laundering, so that any person who engages in money laundering in connection with a Federal health care offense would be subject to existing criminal penalties.

Senate amendment

Similar, with only minor drafting differences.

Conference agreement

The conference agreement includes the House provision.

G. INJUNCTIVE RELIEF RELATING TO HEALTH CARE OFFENSES

(Section 247 of the House bill; section 543 of the Senate amendment.)

Current law

Depending on the facts of a particular case, injunctive relief may be imposed on persons who are committing or about to commit health care fraud under federal racketeering statutes and other related laws.

House bill

If a person is violating or about to commit a Federal health care offense, the Attorney General of the United States could commence a civil action in any Federal court to enjoin such a violation. If a person is alienating or disposing of property or intends to alienate or dispose of property obtained as a result of a Federal health care offense, the Attorney General could seek to enjoin such alienation or disposition, or could seek a restraining order to prohibit the person from withdrawing, transferring, removing, dissipating or disposing of any such property or property of equivalent value and appoint a temporary receiver to administer such restraining order.

Senate amendment

Similar.

Conference agreement

The conference agreement includes the House provision.

H. AUTHORIZED INVESTIGATIVE DEMAND PROCEDURES

(Section 248 of the House bill; section 548 of the Senate amendment.)

Current law

No provision.

House bill

This provision would establish procedures for the Attorney General to make investigative demands in cases regarding health care fraud. Under this section, the Attorney General could issue a summons for records and/or a witness to authenticate the records.

Administrative summons would be authorized for investigations of any scheme to defraud an health care benefit program in connection with the delivery of or payment for health care. This section would provide for service of a subpoena and enforcement of a subpoena in all United States courts, as well as a grant of immunity to persons responding to a subpoena from civil liability for disclosure of such information.

The provision would also provide that health information about an individual that is disclosed under this section may not be used in, or disclosed to any person for use in any administrative, civil, or criminal action or investigation directed against the individual who is the subject of the information unless the action or investigation arises out of, and is directly related to, receipt of health care of payment for health care or action involving a fraudulent claim related to health, or if good cause is shown.

Senate amendment

Contains additional language relating to testimony by a custodian of records, the production of records, witness fees, and administrative summons.

Conference agreement

The conference agreement includes the House provision with an amendment to include Senate bill language relating to testimony by a custodian of records.

I. FORFEITURES FOR FEDERAL HEALTH CARE OFFENSES

(Section 249 of the House bill; section 542 of the Senate amendment.)

Current law

Depending on the facts of a particular case, criminal forfeiture may be imposed on persons convicted under federal money laundering statutes, racketeering statutes, and other related laws.

House bill

A court imposing a sentence on a person convicted of a Federal health care offense could order the person to forfeit all real or personal property that is derived, directly or indirectly, from proceeds traceable to the commission of the offense. After payment of the costs of asset forfeiture have been made, the Secretary of the Treasury would deposit into the Federal Hospital Insurance Trust Fund an amount equal to the net amount realized from the forfeiture of property by reason of a federal health care offense.

Senate amendment

Identical.

Conference agreement

The conference agreement includes the House provision.

J. RELATION TO ERISA AUTHORITY

(Section 250 of the House bill.)

Current law

The Employee Retirement Income Security Act of 1974 sets forth comprehensive requirements for employee pension and welfare benefit plans, including reporting and disclosure requirements and fiduciary standards for trustees and fiduciaries; pension plans are also subject to funding, participation, and vesting requirements.

House bill

The provision states that nothing in this subtitle (Revisions to Criminal law), shall affect the authority of the Secretary of Labor under section 506(b) of ERISA to detect and investigate civil and criminal violations related to ERISA.

Senate amendment

No provision.

Conference agreement

The conference agreement includes the House provision.

2. Administrative simplification

(Sections 251 and 252 of subtitle F of title II of the House bill.)

Current law

No provision.

House bill

The bill would provide that the purpose of the subtitle was to improve the Medicare and Medicaid programs, and the efficiency and effectiveness of the health care system, by encouraging the development of health information network through the establishment of standards and requirements for the electronic transmission of certain health information. Amends title XI of the Social Security Act by adding Part C—Administrative Simplification.

Senate amendment

No provision.

Conference agreement

The conference agreement includes the House provision.

A. DEFINITIONS

(New section 1171 of the Social Security Act.)

Current law

No provision.

House bill

The bill would provide definitions for this part of the Act including the following: clearinghouse, code set, coordination of benefits, health care provider, health information, health plan, individually identifiable health information, standard, and standard setting organization.

Senate amendment

No provision.

Conference agreement

The conference agreement includes the House provision with an amendment to exclude a definition for coordination of benefits and clarifies the definition of health plan.

B. GENERAL REQUIREMENTS FOR ADOPTION OF STANDARDS

(New section 1172 of the Social Security Act.)

Current law

No provision.

House bill

The bill would require that any standard or modification of a standard adopted would apply to the following: (1) a health plan, (2) a clearinghouse, or (3) a health care provider, but only to the extent that the provider was conducting electronic transactions referred to in the bill. The bill would require that any standard or modification of a standard adopted must reduce the administrative cost of providing and paying for health care. The standard setting organization would be required to develop or modify any standard or modification adopted. The Secretary could adopt a standard or modification of a standard that was different from any standard developed by such organization if the different standard or modification was promulgated in accordance with rulemaking procedures and would substantially reduce administrative costs to providers and plans. The Secretary would be required to establish specifications for implementing each of the standards and modifications adopted. The standards adopted would be prohibited from requiring disclosure of trade secrets or confidential commercial information by a participant in the health information network. In complying with the requirements of this part, the Secretary would be required to rely on the recommendations of the Health Information Advisory Committee established by the bill, and consult with appropriate Federal and State agencies and private organizations.

Senate amendment

No provision.

Conference agreement

The conference agreement includes the House provision with a modification that requires the Secretary to rely on the recommendations of the National Committee on Vital and Health Statistics. The standard-setting organization should consult with the National Uniform Billing Committee, the National Uniform Claim Committee, the Working Group for Electronic Data Interchange, and the American Dental Association.

C. STANDARDS FOR INFORMATION TRANSACTIONS AND DATA ELEMENTS

(New section 1173 of the Social Security Act.)

Current law

No provision.

House bill

The bill would require the Secretary to adopt appropriate standards for financial and administrative transactions and data elements exchanged electronically that are consistent with the goals of improving the operation of the health care system and reducing administrative costs. Financial and administrative transactions would include claims, claims attachments, enrollment and disenrollment, eligibility, health care payment and remittance advice, premium payments, first report of injury, claims status, and referral certification and authorization. Standards adopted by the Secretary would be required to accommodate the needs of different types of health care providers.

The Secretary would be required to adopt standards providing for a standard unique health identifier for each individual, employer, health plan, and health care provider for use in the health care system. The Secretary would be required to establish security standards that (1) take into account the technical capabilities of record systems to maintain health information, the costs of security measures, the need for training persons with access to health information, the value of audit trails in computerized record systems used, and the needs and capabilities of small health care providers and rural health care providers; and (2) ensure that a clearinghouse, if it is part of a larger organization, has policies and security procedures which isolate the activities of such service to prevent unauthorized access to such information by such larger organization. The Secretary would be required to establish standards and modifications to such standards regarding the privacy of individually identifiable health information that is in the health information network. The Secretary, in coordination with the Secretary of Commerce, would be required to adopt standards specifying procedures for the electronic transmission and authentication of signatures, compliance with which would be deemed to satisfy Federal and State statutory requirements for written signatures with respect to the transactions specified by the bill. This part would not be construed to prohibit the payment of health care services or health plan premiums by debit, credit, payment card or numbers, or other electronic means. The Secretary would be required to adopt standards for determining the financial liability of health plans when health benefits are payable under two or more health plans, the sequential processing of claims, and other data elements for individuals who have more than one health plan.

Senate amendment

No provision.

Conference agreement

The conference agreement includes the House provision.

The conferees recognize that certain uses of individually identifiable information are appropriate, and do not compromise the privacy of an individual. Examples of such use of information include the transfer of information when making referrals from primary care to specialty care, and the transfer of information from a health plan to an organization for the sole purpose of conducting health care-related research. As health plans and providers continue to focus on outcomes research and innovation, it is important that the exchange and aggregated use of health care data be allowed.

The conference agreement includes a modification that this part would not be construed to regulate the payment of health care services or health care premiums by debit, credit, payment card or other electronic means.

D. TIMETABLES FOR ADOPTION OF STANDARDS

(New section 1174 of the Social Security Act.)

Current law

No provision.

House bill

The bill would require the Secretary to adopt standards relating to the transactions, data elements of health information, security and privacy by not later than 18 months after the date of enactment of the part, except that standards relating to claims attachments would be required to be adopted not later than 30 months after enactment. The Secretary would be required to review the adopted standards and adopt additional or modified standards as appropriate, but not more frequently than once every 6 months, except during the first 12-month period after the standards are adopted unless the Secretary determines that a modification is necessary in order to permit compliance with the standards. The Secretary would also be required to ensure that procedures exist for the routine maintenance, testing, enhancement, and expansion of code sets.

Senate amendment

No provision.

Conference agreement

The conference agreement includes the House provision with a modification that the Secretary would be required to adopt additional or modified standards not more frequently than 12 months.

E. REQUIREMENTS

(New section 1175 of the Social Security Act.)

Current law

No provision.

House bill

The bill would establish that if a person desires to conduct a financial or administrative transaction with a health plan as a standard transaction, (1) the health plan may not refuse to conduct such transaction as a standard transaction, (2) the health plan may not delay such transaction, or otherwise adversely affect, or attempt to adversely affect, the person or the transaction on the grounds that the transaction is a standard transaction, and (3) the information transmitted and received in connection with the transaction would be required to be in a form of standard data elements for health information. Health plans could satisfy the transmission of information by directly transmitting standard data elements of health information, or submitting nonstandard data elements to a clearinghouse for processing in to standard data elements and transmission. Not later than 24 months after the date on which standard or implementation specification was adopted or established under this part, each person to which the standard applied would be required to comply with the standard or specification. Small health plans, determined by the Secretary, would be required to comply not later than 36 months after standards were adopted.

Senate amendment

No provision.

Conference agreement

The conference agreement includes the House provision.

F. GENERAL PENALTY FOR FAILURE TO COMPLY WITH REQUIREMENTS
AND STANDARDS

(Section 1176 of the Social Security Act.)

Current law

No provision.

House bill

The bill would require the Secretary to impose on any person who violates a provision under the bill a penalty of not more than $100 for each such violation of a specific standard or requirement, except that the total amount imposed on the person for all such violations during a calendar year would not exceed $25,000. A penalty would not be imposed if it was established that the person liable for the penalty did not know, and by exercising reasonable diligence would not have known, that such person violated the provision. A penalty would not be imposed if (1) the failure to comply was due to reasonable cause and not willful neglect, and (2) the failure to comply as corrected during the 30-day period beginning on the first date the person liable for the penalty knows, or would have known, that the failure to comply occurred.

Senate amendment

No provision.

Conference agreement.

The conference agreement includes the House provision.

G. WRONGFUL DISCLOSURE OF INDIVIDUALLY IDENTIFIABLE HEALTH
INFORMATION

(New section 1177 of the Social Security Act.)

Current law

No provision.

House bill

The bill would define the offense of wrongful disclosure of individually identifiable health information as instances when a person who knowingly (1) uses or causes to be used a unique health identifier violation of a provision in this part, (2) obtains individually identifiable health information relating to an individual in violation of a provision in this part, or (3) discloses individually identifiable health information to another person in violation of this part. A person committing such an offense would be required to (1) be fined not more than $50,000, imprisoned not more than 1 year, or both; (2) if the offense was committed under false pretenses, be fined not more than $100,000, imprisoned not more than 5 years, or both; and (3) if the offense was committed with intent to sell, transfer, or use individually identifiable health information for commercial advantage, personal gain, or malicious harm, fined not more than $250,000, imprisoned not more than 10 years, or both.

Senate amendment

No provision.

Conference agreement

The conference agreement includes the House provision.

H. EFFECT ON STATE LAW

(New section 1178 of the Social Security Act.)

Current law

No provision.

House bill

The bill would require that a provision, requirement, or standard provided by the bill supersede any contrary provision of state law, including a provision of state law that required medical or health plan records (including billing information) to be maintained or transmitted in written rather that electronic form. A provision under the bill would not supersede a contrary provision of state law if the provision of state law (1) was more stringent than the requirements of the bill with respect to privacy or individually identifiable health information, or (2) was a provision the Secretary determined was necessary to prevent fraud and abuse with respect to controlled substances or for other purposes.

Senate amendment

No provision.

Conference agreement

The conference agreement includes the House provision with a modification, that the provision would not supersede a contrary State law only if the Secretary determines that the State law (1) is necessary to prevent fraud and abuse; (2) to ensure appropriation State regulation of insurance and health plans; (3) for state reporting on health care delivery or costs, or for other purposes; or (4) addresses controlled substances.

The conference agreement also includes the requirement that any standard adopted under this part would not apply to the following: (1) the use or disclosure of information for authorizing, processing, clearing, settling, billing, transferring, collecting, or reconciling a payment for, health plan premiums or health care, where such payment is made by means of a credit, debit, or other payment card, or by an account, check, electronic funds transfer or other such means; (2) the use or disclosure of information relating to a payment described above for transferring receivables, resolving customer disputes or inquiries, auditing, supplying a statement to a consumer of a financial institution regarding the customer's account with such an institution, reporting to customer reporting agencies, or complying with a civil or criminal subpoena or a Federal or State law regulating financial institutions.

The conferees do not intend to exclude the activities of financial institutions or their contractors from compliance with the standards adopted under this part if such activities would be subject to this part. However, conferees intend that this part does not apply to use or disclosure of information when an individual utilizes a payment system to make a payment for, or related to, health plan premiums or health care. For example, the exchange of information between participants in a credit card system in connection with processing a credit card payment for health care would not be covered by this part. Similarly sending a checking account statement to an accountholder who uses a credit or debit card to pay for health care services, would not be covered by this part. However, this part does apply if a company clears health care claims, the health care claims activities remain subject to the requirements of this part.

1. CHANGES IN MEMBERSHIP AND DUTIES OF NATIONAL COMMITTEE ON VITAL AND HEALTH STATISTICS

(Section 253 of the House bill.)

Current law

No provision.

House bill

The bill would amend the membership and duties of the National Committee on Vital and Health Statistics, authorized under section 306(k) of the Public Health Service Act, as amended, by increasing the number of members to 18. The committee would be required to (1) provide assistance and advice to the Secretary on issues related to health statistical and health information; health with complying with the requirements of the bill; (2) study the issues related to the adoption of uniform data standards for patient medical record information and electronic exchange of such information; (3) report to the Secretary not later than 4 years after enactment of the Health Coverage Availability and Affordability Act of 1996, and annually thereafter, recommendations and legislative proposals for such standards and electronic exchange; and (4) be generally responsible for advising the Secretary and the Congress on the status of the future of the health information network. The committee would be required, not later than 1 year after enactment, to report to Congress, health care providers, health plans, and other entities using the health information network regarding (1) the extent to which entities using the network were meeting the standards adopted and working together to form an integrated network that meets the needs of its users; (2) the extent to which entities were meeting the privacy and security standards, and the types of penalties assessed for noncompliance; (3) whether the federal and state governments were receiving information of sufficient quality to meet their responsibilities; (4) any problems that exist with implementation of the network; and (5) the extent to which timetables established by under this part of the bill were being met.

Senate amendment

No provision.

Conference agreement

The conference agreement includes the House provision.

The conference agreement also includes a requirement that the Secretary submit detailed recommendations on standards with respect to the privacy of individually identifiable health information not later than 12 months after enactment. The recommendations would be required to address at least: (1) the rights an individual should have relating to individually identifiable health information; (2) the procedures that should be established for the exercise of such rights; and (3) the uses and disclosures of such information that should be authorized or required. The Secretary would be required to consult with the Attorney General, and the National Committee on Vital and Health Statistics for carrying out this requirement. If Congress fails to enact privacy legislation, the Secretary is required to develop standards with respect to privacy of individually identifiable health information not later than 42 months from the date of enactment.

The conferees recognize that industry experts are essential to the membership of the National Committee on Vital and Health Statistics. It is the conferees' intent that the Committee select representatives from the insurer, HMO, provider, employer, accreditation communities, and a representative from the Workgroup for Electronic Data Interchange (WEDI).

The conferees recognize that technological innovation with respect to electronic transmission of health-care related transactions is progressing rapidly in the marketplace. The conferees do not intend to stifle innovation in this area. Therefore, the conferees intend that the Committee take into account private sector initiatives.

3. Duplication and coordination of Medicare-related plans

(Subtitle G of title II of the House bill.)

A. DUPLICATION AND COORDINATION OF MEDICARE-RELATED PLANS

(Section 281 of House bill.)

Current law

Many Medicare beneficiaries purchase private health insurance to supplement their Medicare coverage. These individually purchased policies are known as Medigap policies. The Omnibus Budget Reconciliation Act of 1990 (OBRA 1990, P.L. 101–508) provided for a standardization of Medigap policies. OBRA also substantially modified the antiduplication provision contained in law. The intent of the OBRA 1990 anti-duplication provision was to prohibit sales of duplicative Medigap policies. However, the statutory language applied, with very limited exceptions, to all "health insurance policies" sold to Medicare beneficiaries. Observers noted that this provision could thus apply to a broad range of policies including hospital indemnity plans, dread disease policies, and long-term care insurance policies.

The Social Security Amendments of 1994 (P.L. 103–432) included a number of technical modifications to the Medigap statute, including modifications to the anti-duplication provisions contained in section 1882(d)(3) of the Act. Under the revised language, it is illegal to sell or issue the following policies to Medicare beneficiaries: (i) a health insurance policy with knowledge that it duplicates Medicare or Medicaid benefits to which a beneficiary is otherwise entitled; (ii) a Medigap policy, with knowledge that the beneficiary already has a Medigap policy; or (iii) a health insurance policy (other than Medigap) with knowledge that it duplicates private health benefits to which the beneficiary is already entitled.

A number of exceptions to these prohibitions are established. The sale of a medigap policy is not in violation of the provisions relating to duplication of Medicaid coverage if: (i) the State Medicaid program pays the premiums for the policy; (ii) in the case of qualified Medicare beneficiaries (QMBs), the policy includes prescription drug coverage; or (iii) the only Medicaid assistance the individual is entitled to is payment of Medicare Part B premiums.

The sale of a health insurance policy (other than a Medigap policy) that duplicates private coverage is not prohibited if the policy pays benefits directly to the individual without regard to other coverage. Further, the sale of a health insurance policy (other than a Medigap policy to an individual entitled to Medicaid) is not in violation of the prohibition relating to selling of a policy duplicating Medicare or Medicaid, if the benefits are paid without regard to the duplication in coverage. This exception is conditional on the prominent disclosure of the extent of the duplication, as part of or together with, the application statement.

P.L. 103–432 provided for the development by the National Association of Insurance Commissioners (NAIC) of disclosure statements describing the extent of duplication for each of the types of private health insurance policies. Statements were to be developed, at a minimum, for policies paying fixed cash benefits directly to the beneficiary and policies limiting benefits to specific diseases. The NAIC identified 10 types of health insurance policies requiring disclosure statements and developed statements for them. These were approved by the Secretary and published in the *Federal Register* on June 12, 1995.

House bill

The provision would modify the anti-duplication provisions. The requirement for obtaining a written application statement would be limited to the sale of Medigap policies to persons already having Medigap policies.

Anti-duplicative provisions would specifically state that a policy which pays benefits to or on behalf of an individual without regard to other health benefit coverage would not be considered to duplicate any health benefits under Medicare, Medicaid, or a health insurance policy. Further, such policies would be excluded from the sales prohibitions.

The provision would specifically state that a health insurance policy (or a rider to an insurance contract which is not a health policy) which provides benefits for long term care, nursing home care, home health care or community-based care and that coordinates or excludes against services covered under Medicare would not be considered duplicative, provided such coordination or exclusion was disclosed in the policy's outline of coverage.

The provision would specify that a health insurance policy (which may be a contract with a health maintenance organization), provided to a disabled beneficiary, that is a replacement product for another policy that is being terminated by the insurer would not be considered duplicative if it coordinates with Medicare.

The provision would prohibit the imposition of criminal or civil penalties, or taking of legal action, with respect to any actions which occurred between enactment of P.L. 103–432 and enactment of this measure, provided the policies met the new requirements.

The provision would prohibit States from imposing duplication requirements with respect to a policy (other than Medigap policy) or rider to an insurance contract which is not a health policy if the policy or rider pays benefits without regard to other benefits coverage or if it is a long-term care policy or policy sold to the disabled (as such policies are described above).

The provision would also delete current language relating to required disclosure statements.

Senate amendment

No provision.

Conference agreement

The conference agreement includes the House provision with modifications. The agreement would clarify that policies offering only long-term care nursing home care, home health care, or community based care, or any combination thereof would be allowed to coordinate benefits with Medicare and not be considered duplicative, provided such coordination was disclosed. The conference agreement does not include the provision relating to replacement policies sold to disabled persons.

The conference agreement would modify, rather than repeal, the current law requirement for disclosure statements for policies that pay regardless of other coverage. Disclosure statements, for the type of policy being applied for, would be furnished to a Medicare beneficiary applying for a health insurance policy. The statement would be furnished as a part of (or together with) the policy application.

The conference agreement would specify that whoever issues or sells a health insurance policy to a Medicare beneficiary and fails to furnish the required disclosure statement would be fined under title 18 of the United States Code, or imprisoned not more than five years or both. In addition, or in lieu of the criminal penalty, a civil money penalty of $25,000 (or $15,000 in the case of someone who is not an issuer) could be imposed for each violation.

The disclosure requirements would not apply to Medigap policies or health insurance policies identified in the July 12, 1995 Federal Register notice (i.e. policies that do not duplicate Medicare (even incidentally), life insurance policies that contain long-term care riders or accelerated death benefits, disability insurance policies, property and casualty policies, employer and union group health plans, managed care organizations with Medicare contracts, and health care prepayment plans (HCPPs) that provide some or all of Part B benefits under an agreement with HCFA.)

The conference agreement would modify existing disclosure statements to remove the wording that implies the policies duplicate Medicare coverage. New language would be substituted which states that: "Some health care services paid for by Medicare may also trigger the payment of benefits under this policy".

The agreement would further modify the required statement for policies providing both nursing home and non-institutional coverage, nursing home benefits only, or home health care benefits only. The reference to Federal law would be modified to read: "Federal law requires us to inform you that in certain situations this insurance may pay for some care also covered by Medicare". All other policies would be required to include the following statement: "This policy must pay benefits without regard to other health benefit coverage to which you may be entitled under Medicare or other insurance."

The conference agreement would further modify the language relating to State actions. The law would specifically state that nothing in the provision restricts or precludes a State's ability to regulate health insurance, including the policies subject to disclosure requirements. However, a State may not declare or specify, in statute, regulation, or otherwise, that a health insurance policy (other than a Medigap policy) or rider to an insurance contract which is not a health insurance policy that pays regardless of other coverage duplicates Medicare or Medigap benefits.

The conference agreement further narrows the language relating to application of penalties and legal action with respect to non-duplication requirements during a transition period, defined as beginning on November 5, 1991 and ending on the date of enactment. No criminal or civil monetary penalty could be imposed for an act or omission that occurred during the transition period relating to policies that pay benefits without regard to other coverage or long-term care policies. No legal action could be brought or continued in any Federal or State court with respect to the sale of such policies insofar as such action includes a cause of action which arose or is based on action occurring during the transition period and relating to non-duplication requirements. This limitation on legal actions would be conditional on the existing disclosure requirements being met with respect to any policy sold during the period beginning on the effective date of the disclosure requirements required by the 1994 Act (i.e. August 11, 1995) and ending 30 days after enactment.

The conference agreement further provides that the new disclosure rules only apply after enactment to health insurance policies that pay regardless of other coverage and 30-days after enactment to another health insurance policy.

The conference agreement would further permit a seller or issuer of a health insurance policy to use current disclosure statements rather than the new disclosure statements.

4. Medical liability reform

(Subtitle H of title II of the House bill; section 310 of title I of the Senate amendment.)

I. General Provisions

A. Federal Reform of Health Care Liability Actions

(Section 271 of House bill.)

Current law

There are no uniform Federal standards governing health care liability actions.

House bill

(1) Applicability. The provision would provide for Federal reform of health care liability actions. It would apply to any health care liability action brought in any State or Federal court. The provisions would not apply to any action for damages arising from a vaccine-related injury or death or to the extent that the provisions of the National Vaccine Injury Compensation Program apply. The provisions would also not apply to actions under the Employment Retirement Income Security Act.

(2) Preemption; Effect on Sovereign Immunity. The provisions would preempt State law to the extent State law provisions were inconsistent with the new requirements. However, it would not preempt State law to the extent State law provisions were more stringent. The provision specifies that nothing in the preemption provision could be construed to: (i) waive or affect any defense of sovereign immunity asserted by any State under any provision of law; (ii) waive or affect any defense of sovereign immunity asserted by the U.S.: (iii) affect any provision of the Foreign Services Immunity Act of 1976; (iv) preempt State choice-of-law rules with respect to claims brought by a Foreign nation or a citizen of a foreign nation; or (v) affect the right of any court to transfer venue or to apply the law of a foreign nation or to dismiss a claim of a foreign nation or of a citizen of a foreign nation on the ground of inconvenient forum.

(3) Amount in Controversy; Federal Court Jurisdiction. The provision would specify that in the case of a health care liability action brought under section 1332 of Title 28 of the U.S. Code, the amount of noneconomic and punitive damages and attorneys fees would not be included in establishing the amount in controversy for purposes of establishing original jurisdiction. Further, the provision would specify that nothing in this subtitle would be construed to establish any jurisdiction in the U.S. district courts over health care liability action on the basis of Federal question grounds specified in section 1331 or 1337 of title 28 of the U.S. Code.

Senate amendment

No provision.

Conference agreement

The conference agreement does not include the House provision.

B. Definitions

(Section 272 of House bill.)

275

Current law

No provision.

House bill

The provision would define the following terms for purposes of the Federal reforms: actual damages; alternative dispute resolution system; claimant; clear and convincing evidence; collateral source payments; drug; economic loss; harm; health benefit plan; health care liability action; health care liability claim; health care provider; health care service; medical device; noneconomic damages; person; product seller; punitive damages; and State.

Senate amendment

No provision.

Conference agreement

The conference agreement does not include the House provision.

C. EFFECTIVE DATE

(Section 273 of House bill.)

Current law

No provision.

House bill

The provision would specify that Federal reforms apply to any health care liability action brought in any State or Federal court that is initiated after the date of enactment. The provision would also apply to any health care liability claim subject to an alternative dispute resolution system, Any health care liability claim or action arising from an injury occurring prior to enactment would be governed by the statute of limitations in effect at the time the injury occurred.

Senate amendment

No provision.

Conference agreement

The conference agreement does not include the House provision.

II. UNIFORM STANDARDS FOR HEALTH CARE LIABILITY ACTIONS

A. STATUTE OF LIMITATIONS

(Section 281 of House bill.)

Current law

To date reforms of the malpractice system have occurred primarily at the State level and have generally involved changes in the rules governing tort cases. (A tort case is a civil action to recover damages, other than for a breach of contract.)

House bill

The provision would establish a uniform statute of limitations. Actions could not be brought more than two years after the injury was discovered or reasonably should have been discovered. In no event could the action be brought more than five years after the date of the alleged injury.

Senate amendment

No provision.

Conference agreement

The conference agreement does not include the House provision.

B. CALCULATION AND PAYMENT OF DAMAGES

(Section 282 of House bill.)

Current bill

No provision.

House bill

1. Noneconomic Damages. The provision would limit noneconomic damages to $250,000 in a particular case. The limit would apply regardless of the number of persons against whom the action was brought or the number of actions brought.

The provision would specify that a defendant would only be liable for the amount of noneconomic damages attributable to that defendant's proportionate share of the fault or responsibility for that claimant's injury.

2. Punitive Damages. The provision would permit the award of punitive damages (to the extent allowed under State law) only if the claimant established by clear and convincing evidence either that the harm was the result of conduct that specifically intended to cause harm or the conduct manifested a conscious flagrant indifference to the rights or safety of others. The amount of punitive damages awarded could not exceed $250,000 or three times the amount of economic damages, whichever was greater. The determination of punitive damages would be determined by the court and not be disclosed to the jury. The provision would not create a cause of action for punitive damages. Further, it would not preempt or supersede any State or Federal law to the extent that such law would further limit punitive damage awards.

The provision would permit either party to request a separate proceeding (bifurcation) on the issue of whether punitive damages should be awarded and in what amount. If a separate proceeding was requested, evidence related only to the claim of punitive damages would be inadmissible in any proceeding to determine whether actual damages should be awarded.

The provision would prohibit the award of punitive damages in a case where the drug or device was subject to premarket approval by the Food and Drug Administration, unless there was misrepresentation or fraud. A manufacturer or product seller would not be held liable for punitive damages related to adequacy of required tamper resistant packaging unless the packaging or labeling was found by clear and convincing evidence to be substantially out of compliance with the regulations.

3. Periodic Payments for Future Losses. The provision would permit the periodic (rather than lump sum) payment of future losses in excess of $50,000. The judgment of a court awarding periodic payments could not, in the absence of fraud, be reopened at any time to contest, amended, or modify the schedule or amount of payments. The provision would not preclude a lump sum settlement.

4. Treatment of Collateral Source Payments. The provision would permit a defendant to introduce evidence of collateral source payments. Such payments are those which are any amounts paid or reasonably likely to be paid by health or accident insurance, disability coverage, workers compensation, or other third party sources. If such evidence was introduced, the claimant could introduce evidence of any amount paid or reasonably likely to be paid to secure the right to such collateral source payments. No provider of collateral source payments would be permitted to recover any amount against the claimant or against the claimant's recovery. The provision would apply to settlements as well as actions resolved by the courts.

Senate amendment

No provision.

Conference agreement

The conference agreement does not include the House provision.

C. ALTERNATIVE DISPUTE RESOLUTION

(Section 283 of House bill.)

Current law

No provision.

House bill

The provision would require that any alternative dispute resolution system used to resolve health care liability actions or claims must include provisions identical to those specified in the bill.

Senate amendment

No provision.

Conference agreement

The conference agreement does not include the House provision.

III. MEDICAL VOLUNTEERS

(Section 310 of Senate bill.)

Current law

The Federally Supported Health Centers Assistance Act of 1992 (P.L. 102–501) provides protection from legal liability for certain health professionals providing services under the Public Health Service Act P.L. 104–73 made the provision permanent.

House bill

No provision.

Senate amendment

Section 310 of the bill would be known as the Medical Volunteer Act. It would provide that under certain circumstances a health care professional would be regarded for purposes of a malpractice claim to be a Federal employee for purposes of the Federal tort claims provisions of title 28 of the U.S. Code. Specifically this would occur when such professional provided services to a medically underserved person without receiving compensation for such services. The professional would be deemed to have provided services without providing compensation only if prior to furnishing services the professional: (i) agreed to furnish services without charge to any person, including any health insurance plan or program under which the recipient is covered; and (ii) provided the recipient with adequate notice (as determined by the Secretary) of the limited liability of the professional. These provisions would preempt any State law to the extent such law was inconsistent; they would not preempt any State law that provided greater incentives or protections.

A medically underserved person would be defined as a person residing in either: (I) a medically underserved area as defined for purposes of determining a medically underserved population under section 330 of the Public Health Service Act; or (ii) a health professional shortage area as defined in section 332 of that Act. Further the individual would have to receive care in a facility substantially comparable to any of those designated in the Federally-Supported Health Centers Act, as determined in regulations of the Secretary.

Conference agreement

The conference agreement includes the Senate provision. This provision extends Federal Tort Claims Act coverage to certain medical volunteers in free clinics in order to expand access to health care services to low-income individuals in medically underserved areas. Such coverage is currently provided in the Public Health Service Act to certain community and other health centers under the Federally Supported Health Centers Assistance Act. The provision tracks to the extent possible the provisions of that Act with respect to the coverage provided, quality assurance, and the process by which a free clinic applies to have a free clinic health professional deemed an employee of the Public Health Service.

Health professionals must meet certain conditions before they are deemed employees of the Public Health Service Act. They must be licensed or certified in accordance with applicable law and they must be volunteers; they may not receive compensation for the services in the form of salary, fees, or third-party payments. However, they may receive reimbursement from the clinic for reasonable expenses, such as costs of transportation and the cost of supplies they provide. Further, the free clinic may receive a voluntary donation from the individual served.

Eligible health professionals must provide qualifying services (i.e., otherwise available for Medicaid reimbursement) at a free clinic or through programs or events conducted by the clinic. These programs or events may include the provision of health services in a clinic-owned or clinic-operated mobile van or at a booth in a health fair. They may not include the provision of health services in a private physician's office following a referral from the free clinic. The health care professional or the free clinic must provide prior written notice of the extent of the limited liability to the individual. This notice should include written disclosure, understandable to a reasonable person, given a reasonable amount of time prior to the provision of services. Separate notice need not be provided by each professional nor prior to each discrete service but adequate written notice must be received by each individual.

The free clinic must be licensed or certified under applicable law and may not impose a charge on or accept reimbursement from any private or public third-party payor. The free clinic may, however, receive voluntary donations from individuals receiving health care services and is not precluded from receiving donations, grants, contracts, or awards from private or public sources for the general support of the clinic, or for specific purposes other than for payment or reimbursement for a health care service.

A free clinic must apply, consistent with the provisions applicable to community health centers, to have each health care professional "deemed" an employee of the Public Health Service Act, and therefore eligible for coverage under the Federal Tort Claims Act. A free clinic may not be deemed such an employee under this provision.

The Committee is aware that each of the 50 states have passed laws to limit the liability of volunteers in a variety of circumstances. This provision does not preempt those laws beyond the preemption provided in the Federal Tort Claims Act. Instead, the United States shall be liable in the same manner and to the same extent as a private individual in the same circumstances under State law.

The provision applies only to causes of action filed against a health professional for acts or omissions occurring on or after the date on which the health professional is determined by the Secretary to be a "free clinic health professional."

The provision establishes for free clinics funding and estimating mechanisms that match to the extent possible those for community health centers. No funds appropriated for purposes of community health centers will be available to free clinics.

4. Other provisions

I. EXTENSION OF MEDICARE SECONDARY PAYER PROVISIONS

(Sec. 621 of Senate Amendment.)

Current law

Generally Medicare is the "primary payer," that is, it pays health claims first, with an individual's private or other public insurance filling in some or all of Medicare's coverage gaps. However, in certain instances, the individual's other coverage pays first, while Medicare is the secondary payer. This phenomenon is referred to as the MSP program. A group health plan offered by an employer (with 20 or more employees is required to offer workers age 65 or over (and workers spouses age 65 or over) the same group health insurance coverage as is offered to younger workers. If the worker accepts the coverage, the employer is the primary payer, with Medicare becoming the secondary payer.

Similarly, a group health plan offered by a large employer (100 or more employees) is the primary payer for employees or their dependents who are on the Medicare disability program. The provision applies only to persons covered under the group plan because the employee is in "current employment status" (i.e. is an employee or is treated as an employee by the employer). The MSP provision for the disabled population expires October 1, 1998.

The MSP provisions apply to end-stage renal (ESRD) beneficiaries with employer group health plans, regardless of employer size. The group health plan is the primary payer for 18 months for persons who become eligible for Medicare ESRD benefits. The employer's role as primary payer is limited to a maximum of 21 months (18 months plus the usual 3-month waiting period for Medicare ESRD coverage). The 18-month MSP provisions for the ESRD population expire October 1, 1998; at that time the period would revert to 12 months.

The law authorizes a data match program which is intended to identify potential secondary payer situations. Medicare beneficiaries are matched against data contained in Social Security Administration (SSA) and Internal Revenue Service (IRS) files to identify cases in which a working beneficiary (or working spouse) may have employer-based health insurance coverage. Cases of previous incorrect Medicare payments are identified and recoveries are attempted. The authority for the program extends through Sept. 30, 1998.

House bill

No provision.

Senate Amendment

The provision would make permanent the MSP provisions for the disabled and the 18-month period for the ESRD population. It would also make permanent the data match requirement.

Conference agreement

The conference agreement does not include the Senate provision.

TITLE III. TAX-RELATED HEALTH PROVISIONS

A. MEDICAL SAVINGS ACCOUNTS

(Sec. 301 of the House bill.)

Present law

The tax treatment of health expenses depends on whether the individual is an employee or self employed, and whether the individual is covered under an employer-sponsored health plan. Employer contributions to a health plan for coverage for the employee and the employee's spouse and dependents is excludable from the employee's income and wages for social security tax purposes. Self-employed individuals are entitled to deduct 30 percent of the amount paid for health insurance for a self-employed individual and his or her spouse or dependents. Any individual who itemizes tax deductions may deduct unreimbursed medical expenses (including expenses for medical insurance) paid during the year to the extent that the total of such expenses exceeds 7.5 percent of the individual's adjusted gross income ("AGI"). Present law does not contain any special rules for medical savings accounts.

House bill

In general

Within limits, contributions to a medical savings account ("MSA") are deductible if made by an eligible individual and are excludable from income (and wages for social security purposes) if made by the employer of an eligible individual. Earnings on amounts in an MSA are not currently taxable. Distributions from an MSA for medical expenses are not taxable.

Eligible individuals

An individual is eligible to make a deductible contribution to an MSA (or to have employer contributions made on his or her behalf) if the individual is covered under a high deductible health plan and is not covered under another health plan (other than a plan that provides certain permitted coverage). An individual with other coverage in addition to a high deductible plan is still eligible for an MSA if such other coverage is certain permitted insurance or is coverage (whether provided through insurance to otherwise) for accidents, disability, dental care, vision care, or long-term care. Permitted insurance is (1) Medicare supplemental insurance; (2) insurance if substantially all of the coverage provided under such insurance relates to (a) liabilities incurred under worker's compensation law, (b) tort liabilities, (c) liabilities relating to ownership or use of property (e.g., auto insurance), or (d) such other similar liabilities as the Secretary may prescribe by regulations, (3) insurance for a specified disease or illness, and (4) insurance that provides a fixed payment for hospitalization. An individual is not eligible to make deductible contributions to an MSA for a year if any employer contributions are made to an MSA on behalf of the individual for the year.

Tax treatment of and limits on contributions

Individuals contributions to an MSA are deductible (within limits) in determining AGI. Employer contributions are excludable (within the same limits) from gross income and wages for employment tax purposes, except that this exclusion does not apply to contributions made through a cafeteria plan. The maximum amount of contributions that can be deducted or excluded for a year is equal to the lesser of (1) the deductible under the high deductible health plan or (2) $2,000 in the case of single coverage and $4,000 if the high deductible plan covers the individual and a spouse or dependent. The annual limit is the sum of the limits determined separately for each month, based on the individual's status as of the first day of the month. The maximum contribution limit to an MSA is determined separately for each spouse in a married couple. In no event can the maximum contribution limit exceed $4,000 for a family. The dollar limits are indexed for medical inflation and rounded to the nearest multiple of $50.

Definition of high deductible health plan

A high deductible health plan is a health plan with a deductible of at least $1,500 in the case of single coverage and $3,000 in the case of coverage of more than one individual. These dollar limits are indexed for medical inflation, rounded to the nearest multiple of $50.

Tax treatment of MSAs

Earnings on amounts in an MSA are not currently includible in income.

Taxation of distributions

Distributions from an MSA for the medical expenses of the individual and his or her spouse or dependents are excludable from income. For this purpose, medical expenses do not include expenses for insurance other than long-term care insurance, premiums for health care continuation coverage, and premiums for health care coverage while an individual is receiving unemployment compensation under Federal or State law.

Distributions that are not for medical expenses are includible in income. Such distributions are also subject to an additional 10-percent tax unless made after age 59½, death or disability.

Upon death, if the beneficiary is the individual's surviving spouse, the spouse may continue the MSA as his or her own. Otherwise, the beneficiary must include the MSA balance in income in the year of death. If there is no beneficiary, the MSA balance is includible on the final return of the decedent. In any case, no estate tax applies.

Definition of MSA

In general, an MSA is a trust or custodial account created exclusively for the benefit of the account holder and is subject to rules similar to those applicable to individual retirement arrangements.

Effective date

Taxable years beginning after December 31, 1996.

Senate amendment

The Senate amendment does not contain provisions providing favorable tax treatment for MSAs. However, the Senate amendment amends the Public Health Services Act to permit health maintenance organizations to charge deductibles to individuals with an MSA. In addition, the Senate amendment provides that it is the sense of the Committee on Labor and Human Resources that the establishment of MSAs should be encouraged as part of any health insurance legislation passed by the Senate through the use of tax incentives relating to contributions to, the income growth of, and the qualified use of, MSAs. The Senate amendment also provides that it is the sense of the Senate that the Congress should take measures to further the purposes of the Senate amendment, including any necessary changes to the Internal Revenue Code to encourage groups and individuals to obtain health coverage, and to promote access, equity, portability, affordability, and security of health benefits.

Conference agreement

The conference agreement follows the House bill, with modifications.

In general

Within limits, contributions to a medical savings account ("MSA") are deductible if made by an eligible individual and are excludable if made by the employer of an eligible individual. Earnings on amounts in an MSA are not currently taxable. Distributions from an MSA for medical expenses are not taxable.

Eligible individuals

Beginning in 1997, MSAs are available to employees covered under an employer-sponsored high deductible plan of a small employer and self-employed individuals. An employer is a small employer if it employed, on average, no more than 50 employees during either the preceding or the second preceding year.

In determining whether an employer is a small employer, a preceding year is not taken into account unless the employer was in existence throughout such year. In the case of an employer that was not in existence through the first preceding year, the determination of whether the employer has no more than 50 employees is based on the average number of employees that the employer reasonably expects to employ in the current year. In determining the number of employees of an employer, employers under common control are treated as a single employer.

In order for an employee of an eligible employer to be eligible to make MSA contributions (or to have employer contributions made on his or her behalf), the employee must be covered under an employer-sponsored high deductible health plan and must not be covered under any other health plan (other than a plan that provides certain permitted coverage). In the case of an employee, contributions can be made to an MSA either by the individual or by the individual's employer. However, an individual is not eligible to make contributions to an MSA for a year if any employer contributions are made to an MSA on behalf of the individual for the year.

Similarly, in order to be eligible to make contributions to an MSA, a self-employed individual must be covered under a high deductible health plan and no other health plan (other than a plan that provides certain permitted coverage).

An individual with other coverage in addition to a high deductible plan is still eligible for an MSA if such other coverage is certain permitted insurance or is coverage (whether provided through insurance to otherwise) for accidents, disability, dental care, vision care, or long-term care. Permitted insurance is: (1) Medicare supplemental insurance; (2) insurance if substantially all of the coverage provided under such insurance relates to (a) liabilities incurred under worker's compensation law, (b) tort liabilities, (c) liabilities relating to ownership or use of property (e.g., auto insurance), or (d) such other similar liabilities as the Secretary may prescribe by regulations, (3) insurance for a specified disease or illness, and (4) insurance that provides a fixed payment for hospitalization.

If a small employer with an MSA plan (i.e., the employer or its employees made contributions to an MSA) ceases to become a small employer (i.e., exceeds the 50-employee limit), then the employer (and its employees) can continue to establish and make contributions to MSAs (including contributions for new employees and employees that did not previously have an MSA) until the year following the first year in which the employer has more than 200 employees. After that, those employees who had an MSA (to which individual or employer contributions were made in any year) can continue to make contributions (or have contributions made on their behalf) even if the employer has more than 200 employees. For example, suppose Employer A has 48 employees in 1995 and 1996, and 205 employees in 1997 and 1998. A would be a small employer in 1997 and 1998 because it has 50 or fewer employees in the preceding or the second preceding year. Employer A would still be considered a small employer in 1999. However, in years after 1999, Employer A would not be considered a small employer (even if the number of employees fell to 50 or below), and in years after 1999, only employees who previously had MSA contributions could make new MSA contributions (or have employer contributions made on their behalf).

Tax treatment of and limits on contributions

Individual contributions to an MSA are deductible (within limits) in determining AGI (i.e., "above the line"). In addition, employer contributions are excludable (within the same limits), except that this exclusion does not apply to contributions made through a cafeteria plan.

In the case of a self-employed individual, the deduction cannot exceed the individual's earned income from the trade or business with respect to which the high deductible plan is established. In the case of an employee, the deduction cannot exceed the individual's compensation attributable to the employer sponsoring the high deductible plan in which the individual is enrolled.

The maximum annual contribution that can be made to an MSA for a year is 65 percent of the deductible under the high deductible plan in the case of individual coverage and 75 percent of the deductible in the case of family coverage. No other dollar limits on the maximum contribution apply. The annual contribution limit is the sum of the limits determined separately for each month, based on the individual's status and health plan coverage as of the first day of the month.

Contributions for a year can be made until the due date for the individual's tax return for the year (determined without regard to extensions).

In order to facilitate application of the cap on the number of MSA participants, described below, the employer is required to report employer MSA contributions, and the individual is required to report such employer MSA contributions on the individual's tax return.

Comparability rule for employer contributions

If an employer provides high deductible health plan coverage coupled with an MSA to employees and makes employer contributions to the MSAs, the employer must make available a comparable contribution on behalf of all employees with comparable coverage during the same period. Contributions are considered comparable if they are either of the same amount or the same percentage of the deductible under the high deductible plan. The comparability rule is applied separately to part-time employees (i.e., employees who are customarily employed for fewer than 30 hours per week). No restrictions are placed on the ability of the employer to offer different plans to different groups of employees.

For example, suppose an employer maintains two high deductible plans, Plan A, with a deductible of $1,500 for individual coverage and $3,000 for family coverage, and Plan B, with a deductible of $2,000 for individual coverage and $4,000 for family coverage. The employer offers an MSA contribution to full-time employees in Plan A of $500 for individual coverage and $750 for family coverage. In order to satisfy the comparability rule, the employer would have to offer full-time employees covered under Plan B one of the following MSA contributions: (1) $500 for employees with individual coverage and $750 for employees with family coverage or (2) $667 for employees with individual coverage and $1,000 for employees with family coverage. Different contributions (or no contributions) could be made for part-time employees covered under either high deductible plan.

If employer contributions do not comply with the comparability rule during a period, then the employer is subject to an excise tax equal to 35 percent of the aggregate amount contributed by the employer to MSAs of the employer for that period. The excise tax is designed as a proxy for the denial of employer contributions. In the case of a failure to comply with the comparability rule which is due to reasonable cause and not to willful neglect, the Secretary may waive part of all of the tax imposed to the extent that the payment of the tax would be excessive relative to the failure involved.

For purposes of the comparability rule, employers under common control are aggregated in the same manner as in determining whether the employer is a small employer. The comparability rule does not fail to be satisfied in a year if the employer is precluded from making contributions for all employees with high deductible plan coverage because the employer has more than 200 employees or due to operation of the cap during the initial 4-year period.

Definition of high deductible plan

A high deductible plan is a health plan with an annual deductible of at least $1,500 and no more than $2,250 in the case of individual coverage and at least $3,000 and no more than $4,500 in the case of family coverage. In addition, the maximum out-of-pocket expenses with respect to allowed costs (including the deductible) must be no more than $3,000 in the case of individual coverage and no more than $5,500 in the case of family coverage. Beginning after 1998, these dollar amounts are indexed for inflation in $50 dollar increments based on the consumer price index. A plan does not fail to qualify as a high deductible plan merely because it does not have a deductible for preventive care as required by State law.

As under present law, State insurance commissions would have oversight over the issuance of high deductible plans issued in conjunction with MSAs and could impose additional consumer protections. It is intended that the National Association of Insurance Commissioners ("NAIC") will develop model standards for high deductible plans that individual States could adopt.

Tax treatment of MSAs

Earnings on amounts in an MSA are not currently includible in income.

Taxation of distributions

Distributions from an MSA for the medical expenses of the individual and his or her spouse or dependents generally are excludable from income. However, in any year for which a contribution is made to an MSA, withdrawals from an MSA maintained by that individual are excludable from income only if the individual for whom the expenses were incurred was eligible to make an MSA contribution at the time the expenses were incurred. This rule is designed to ensure that MSAs are in fact used in conjunction with a high deductible plan, and that they are not primarily used by other individuals who have health plans that are not high deductible plans. For example, suppose that, in 1997, individual A is covered by a high deductible plan, and A's spouse ("B") is covered by a health plan that is not a high deductible plan. A makes contributions to an MSA for 1997. Withdrawals from the MSA to pay B's medical expenses incurred in 1997 would be includible in income (and subject to the additional tax on nonmedical withdrawals) because B is not covered by a high deductible plan.

For this purpose, medical expenses are defined as under the itemized deduction for medical expenses, except that medical expenses do not include expenses for insurance other than long-term care insurance, premiums for health care continuation coverage, and premiums for health care coverage while an individual is receiving unemployment compensation under Federal or State law.

Distributions that are not for medical expenses are includible in income. Such distributions are also subject to an additional 15-percent tax unless made after age 65, death, or disability.

Estate tax treatment

Upon death, any balance remaining in the decedent's MSA is includible in his or her gross estate.

If the account holder's surviving spouse is the named beneficiary of the MSA, then, after the death of the account holder, the MSA becomes the MSA of the surviving spouse and the amount of the MSA balance may be deducted in computing the decedent's taxable estate, pursuant to the estate tax marital deduction provided in Code section 2056. The MSA qualifies for the marital deduction because the account holder has sole control over disposition of the assets in the MSA. The surviving spouse is not required to include any amount in income as a result of the death; the general rules applicable to MSAs apply to the surviving spouse's MSA (e.g., the surviving spouse is subject to income tax only on distributions from the MSA for nonmedical purposes). The surviving spouse can exclude from income amounts withdrawn from the MSA for expenses incurred by the decedent prior to death, to the extent they otherwise are qualified medical expenses.

If, upon death, the MSA passes to a named beneficiary other than the decedent's surviving spouse, the MSA ceases to be an MSA as of the date of the decedent's death, and the beneficiary is required to include the fair market value of MSA assets as of the date of death in gross income for the taxable year that includes the date of death. The amount includable in income is reduced by the amount in the MSA used, within one year of the death, to pay qualified medical expenses incurred prior to the death. As is the case with other MSA distributions, whether the expenses are qualified medical expenses is determined as of the time the expenses were incurred. In computing taxable income, the beneficiary may claim a deduction for that portion of the Federal estate tax on the decendent's estate that was attributable to the amount of the MSA balance (calculated in accordance with the present-law rules relating to income in respect of a decedent set forth in sec. 691(c)).

If there is no named beneficiary for the decedent's MSA, the MSA ceases to be an MSA as of the date of death, and the fair market value of the assets in the MSA as of such date are includible in the decedent's gross income for the year of the death. This rule applies in all cases in which there is no named beneficiary, even if the surviving spouse ultimately obtains the right to MSA assets (e.g., if the surviving spouse is the sole beneficiary of the decedent's estate). Because of the significant tax consequences if a married individual fails to name his or her spouse as the MSA beneficiary, even if the rights to MSA assets are otherwise acquired by the surviving spouse, it is anticipated that the marketing materials describing other tax aspects of MSAs will explain the consequences of failure to name the spouse as the beneficiary.

Cap on taxpayers utilizing MSAs

In general.—The number of taxpayers benefiting annually from an MSA contribution is limited to a threshold level (generally 750,000 taxpayers). If it is determined in a year that the threshold level has been exceeded (called a "cut-off" year) then, in general, for succeeding years during the 4-year pilot period 1997–2000, only those individuals who (1) made an MSA contribution or had an employer MSA contribution for the year or a preceding year (i.e. are active MSA participants) or (2) are employed by a participating employer, would be eligible for an MSA contribution. In determining whether the threshold for any year has been exceeded, MSAs of individuals who were not covered under a health insurance plan for the six month period ending on the date on which coverage under a high deductible plan commences would not be taken into account.[1] However, if the threshold level is exceeded in a year, previously uninsured individuals would be subject to the same restriction on contributions in succeeding years as other individuals. That is, they would not be eligible for an MSA contribution for a year following a cut-off-year unless they are an active MSA participant (i.e. had an MSA contribution for the year or a preceding year) or are employed by a participating employer.

In a year after a cut-off year, employees of a participating employer can establish new MSAs and make new contributions (even if the employee is a new employee or did not previously have an MSA). An employer is a participating employer if (1) the employer made any MSA contributions on behalf of employees in any preceding year or (2) at least 20 percent of the employees covered under a high deductible plan made an MSA contribution of at least $100 in the preceding year.

In the case of a cut-off year before 2000, an individual is not an eligible individual or an active MSA participant unless the individual was first covered under a high deductible plan on or before the cut-off date. The cut-off date is generally October 1 of the cut-off year. However, if the individual was enrolled in a plan pursuant to a regularly scheduled enrollment period, then the cut-off date is December 31. Similarly, an employer is not considered a participating employer if it first offered coverage after October 1 of a cut-off year unless the high deductible plan is offered pursuant to a regularly scheduled enrollment period. In addition, a self-employed individual is not considered an eligible individual or an active MSA participant unless the individual was covered under a high deductible plan on or before November 1 of a cut-off year.

These rules are designed to prevent high deductible plans from being first offered just before the limitation on MSAs is effective in order to avoid application of the cap. They are not, however, intended to preclude individuals who first enroll in an employer-sponsored high deductible health plan or employees of employers that adopt a high deductible plan in a cut-off year due to normal health plan operation from having MSAs. For example, suppose a small employer offers a high deductible plan that provides that new employees may be covered under the plan beginning the first day of the month after the month in which they are hired. New employee A (whose previous coverage was not high deductible coverage) is hired on October 15, and is enrolled in the high deductible plan November 1 of that year. If the year is a cut-off year, Employee A is an eligible individual and, if he has an MSA contribution for the year, an active participant for the year because he was enrolled pursuant to a regularly scheduled enrollment period. Similarly, suppose that employer A is a small employer and does not currently offer health care coverage. In 1997, A decides to offer health plan coverage to its employees, including a high deductible

---

[1] Permitted coverage, as described above, does not constitute coverage under a health insurance plan for this purpose.

plan coupled with an MSA. A takes steps to provide such coverage on or before October 1 of the year (e.g., making arrangements with insurance companies or distributing plan material to employees). The first enrollment period for the health plans begins September 1, and coverage under the plan will begin November 1. If the year is a cut-off year, the employer is a participating employer because the plan was established pursuant to a regularly scheduled enrollment period.

Under certain circumstances, MSA participation may be re-opened after a cut-off year so that MSAs are again available to all individuals in the qualifying group of self-employed individuals and employees of small employers.

For the 1997 tax year, taxpayers are permitted to establish MSAs provided that they are in the qualifying group of self-employed individuals or employees working for small employers.

Rules for 1997

On or before June 1, 1997, each trustee or custodian of an MSA (e.g., insurance company or financial institution) is required to report to the Internal Revenue Service ("IRS") the total number of MSAs established as of April 30, 1997, for which it acts as trustee or custodian, including the number of MSAs established for previously uninsured individuals.[2] If, based on this reporting, the number of MSAs established (but excluding those established for previously uninsured individuals) as of April 30, 1997, exceeds 375,000 (50 percent of 750,000), on or before September 1, 1997, the IRS would publish guidance providing that only active MSA participants or employees of participating employers would be eligible for an MSA contribution for the 1998 tax year and thereafter. If this threshold is exceeded, an individual who is first covered by an employer-sponsored high deductible health plan after September 1, 1997, is not an eligible individual or an active MSA participant (and therefore cannot have an MSA for 1997 or a subsequent year) unless the high deductible coverage is elected pursuant to a regularly scheduled enrollment period. Similarly, an employer is not considered a participating employer if it first offered a high deductible plan after September 1, 1997, unless the plan was offered pursuant to a regularly scheduled enrollment period. Also, a self-employed individual would not be an eligible individual or an active MSA participant unless the individual was first covered under a high deductible plan on or before October 1, 1997.

If the 375,000 cap is not exceeded, then another determination of MSA participation will be made, as follows. On or before August 1, 1997, each trustee or custodian of an MSA (e.g., insurance company or financial institution) is required to report to the Internal Revenue Service ("IRS") the total number of MSAs established as of June 30, 1997, for which it acts as trustee or custodian, including the number of MSAs established for previously uninsured individuals. If, based on this reporting, the number of MSAs established (but excluding those established for previously uninsured in-

---

[2] This report would include the name and social security number of taxpayers establishing an MSA. Failures to report are subject to a penalty of $25 for each MSA up to a maximum of $5,000. A trustee or custodian required to report could elect to do so on a company-wide or branch-by-branch basis.

dividuals) exceeds the 1997 threshold level of 525,000 (70 percent of 750,000), on or before October 1, 1997, the IRS would publish guidance providing that only active MSA participants or employees of participating employers would be eligible for an MSA contribution for the 1998 tax year and thereafter. If the 1997 threshold is exceeded, an individual who is first covered by an employer-sponsored high deductible health plan after October 1, 1997, is not an eligible individual or an active MSA participant (and therefore cannot have an MSA for 1997 or a subsequent year) unless the high deductible coverage is elected pursuant to a regularly scheduled enrollment period. Similarly, an employer is not considered a participating employer if it first offered a high deductible plan after October 1, 1997, unless the plan was offered pursuant to a regularly scheduled enrollment period. Also, a self-employed individual would not be an eligible individual or an active MSA participant unless the individual was first covered under a high deductible plan on or before November 1, 1997.

If the 1997 threshold level is not exceeded, all taxpayers in the qualifying eligible group (i.e., self-employed individuals and employees working for employers with 50 or fewer employees) would be permitted to have MSA contributions for the 1998 tax year.

Rules for 1998 and succeeding years

In general.—In 1998 and succeeding years, on or before August 1 of the year, each trustee or custodian of an MSA is required to report to the IRS the total number of MSAs established as of June 30 for the current year,[3] including the number of such MSAs established for previously uninsured individuals. In addition, the IRS is directed to collect data with respect to the number of taxpayers showing an MSA contribution on their individual income tax returns for the prior year and the extent to which such taxpayers were previously uninsured.[4] If, based on this information, the IRS determines as described below that the number of taxpayers anticipated to have MSA contributions (disregarding previously uninsured individuals) exceeds the applicable threshold level, the IRS is required to issue guidance to the public by no later than October 1. If this guidance is issued, then only taxpayers who are active MSA participants or who are employed by a participating employer would be entitled to MSA contributions in tax years following the year the guidance is issued.

For 1998 and succeeding years, the threshold is exceeded if either of the following limits are exceeded. The numerical limit is exceeded if: (1) the number of MSA returns filed on or before April 1 of the year, plus the estimate of the number of MSA returns for such year that will be filed after such date exceeds the threshold, or (2) 90 percent of the amount determined under (1), plus 15/6ths of the MSAs established for the year before July 1 exceeds $750,000.

---

[3] That is, the report would not include MSAs to which contributions are made for the prior year.
[4] Each income tax return on which an MSA contribution is shown is treated as one taxpayer for purposes of the cap. It is anticipated that the IRS would adjust the actual return information to take into account MSAs that may have been established by late filers.

1998.—In 1998, the IRS would analyze the return data from the filing of 1997 tax year returns and would determine, based on this data, the number of taxpayers with MSA contributions for 1997 and who were not previously uninsured. If the IRS determines that (1) MSA returns filed on or before April 15, 1998, plus the estimated number of MSA returns for 1997 filed after such date exceeds 600,000, or (2) that 90 percent of the MSA returns in (1), plus 15/6ths of the number of MSAs established for 1998 between January 1 and July 1, 1998, the IRS would publish guidance on or before October 1, 1998, advising taxpayers that only taxpayers who had previously had MSA contributions (i.e., for either the 1997 or 1998 tax year) or who are employed by a participating employer would be eligible for MSA contributions in succeeding tax years. If the 1998 threshold is exceeded, an individual who is first covered by an employer-sponsored high deductible health plan after October 1, 1998, is not an eligible individual or an active MSA participant (and therefore cannot have an MSA for 1998 or a subsequent year) unless the high deductible coverage is elected pursuant to a regularly scheduled enrollment period. Similarly, an employer is not considered a participating employer if it first offered a high deductible plan after October 1, 1998, unless the plan was offered pursuant to a regularly scheduled enrollment period. Also, a self-employed individual would not be an eligible individual or an active MSA participant unless the individual was first covered under a high deductible plan on or before November 1, 1998.

In the event that the threshold level had not been exceeded, all taxpayers in the qualifying eligible group would be permitted to establish MSAs during the 1999 tax year.

1999.—In 1999, the IRS would analyze the return data from the filing of 1998 tax year returns and would determine, based on this data, the number of taxpayers with MSA contributions for 1998 and who were not previously uninsured. If the IRS determines that (1) MSA returns filed on or before April 15, 1999, plus the estimated number of MSA returns for 1998 filed after such date exceeds 600,000, or (2) that 90 percent of the MSA returns in (1), plus 15/6ths of the number of MSAs established for 1998 between January 1 and July 1, 1999, the IRS would publish guidance on or before October 1, 1999, advising taxpayers that only taxpayers who had previously had MSA contributions (i.e., for the 1997, 1998, or 1999 tax year) or who are employed by a participating employer would be eligible for MSA contributions in succeeding tax years. If the 1999 threshold is exceeded, an individual who is first covered by an employer-sponsored high deductible health plan after October 1, 1999, is not an eligible individual or an active MSA participant (and therefore cannot have an MSA for 1999 or a subsequent year) unless the high deductible coverage is elected pursuant to a regularly scheduled enrollment period. Similarly, an employer is not considered a participating employer if it first offered a high deductible plan after October 1, 1999, unless the plan was offered pursuant to a regularly scheduled enrollment period. Also, a self-employed individual would not be an eligible individual or an active MSA participant unless the individual was first covered under a high deductible plan on or before November 1, 1999.

In the event that the threshold level had not been exceeded, all taxpayers in the qualifying eligible group would be permitted to establish MSAs during the 2000 tax year.

Reopening of MSA participation.—If 1997 is a cut-off year, then in 1998, the IRS would (as described above) analyze the return data from the filing of 1997 tax year returns and would determine, based on this data, the number of taxpayers with MSA contributions for 1997 and who were not previously uninsured. If the IRS determines that MSA returns filed on or before April 15, 1998, plus the estimated number of MSA returns for 1997 filed after such date (disregarding MSAs of previously uninsured individuals) exceeds 750,000, then the IRS will announce by October 1, 1998, that MSAs will be available to all eligible individuals in the qualifying eligible group of self-employed individuals and employees of small employers covered under a high deductible health plan during the first 6 months of 1999. Similarly, if 1998 is a cut-off year, then in 1999, MSA returns filed on or before April 15, 1999, plus the estimated number of MSA returns for 1998 filed after such date (disregarding MSAs of previously uninsured individuals) exceeds 750,000, then IRS will announce by October 1, 1998, that MSAs will be available to all eligible individuals in the qualifying eligible group of self-employed individuals and employees of small employers with high deductible plan coverage during the first 6 months of 2000.

End of pilot project

After December 31, 2000, no new contributions may be made to MSAs except by or on behalf of individuals who previously had MSA contributions and employees who are employed by a participating employer. An employer is a participating employer if (1) the employer made any MSA contributions for any year to an MSA on behalf of employees or (2) at least 20 percent of the employees covered under a high deductible plan made MSA contributions of at least $100 in the year 2000.

Self-employed individuals who made contributions to an MSA during the period 1997–2000 also may continue to make contributions after 2000.

Measuring the effects of MSAs

During 1997–2000, the Department of the Treasury will evaluate MSA participation and the reduction in Federal revenues due to such participation and make such reports of such evaluations to the Congress as the Secretary determines appropriate.

The General Accounting Office is directed to contract with an organization with expertise in health economics, health insurance markets and actuarial science to conduct a study regarding the effects of MSAs in the small group market on (1) selection (including adverse selection), (2) health costs, including the impact on premiums of individuals with comprehensive coverage, (3) use of preventive care, (4) consumer choice, (5) the scope of coverage of high deductible plans purchased in conjunction with an MSA and (6) other relevant issues, to be submitted to the Congress by January 1, 1999.

The conferees intend that the study be broad in scope, gather sufficient data to fully evaluate the relevant issues, and be adequately funded. The conferees expect the study to utilize appropriate techniques to measure the impact of MSAs on the broader health care market, including in-depth analysis of local markets with high penetration. The conferees expect the study to evaluate the impact of MSAs on individuals and families experiencing high health care costs, especially low- and middle-income families.

Definiton of MSA

In general, an MSA is a trust or custodial account created exclusively for the benefit of the account holder and subject to rules similar to those applicable to individual retirement arrangements.

Effective date

The provisions are effective for taxable years beginning after December 31, 1996.

B. INCREASE IN DEDUCTION FOR HEALTH INSURANCE EXPENSES OF SELF-EMPLOYED INDIVIDUALS

(Sec. 311 of the House bill and sec. 401 of the Senate amendment.)

Present law

Under present law, self-employed individuals are entitled to deduct 30 percent of the amount paid for health insurance for the self-employed individual and the individual's spouse and dependents. The deduction is not available for any month in which the taxpayer is eligible to participate in a subsidized health plan maintained by the employer of the taxpayer or the taxpayer's spouse. The 30-percent deduction is available in the case of self insurance as well as commercial insurance. The self-insured plan must in fact be insurance (e.g., there must be appropriate risk shifting) and not merely a reimbursement arrangement.

House bill

Under the House bill, the deduction for health insurance for self-employed individuals is phased up to 50 percent as follows: for taxable years beginning in 1998, the amount of the deduction would be 35 percent of health insurance expenses; for taxable years beginning in 1999, 2000, and 2001, 40 percent; for taxable years beginning in 2002, 45 percent; and for taxable years beginning in 2003 and thereafter, 50 percent.

Effective date.—The provision is effective for taxable years beginning after December 31, 1997.

Senate amendment

Beginning in 1997, the Senate amendment phases up the deduction in 5 percent increments until it is 80 percent in 2006 and thereafter.

Effective date.—The provision is effective for taxable years beginning after December 31, 1996.

Conference agreement

The conference agreement increases the deduction for health insurance of self-employed individuals as follows: the deduction would be 40 percent in 1997; 45 percent in 1998 through 2002; 50 percent in 2003; 60 percent in 2004; 70 percent in 2005; and 80 percent in 2006 and thereafter.

The conference agreement also provides that payments for personal injury or sickness through an arrangements having the effect of accident or health insurance (and that are not merely reimbursement arrangements) are excludable from income. In order for the exclusion to apply, the arrangement must be insurance (e.g., there must be adequate risk shifting). This provision equalizes the treatment of payments under commercial insurance and arrangements other than commercial insurance that have the effect of insurance. Under this provision, a self-employed individual who receives payments from such an arrangement could exclude the payments from income.

Effective date.—The provision is effective for taxable years beginning after December 31, 1996. No inference is intended with respect to the excludability of payments under arrangements having the effect of accident or health insurance under present law.

C. TREATMENT OF LONG-TERM CARE INSURANCE AND SERVICES

(Secs. 321–323 and 325–328 of the House bill and secs. 411–415 and 421–424 of the Senate amendment.)

Present law

In general

Present law generally does not provide explicit rules relating to the tax treatment of long-term care insurance contracts or long-term care services. Thus, the treatment of long-term care contracts and services is unclear. Present law does provide rules relating to medical expenses and accident or health insurance.

Itemized deduction for medical expenses

In determining taxable income for Federal income tax purposes, a taxpayer is allowed an itemized deduction for unreimbursed expenses that are paid by the taxpayer during the taxable year for medical care of the taxpayer, the taxpayer's spouse, or a dependent of the taxpayer, to the extent that such expenses exceed 7.5 percent of the adjusted gross income of the taxpayer for such year (sec. 213). For this purpose, expenses paid for medical care generally are defined as amounts paid: (1) for the diagnosis, cure, mitigation, treatment, or prevention of disease (including prescription medicines or drugs and insulin), or for the purpose of affecting any structure or function of the body (other than cosmetic surgery not related to disease, deformity, or accident); (2) for transportation primarily for, and essential to, medical care referred to in (1); or (3) for insurance (including Part B Medicare premiums) covering medical care referred to in (1) and (2).

Exclusion for amounts received under accident or health insurance

Amounts received by a taxpayer under accident or health insurance for personal injuries or sickness generally are excluded from gross income to the extent that the amounts received are not attributable to medical expenses that were allowed as a deduction for a prior taxable year (sec. 104).

Treatment of accident or health plans maintained by employers

Contributions of an employer to an accident or health plan that provides compensation (through insurance or otherwise) to an employee for personal injuries or sickness of the employee, the employee's spouse, or a dependent of the employee, are excluded from the gross income of the employee (sec. 106). In addition, amounts received by an employee under such a plan generally are excluded from gross income to the extent that the amounts received are paid, directly or indirectly, to reimburse the employee for expenses for the medical care of the employee, the employee's spouse, or a dependent of the employee (sec. 105). for this purpose, expenses incurred for medical care are defined in the same manner as under the rules regarding the deduction for medical expenses.

A cafeteria plan is an employer-sponsored arrangement under which employees can elect among cash and certain employer-provided qualified benefits. No amount is included in the gross income of a participant in a cafeteria plan merely because the participant has the opportunity to make such an election (sec. 125). Employer-provided accident or health coverage is one of the benefits that may be offered under a cafeteria plan.

A flexible spending arrangement ("FSA") is an arrangement under which an employee is reimbursed for medical expenses or other nontaxable employer-provided benefits, such as dependent care, and under which the maximum amount of reimbursement that is reasonably available to a participant for a period of coverage is not substantially in excess of the total premium (including both employee-paid and employer-paid portions of the premium) for such participant's coverage. Under proposed Treasury regulations, a maximum amount of reimbursement is not substantially in excess of the total premium if such maximum amount is less than 500 percent of the premium. An FSA may be part of a cafeteria plan or provided by an employer outside a cafeteria plan. FSAs are commonly used to reimburse employees for medical expenses not covered by insurance. If certain requirements are satisfied,[5] amounts reimbursed for nontaxable benefits from an FSA are excludable from income.

Health care continuation rules

The health care continuation rules require that an employer must provide qualified beneficiaries the opportunity to continue to participate for a specified period in the employer's health plan after

---

[5] These requirements include a requirement that a health FSA can only provide reimbursement for medical expenses (as defined in sec. 213) and cannot provide reimbursement for premium payments for other health coverage and that the maximum amount of reimbursement under a health FSA must be available at all times during the period of coverage.

the occurrence of certain events (such as termination of employment) that would have terminated such participation (sec. 4980B). Individuals electing continuation coverage can be required to pay for such coverage.

House bill

Tax treatment and definition of long-term care insurance contracts and qualified long-term care services

Exclusion of long-term care proceeds.—A long-term care insurance contract generally is treated as an accident and health insurance contract. Amounts (other than policyholder dividends or premium refunds) received under a long-term care insurance contract generally are excludable as amounts received for personal injuries and sickness, subject to a cap of $175 per day, or $63,875 annually, on per diem contracts only. If the aggregate amount of periodic payments under all qualified long-term care contracts exceeds the dollar cap for the period, then the amount of such excess payments is excludable only to the extent of the individual's costs (that are not otherwise compensated for by insurance or otherwise) for long-term care services during the period. The dollar cap is indexed by the medical care cost component of the consumer price index.

Exclusion for employer-provided long-term care coverage.—A plan of an employer providing coverage under a long-term care insurance contract generally is treated as an accident and health plan. Employer-provided coverage under a long-term care insurance contract is not, however, excludable by an employee if provided through a cafeteria plan; similarly, expenses for long-term care services cannot be reimbursed under an FSA.[6]

Definition of long-term care insurance contract.—A long-term care insurance contract is defined as any insurance contract that provides only coverage of qualified long-term care services and that meets other requirements. The other requirements are that (1) the contract is guaranteed renewable, (2) the contract does not provide for a cash surrender value or other money that can be paid, assigned, pledged or borrowed, (3) refunds (other than refunds on the death of the insured or complete surrender or cancellation of the contract) and dividends under the contract may be used only to reduce future premiums or increase future benefits, and (4) the contract generally does not pay or reimburse expenses reimbursable under Medicare (except where Medicare is a secondary payor, or the contract makes per diem or other periodic payments without regard to expenses).

A contract does not fail to be treated as a long-term care insurance contract solely because it provides for payments on a per diem or other periodic basis without regard to expenses incurred during the period.

Medicare duplication rules.—The bill provides that no provision of law shall be construed or applied so as to prohibit the offering of a long-term care insurance contract on the basis that the

---

[6] The bill does not otherwise modify the requirements relating to FSAs. An FSA is defined as a benefit program providing employees with coverage under which specified incurred expenses may be reimbursed (subject to maximums and other reasonable conditions), and the maximum amount of reimbursement that is reasonably available to a participant is less than 500 percent of the value of the coverage.

contract coordinates its benefits with those provided under Medicare. Thus, long-term care insurance contracts are not subject to the rules requiring duplication of Medicare benefits.

Definition of qualified long-term care services.—Qualified long-term care services means necessary diagnostic, preventive, therapeutic, curing, treating, mitigating and rehabilitative services, and maintenance or personal care services that are required by a chronically ill individual and that are provided pursuant to a plan of care prescribed by a licensed health care practitioner.

Chronically ill individual.—A chronically ill individual is one who has been certified within the previous 12 months by a licensed health care practitioner as (1) being unable to perform (without substantial assistance) at least 2 activities of daily living for at least 90 days[7] due to a loss of functional capacity, (2) having a similar level of disability as determined by the Secretary of the Treasury in consultation with the Secretary of Health and Human Services, or (3) requiring substantial supervision to protect such individual from threats to health and safety due to severe cognitive impairment. Activities of daily living are eating, toileting, transferring, bathing, dressing and continence.[8]

It is intended that an individual who is physically able but has a cognitive impairment such as Alzheimer's disease or another form of irreversible loss of mental capacity be treated similarly to an individual who is unable to perform (without substantial assistance) at least 2 activities of daily living. Because of the concern that eligibility for the medical expense deduction not be diagnosis-driven, the provision requires the cognitive impairment to be severe. It is intended that severe cognitive impairment mean a deterioration or loss in intellectual capacity that is measured by clinical evidence and standardized tests which reliably measure impairment in: (1) short- or long-term memory; (2) orientation to people, places or time; and (3) deductive or abstract reasoning. In addition, it is intended that such deterioration or loss place the individual in jeopardy of harming self or others and therefore require substantial supervision by another individual.

A licensed health care practitioner is a physician (as defined in sec. 1861(r)(1) of the Social Security Act) and any registered professional nurse, licensed social worker or other individual who meets such requirements as may be prescribed by the Secretary of the Treasury.

Expenses for long-term care services treated as medical expenses.—Unreimbursed expenses for qualified long-term care services provided to the taxpayer or the taxpayer's spouse or dependents are treated as medical expenses for purposes of the itemized deduction for medical expenses (subject to the present-law floor of 7.5 percent of adjusted gross income). For this purpose, amounts received under a long-term care insurance contract (regardless of whether the contract reimburses expenses or pays benefits on a per

---

[7] The 90-day period is not a waiting period. Thus, for example, an individual can be certified was chronically ill if the licensed health care practitioner certifies that the individual will be unable to perform at least 2 activities of daily living for at least 90 days.

[8] Nothing in the bill requires the contract to take into account all of the activities of daily living. For example, a contract could require that an individual be unable to perform (without substantial assistance) 2 out of any 5 such activities, or for another example, 3 out of the 6 activities.

diem or other periodic basis) are treated as reimbursement for expenses actually incurred for medical care.

For purposes of the deduction for medical expenses, qualified long-term care services do not include services provided to an individual by a relative or spouse (directly, or through a partnership, corporation, or other entity), unless the relative is a licensed professional with respect to such services, or by a related corporation (within the meaning of Code section 267(b) or 707(b)).[9]

Long-term care insurance premiums treated as medical expenses.—Long-term care insurance premiums that do not exceed specified dollar limits are treated as medical expenses for purposes of the itemized deduction for medical expenses.[10] The limits are as follows:

In the case of an individual with an attained age before the close of the taxable year of:	The limitation on premiums paid for such taxable years is:
Not more than 40	$200
More than 40 but not more than 50	375
More than 50 but not more than 60	750
More than 60 but not more than 70	2,000
More than 70	2,500

For taxable years beginning after 1997, these dollar limits are indexed for increases in the medical care component of the consumer price index. The Secretary of the Treasury, in consultation with the Secretary of Health and Human Services, is directed to develop a more appropriate index to be applied in lieu of the foregoing. Such an alternative might appropriately be based on increases in skilled nursing facility and home health care costs. It is intended that the Treasury Secretary annually publish the indexed amount of the limits as early in the year as they can be calculated.

Deduction for long-term care insurance of self-employed individuals.—The present-law 30 percent deduction for health insurance expenses of self-employed individuals is phased up to 50 percent under the bill. Because the bill treats payments of eligible long-term care insurance premiums in the same manner as medical insurance premiums, the self-employed health insurance deduction applies to eligible long-term care insurance premiums under the bill.

Long-term care riders on life insurance contracts.—In the case of long-term care insurance coverage provided by a rider on or as part of a life insurance contract, the requirements applicable to long-term care insurance contracts apply as if the portion of the contract providing such coverage were a separate contract. The term "portion" means only the terms and benefits that are in addition to the terms and benefits under the life insurance contract without regard to long-term care coverage. As a result, if the applicable requirements are met by the long-term care portion of the contract, amounts received under the contract as provided by the

---

[9] The rule limiting such services provided by a relative or a related corporation does not apply for purposes of the exclusion for amounts received under a long-term care insurance contract, whether the contract is employer-provided or purchased by an individual. The limitation in unnecessary in such cases because it is anticipated that the insurer will monitor reimbursements to limit opportunities for fraud in connection with the performance of services by the taxpayer's relative or a related corporation.

[10] Similarly, within certain limits, in the case of a rider to a life insurance contract, charges against the life insurance contract's cash surrender value that are includible in income are treated as medical expenses (provided the rider constitutes a long-term care insurance contract).

rider are treated in the same manner as long-term care insurance benefits, whether or not the payment of such amounts causes a reduction in the contract's death benefit or cash surrender value. The guideline premium limitation applicable under section 7702(c)(2) is increased by the sum of charges (but not premium payments) against the life insurance contract's cash surrender value, the imposition of which reduces premiums paid for the contract (within the meaning of sec. 7702(f)(1)). In addition, it is anticipated that Treasury regulations will provide for appropriate reduction in premiums paid (within the meaning of sec. 7702(f)(1)) to reflect the payment of benefits under the rider that reduce the cash surrender value of the life insurance contract. A similar rule should apply in the case of a contract governed by section 101(f) and in the case of the payments under a rider that are excludable under section 101(g) of the Code (as added by this bill).

Health care continuation rules.—The health care continuation rules do not apply to coverage under a long-term care insurance contract.

Inclusion of excess long-term care benefits

In general, the bill provides that the maximum annual amount of long-term care benefits under a per diem type contract that is excludable from income with respect to an insured who is chronically ill (not including amounts received by reason of the individual being terminally ill)[11] cannot exceed the equivalent of $175 per day for each day the individual is chronically ill. Thus, for per diem type contracts, the maximum annual exclusion for long-term care benefits with respect to any chronically ill individual (not including amounts received by reason of the individual being terminally ill) is $63,875 (for 1997). If payments under such contracts exceed the dollar limit, then the excess is excludable only to the extent the individual has incurred actual costs for long-term care services. If the insured is not the same as the holder of the contract, the insured may assign some or all of this limit to the contract holder at the time and manner prescribed by the Secretary.

This $175 per day limit is indexed for inflation after 1997 for increases in the medical care component of the consumer price index. The Treasury Secretary, in consultation with the Secretary of Health and Human Services, is directed to develop a more appropriate index, to be applied in lieu of the foregoing. Such an alternative might appropriately be based on increases in skilled nursing facility and home health care costs. It is intended that the Treasury Secretary annually publish the indexed amount of the limit as early in the year as it can be calculated.

A payor of long-term care benefits (defined for this purpose to include any amount paid under a product advertised, marketed or offered as long-term care insurance) is required to report to the IRS the aggregate amount of such benefits paid to any individual during any calendar year, and the name, address and taxpayer identification number of such individual. A copy of the report must be

---

[11] Terminally ill is defined as under the provision of the bill relating to accelerated death benefits. In general, under that provision, an individual is considered to be terminally ill if he or she is certified as having an illness or physical condition that reasonably can be expected to result in death within 24 months of the date of the certification.

provided to the payee by January 31 following the year of payment, showing the name of the payor and the aggregate amount of benefits paid to the individual during the calendar year. Failure to file the report or provide the copy to the payee is subject to the generally applicable penalties for failure to file similar information reports.

Consumer protection provisions

Under the bill, long-term care insurance contracts, and issuers of contracts, are required to satisfy certain provisions of the long-term care insurance model Act and model regulations promulgated by the National Association of Insurance Commissioners (as adopted as of January 1993). The policy requirements relate to disclosure, nonforfeitability, guaranteed renewal or noncancellability, prohibitions on limitations and exclusions, extension of benefits, continuation or conversion of coverage, discontinuance and replacement of policies, unintentional lapse, post-claims underwriting, minimum standards, inflation protection, preexisting conditions, and prior hospitalization. The bill also provides disclosure and nonforfeiture requirements. The nonforfeiture provision gives consumers the option of selecting reduced paid-up insurance, extended term insurance, or a shortened benefit period in the event a policyholder who elects a nonforfeiture provision is unable to continue to pay premiums. The requirements for issuers of long-term care insurance contracts relate to application forms, reporting requirements, marketing, appropriateness of purchase, format, delivering a shopper's guide, right to return, outline of coverage, group plans, policy summary, monthly reports on accelerated death benefits, and incontestability period. A tax is imposed equal to $100 per policy per day for failure to satisfy these requirements.

Nothing in the bill prevents a State from establishing, implementing or continuing standards related to the protection of policyholders of long-term care insurance policies, if such standards are not inconsistent with standards established under the bill.

Effective date

The provisions defining long-term care insurance contracts and qualified long-term care services apply to contracts issued after December 31, 1996. Any contract issued before January 1, 1997, that met the long-term care insurance requirements in the State in which the policy was sitused at the time it was issued shall be treated as a long-term care insurance contract, and services provided under or reimbursed by the contract treated as qualified long-term care services.

A contract providing for long-term care insurance may be exchanged for a long-term care insurance contract (or the former cancelled and the proceeds reinvested in the latter within 60 days) tax free between the date of enactment and January 1, 1998. Taxable gain would be recognized to the extent money or other property is received in the exchange.

The issuance or conformance of a rider to a life insurance contract providing long-term care insurance coverage is not treated as a modification or a material change for purposes of applying sections 101(f), 7702, and 7702A of the Code.

The provision relating to treatment of eligible long-term care premiums as a medical expense is effective for taxable years beginning after December 31, 1996. The provision treating amounts paid for long-term care services as a medical expense (for purposes of the medical expense deduction) is effective for services furnished in taxable years beginning after December 31, 1997.

The provisions relating to the maximum exclusion for certain long-term care benefits and reporting are effective for taxable years beginning after December 31, 1996. Thus, the initial year in which reports will be filed with the IRS and copies provided to the payee will be 1998, with respect to long-term care benefits paid in 1997.

Senate amendment

The Senate amendment is the same as the House bill, except as follows.

Life insurance company reserves

In determining reserves for insurance company tax purposes, the Senate amendment provides that the Federal income tax reserve method applicable for a long-term care insurance contract issued after December 31, 1996, is the method prescribed by the National Association of Insurance Commissioners ("NAIC") (or, if no reserve method has been so prescribed, a method consistent with the tax reserve method for life insurance, annuity or noncancellable accident and health insurance contracts, whichever is most appropriate). The method currently prescribed by the NAIC for long-term care insurance contracts is the one-year full preliminary term method. As under present law, however, in no event may the tax reserve for a contract as of any time exceed the amount which would be taken into account with respect to the contract as of such time in determining statutory reserves.

Exchanges of life insurance and other contracts for long-term care insurance contracts

The exchange of a life insurance contract or an endowment or annuity contract for a qualified long-term care insurance contract is not taxable under the Senate amendment.

Distributions from IRAs and retirement plans for long-term care insurance

The Senate amendment permits certain plans to make distributions to pay premiums for long-term care insurance for the individual or the individual's spouse and provides that the 10-percent tax on early withdrawals does not apply to such distributions. The provision applies to distributions from individual retirement arrangements ("IRAs") and distributions attributable to elective deferrals to qualified cash or deferred arrangements (sec. 401(k) plans), tax-sheltered annuities (sec. 403(b) plans), nonqualified deferred compensation plans of governmental or tax-exempt employers (sec. 457 plans), and section 501(c)(18) plans used to pay premiums for long-term care insurance for the individual or the individual's spouse. Such distributions are includable in income (as under present law).

Effective dates

The effective dates are the same as the House bill, except as follows.

The provision treating long-term care services as a medical expense is effective for taxable years beginning after December 31, 1996.

The change in treatment of reserves for long-term care insurance contracts is effective for contracts issued after December 31, 1996.

The provision relating to tax-free exchanges of life insurance, endowment and annuity contracts for long-term care insurance contracts is effective for taxable years beginning after December 31, 1997.

The provision relating to certain distributions from IRAs and elective deferrals used to pay long-term care insurance premiums is effective for payments and distributions after December 31, 1996.

Conference agreement

The conference agreement generally follows the House bill, except as follows.

Tax treatment and definition of long-term care insurance contracts and qualified long-term care services

Chronically ill individual.—The conference agreement provides that, for purposes of determining whether an individual is chronically ill, the number of activities of daily living that are taken into account under the contract may not be less than five. For example, a contract could require that an individual be unable to perform (without substantial assistance) two out of any five of the activities listed in the bill. By contrast, a contract does not meet this requirement if it required that an individual be unable to perform two out of any four of the activities listed in the bill.

In addition, the conference agreement modifies the second test for whether an individual is chronically ill (i.e., that the individual has a level of disability similar to an individual who is unable to perform (without substantial assistance) at least two activities of daily living). Under the conference agreement, this test is met if the individual has been certified within the previous 12 months by a licensed health care practitioner as having a similar level of disability, as determined under regulations prescribed by the Secretary in consultation with the Secretary of Health and Human Services.

Health care continuation rules.—The health care continuation rules do not apply to coverage under a plan, substantially all of the coverage under which is for qualified long-term care services.

State-maintained plans.—The conference agreement modifies the definition of a qualified long-term care insurance contract. Under the conference agreement, an arrangement is treated as a qualified long-term care insurance contract if an individual receives coverage for qualified long-term care services under a State long-term care plan, and the terms of the arrangement would satisfy the requirements for a long-term care insurance contract under the provision, were the arrangement an insurance contract. For this purpose, a State long-term care plan is any plan established and maintained by a State (or instrumentality of such State) under which only employees (and former employees, including retirees) of a State or of a political subdivision or instrumentality of the State, and their relatives, and their spouses and spouses' relatives, may receive coverage only for qualified long-term care services. Relative is defined as under section 152(a)(1)–(8). No inference is intended with respect to the tax consequences of such arrangements under present law.

Inclusions of excess long-term care benefits

The conference agreement modifies the calculation of the dollar cap applicable to aggregate payments under per diem type long-term care insurance contracts and amounts received with respect to a chronically ill individual pursuant to a life insurance contract.[12] The amount of the dollar cap with respect to any one chronically ill individual (who is not terminally ill) is $175 per day ($63,875 annually, as indexed), reduced by the amount of reimbursements and payments received by anyone for the cost of qualified long-term care services for the chronically ill individual. If more than one payee receives payments with respect to any one chronically ill individual, then everyone receiving periodic payments with respect to the same insured is treated as one person for purposes of the dollar cap. The amount of the dollar cap is utilized first by the chronically ill person, and any remaining amount is allocated in accordance with Treasury regulations. If payments under such contracts exceed the dollar cap, then the excess is excludable only to the extent of actual costs (in excess of the dollar cap) incurred for long-term care services. Amounts in excess of the dollar cap, with respect to which no actual costs were incurred for long-term care services, are fully includable in income without regard to rules relating to return of basis under Code section 72.

The managers of the bill wish to clarify that, although the legislation imposes a daily (or equivalent) dollar cap on the amount of excludable benefits under certain types of long-term care insurance in certain circumstances, this limitation is not intended to suggest a preference or otherwise convey or facilitate a competitive advantage to one type of long-term care insurance compared to another type of long-term care insurance.

The Chairmen of the House Committee on Ways and Means and the Senate Finance Committee shall jointly request that the NAIC, in consultation with representatives of the insurance industry and consumer organizations, develop and conduct a study to determine the marketing and other effects, if any, of the dollar limit on excludable long-term care benefits under certain types of long-term care insurance contracts under the bill. Such Chairmen are to request that the NAIC, if it agrees to such request, shall submit the results of its study to the such Committees by no later than two years after agreeing to the request.

The conference agreement modifies the reporting requirement for payors of amounts excludable under the provision. Thus, in addition to the reporting requirements of the House bill, a payor is required to report the name, address, and taxpayer identification

---

[12] See item D, below.

number of the chronically ill individual on account of whose condition such amounts are paid, and whether the contract under which the amount is paid is a per diem-type contract.

A grandfather rule is provided under the conference agreement in the case of a per diem type contract issued to a policyholder on or before July 31, 1996. Under the grandfather rule, the amount of the dollar cap with respect to such a per diem contract is calculated without any reduction for reimbursements for qualified long-term care services under any other contract issued with respect to the same insured on or before July 31, 1996. The other provisions of the dollar cap are not affected by the grandfather rule. The grandfather rule ceases to apply as of the time that any of the contracts issued on or before July 31, 1996, with respect to the insured are exchanged, or benefits are increased.

Life insurance company reserves

The conference agreement includes the Senate amendment provision with respect to life insurance reserves. Thus, under the conference agreement, in determining reserves for insurance company tax purposes, the Senate amendment provides that the Federal income tax reserve method applicable for a long-term care insurance contract is the method prescribed by the NAIC (or, if no reserve method has been so prescribed, a method consistent with the tax reserve method for life insurance, annuity or noncancellable accident and health insurance contracts, whichever is most appropriate). As under present law, in no event may the tax reserve for a contract as of any time exceed the amount which would be taken into account with respect to the contract as of such time in determining statutory reserves.

Consumer protection provisions

The conference agreement clarifies and modifies the category of contracts to which the consumer protection provisions apply. The conference agreement clarifies that the consumer protection provisions that apply with respect to the terms of the contract apply only for purposes of determining whether a contract is a qualified long-term care insurance contract (within the meaning of the bill).

The conference agreement provides that, for purposes of both the requirements as to contract terms and the requirements relating to issuers of contracts, the determination of whether any requirement of a model regulation or model Act has been met is made by the Secretary of the Treasury. It is not intended that the Secretary create a Federal standard, but rather, look to applicable or appropriate State standards or to those provided specifically in the model regulation or model Act.

The conference agreement modifies the $100-per-day tax on failure to satisfy the requirements for issuers of contracts, to provide that the amount of the tax imposed is $100 per insured per day. The conference agreement provides that the consumer protection requirements for issuers of contracts apply with respect to contracts that are qualified long-term care insurance contracts (within the meaning of the bill).

The conference agreement modifies the rule relating to State establishment of standards relating to contract terms or issuers of contracts. The conference agreement provides that an otherwise qualified long-term care insurance contract will not fail to be a qualified long-term care insurance contract, and will not be treated as failing to meet the analogous requirement under the conference agreement, solely because it satisfies a consumer protection standard imposed under applicable State law that is more stringent than the analogous standard provided in the bill. The conference agreement does not preclude States from enacting more stringent consumer protection provisions than the analogous standards under the bill.

Effective date

The conference agreement follows the Senate amendment with respect to the effective date of the provision treating long-term care services as a medical expense. Thus, under the conference agreement, this provision is effective for taxable years beginning after December 31, 1996.

The conference agreement provides that the provision relating to life insurance company reserves is effective for contracts issued after December 31, 1997.

D. TREATMENT OF ACCELERATED DEATH BENEFITS UNDER LIFE INSURANCE CONTRACTS

(Secs. 331–332 of the House bill and secs. 431–432 of the Senate amendment).

Present law

Treatment of amounts received under a life insurance contract

If a contract meets the definition of a life insurance contract, gross income does not include insurance proceeds that are paid pursuant to the contract by reason of the death of the insured (sec. 101(a)). In addition, the undistributed investment income ("inside buildup") earned on premiums credited under the contract is not subject to current taxation to the owner of the contract. The exclusion under section 101 applies regardless of whether the death benefits are paid as a lump sum or otherwise.

Amounts received under a life insurance contract (other than a modified endowment contract) prior to the death of the insured are includible in the gross income of the recipient to the extent that the amount received constitutes cash value in excess of the taxpayer's investment in the contract (generally, the investment in the contract is the aggregate amount of premiums paid less amounts previously received that were excluded from gross income).

If a contract fails to be treated as a life insurance contract under section 7702(a), inside buildup on the contract is generally subject to tax (sec. 7702(g)).

Requirements for a life insurance contract

To qualify as a life insurance contract for Federal income tax purposes, a contract must be a life insurance contract under the applicable State or foreign law and must satisfy either of two alternative tests: (1) cash value accumulation test or (2) a test consisting of a guideline premium requirement and a cash value corridor requirement (sec. 7702(a)). A contract satisfies the cash value accumulation test if the cash surrender value of the contract may not at any time exceed the net single premium that would have to be paid at such time to fund future benefits under the contract. A contract satisfies the guideline premium and cash value corridor tests if the premiums paid under the contract do not at any time exceed the greater of the guideline single premium or the sum of the guideline level premiums, and if the death benefit under the contract is not less than a varying statutory percentage of the cash surrender value of the contract.

Proposed regulations on accelerated death benefits

The Treasury Department has issued proposed regulations [13] under which certain "qualified accelerated death benefits" paid by reason of the terminal illness of an insured would be treated as paid by reason of the death of the insured and therefore qualify for exclusion under section 101. In addition, the proposed regulations would permit an insurance contract that includes a qualified accelerated death benefit rider to qualify as a life insurance contract under section 7702. Thus, the proposed regulations provide that including this benefit would not cause an insurance contract to fail to meet the definition of a life insurance contract.

Under the proposed regulations, a benefit would qualify as a qualified accelerated death benefit only if it meets three requirements. First, the accelerated death benefit can be payable only if the insured becomes terminally ill. Second, the amount of the benefit must equal or exceed the present value of the reduction in the death benefit otherwise payable.[14] Third, the cash surrender value and the death benefit payable under the policy must be reduced proportionately as a result of the accelerated death benefit.

For purposes of the proposed regulations, an insured would be treated as terminally ill if he or she has an illness that, despite appropriate medical care, the insurer reasonably expects to result in death within twelve months from the payment of the accelerated death benefit. The proposed regulations would not apply to viatical settlements.

House bill

The House bill provides an exclusion from gross income as an amount paid by reason of the death of an insured for (1) amounts received under a life insurance contract and (2) amount received for the sale or assignment of a life insurance contract to a qualified viatical settlement provider, provided that the insured under the life insurance contract is either terminally ill or chronically ill. The exclusion for amounts received under a life insurance contract on the life of an insured who is chronically ill applies if the amount is received under a rider or other provision of the contract that is

---

[13] Prop. Treas. Reg. Secs. 1.101–8, 1.7702–0, 1.7702–2, and 1.7702A–1 (December 15, 1992).

[14] For purposes of determining the present value under the proposed regulations, the maximum permissible discount rate would be the greater of (1) the applicable Federal rate that applies under the discounting rules for property and casualty insurance loss reserves, and (2) the interest rate applicable to policy loans under the contract. Also, the present value would be determined assuming that the death benefit would have been paid twelve months after payment of the accelerated death benefit.

treated as a long-term care insurance contract under section 7702B (as added by the bill), and the amount is excludable as a payment for long-term care services under section 7702B (including under the dollar cap on per diem type payments ($175 per day, or $63,875 annually, in 1997).

The provision does not apply in the case of an amount paid to any taxpayer other than the insured, if such taxpayer has an insurable interest by reason of the insured being a director, officer or employee of the taxpayer, or by reason of the insured being financial interested in any trade or business carried on by the taxpayer.

A terminally ill individual is defined as one who has been certified by a physician as having an illness or physical condition that reasonably can be expected to result in death within 24 months of the date of certification. A physician is defined for this purpose in the same manner as under the long-term care insurance rules of the bill.[15]

A chronically ill individual is defined under the long-term care provisions of the bill.[16] In the case of amounts received with respect to a chronically ill individual (but not amounts received by reason of the individual being terminally ill), the $175 per day ($63,875 annual) limitation on excludable benefits that applies for per diem type long-term care insurance contracts also limits amounts that are excludable with respect to such contracts under this provision.

The payor of a payment to which this provision applies is required to report to the IRS the aggregate amount of such benefits paid to any individual during any calendar year, and the name, address and taxpayer identification number of such individual. A copy of the report must be provided to the payee by January 31 following the year of payment, showing the name of the payer and the aggregate amount of such benefits paid to the individual during the calendar year. Failure to file the report or provide the copy to the payee is subject to the generally applicable penalties for failure to file similar information reports.

A qualified viatical settlement provider is any person that regularly purchases or takes assignments of life insurance contracts on the lives of the terminally ill individuals and either (1) is licensed for such purposes in the State in which the insured resides; or (2) if the person is not required to be licensed by that State, menets the requirements of sections 8 and 9 of the Viatical Settlements Model Act (issued by the National Association of Insurance Commissioners (NAIC)), and also meets the section of the NAIC

---

[15] A physician is defined for these purposes as in section 1861(r)(1) of the Social Security Act, which provides that a physician means a doctor of medicine or osteopathy legally authorized to practice medicine and surgery by the State in which he performs such function or action (including a physician within the meaning of section 1101(a)(7) of that Act). Section 1101(a)(7) of that Act provides that the term physician includes osteopathic practitioners within the scope of their practice as defined by State law.

[16] Thus, a chronically ill individual is one who has been certified within the previous 12 months by a licensed health care practitioner as (1) being unable to perform (without substantial assistance) at least 2 activities of daily living for at least 90 days due to a loss of functional capacity, (2) having a similar level of disability as determined by the Secretary of the Treasury in consultation with the Secretary of Health and Human Services, or (3) requiring substantial supervision to protect such individual from threats to health and safety due to severe cognitive impairment. Activities of daily living are eating, toileting, transferring, bathing, dressing and continence. Nothing in the bill requires the contract to take into account all of the activities of daily living.

Viatical Settlements Model Regulation relating to standards for evaluation of reasonable payments, including discount rates, in determining amounts paid by the viatical settlement provider.

For life insurance company tax purposes, the bill provides that a life insurance contract is treated as including a reference to a qualified accelerated death benefit rider to a life insurance contract (except in the case of any rider that is treated as a long-term care insurance contract under section 7702B, as added by the bill). A qualified accelerated death benefit rider is any rider on a life insurance contract that provides only for payments of a type that are excludable under this provision.

Effective date

The provision applies to amounts received after December 31, 1996. The provision treating a qualified accelerated death benefit rider as life insurance for life insurance company tax purposes takes effect on January 1, 1997. The issuance of a qualified accelerated death benefit rider to a life insurance contract, or the addition of any provision required to conform an accelerated death benefit rider to these provisions, is not treated as a modification or material change to the contract (and is not intended to affect the issue date of any contract under section 101(f)).

Senate amendment

The Senate amendment is the same as the House bill, except that, in the case of a chronically ill insured, while the Senate amendment does provide that the exclusion for amounts received under a life insurance contract applies if the amount is received under a rider or other provision of the contract that is treated as a long-term care insurance contract under section 7702B (as added by the bill), the Senate amendment does not include the explicit language of the House bill requiring that the amount be treated as a payment for long-term care services under section 7702B.

Conference agreement

The conference agreement follows the House bill and the Senate amendment, with technical modifications and clarifications.

The conference agreement provides that the amount paid for the sale or assignment of any portion of the death benefit under a life insurance contract on the life of a terminally or chronically ill individual to a viatical settlement provider is excludable by the recipient as an amount paid under the contract by reason of the death of the insured. For example, the sale or assignment of a life insurance contract that has a rider providing for long-term care insurance, payments under which rider are funded by and reduce the death benefit, is considered the sale or assignment of the death benefit. Sale or assignment of a stand-alone rider providing for long-term care insurance (where payments under the rider are not funded by reductions in the death benefit), however, is not considered the sale or assignment of the death benefit.

The conference agreement provides that a viatical settlement provider is any person regularly engaged in the trade or business of purchasing or taking assignments of life insurance contracts on the lives of insured individuals who are terminally ill or chronically ill, so long as the viatical settlement provider meets certain requirements. The viatical settlement provider must either (1) be licensed, in the State where the insured resides, to engage in such transactions with terminally ill individuals (if the insured is terminally ill) or with chronically ill individuals (if the insured is chronically ill), or (2) if such licensing with respect to the insured individual is not required in the State, meet other requirements depending on whether the insured is terminally or chronically ill. If the insured is terminally ill, the viatical settlement provider must meet the requirements of sections 8 and 9 of the Viatical Settlements Model Act, relating to disclosure and general rules (issued by the National Association of Insurance Commissioner (NAIC)), and also meet the section of the NAIC Viatical Settlements Model Regulation relating to standards for evaluation of reasonable payments, including discount rates, in determining amounts paid by the viatical settlement provider. If the insured is chronically ill, the viatical settlement provider must meet requirements similar to those of sections 8 and 9 of the NAIC Viatical Settlements Model Act, and also must meet the standards, if any, promulgated by the NAIC for evaluating the reasonableness of amounts paid in viatical settlement transactions with chronically ill individuals.

The conference agreement clarifies the rules for chronically ill insureds so that the tax treatment of payments with respect to chronically ill individuals is reasonably similar under the long-term care rules of the bill and under this provision. In the case of a chronically ill individual, the exclusion under this provision with respect to amounts paid under a life insurance contract and amounts paid in a sale or assignment to a viatical settlement provider applies if the payment received is for costs incurred by the payee (not compensated by insurance or otherwise) for qualified long-term care services (as defined under the long-term care rules of the bill) for the insured person for the period, and two other requirements (similar to requirements applicable to long-term care insurance contracts under the bill) are met. The first requirement is that under the terms of the contract giving rise to the payment, the payment is not a payment or reimbursement of expenses reimbursable under Medicare (except where Medicare is a secondary payor under the arrangement, or the arrangement provides for per diem or other periodic payments without regard to expenses for qualified long-term care services). The conference agreement provides that no provision of law shall be construed or applied so as to prohibit the offering of such a contract giving rise to such a payment on the basis that the contract coordinates its payments with those provided under Medicare. The second requirement is that the arrangement complies with those consumer protection provisions applicable under the bill to long-term care insurance contracts and issuers that are specified in Treasury regulations. It is intended that such guidance incorporate rules similar to those of section 6F (relating to right to return, permitting the payee 30 days to rescind the arrangement) of the NAIC Long-Term Care Insurance Model Act, and section 13 (relating to requirements for application, requiring that the payee be asked if he or she already has long-term care insurance, Medicaid, or similar coverage) of the NAIC Long-Term Care Insurance Model Regulations. If the NAIC or the State in which the policyholder resides issues standards relating to chronically ill individuals, then the analogous requirements under Treasury regulations cease to apply.

An individual who meets the definition of a terminally ill individual is not treated as chronically ill, for purposes of this provision.

Payments made on a per diem or other periodic basis, without regard to expenses incurred for qualified long-term care services, are nevertheless excludable under this provision, subject to the dollar cap on excludable benefits that applies for amounts that are excludable under per diem type long-term care insurance contracts. The conference agreement modifies the calculation of the dollar cap applicable to aggregate payments under per diem type long-term care insurance contracts and amounts received with respect to a chronically ill individual pursuant to a life insurance contract.[17] The amount of the dollar cap with respect to the aggregate amount received under per diem type long-term care insurance contracts and this provision with respect to any one chronically ill individual (who is not terminally ill) is $175 per day ($63,875 annually) (indexed), reduced by the amount of reimbursements and payments received by anyone for the cost of qualified long-term care services for the chronically ill individual. If more than one payee receives payments with respect to any one chronically ill individual, the amount of the dollar cap is utilized first by the chronically ill person, and any remaining amount is allocated in accordance with Treasury regulations. If payments under such contracts exceed the dollar cap, then the excess is excludable only to the extent of actual costs incurred for long-term care services. Amounts in excess of the dollar cap, with respect to which no actual costs (in excess of the dollar cap) were incurred for long-term care services, are fully includable in income without regard to rules relating to return of basis under Code section 72.

The conference agreement modifies the reporting requirement for payors of amounts excludable under the provision. Thus, in addition to the reporting requirements of the House bill, a payor is required to report the name, address, and taxpayer identification number of the chronically ill individual on account of whose condition such amounts are paid, and whether the contract under which the amount is paid is a per diem-type contract.

E. EXEMPTION FROM INCOME TAX FOR STATE-SPONSORED ORGANIZATIONS PROVIDING HEALTH COVERAGE FOR HIGH-RISK INDIVIDUALS; EXEMPTION FROM INCOME TAX FOR STATE-SPONSORED WORKERS' COMPENSATION REINSURANCE ORGANIZATIONS

(Sec. 341 of the House bill and sec. 451 of the Senate amendment).

Present law

In general, the Internal Revenue Service ("IRS") takes the position that organizations that provide insurance for their members or other individuals are not considered to be engaged in a tax-exempt activity. The IRS maintains that such insurance activity is ei-

---

[17] See item C, above.

ther (1) a regular business of a kind ordinarily carried on for profit, or (2) an economy or convenience in the conduct of members' businesses because it relieves the members from obtaining insurance on an individual basis.

Certain insurance risk pools have qualified for tax exemption under Code section 501(c)(6). In general, these organizations (1) assign any insurance policies and administrative functions to their member organizations (although they may reimburse their members for amounts paid and expenses), (2) serve an important common business interest of their members, and (3) must be membership organizations financed, at least in part, by membership dues.

State insurance risk pools may also qualify for tax-exempt status under section 501(c)(4) as a social welfare organization or under section 115 as serving an essential governmental function of a State. In seeking qualification under section 501(c)(4), insurance organizations generally are constrained by the restrictions on the provision of "commercial-type insurance" contained in section 501(m). Section 115 generally provides that gross income does not include income derived from the exercise of any essential governmental function and accruing to a State or any political subdivision thereof. However, the IRS may be reluctant to rule that particular State risk-pooling entities satisfy the section 501(c)(4) or 115 requirements for tax-exempt status.

House bill

Health coverage for high-risk individuals

The House bill provides tax-exempt status to any membership organization that is established by a State exclusively to provide coverage for medical care on a nonprofit basis to certain high-risk individuals, provided certain criteria are satisfied.[18] The organization may provide coverage for medical care either by issuing insurance itself or by entering into an arrangement with a health maintenance organization ("HMO").

High-risk individuals eligible to receive medical care coverage from the organization must be residents of the State who, due to a pre-existing medical condition, are unable to obtain health coverage for such condition through insurance or an HMO, or are able to acquire such coverage only at a rate that is substantially higher than the rate charged for such coverage by the organization. The State must determine the composition of membership in the organization. For example, a State could mandate that all organizations that are subject to insurance regulation by the State must be members of the organization.

The House bill further requires the State or members of the organization to fund the liabilities of the organization to the extent that premiums charged to eligible individuals are insufficient to cover such liabilities. Finally, no part of the net earnings of the organization can inure to the benefit of any private shareholder or individual.

Effective date.—The provision applies to taxable years beginning after December 31, 1996.

---

[18] No inference is intended as to the tax treatment of other types of State-sponsored organizations.

Workers' compensation reinsurance organizations

No provision.

Senate amendment

The Senate amendment is the same as the House bill.

Conference agreement

Health coverage for high-risk individuals

The conference agreement follows the House bill and the Senate amendment.

Workers' compensation reinsurance organizations

The conference agreement provides tax-exempt status to any membership organization that is established by a State before June 1, 1996, exclusively to reimburse its members for workers' compensation insurance losses, and that satisfies certain other conditions. A State must require that the membership of the organization consist of all persons who issue insurance covering workers' compensation losses in such State, and all persons and governmental entities who self-insure against such losses. In addition, the organization must operate as a nonprofit organization by returning surplus income to members or to workers' compensation policyholders on a periodic basis and by reducing initial premiums in anticipation of investment income.

Effective date.—The provision applies to taxable years ending after the date of enactment.

F. HEALTH INSURANCE ORGANIZATIONS ELIGIBLE FOR BENEFITS OF SECTION 833

(Sec. 351 of the House bill).

Present law

An organization described in sections 501(c)(3) or (4) of the Code is exempt from tax only if no substantial part of its activities consists of providing commercial-type insurance (sec. 501(m)). Special rules apply to certain eligible health insurance organizations. Eligible health insurance organizations are (1) Blue Cross and Blue Shield organizations existing on August 16, 1986, which have not experienced a material change in structure or operations since that date, and (2) other organizations that meet certain community-service related requirements and substantially all of whose activities involve the providing of health insurance. Section 833 provides that eligible organizations are generally treated as stock property and casualty insurance companies.

Section 833 provides a special deduction for eligible organizations, equal to 25 percent of the claims and expenses incurred during the year, less the adjusted surplus at the beginning of the year. This deduction is calculated by computing surplus, taxable income, claims incurred, expenses incurred, tax-exempt income, net operating loss carryovers, and other items attributable to health expenses. The deduction may not exceed taxable income attributable to health business for the year (calculated without regard to this deduction).

313

In addition, section 833 eliminates, for eligible organizations, the 20 percent reduction in unearned premium reserves that applies generally to all property and casualty insurance companies.

House bill

The House bill applies the special rules under section 833 to the same extent they are provided to certain existing Blue Cross or Blue Shield organizations, in the case of any organization that (1) is not a Blue Cross or Blue Shield organization existing on August 16, 1986, and (2) otherwise meets the requirements of section 833(c)(2) (including the requirement of no material change in operations or structure since August 16, 1986). Under the provision, an organization qualifies for this treatment only if (1) it is not a health maintenance organization and (2) it is organized under and governed by State laws which are specifically and exclusively applicable to not-for-profit health insurance or health service type organizations.

Effective date.—The provision is effective for taxable years ending after December 31, 1996.

Senate amendment

No provision.

Conference agreement

The conference agreement follows the House bill.

G. PENALTY-FREE WITHDRAWALS FROM IRAS FOR MEDICAL EXPENSES

(Sec. 461 of the Senate amendment).

Present law

Amounts withdrawn from an individual retirement arrangement ("IRA") are includible in income (except to the extent of any nondeductible contributions). In addition, a 10-percent additional tax applies to withdrawals from IRAs made before age 59½, unless the withdrawal is made on account of death or disability or is made in the form of annuity payments.

A similar additional tax applies to early withdrawals from employer-sponsored tax-qualified pension plans. However, the 10-percent additional tax does not apply to withdrawals from such plans to the extent used for medical expenses that exceed 7.5 percent of adjusted gross income ("AGI").

House bill

No provision.

Senate amendment

The Senate amendment extends the exception to the 10-percent tax for medical expenses in excess of 7.5 percent of AGI to withdrawals from IRAs. In addition, the Senate amendment provides that the 10-percent additional tax does not apply to withdrawals for medical insurance (without regard to the 7.5 percent of AGI floor) if the individual (including a self-employed individual) has received unemployment compensation under Federal or State law for at least 12 weeks, and the withdrawal is made in the year such unemployment compensation is received or the following year. If a self-employed individual is not eligible for unemployment compensation under applicable law, then, to the extent provided in regulations, a self-employed individual is treated as having received unemployment compensation for at least 12 weeks if the individual would have received unemployment compensation but for the fact that the individual was self-employed.

Effective date.—The provision is effective for taxable years beginning after December 31, 1996.

Conference agreement

The conference agreement follows the Senate amendment, with the modification that the exception ceases to apply if the individual has been reemployed for at least 60 days.

H. REQUIRE TREASURY TO INCLUDE ORGAN AND TISSUE DONATION INFORMATION WITH TAX REFUNDS

(Sec. 307 of the Senate amendment).

Present law

There is no statutory requirement that Treasury include organ and tissue donation information with any payment of a refund of individual income taxes.

House bill

No provision.

Senate amendment

The Senate amendment requires Treasury to include organ and tissue donation information with any payment of a refund of individual income taxes made on or after February 1, 1997, through June 30, 1997.

Effective date.—The provision is effective for refunds made on or after February 1, 1997, through June 30, 1997.

Conference agreement

The conference agreement generally follows the Senate amendment, with two technical modifications. The first modification requires that the organ donor card be included to the extent particable. The second modification clarifies that the organ donor card is to be included with the mailing of any payment of a refund of individual income taxes.

Effective date.—The provision is effective for refunds made on or after February 1, 1997, through June 30, 1997.

TITLE IV. APPLICATION AND ENFORCEMENT OF GROUP HEALTH PLAN REQUIREMENTS

A. APPLICATION AND ENFORCEMENT OF GROUP HEALTH PLAN PORTABILITY, ACCESS, AND RENEWABILITY REQUIREMENTS

(Sec. 104(b) of the House bill).

Present Law

Under present law, the health care continuation rules (referred to as "COBRA" rules, after the Consolidated Omnibus Budget Reconciliation Act of 1985 in which they were enacted) require that most employer-sponsored group health plans must offer certain employees and their dependents ("qualified beneficiaries") the option of purchasing continued health coverage in the case of certain qualifying events. These qualifying events include: termination or reduction in hours of employment, death, divorce or legal separation, enrollment in Medicare, or the end of a child's dependency under a parent's health plan. In general, the maximum period of COBRA coverage is 18 months. An employer is permitted to charge qualified beneficiaries 102 percent of the applicable premium for COBRA coverage.

A tax is imposed on the failure of a group health plan to satisfy the COBRA rules. The tax may be imposed on the employer sponsoring the plan in the case of a plan other than a multiemployer plan, on the plan in the case of a multiemployer plan, or on each person who is responsible for administering or providing benefits under the plan if such person has, by written agreement, assumed responsibility for performing the act pursuant to which the violation occurs.

The amount of the tax is generally equal to $100 per day for each day on which there is a violation. The tax applies separately with respect to each qualified beneficiary for whom a failure occurs. In general, a tax will not be imposed if the violation was unintentional and is corrected within 30 days. The maximum tax for unintentional violations that can be imposed for a taxable year generally is the lesser of (1) 10 percent of the employer's payments under group health plans (or under the trust funding the plan in the case of a multiemployer plan), or (2) $500,000. If the tax is imposed on another person responsible for administering or providing benefits under the plan, the maximum penalty for failures during the year is $2 million. The Secretary may waive all or part of the tax to the extent that payment of the tax would be excessive relative to the failure involved.

Other than the COBRA rules, there are no other requirements in the Code which apply to group health plans (or insurers or health maintenance organizations ("HMOs")) regarding portability through limitations on preexisting condition exclusions, prohibitions on excluding individuals from coverage based on health status, and guaranteed renewability of health plan coverage.

House bill

Under the House bill, group health plans, insurers, and HMOs are subject to certain requirements regarding portability through limitations on preexisting condition exclusions and prohibitions on excluding individuals from coverage based on health status. The House bill generally extends the tax for failures to satisfy the COBRA rules to failures to comply with these requirements.

No tax is imposed on an insurer or HMO that is governed under a State law that the Secretary of Health and Human Services has determined to provide enforcement of similar requirements. In addition, no tax may be imposed on a small employer (defined as an employer who employs at least 2, but fewer than 51 employees on a typical business day) that provides health care benefits through a contract with an insurer or HMO and the violation is solely because of the product offered by the insurer or HMO under such contract. In addition, no tax is imposed if there has been enforcement by the Secretary of Labor or the Secretary of Health and Human Services.

Effective date.—The provision generally is effective with respect to plan years beginning on or after January 1, 1998.

Senate amendment

No provision. The requirements in the Senate amendment on group health plans, insurers, and HMOs regarding portability through limitations on preexisting condition exclusions and prohibitions on excluding individuals from coverage based on health status are not applied or enforced through the Code.

Conference agreement

Under the conference agreement, group health plans are subject to certain requirements regarding portability through limitations on preexisting condition exclusions, prohibitions on excluding individuals from coverage based on health status, and guaranteed renewability of health insurance coverage.[19] The conference agreement incorporates these requirements into the Code and generally imposes a tax with respect to any failure of a group health plan to comply with the requirements. The tax may generally be imposed on the employer sponsoring the plan. However, the tax may be imposed on the plan in the case of a multiemployer plan, and, with respect to violations of the requirements relating to guaranteed renewability, on the arrangement in the case of a multiple employer welfare arrangement.

The group health plan requirements contained in the Code do not apply to governmental plans and plans which on the first day of the plan year cover less than 2 current employees. In addition, no tax may be imposed on a small employer (defined as an employer who employed an average of 50 or fewer employees on business days during the preceding calendar year) that provides health care benefits through a contract with an insurer or HMO and the violation is solely because of the coverage offered by the insurer or HMO.

The amount of the tax is generally equal to $100 per day for each day during which a failure occurs until the failure is corrected. The tax applies separately with respect to each individual affected by the failure. In general, a tax will not be imposed if the violation was unintentional and is corrected within 30 days.[20] The maximum tax for unintentional violations that can be imposed generally is the lesser of (1) 10 percent of the employer's payments during the taxable year in which the failure occurred under group health plans (or 10 percent of the amount paid by the multiemployer plan or multiple employer welfare arrangement during the

---

[19] These requirements are discussed earlier in greater detail.

[20] In the case of a church plan, this correction is generally extended to 270 days after the date of mailing by the Secretary of a notice of default with respect to a failure to comply with the group health plan requirements.

plan year in which the failure occurred for medical care, if applicable), or (2) $500,000. The Secretary may waive all or part of the tax to the extent that payment of the tax would be excessive relative to the failure involved.

Effective date.—The provision applies with respect to failures of group health plans to satisfy the requirements regarding portability through limitations on preexisting condition exclusions, prohibitions on excluding individuals from coverage based on health status, and guaranteed renewability of health insurance coverage.

B. CLARIFICATION OF CERTAIN COBRA HEALTH CARE CONTINUATION REQUIREMENTS

(Sec. 121 of the Senate amendment).

Present law

Under present law, the health care continuation rules (referred to as "COBRA" rules, after the Consolidated Omnibus Budget Reconciliation Act of 1985 in which they were enacted) require that most employer-sponsored group health plans must offer certain employees and their dependents ("qualified beneficiaries") the option of purchasing continued health coverage in the case of certain qualifying events. These qualifying events include; termination or reduction in hours of employment, death, divorce or legal separation, enrollment in Medicare, or the end of a child's dependency under a parent's health plan. In general, the maximum period of COBRA coverage is 18 months. An employer is permitted to charge qualified beneficiaries 102 percent of the applicable premium for COBRA coverage. A $100 per day tax generally may be assessed against employers (plans in the case of multiemployer plans) for failures to comply with the COBRA rules, subject to certain exceptions and limitations.

The 18-month maximum COBRA coverage period is extended to 29 months if the qualified beneficiary is determined under the Social Security Act to have been disabled at the time of the qualifying event and the qualified beneficiary provides notice of such determination to the employer before the end of the 18-month period. A qualified beneficiary has 60 days to notify the employer of a disability determination. During the 11-month period of extended COBRA coverage, the qualified beneficiary may be charged 150 percent of the applicable premium.

COBRA coverage may be terminated before the 18-month maximum coverage period in the case of certain events. These include: the employer ceases to maintain any group health plan, the qualified beneficiary fails to pay the premium, the qualified beneficiary becomes covered under another group health plan with no preexisting condition limitation or exclusion, or the qualified beneficiary becomes entitled to Medicare.

Under present law, the term qualified beneficiary only includes individuals who were either the spouse or the dependent of the covered employee at the time of the qualifying event.

A group health plan is required to notify each covered employee and the covered employee's spouse of their COBRA rights upon commencement of participation in the plan. Further, the group health plan administrator must notify each qualified beneficiary of their COBRA rights within 14 days after notification of the occurrence of a qualifying event.

House bill

No provision. However, the House bill modifies the COBRA rules so that the penalties applicable to failures to comply with the COBRA rules generally apply to failures to comply with the requirements in the House bill on group health plans, insurers, and health maintenance organizations ("HMOs") regarding portability through limitations on preexisting condition exclusions and prohibitions on excluding individuals from coverage based on health status.

Senate amendment

The Senate amendment modifies the COBRA rules by clarifying that the extended maximum COBRA coverage period of 29 months in cases of disability also applies to the disabled qualified beneficiary of the covered employee. In addition, the Senate amendment provides the extended COBRA coverage if the disability exists at any time during the initial 18-month COBRA coverage period as opposed to requiring the disability to exist at the time of the qualifying event. As under present law, the disability determination still has to be made, and the notice of the disability still has to be given, before the end of the initial COBRA coverage period.

The Senate amendment coordinates the COBRA rules with the new requirements regarding preexisting condition exclusions so that COBRA coverage can be terminated if a qualified beneficiary becomes covered under another group health plan, even if such group health plan contains a preexisting condition limitation or exclusion, provided the preexisting condition limitation or exclusion does not apply to the qualified beneficiary by reason of the new requirements restricting the application of preexisting condition limitations and exclusions.

The Senate amendment also modifies the definition of qualified beneficiary to include a child born to our placed for adoption with the covered employee during the period of COBRA coverage. Consequently, since the health care availability provisions in the Senate amendment require group health plans to allow participants to change their coverage status (i.e., to change from individual coverage to family coverage, or to add on the new child) upon the birth or adoption of a new child, COBRA participants would also be allowed to change their coverage status upon the birth or adoption of a new child.

The Senate amendment requires a group health plan to notify each qualified beneficiary who has elected COBRA coverage of the changes to the COBRA rules contained in the Senate amendment no later than November 1, 1996.

Effective date.—The provision applies to qualifying events occurring on or after the date of enactment for plan years beginning after December 31, 1997.

Conference agreement

The conference agreement follows the Senate amendment, except the extended period of COBRA coverage in cases of disability applies if the disability exists at any time during the first 60 days of COBRA coverage.

Effective date.—The provision is effective on January 1, 1997, regardless of whether the qualifying event occurred before, on, or after such date.

TITLE V. REVENUE OFFSETS

A. DISALLOW INTEREST DEDUCTION FOR CORPORATE-OWNED LIFE INSURANCE POLICY LOANS

(Sec. 495 of the Senate amendment).

Present law

No Federal income tax generally is imposed on a policyholder with respect to the earnings under a life insurance contract ("inside buildup"). [21] Further, an exclusion from Federal income tax is provided for amounts received under a life insurance contract paid by reason of the death of the insured (sec. 101(a)). The policyholder may borrow with respect to the life insurance contract without affecting these exclusions, subject to certain limitations.

The limitations on borrowing with respect to a life insurance contract under present law provide that no deduction is allowed for any interest paid or accrued on any indebtedness with respect to one or more life insurance policies owned by the taxpayer covering the life of any individual who (1) is an officer or employee of, or (2) is financially interested in, any trade or business carried on by the taxpayer to the extent that the aggregate amount of such debt with respect to policies covering the individual exceeds $50,000 (sec. 264(a)(4)).

Further, no deduction is allowed for any amount paid or accrued on debt incurred or continued to purchase or carry a life insurance, endowment, or annuity contract pursuant to a plan of purchase that contemplates the systematic direct or indirect borrowing of part or all of the increases in the cash value of the contract.[22] An exception to the latter rule is provided, permitting deductibility of interest on bona fide debt that is part of such a plan, if no part of 4 of the annual premiums due during the first 7 years is paid by means of debt (the "4-out-of-7 rule") (sec. 264(c)(1)). Provided the transaction gives rise to debt for Federal income tax purposes, and

---

[21] This favorable tax treatment is available only if a life insurance contract meets certain requirements designed to limit the investment character of the contract (sec. 7702). Distributions from a life insurance contract (other than a modified endowment contract) that are made prior to the death of the insured generally are includible in income, to the extent that the amounts distributed exceed the taxpayer's basis in the contract; such distributions generally are treated first as a tax-free recovery of basis, and then as income (sec. 72(e)). In the case of a modified endowment contract, however, in general, distributions are treated as income first, loans are treated as distributions (i.e., income rather than basis recovery first), and an additional 10 percent tax is imposed on the income portion of distributions made before age 59½ and in certain other circumstances (secs. 72 (e) and (v)). A modified endowment contract is a life insurance contract that does not meet a statutory "7-pay" test, i.e., generally is funded more rapidly than 7 annual level premiums (sec. 7702A).

[22] The statute provides that the $50,000 limitation applies only with respect to contracts purchased after June 20, 1986. However, additional limitations are imposed on the deductibility of interest with respect to single premium contracts (sec. 264(a)(2)), and on the deductibility of premiums paid on a life insurance contract covering the life of any officer or employee or person financially interested in a trade or business of the taxpayer when the taxpayer is directly or indirectly a beneficiary under the contract (sec. 264(a)(1)).

provided the 4-out-of-7 rule is met,[23] a company may under present law borrow up to $50,000 per employee, officer, or financially interested person to purchase or carry a life insurance contract covering such a person, and is not precluded under section 264 from deducting the interest on the debt, even though the earnings inside the life insurance contract (inside buildup) are tax-free, and in fact the taxpayer has full use of the borrowed funds.

House bill

No provision.

Senate amendment

Under the Senate amendment, no deduction is allowed for interest paid or accrued on any indebtedness with respect to one or more life insurance policies or annuity or endowment contracts owned by the taxpayer covering any individual who is (1) an officer or employee of, or (2) financially interested in, any trade or business carried on by the taxpayer, regardless of the aggregate amount of debt with respect to policies or contracts covering the individual.

An exception is provided retaining present law for interest on indebtedness with respect to life insurance policies covering up to 10 key persons. A key person is an individual who is either an officer or a 20-percent owner of the taxpayer. The number of individuals that can be treated as key persons may not exceed the greater of (1) 5 individuals, or (2) the lesser of 5 percent of the total number of officers and employees of the taxpayer or 10 individuals. Interest paid or accrued on debt with respect to a life insurance contract covering a key person is deductible only to the extent the rate of interest does not exceed Moody's Corporate Bond Yield Average—Monthly Average Corporates for each month interest is paid or accrued.

Effective date.—The Senate amendment provision generally is effective with respect to interest paid or accrued after December 31, 1995 (subject to a phase-in rule).

The phase-in rule provides that with respect to debt incurred before January 1, 1996, any otherwise deductible interest paid or accrued after October 13, 1995, and before January 1, 1999, is allowed to the extent the rate of interest does not exceed the lesser of (1) the borrowing rate specified in the contract as of October 13, 1995, or (2) a percentage of Moody's Corporate Bond Yield Average—Monthly Average Corporates for each month the interest is paid or accrued. For interest paid or accrued after October 13, 1995, and before January 1, 1996, the percentage of the Moody's rate is 100 percent; for interest paid or accrued in 1996, the percentage is 90 percent; for interest paid or accrued in 1997, the percentage is 80 percent; for 1998, the percentage is 70 percent; for 1999 and thereafter, the percentage is 0 percent. Only interest that would have been allowed as a deduction but for the provision is allowed under the phase-in. Interest that is deductible under the

---

[23] Interest deductions are disallowed if any of the disallowance rules of section 264(a)(2)–(4) apply. The disallowance rule of section 264(a)(3) is not applicable if one of the exceptions of section 264(c), such as the 4-out-of-7 rule (sec. 264(c)(1)) is satisfied. In addition to the specific disallowance rules of section 264, generally applicable principles of tax law apply.

phase-in rules does not include interest on borrowings by the taxpayer with respect to contracts on the lives of more than 20,000 insured individuals, effective for interest paid or accrued after December 31, 1995. For this purpose, all persons treated as a single employer are treated as one taxpayer.

An exception is provided under the effective date with respect to any life insurance contract entered into during 1994 or 1995. In the case of such contracts, with respect to debt incurred before January 1, 1997, a deduction is allowed for interest (that is otherwise deductible) only (1) with respect to policies that satisfy the key person exception, and (2) as provided under the phase-in rule. Thus, with respect to interest on amounts borrowed during 1996 with respect to such a contract, the phase-in rule applies, capping the rate for determining the amount of deductible interest at the lesser of (1) the borrowing rate specified in the contract as of October 13, 1995, or (2) the applicable percentage of Moody's Corporate Bond Yield Average—Monthly Average Corporates for each month the interest is paid or accrued. For example, for interest paid or accrued in 1996 on amounts borrowed in 1996 with respect to such a contract, the applicable percentage is 90 percent.

The provision generally does not apply to interest on debt with respect to contracts purchased on or before June 20, 1986 (thus generally continuing the effective date provision of the $50,000 limitation enacted in the 1986 Act.) If the policy loan interest rate under such a contract provides for a fixed rate of interest, then interest on such a contract paid or accrued after October 13, 1995, is allowable only to the extent the fixed rate of interest does not exceed Moody's Corporate Bond Yield Average—Monthly Average Corporates for the month in which the contract was purchased. If the policy loan interest rate under such a contract does not provide for a fixed rate of interest, then interest on such a contract paid or accrued after October 13, 1995, is allowable only to the extent the rate of interest for each fixed period selected by the taxpayer does not exceed Moody's Corporate Bond Yield Average—Monthly Average Corporates, for the month immediately preceding the beginning of the fixed period. The fixed period must be 12 months or less. It is intended that conforming a contract to satisfy this interest rate limitation not be treated as a material modification for purposes of this grandfather rule or sections 101(f), 7702 or 7702A. No inference is intended as to whether such a change is a material modification under present law.

Any amount included in income during 1996, 1997, or 1998, that is received under a contract described in the proposal on the complete surrender, redemption or maturity of the contract or in full discharge of the obligation under the contract that is in the nature of a refund of the consideration paid for the contract, is includable ratably over the first 4 taxable years beginning with the taxable year the amount would otherwise have been includable. Utilization of this 4-year income-spreading rule does not cause interest paid or accrued prior to January 1, 1999, to be nondeductible solely by reason of (1) failure to meet the 4-out-or-7 rule, or (2) causing the contract to be treated as single premium contract within the meaning of section 264(b)(1) (i.e., a contract in which substantially all of the premiums are paid within 4 years after the date of purchase). In addition, the lapse of a contract after October 13, 1995, due to nonpayment of premiums does not cause interest paid or accrued prior to January 1, 1999, to be nondeductible solely by reason of (1) failure to meet the 4-out-of-7 rule, or (2) causing the contract to be treated as a single premium contract within the meaning of section 264(b)(1).

In the case of an insurance company, the unamortized balance of policy expense attributable to a contract with respect to which the 4-year income-spreading treatment is allowed to the policyholder is deductible in the year in which the transaction giving rise to income-spreading occurs.

No inference, is intended as to the treatment of interest paid or accrued under present law.

Conference agreement

The conference agreement follows the Senate amendment, with the following modifications.

The exception relating to key persons is modified to apply to life insurance policies covering up to 20 key persons. Thus, under the conference agreement, the number of individuals that can be treated as key persons may not exceed the greater of (1) 5 individuals, or (2) the lesser of 5 percent of the total number of officers and employees of the taxpayer or 20 individuals.

The cap (based on Moody's Corporate Bond Yield Average—Monthly Average Corporates) on deductible interest paid or accrued with respect to (1) interest paid or accrued on debt with respect to a life insurance contract covering a key person, and (2) interest on debt with respect to contracts purchased on or before June 20, 1986, applies only for interest paid or accrued for any month beginning after December 31, 1995.

In addition, in the case of a contract purchased on or before June 20, 1986, where the policy loan interest rate under the contract does not provide for a fixed rate of interest, the interest is allowable only to the extent the rate of interest for each period does not exceed Moody's Corporate Bond Yield Average—Monthly Average Corporates for the third month preceding the first month preceding the period.

Effective date.—The conference agreement modifies the percentages of the Moody's Corporate Bond Yield Average—Monthly Average Corporates that apply with respect to qualified interest under the phase-in rule. Thus, under the conference agreement, the percentage of the Moody's rate is 100 percent for interest paid or accrued in 1996; 90 percent for interest paid or accrued in 1997; 80 percent for interest paid or accrued in 1998; and 0 percent thereafter. The rule limiting deductible interest to the applicable percentage of the Moody's rate does not apply for interest paid or accrued in any month beginning before January 1, 1996.

B. EXPATRIATION TAX PROVISIONS

(Secs. 421–423 of the House bill and secs. 471–473 of the Senate amendment.)

Present law

Individuals who relinquish U.S. citizenship with a principal purpose of avoiding U.S. taxes are subject to special tax provisions for 10 years after expatriation. The determination of who is a U.S. citizen for tax purposes, and when such citizenship is lost, is governed by the provisions of the Immigration and Nationality Act, 8 U.S.C. section 1401, et seq.

An individual who relinquishes his U.S. citizenship with a principal purpose of avoiding U.S. taxes is subject to tax on his or her U.S. source income at the rates applicable to U.S. citizens, rather than the rates applicable to other non-resident aliens, for 10 years after expatriation. In addition, the scope of items treated as U.S. source income for this purpose is broader than those items generally considered to be U.S. source income. For example, gains on the sale of personal property located in the United States and gains on the sale or exchange of stock or securities issued by U.S. persons are treated as U.S. source income. This alternative method of income taxation applies only if it results in higher U.S. tax liability.

Rules applicable in the estate and gift tax contexts expand the categories of items that are subject to the gift and estate taxes in the case of a U.S. citizen who relinquished citizenship with a principal purpose of avoiding U.S. taxes within the 10-year period ending on the date of the transfer. For example, U.S. property held through a foreign corporation controlled by such individual and related persons is included in his or her estate and gifts of U.S.-situs intangible property by such individual are subject to the gift tax.

House bill

Overview

The House bill expands and substantially strengthens in several ways the present-law provisions that subject U.S. citizens who lose their citizenship for tax avoidance purposes to special tax rules for 10 years after such loss of citizenship (secs. 877, 2107, and 2501(a)(3)). First, the House bill extends the expatriation tax provisions to apply not only to U.S. citizens who lose their citizenship but also to certain long-term residents of the United States whose U.S. residency is terminated. Second, the House bill subjects certain individuals to the expatriation tax provisions without inquiry as to their motive for losing their U.S. citizenship or residency, but allows certain categories of citizens to show an absence of tax-avoidance motive if they request a ruling from the Secretary of the Treasury as to whether the loss of citizenship had a principal purpose of tax avoidance. Third, the House bill expands the categories of income and gains that are treated as U.S. source (and therefore subject to U.S. income tax under section 877) if earned by an individual who is subject to the expatriation tax provisions and includes provisions designed to eliminate the ability to engage in certain transactions that under current law partially or completely circumvent the 10-year reach of section 877. Further, the House bill provides relief from double taxation in circumstances where another country imposes tax on items that would be subject to U.S. tax under the expatriation tax provisions.

The House bill also contains provisions to enhance compliance with the expatriation tax provisions. The House bill imposes information reporting obligations on U.S. citizens who lose their citizenship and long-term residents whose U.S. residency is terminated at the time of expatriation. In addition, the House bill directs the Treasury Department to undertake a study regarding compliance by individuals living abroad with their U.S. tax reporting obligations and to make recommendations with respect to improving such compliance.

Individuals covered

The present-law expatriation tax provisions apply only to certain U.S. citizens who lose their citizenship. The House bill extends these expatriation tax provisions to apply also to long-term residents of the United States whose U.S. residency is terminated. For this purpose, a long-term resident is any individual who was a lawful permanent resident of the United States for at least 8 out of the 15 taxable years ending with the year in which such termination occurs. In applying this 8-year test, an individual is not considered to be a lawful permanent resident for any year in which the individual is taxed as a resident of another country under a treaty tie-breaker rule. An individual's U.S. residency is considered to be terminated when either the individual ceases to be a lawful permanent resident pursuant to section 7701(b)(6) (i.e., the individual loses his or her green-card status) or the individual is treated as a resident of another country under a tie-breaker provision of a tax treaty (and the individual does not elect to waive the benefits of such treaty). Furthermore, a long-term resident may elect to use the fair market value basis of property on the date the individual became a U.S. resident (rather than the property's historical basis) to determine the amount of gain subject to the expatriation tax provisions if the asset is sold within the 10-year period.

Under present law, the expatriation tax provisions are applicable to a U.S. citizen who loses his or her citizenship unless such loss did not have as a principal purpose the avoidance of taxes. Under the House bill, U.S. citizens who lose their citizenship and long-term residents whose U.S. residency is terminated are generally treated as having lost such citizenship or terminated such residency with a principal purpose of the avoidance of taxes if either: (1) the individual's average annual U.S. Federal income tax liability for the 5 taxable years ending before the date of such loss or termination is greater than $100,000 (the "tax liability test"), or (2) the individual's net worth as of the date of such loss or termination is $500,000 or more (the "net worth test"). The dollar amount thresholds contained in the tax liability test and the net worth test are indexed for inflation in the case of a loss of citizenship or termination of residency occurring in any calendar year after 1996. An individual who falls below the thresholds specified in both the tax liability test and the net worth test is subject to the expatriation tax provisions unless the individual's loss of citizenship or termination of residency did not have as a principal purpose the avoidance of tax (as under present law in the case of U.S. citizens).

A U.S. citizen, who loses his or her citizenship and who satisfies either the tax liability test or the net worth test, is not subject to the expatriation tax provisions if such individual can demonstrate that he or she did not have a principal purpose of tax avoidance and the individual is within one of the following categories: (1) the individual was born with dual citizenship and retains only the non-U.S. citizenship; (2) the individual becomes a citizen of the country in which the individual, the individual's spouse, or one of the individual's parents, was born; (3) the individual was present in the United States for no more than 30 days during any year in the 10-year period immediately preceding the date of his or her loss of citizenship; (4) the individual relinquishes his or her citizenship before reaching age 18½; or (5) any other category of individuals prescribed by Treasury regulations. In all of these situations, the individual would have been subject to tax on his or her worldwide income (as are all U.S. citizens) until the time of expatriation. In order to qualify for one of these exceptions, the former U.S. citizen must, within one year from the date of loss of citizenship, submit a ruling request for a determination by the Secretary of the Treasury as to whether such loss had as one of its principal purposes the avoidance of taxes. A former U.S. citizen who submits such a ruling request is entitled to challenge an adverse determination by the Secretary of the Treasury. However, a former U.S. citizen who fails to submit a timely ruling request is not eligible for these exceptions. It is expected that in making a determination as to the presence of a principal purpose of tax avoidance, the Secretary of the Treasury will take into account factors such as the substantiality of the former citizen's ties to the United States (including ownership of U.S. assets) prior to expatriation, the retention of U.S. citizenship by the former citizen's spouse, and the extent to which the former citizen resides in a country that imposes little or no tax.

The foregoing exceptions are not available to long-term residents whose U.S. residency is terminated. However, the House bill authorizes the Secretary of the Treasury to prescribe regulations to exempt certain categories of long-term residents from the House bill's provisions.

Items subject to section 877

Under section 877, an individual covered by the expatriation tax provisions is subject to tax on U.S. source income and gains for a 10-year period after expatriation at the graduated rates applicable to U.S. citizens.[24] The tax under section 877 applies to U.S. source income and gains of the individual for the 10-year period, without regard to whether the property giving rise to such income or gains was acquired before or after the date the individual became subject to the expatriation tax provisions. For example, a

---

[24] Under present law, all nonresident aliens (including expatriates) are subject to U.S. income tax at graduated rates on certain types of income. Such income includes income effectively connected with a U.S. trade or business and gains from the disposition of interests in U.S. real property. For example, compensation (including deferred compensation) paid with respect to services performed in the United States is subject to such tax. Thus, under current law, a U.S. citizen who earns a stock option while employed in the United States and delays the exercise of such option until after such individual loses his or her citizenship is subject to U.S. tax on the compensation income recognized upon exercise of the stock option (even if the stock received upon the exercise is stock in a foreign corporation).

U.S. citizen who inherits an appreciated asset immediately before losing citizenship and disposes of the asset immediately after such loss would not recognize any taxable gain on such disposition (because of the date of death fair market value basis accorded to inherited assets), but the individual would continue to be subject to tax under section 877 on the income or gain derived from any U.S. property acquired with the proceeds from such disposition.

In addition, section 877 currently recharacterizes as U.S. source income certain gains of individuals who are subject to the expatriation tax provisions, thereby subjecting such individuals to U.S. income tax on such gains. Under this rule, gain on the sale or exchange of stock of a U.S. corporation or debt of a U.S. person is treated as U.S. source income. In this regard, under current law, the substitution of a foreign obligor for a U.S. obligor is generally treated as a taxable exchange of the debt instrument, and therefore any gain on such exchange is subject to tax under section 877. The House bill extends this recharacterization to income and gains derived from property obtained in certain transactions on which gain or loss is not recognized under present law. An individual covered by section 877 who exchanges property that would produce U.S. source income for property that would produce foreign source income is required to recognize immediately as U.S. source income any gain on such exchange (determined as if the property had been sold for its fair market value on such date). To the extent gain is recognized under this provision, the property would be accorded the step-up in basis provided under current law. This rule requiring immediate gain recognition does not apply if the individual enters into an agreement with the Secretary of the Treasury specifying that any income or gains derived from the property received in the exchange during the 10-year period after the loss of citizenship (or termination of U.S. residency, as applicable) would be treated as U.S. source income. Such a gain recognition agreement terminates if the property transferred in the exchange is disposed of by the acquiror, and any gain that had not been recognized by reason of such agreement is recognized as U.S. source as of such date. It is expected that a gain recognition agreement would be entered into not later than the due date for the tax return for the year of the exchange. In this regard, the Secretary of the Treasury is authorized to issue regulations providing similar treatment for nonrecognition transactions that occur within 5 years immediately prior to the date of loss of citizenship (or termination of U.S. residency, as applicable).

The Secretary of Treasury is authorized to issue regulations to treat removal of tangible personal property from the United States, and other circumstances that result in a conversion of U.S. source income to foreign source income without recognition of any unrealized gain, as exchanges for purposes of computing gain subject to section 877. The taxpayer may defer the recognition of the gain if he or she enters into a gain recognition agreement as described above. For example, a former citizen who removes appreciated artwork that he or she owns from the United States could be subject to immediate tax on the appreciation under this provision unless the individual enters into a gain recognition agreement.

The foregoing rules regarding the treatment under section 877 of nonrecognition transactions are illustrated by the following examples: Ms. A loses her U.S. citizenship on January 1, 1996, and is subject to section 877. On June 30, 1997, Ms. A transfers the stock she owns in a U.S. corporation, USCo, to a wholly-owned foreign corporation, FCo, in a transaction that qualifies for tax-free treatment under section 351. At the time of such transfer, A's basis in the stock of USCo is $100,000 and the fair market value of the stock is $150,000. Under present law, Ms. A. would not be subject to U.S. tax on the $50,000 of gain realized on the exchange. Moreover, Ms. A would not be subject to U.S. tax on any distribution of the proceeds from a subsequent disposition of the USCo stock by FCo. Under the House bill, if Ms. A does not enter into a gain recognition agreement with the Secretary of the Treasury, Ms. A would be deemed to have sold the USCo stock for $150,000 on the date of the transfer, and would be subject to U.S. tax in 1997 on the $50,000 of gain realized. Alternatively, if Ms. A enters into a gain recognition agreement, she would not be required to recognize for U.S. tax purposes in 1997 the $50,000 of gain realized upon the transfer of the USCo stock to FCo. However, under the gain recognition agreement, for the 10-year period ending on December 31, 2005, any income (e.g., dividends) or gain with respect to the FCo stock would be treated as U.S. source, and therefore Ms. A would be subject to tax on such income or gain under section 877. If FCo disposes of the USCo stock on January 1, 2002, Ms. A's gain recognition agreement would terminate on such date, and Ms. A would be required to recognize as U.S. source income at that time the $50,000 of gain that she previously deferred under the gain recognition agreement. (The amount of gain required to be recognized by Ms. A in this situation would not be affected by any changes in the value of the USCo stock since her June 30, 1997 transfer of such stock to FCo.)

The House bill also extends the recharacterization rules of section 877 to treat as U.S. source any income and gains derived from stock in a foreign corporation if the individual losing citizenship or terminating residency owns, directly or indirectly, more than 50 percent of the vote or value of the stock of the corporation on the date of such loss or termination or at any time during the 2 years preceding such date. Such income and gains are recharacterized as U.S. source only to the extent of the amount of earnings and profits attributable to such stock earned or accumulated prior to the date of loss of citizenship (or termination of residency, as applicable) and while such ownership requirement is satisfied.

The following example illustrates this rule: Mr. B loses his U.S. citizenship on July 1, 1996 and is subject to section 877. Mr. B has owned all of the stock of a foreign corporation, FCo, since its incorporation in 1991. As of FCo's December 31, 1995 year-end, FCo has accumulated earnings and profits of $500,000. FCo has earnings and profits of $100,000 for 1996 and does not have any subpart F income (as defined in sec. 952). FCo makes a $100,000 distribution to Mr. B in each of 1997 and 1998. On January 1, 1999, Mr. B disposes of all his stock of FCo and realizes $400,000 of gain. Under present law, neither the distributions from FCo nor the gain on the disposition of the FCo stock would be subject to

U.S. tax. Under the House bill, the distributions from FCo and the gain on the sale of the stock of FCo would be treated as U.S. source income and would be taxed to Mr. B under section 877, subject to the earnings and profits limitation. For this purpose, the amount of FCo's earnings and profits for 1996 is prorated based on the number of days during 1996 that Mr. B is a U.S. citizen. Thus, the amount of FCo's earnings and profits earned or accumulated before Mr. B's loss of citizenship is $550,000. Accordingly, the $100,000 distributions from FCo in 1997 and 1998 would be treated as U.S. source income taxable to Mr. B under section 877 in such years. In addition, $350,000 of the gain realized from the sale of the stock of FCo in 1999 would be treated as U.S. source income taxable to Mr. B under section 877 in that year.

Special rule for shift in risks of ownership

Section 877 applies to income and gains for the 10-year period following the loss of citizenship (or termination of residency, as applicable). For purposes of applying section 877, the House bill suspends this 10-year period for gains derived from a particular property during any period in which the individual's risk of loss with respect to such property is substantially diminished. For example, Ms. C loses her citizenship on January 1, 1996 and is subject to section 877. On that date Ms. C owns 10,000 shares of stock of a U.S. corporation, USCo, with a value of $1 million. On the same date Ms. C enters into an equity swap with respect to such USCo stock with a 5-year term. Under the transaction, Ms. C will transfer to the counter-party an amount equal to the dividends on the USCo stock and any increase in the value of the USCo stock for the 5-year period. The counter-party will transfer to Ms. C an amount equal to a market rate of interest on $1 million and any decrease in the value of the USCo stock for the same period. Ms. C's risk of loss with respect to the USCo stock is substantially diminished during the 5-year period in which the equity swap is in effect, and therefore, under the House bill, the 10-year period under section 877 is suspended during such period. Accordingly, under the House bill, if Ms. C sells her USCo stock for a gain on January 1, 2010, such gain would be treated as U.S. source income taxable to Ms. C under section 877. Such gain would not be subject to U.S. tax under present law.

Double tax relief

In order to avoid the double taxation of individuals subject to the expatriation tax provisions, the House bill provides a credit against the U.S. tax imposed under such provisions for any foreign income, gift, estate or similar taxes paid with respect to the items subject to such taxation. This credit is available only against the tax imposed solely as a result of the expatriation tax provisions, and is not available to be used to offset any other U.S. tax liability. For example, Mr. D loses his citizenship on January 1, 1996 and is subject to section 877. Mr. D becomes a resident of Country X. During 1996, Mr. D recognizes a $100,000 gain upon the sale of stock of a U.S. corporation, USCo. Country X imposes $20,000 tax on this capital gain. But for the double tax relief provision, Mr. D would be subject to tax of $28,000 on this gain under section 877.

However, Mr. D's U.S. tax under section 877 would be reduced by the $20,000 of foreign tax paid, and Mr. D's resulting U.S. tax on this gain would be $8,000.

Effect on tax treaties

While it is believed that the expatriation tax provisions, as amended by the House bill, are generally consistent with the underlying principles of income tax treaties to the extent the House bill provides a foreign tax credit for items taxed by another country, it is intended that the purpose of the expatriation tax provisions, as amended, not be defeated by any treaty provision. The Treasury Department is expected to review all outstanding treaties to determine whether the expatriation tax provisions, as revised, potentially conflict with treaty provisions and to eliminate any such potential conflicts through renegotiation of the affected treaties as necessary. Beginning on the tenth anniversary of the enactment of the House bill, any conflicting treaty provisions that remain in force would take precedence over the expatriation tax provisions as revised.

Required information reporting and sharing

Under the House bill, a U.S. citizen who loses his or her citizenship is required to provide a statement to the State Department (or other designated government entity) which includes the individual's social security number, forwarding foreign address, new country of residence and citizenship and, in the case of individuals with a net worth of at least $500,000, a balance sheet. The entity to which such statement is to be provided is required to provide the Secretary of the Treasury copies of all statements received and the names of individuals who refuse to provide such statements. A long-term resident whose U.S. residency is terminated is required to attach a similar statement to his or her U.S. income tax return for the year of such termination. An individual's failure to provide the required statement results in the imposition of a penalty for each year the failure continues equal to the greater of (1) 5 percent of the individual's expatriation tax liability for such year, or (2) $1,000.

The House bill requires the State Department to provide the Secretary of the Treasury with a copy of each certificate of loss of nationality (CLN) approved by the State Department. Similarly, the House bill requires the agency administering the immigration laws to provide the Secretary of the Treasury with the name of each individual whose status as a lawful permanent resident has been revoked or has been determined to have been abandoned.

Further, the House bill requires the Secretary of the Treasury to publish in the Federal Register the names of all former U.S. citizens from whom it receives the required statements or whose names it receives under the foregoing information-sharing provisions.

Treasury report on tax compliance by U.S. citizens and residents living abroad

The Treasury Department is directed to undertake a study on the tax compliance of U.S. citizens and green-card holders residing outside the United States and to make recommendations regarding the improvement of such compliance. The findings of such study and such recommendations are required to be reported to the House Committee on Ways and Means and the Senate Committee on Finance within 90 days of the date of enactment.

During the course of the 1995 Joint Committee on Taxation staff study on expatriation (see Joint Committee on Taxation, Issues Presented by Proposals to Modify the Tax Treatment of Expatriation (JCS–17–95), June 1, 1995), a specific issue was identified regarding the difficulty in determining when a U.S. citizen has committed an expatriating act with the requisite intent, and thus no longer has the obligation to continue to pay U.S. taxes on his or her worldwide income due to the fact that the individual is no longer a U.S. citizen. Neither the Immigration and Nationality Act nor any other Federal law requires an individual to request a CLN within a specified amount of time after an expatriating act has been committed, even though the expatriating act terminates the status of the individual as a U.S. citizen for all purposes, including the status of being subject to U.S. tax on worldwide income. Accordingly, it is anticipated that the Treasury report, in evaluating whether improved coordination between executive branch agencies could improve compliance with the requirements of the Internal Revenue Code, will review the process through which the State Department determines when citizenship has been lost, and make recommendations regarding changes to such process to recognize the importance of such date for tax purposes. In particular, it is anticipated that the Treasury Department will explore ways of working with the State Department to insure that the State Department will not issue a CLN confirming the commission of an expatriating act with the requisite intent necessary to terminate citizenship in the absence of adequate evidence of both the occurrence of the expatriating act (e.g., the joining of a foreign army) and the existence of the requisite intent.

Effective date

The expatriation tax provisions as modified by the House bill generally apply to any individual who loses U.S. citizenship, and any long-term residents whose U.S. residency is terminated, on or after February 6, 1995. For citizens, the determination of the date of loss of citizenship remains the same as under present law (i.e., the date of loss of citizenship is the date of the expatriating act). However, a special transition rule applies to individuals who committed an expatriating act within one year prior to February 6, 1995, but had not applied for a CLN as of such date. Such an individual is subject to the expatriation tax provisions as amended by the House bill as of the date of application for the CLN, but is *not* retroactively liable for U.S. income taxes on his or her worldwide income. In order to qualify for the exceptions provided for individuals who fall within one of the specified categories, such individual is required to submit a ruling request within 1 year after the date of enactment of the House bill.

The special transition rule is illustrated by the following example. Mr. E joined a foreign army on October 1, 1994 with the intent to relinquish his U.S. citizenship, but Mr. E does not apply for a

CLN until October 1, 1995. Mr. E would be subject to the expatriation tax provisions (as amended) for the 10-year period beginning on October 1, 1995. Moreover, if Mr. E falls within one of the specified categories (i.e., Mr. E is age 18 when he joins the foreign army), in order to qualify for the exception provided for such individuals, Mr. E would be required to submit his ruling request within 1 year after the date of enactment of the House bill. Mr. E would not, however, be liable for U.S. income taxes on his worldwide income for any period after October 1, 1994.

Senate amendment

In general

The Senate amendment replaces the present-law expatriation income tax rules with rules that generally subject certain U.S. citizens who relinquish their U.S. citizenship and certain long-term U.S. residents who relinquish their U.S. residency to tax on the net unrealized gain in their property as if such property were sold for fair market value on the expatriation date. The Senate amendment also imposes information reporting obligations on U.S. citizens who relinquish their citizenship and long-term residents whose U.S. residency is terminated.

Individuals covered

The Senate amendment applies the expatriation tax to certain U.S. citizens and long-term residents who terminate their U.S. citizenship or residency. For this purpose, a long-term resident is any individual who was a lawful permanent resident of the United States for at least 8 out of the 15 taxable years ending with the year in which the termination of residency occurs. In applying this 8-year test, an individual is not considered to be a lawful permanent resident of the United States for any year in which the individual is taxed as a resident of another country under a treaty tie-breaker rule. An individual's U.S. residency is considered to be terminated when either the individual ceases to be a lawful permanent resident pursuant to section 7701(b)(6) (i.e., the individual loses his or her green-card status) or the individual is treated as a resident of another country under a tie-breaker provision of a tax treaty (and the individual does not elect to waive the benefits of such treaty).

The expatriation tax under the Senate amendment applies only to individuals whose average income tax liability or net worth exceeds specified levels. U.S. citizens who lose their citizenship and long-term residents who terminate U.S. residency are subject to the expatriation tax if they meet either of the following tests: (1) the individual's average annual U.S. Federal income tax liability for the 5 taxable years ending before the date of such loss or termination is greater than $100,000, or (2) the individual's net worth as of the date of such loss or termination is $500,000 or more. The dollar amount thresholds contained in these tests are indexed for inflation in the case of a loss of citizenship or termination of residency occurring in any calendar year after 1996.

Exceptions from the expatriation tax under the Senate amendment are provided for individuals in two situations. The first exception applies to an individual who was born with citizenship both in the United States and in another country, provided that (1) as of the date of relinquishment of U.S. citizenship the individual continues to be a citizen of, and is taxed as a resident of, such other country, and (2) the individual was a resident of the United States for no more than 8 out of the 15 taxable years ending with the year in which the relinquishment of U.S. citizenship occurred. The second exception applies to a U.S. citizen who relinquishes citizenship before reaching age 18½, provided that the individual was a resident of the United States for no more than 5 taxable years before such relinquishment.

Deemed sale of property upon expatriation

Under the Senate amendment, individuals who are subject to the expatriation tax generally are treated as having sold all of their property at fair market value immediately prior to the relinquishment of citizenship or termination of residency. Gain or loss from the deemed sale of property is recognized at that time, generally without regard to provisions of the Code that would otherwise provide nonrecognition treatment. The net gain, if any, on the deemed said of all such property is subject to U.S. tax at such time to the extent it exceeds $600,000 ($1.2 million in the case of married individuals filing a joint return, both of whom expatriate).

The deemed sale rule of the Senate amendment generally applies to all property interests held by the individual on the date of relinquishment of citizenship or termination of residency, provided that the gain on such property interest would be includible in the individual's gross income if such property interest were sold for its fair market value on such date. Special rules apply in the case of trust interests (see "Interests in trusts," below). U.S. real property interests, which remain subject to U.S. taxing jurisdiction in the hands of nonresident aliens, generally are excepted from the Senate amendment. An exception also applies to interests in qualified retirement plans and, subject to a limit of $500,000, interests in certain foreign pension plans as prescribed by regulations. The Secretary of the Treasury is authorized to issue regulations exempting other property interests as appropriate. For example, an exclusion may be provided for an interest in a nonqualified compensation plan of a U.S. employer, where payments from such plan to the individual following expatriation would continue to be subject to U.S. withholding tax.

Under the Senate amendment, an individual who is subject to the expatriation tax is required to pay a tentative tax equal to the amount of tax that would be due for a hypothetical short tax year ending on the date the individual relinquished citizenship or terminated residency. Thus, the tentative tax is based on all income, gain, deductions, loss and credits of the individual for the year through such date, including amounts realized from the deemed sale of property. The tentative tax is due on the 90th day after the date of relinquishment of citizenship or termination of residency.

Deferral of payment of tax

Under the Senate amendment, an individual is permitted to elect to defer payment of the expatriation tax with respect to the deemed sale of any property. Under this election, the expatriation tax with respect to a particular property, plus interest thereon, is due when the property is subsequently disposed of. For this purpose, except as provided in regulations, the disposition of property in a nonrecognition transaction constitutes a disposition. In addition, if an individual holds property until his or her death, the individual is treated as having disposed of the property immediately before death. In order to elect deferral of the expatriation tax, the individual is required to provide adequate security to ensure that the deferred expatriation tax and interest ultimately will be paid. A bond in the amount of the deferred tax and interest constitutes adequate security. Other security mechanisms are also permitted provided that the individual establishes to the satisfaction of the Security of the Treasury that the security is adequate. In the event that the security provided with respect to a particular property subsequently becomes inadequate and the individual fails to correct such situation, the deferred expatriation tax and interest with respect to such property will become due. As a further condition to making this election, the individual is required to consent to the waiver of any treaty rights that would preclude the collection of the expatriation tax.

Interests in trusts

In general.—Under the Senate amendment, special rules apply to trust interests held by the individual at the time of relinquishment of citizenship or termination of residency. The treatment of trust interests depends upon whether the trust is a qualified trust. For this purpose, a "qualified trust" is a trust that is organized under and governed by U.S. law and that is required by its instruments to have at least one U.S. trustee.

Constructive ownership rules apply to a trust beneficiary that is a corporation, partnership, trust or estate. In such cases, the shareholders, partners or beneficiaries of the entity are deemed to be the direct beneficiaries of the trust for purposes of applying these provisions. In addition, an individual who holds (or who is treated as holding) a trust interest at the time of relinquishment of citizenship or termination of residency is required to disclose on his or her tax return the methodology used to determine his or her interest in the trust, and whether such individual knows (or has reason to know) that any other beneficiary of the trust uses a different method.

Nonqualified trusts.—If an individual holds an interest in a trust that is not a qualified trust, a special rule applies for purposes of determining the amount of the expatriation tax due with respect to such trust interest. The individuals interest in the trust is treated as a separate trust consisting of the trust assets allocable to such interest. Such separate trust is treated as having sold its assets as of the date of relinquishment of citizenship or termination of residency and having distributed all proceeds to the individual, and the individual is treated as having recontributed such proceeds to the trust. The individual is subject to the expatriation tax with respect to any net income or gain arising from the deemed distribution from the trust. The election to defer payment is available for the expatriation tax attributable to a nonqualifed trust interest.

A beneficiary's interest in a nonqualified trust is determined on the basis of all facts and circumstances. These include the terms of the trust instrument itself, any letter of wishes or similar document, historical patterns of trust distributions, and the role of any trust protector or similar advisor.

Qualified trusts.—If the individual has an interest in a qualified trust, a different set of rules applies. Under these rules, the amount of unrealized gain allocable to the individual's trust interest is calculated at the time of expatriation. In determining this amount, all contingencies and discretionary interests are assumed to be resolved in the individual's favor (i.e., the individual is allocated the maximum amount that he or she potentially could receive under the terms of the trust instrument). The expatriation tax imposed on such gains generally is collected when the individual receives distributions from the trust, or, if earlier, upon the individual's death. Interest is charged for the period between the date of expatriation and the date on which the tax is paid.

If an individual has an interest in a qualified trust, the individual is subject to expatriation tax upon the receipt of any distribution from the trust. Such distributions may also be subject to U.S. income tax. For any distribution from a qualified trust made to an individual after he or she has expatriated, expatriation tax is imposed in an amount equal to the amount of the distribution multiplied by the highest tax rate generally applicable to trusts and estates, but in no event will the tax imposed exceed the deferred tax amount with respect to such trust interest. The "deferred tax amount" would be equal to (1) the tax calculated with respect to the unrealized gain allocable to the trust interest at the time of expatriation, (2) increased by interest thereon, and (3) reduced by the tax imposed under this provision with respect to prior trust distributions to the individual.

If an individual's interest in a trust is vested as of the expatriation date (e.g., if the individual's interest in the trust is non-contingent and non-discretionary), the gain allocable to the individual's trust interest is determined based on the truth assets allocable to his or her trust interest. If the individual's interest in the trust is not vested as of the expatriation date (e.g., if the individual's trust interest is a contingent or discretionary interest), the gain allocable to his or her trust interest is determined based on all of the trust assets that could be allocable to his or her trust interest, determined by resolving all contingencies and discretionary powers in the individual's favor. In the case where more than one trust beneficiary is subject to the expatriation tax with respect to trust interests that are not vested, the rules are intended to apply so that the same unrealized gain with respect to assets in the trust is not taxed to both individuals.

If the individual disposes of his or her trust interest, the trust ceases to be a qualified trust, or the individual dies, expatriation tax is imposed as of such date. The amount of such tax equal to the lesser of (1) the tax calculated under the rules for nonqualified trust interests applied as of such date or (2) the deferred tax amount with respect to the trust interest as of such date.

If the individual agrees to waive any treaty rights that would preclude collection of the tax, the tax is imposed under this provision with respect to distributions from a qualified trust to the individual deducted and withheld from distributions. If the individual does not agree to such a waiver of treaty rights, the tax with respect to distributions to the individual is imposed on the trust, the trustee is personally liable therefore, and any other beneficiary of the trust has a right of contribution against such individual with respect to such tax. Similarly, in the case of the tax imposed in connection with an individual's disposition of a trust interest, the individual's death while holding a trust interest or the individual's holding of an interest in a trust that ceases to be qualified, the tax is imposed on the trust, the trustee is personnaly liable therefor, and any other beneficiary of the trust has a right of contribution against such individual with respect to such tax.

Election to be treated as a U.S. citizen

Under the Senate amendment, an individual is permitted to make an irrevocable election to continue to be taxed as a U.S. citizen with respect to all property that otherwise is covered by the expatriation tax. This election is an "all-or-nothing" election; an individual is *not* permitted to elect this treatment for some property but not other property. The election, if made, applies to all property that would be subject to the expatriation tax and to any property the basis of which is determined by reference to such property. Under this election, the individual continues to pay U.S. income taxes at the rates applicable to U.S. citizens following expatriation on any income generated by the property and on any gain realized on the disposition of the property, as well as any excise tax imposed with respect to property (see, e.g., sec. 1491). In addition, the property continues to be subject to U.S. gift, estate, and generation-shipping taxes. However, the amount of any transfer tax so imposed is limited to the amount of income tax that would have been due if the property had been sold for its fair market value immediately before the transfer or death. The $600,000 exclusion provided with respect to the expatriation tax under the Senate amendment is available to reduce the tax imposed by reason of this election. In order to make this election, the taxpayer is required to waive any treaty rights that would preclude the collection of the tax. The individual is also required to provide security to ensure payment of the tax under this election in such form, manner, and amount as the Secretary of the Treasury requires.

Date of relinquishment of citizenship

Under the Senate amendment, as individual is treated as having relinquished U.S. citizenship on the date that the individual first makes known to U.S. government of consular officer his or her intention to relinquish U.S. citizenship. Thus, a U.S. citizen who relinquishes citizenship by formally renouncing his or her U.S. nationality before a diplomatic or consular officer for the United States is treated as having relinquished ciizenship on that date, provided that the renunciation is later confirmed by the issuance of a CLN. A U.S. citizen who furnishes to the State Department a signed statement of voluntary relinquishment of U.S. nationality confirming the performance of an expatriating act with the requisite interest to relinquish his or her citizenship is treated as having relinquished his or her citizenship on the date the statement is so furnished (regardless of when the expatriating act was performed), provided that the voluntary relinquishment is later confirmed by the issuance of a CLN. If neither of these circumstances exist, the individual is treated as having relinquished citizenship on the date a CLN is issued or a certificate of naturalization is cancelled. The date of relinquishment of citizenship determined under the Senate amendment applies for all purposes.

Effect on present-law expatriation provisions

Under the Senate amendment, the present-law income tax provisions with respect to U.S. citizens who expatriate with a principal purpose of avoiding tax (sec. 877) and certain aliens who have a break in residency status (sec. 7701(b)(10)) do applying to U.S. citizens who are treated as relinquishing their citizenship on or after February 6, 1995 or to long-term U.S. residents who terminate their residency on or after such date. The special estate and gift tax provisions with respect to individuals who expatriate with a principal purpose of avoiding tax (secs. 2107 and 2501(a)(3)), however, continue to apply; a credit against the tax imposed solely by reason of such special provisions is allowed for the expatriation tax imposed with respect to the same property.

Treatment of gifts and inheritances from an expatriate

Under the Senate amendment, the exclusion from income provided in section 102 does not apply to the value of any property received by gift or inheritance from an individual who was subject to the expatriation tax (i.e., an individual who relinquished citizenship or terminated residency and to whom the expatriation tax was applicable). Accordingly, a U.S. taxpayer who receives a gift or inheritance from such an individual is required to include the value of such gift or inheritance in gross income and is subject to U.S. income tax on such amount.

Required information reporting and sharing

Under the Senate amendment, an individual who relinquishes citizenship or terminates residency is required to provide a statement which includes the individual's social security number, forwarding foreign address, new country of residence and citizenship and, in the case of individuals with a net worth of at least $500,000, a balance sheet. In the case of a former citizen, such statement is due not later than the date the individual's citizenship is treated as relinquished and is to be provided to the State Department (or other government entity involved in the administration of such relinquishment). The entity to which the statement is to be provided by former citizens is required to provide to the Secretary of the Treasury copies of all statements received and the names of individuals who refuse to provide such statements. In the case of a former long-term resident, the statement is provided to the Secretary of the Treasury with the individual's tax return for the year in which the individual's U.S. residency is terminated. An individual's failure to provide the statement required under this provision results in the imposition of a penalty for each year the failure continues equal to the greater of (1) 5 percent of the individual's expatriation tax liability for such year or (2) $1,000.

The Senate amendment requires the State Department to provide the Secretary of the Treasury with a copy of each CLN approved by the State Department. Similarly, the Senate amendment requires the agency administering the immigration laws to provide the Secretary of the Treasury with the name of each individual whose status as a lawful permanent resident has been revoked or has been determined to have been abandoned.

Further, the Senate amendment requires the Secretary of the Treasury to publish in the Federal Register the names of all former U.S. citizens with respect to whom it receives the required statements or whose names it receives under the foregoing information-sharing provisions.

Treasury report on tax compliance by U.S. citizens and residents living abroad

The Treasury Department is directed to undertake a study on the tax compliance of U.S. citizens and green-card holders residing outside the United States and to make recommendations regarding the improvement of such compliance. The findings of such study and such recommendations are required to be reported to the House Committee on Ways and Means and the Senate Committee on Finance within 90 days of the date of enactment.

Effective date

The provision is effective for U.S. citizens whose date of relinquishment of citizenship (as determined under the Senate amendment, see "Date of relinquishment of citizenship" above) occurs on or after February 6, 1995. Similarly, the provision is effective for long-term residents who terminate their U.S. residency on or after February 6, 1995.

U.S. citizens who committed an expatriating act with the requisite intent to relinquish their U.S. citizenship prior to February 6, 1995, but whose date of relinquishment of citizenship (as determined under the Senate amendment) does not occur until after such date, are subject to the expatriation tax under the Senate amendment as of date of relinquishment of citizenship. However, the individual is not subject retroactively to worldwide tax as a U.S. citizen for the period after he or she committed the expatriating act (and therefore ceased being a U.S. citizen for tax purposes under present law). Such an individual continues to be subject to the expatriation tax imposed by present-law section 877 until the individual's date of relinquishment of citizenship (at which time the individual would be subject to the expatriation tax of the Senate amendment). The rules described in this paragraph do not apply to an individual who committed an expatriating act prior to February 6, 1995, but did not do so with the requisite intent to relinquish his or her U.S. citizenship.

The tentative tax is not required to be paid, and the reporting requirements would not be required to be met, until 90 days after the date of enactment. Such provisions apply to all individuals whose date of relinquishment of U.S. citizenship or termination of U.S. residency occurs on or after February 6, 1995.

Conference agreement

The conference agreement follows the House bill with modifications. Under the conference agreement, modified rules apply if an individual who is covered by section 877 contributes property that would produce U.S. source income to a foreign corporation if (1) the individual, directly or indirectly, owns 10 percent or more (by vote) of the stock of such corporation and (2) the individual, directly, indirectly or constructively, owns more than 50 percent (by vote or by value) of the stock of such corporation. For purposes of determining indirect and constructive ownership, the rules of section 958 apply. Under the modified rules, for the ten-year period following expatriation the individual is treated as receiving or accruing directly the income or gains received or accrued by the foreign corporation with respect to the contributed property (or other property which has a basis determined by reference to the basis of such contributed property). Moreover, if the individual disposes of the stock of the foreign corporation, the individual is subject to U.S. tax on the gain that would have been recognized if the corporation had sold such property immediately before the disposition. If the individual disposes of less than all of his or her stock in the foreign corporation, such disposition is treated as a disposition of a pro rata share (determined based on value) of such contributed property (e.g., if the individual owns 100 shares of the foreign corporation's stock and disposes of 10 of such shares, such disposition is treated as a disposition of 10 percent of the property contributed to the foreign corporation). Regulatory authority is provided to prescribe regulations to prevent the avoidance of this rule. Information reporting will be required as necessary to carry out the purposes of this rule. In addition, under the conference agreement, in the case of any former U.S. citizen, a request for a ruling that such individual did not have the avoidance of U.S. tax as a principal purpose for such individual's loss of citizenship would be due not earlier than 90 days after date of enactment.

C. TREATMENT OF BAD DEBT DEDUCTIONS OF THRIFT INSTITUTIONS

(Sec. 401 of the House bill and and sec. 611 of the Senate amendment.)

Present law

Generally, a taxpayer engaged in a trade or business may deduct the amount of any debt that becomes wholly or partially worthless during the year (the "specific charge-off" method of sec. 166). Certain thrift institutions (building and loan associations, mutual savings banks, or cooperative banks) are allowed deductions for bad debts under methods more favorable than those granted to other taxpayers (and more favorable than the rules applicable to other financial institutions). Qualified thrift institutions may compute deductions for bad debts using either the specific charge-off method or the reserve method of section 593.

Under section 593, a thrift institution annually may elect to deduct bad debts under either (1) the "percentage of taxable income" method applicable only to thrift institutions, or (2) the "experience" method that also is available to small banks. Under the "percentage of taxable income" method, a thrift institution generally is allowed a deduction for an addition to its bad debt reserve equal to 8 percent of its taxable income (determined without regard to this deduction and with additional adjustments). Under the experience method, a thrift institution generally is allowed a deduction for an addition to its bad debt reserve equal to the greater of: (1) an amount based on its actual average experience for losses in the current and five preceding taxable years, or (2) an amount necessary to restore the reserve to its balance as of the close of the base year.

If a thrift institution becomes ineligible to use the section 593 method, it is required to change its method of accounting for bad debts and, under proposed Treasury regulations, is required to recapture all or a portion of its bad debt reserve. In addition, a thrift institution eligible to use the section 593 method may be subject to a form of reserve recapture if the institution makes certain excessive distributions to its shareholders (sec. 593(e)).

House bill

Repeal of section 593

The House bill repeals the section 593 reserve method of accounting for bad debts by thrift institutions, effective for taxable years beginning after 1995. Thrift institutions that would be treated as small banks are allowed to utilize the experience method applicable to such institutions, while thrift institutions that are treated as large banks are required to use only the specific charge-off method. Thus, the percentage of taxable income method of accounting for bad debts is no longer available for any financial institution.

Treatment of recapture of bad debt reserves

A thrift institution required to change its method of computing reserves for bad debts will treat such change as a change in a method of accounting, initiated by the taxpayer, and having been made with the consent of the Secretary of the Treasury. Any section 481(a) adjustment required to be recaptured with respect to such change generally will be determined solely with respect to the "applicable excess reserves" of the taxpayer. The amount of applicable excess reserves will be taken into account ratably over a six-taxable year period, beginning with the first taxable year beginning after 1995, subject to the residential loan requirement described below. In the case of a thrift institution that becomes a large bank, the amount of the institution's applicable excess reserves generally is the excess of (1) the balances of its reserve for losses on qualifying real property loans and its reserve for losses on nonqualifying loans as of the close of its last taxable year beginning before January 1, 1996, over (2) the balances of such reserves as of the close of its last taxable year beginning before January 1, 1988 (i.e., the "pre-1988 reserves.") Similar rules are provided for small banks that are allowed to use the experience method.

For taxable years that begin after December 31, 1995, and before January 1, 1998, if the taxpayer continues to make a certain level of residential loans, the recapture of the applicable excess reserves otherwise required to be taken into account for such years will be suspended.

The balance of the pre-1988 reserves is subject to the provisions of section 593(e), as modified by the House bill (requiring recapture in the case of certain excessive distributions to shareholders.)

Other special recapture rules are provided if a thrift institution no longer qualifies as a bank or if a thrift institution becomes a credit union.

Effective date

The provision generally is effective for taxable years beginning after December 31, 1995.

Senate amendment

The Senate amendment generally is the same as the House bill, with certain modifications.

Conference agreement

The conference agreement does not include either the provision in the House bill or the provision in the Senate amendment.

D. EARNED INCOME CREDIT PROVISIONS

(Sec. 411 of the House bill.)

Present law

In general

Certain eligible low-income workers are entitled to claim a refundable credit on their income tax return. The amount of the credit an eligible individual may claim depends upon whether the individual has one, more than one or no qualifying children and is determined by multiplying the credit rate by the individual's [25] earned income up to an earned income amount. The maximum amount of the credit is the product of the credit rate and the earned income amount. For individuals with earned income (or adjusted gross income (AGI), if greater) in excess of the beginning of the phaseout range, the maximum credit amount is reduced by the phaseout rate multiplied by the amount of earned income (or AGI, if greater) in excess of the beginning of the phaseout range. For individuals with earned income (or AGI, if greater) in excess of the end of the phaseout range, no credit is allowed.

The parameters for the credit depend upon the number of qualifying children the individual claims. For 1996, the parameters are given in the following table:

	Two or more qualifying children—	One qualifying child—	No qualifying children—
Credit rate (percent)	40.00	34.00	7.65
Earned income amount	$8,890	$6,330	$4,220
Maximum credit	$3,356	$2,152	$323
Phaseout begins	$11,610	$11,610	$5,280

---

[25] In the case of a married individual who files a joint return with his or her spouse, the income for purposes of these tests is the combined income of the couple.

	Two or more qualifying children—	One qualifying child—	No qualifying children—
Phaseout rate (percent)	21.06	15.98	7.65
Phaseout ends	$28,495	$25,078	$9,500

For years after 1996, the credit rates and the phaseout rates will be the same as in the preceding table. The earned income amount and the beginning of the phaseout range are indexed for inflation; because the end of the phaseout range depends on those amounts as well as the phaseout rate and the credit rate, the end of the phaseout range will also increase if there is inflation.

In order to claim the credit, an individual must either have a qualifying child or meet other requirements. A qualifying child must meet a relationship test, an age test, an identification test, and a residence test. In order to claim the credit without a qualifying child, an individual must not be a dependent and must be over age 24 and under age 65.

To satisfy the identification test, individuals must include on their tax return the name and age of each qualifying child. For returns filed with respect to tax year 1996, individuals must provide a taxpayer identification number (TIN) for all qualifying children born on or before November 30, 1996. For returns filed with respect to tax year 1997 and all subsequent years, individuals must provide TINs for all qualifying children, regardless of their age. An individual's TIN is generally that individual's social security number.

Mathematical or clerical errors

The IRS may summarily assess additional tax due as a result of a mathematical or clerical error without sending the taxpayer a notice of deficiency and giving the taxpayer an opportunity to petition the Tax Court. Where the IRS uses the summary assessment procedure for mathematical or clerical errors, the taxpayer must be given an explanation of the asserted error and a period of 60 days to request that the IRS abate its assessment. The IRS may not proceed to collect the amount of the assessment until the taxpayer has agreed to it or has allowed the 60-day period for objecting to expire. If the taxpayer files a request for abatement of the assessment specified in the notice, the IRS must abate the assessment. Any reassessment of the abated amount is subject to the ordinary deficiency procedures. The request for abatement of the assessment is the only procedure a taxpayer may use prior to paying the assessed amount in order to contest an assessment arising out of a mathematical or clerical error. Once the assessment is satisfied, however, the taxpayer may file a claim for refund if he or she believes the assessment was made in error.

House bill

Under the House bill, individuals are not eligible for the credit if they do not include their taxpayer identification number (and, if married, their spouse's taxpayer identification number) on their tax return. Solely for these purposes and for purposes of the present-law identification test for a qualifying child, a taxpayer identification number is defined as a social security number issued to an individual by the Social Security Administration other than a number issued under section 205(c)(2)(B)(i)(II) (or that portion of sec. 205(c)(2)(B)(i)(III) relating to it) of the Social Security Act (regarding the issuance of a number to an individual applying for or receiving Federally funded benefits).

If an individual fails to provide a correct taxpayer identification number, such omission will be treated as a mathematical or clerical error. If an individual who claims the credit with respect to net earnings from self-employment fails to pay the proper amount of self-employment tax on such net earnings, the failure will be treated as a mathematical or clerical error for purposes of the amount of credit allowed.

Effective date.—The provision is effective for taxable years beginning after December 31, 1995.

Senate amendment

No provision.

Conference agreement

The conference agreement does not include the House bill provision.

E. MODIFY TREATMENT OF FOREIGN TRUSTS

(Secs. 601–606 of the Senate amendment).

Present law

Inbound grantor trusts with foreign grantors

Under the grantor trust rules (secs. 671–679), a grantor that retains certain rights or powers generally is treated as the owner of the trust's assets without regard to whether the grantor is a domestic or foreign person. Under these rules, U.S. trust beneficiaries are not subject to U.S. tax on distributions from a trust where a foreign grantor is treated as owner of the trust, even though no tax may be imposed on the trust income by any jurisdiction. In addition, a special rule provides that if a U.S. beneficiary of an inbound grantor trust transfers property to the foreign grantor by gift, that U.S. beneficiary is treated as the grantor of the trust to the extent of the transfer.

Foreign trusts that are not grantor trusts

Under the accumulation distribution rules (which generally apply to distributions from a trust in excess of the trust's distributable net income for the taxable year), a distribution by a foreign nongrantor trust of previously accumulated income generally is taxed at the U.S. beneficiary's average marginal rate for the prior 5 years, plus interest (secs. 666 and 667). Interest is computed at a fixed annual rate of 6 percent, with no compounding (sec. 668). If adequate records of the trust are not available to determine the proper application of the rules relating to accumulation distributions to any distribution from a trust, the distribution is treated as an accumulation distribution out of income earned during the first year of the trust (sec. 666(d)).

If a foreign nongrantor trust makes a loan to one of its beneficiaries, the principal of such a loan generally is not taxable as income to the beneficiary.

Outbound foreign grantor trusts with U.S. grantors

Under the grantor trust rules, a U.S. person that transfers property to a foreign trust generally is treated as the owner of the portion of the trust comprising that property for any taxable year in which there is a U.S. beneficiary of any portion of the trust (sec. 679(a)). This treatment generally does not apply, however, to transfers by reason of death, to transfers made before the transferor became a U.S. person, or to transfers that represent sales or exchanges of property at fair market value where gain is recognized to the transferor.

Residence of trusts and estates

An estate or trust is treated as foreign if it is not subject to U.S. income taxation on its income that is neither derived from U.S. sources nor effectively connected with the conduct of a U.S. trade or business. Thus, if a trust is taxed in a manner similar to a nonresident alien individual, it is considered to be a foreign trust. Any other trust is treated as domestic.

Section 1491 generally imposes a 35-percent excise tax on a U.S. person that transfers appreciated property to certain foreign entities, including a foreign trust. In the case of a domestic trust that changes its situs and becomes a foreign trust, it is unclear whether property has been transferred from a U.S. person to a foreign entity and, thus, whether the transfer is subject to the excise tax.

Information reporting and penalties related to foreign trusts

Any U.S. person that creates a foreign trust or transfers money or property to a foreign trust is required to report that event to the Treasury Department without regard to whether the trust is a grantor trust or a nongrantor trust. Similarly, any U.S. person that transfers property to a foreign trust that has one or more U.S. beneficiaries is required to report annually to the Treasury Department. In addition, any U.S. person that makes a transfer described in section 1491 is required to report the transfer to the Treasury Department.

Any person that fails to file a required report with respect to the creation of, or a transfer to, a foreign trust may be subject to a penalty of 5 percent of the amount transferred to the foreign trust. Similarly, any person that fails to file a required annual report with respect to a foreign trust with U.S. beneficiaries may be subject to a penalty of 5 percent of the value of the corpus of the trust at the close of the taxable year. The maximum amount of the penalty imposed under either case may not exceed $1,000. A reasonable cause exception is available.

Reporting of foreign gifts

There is no requirement to report gifts or bequests from foreign sources.

House bill

No provision.

Senate amendment

Inbound grantor trusts with foreign grantors

The Senate amendment generally applies the grantor trust rules only to the extent that they result, directly or indirectly, in income or other amounts being currently taken into account in computing the income of a U.S. citizen or resident or a domestic corporation. Certain exceptions apply to this general rule. Under one exception, the grantor trust rules continue to apply to a revocable trust. Under another exception, the grantor trust rules continue to apply to a trust where the only amounts distributable during the lifetime of the grantor are to the grantor or the grantor's spouse. The general rule denying grantor trust status does not apply to trusts established to pay compensation, and certain trusts in existence as of September 19, 1995 provided that such trust is treated as owned by the grantor under section 676 or 677 (other than sec. 677(a)(3)).[26] In addition, the grantor trust rules generally apply where the grantor is a controlled foreign corporation (as defined in sec. 957). Finally, the grantor trust rules continue to apply in determining whether a foreign corporation is characterized as a passive foreign investment company ("PFIC"). Thus, a foreign corporation cannot avoid PFIC status by transferring its assets to a grantor trust.

If a U.S. beneficiary of an inbound grantor trust transfers property to the foreign grantor, such beneficiary generally is treated as a grantor of a portion of the trust to the extent of the transfer. This rule applies without regard to whether the foreign grantor is otherwise treated as the owner of any portion of such trust. However, this rule does not apply if the transfer is a gift that qualifies for the annual exclusion described in section 2503(b).

The Senate amendment provides a special rule that allows the Secretary of the Treasury to recharacterize a transfer, directly or indirectly, from a partnership or foreign corporation which the transferee treats as a gift or bequest, to prevent the avoidance of the purpose of section 672(f). In a case where a foreign person (that would be treated as the owner of a trust but for the above rule) actually pays tax on the income of the trust to a foreign country, it is anticipated that Treasury regulations will provide that, for foreign tax credit purposes, U.S. beneficiaries that are subject to U.S. income tax on the same income will be treated as having paid the foreign taxes that are paid by the foreign grantor. Any resulting foreign tax credits will be subject to applicable foreign tax credit limitations.

Effective date.—The provisions described in this part are effective on the date of enactment.

---

[26] The exception does not apply to the portion of any such trust attributable to any transfers made after September 19, 1995.

Foreign trusts that are not grantor trusts

The Senate amendment changes the interest rate applicable to accumulation distributions from foreign trusts from simple interest at a fixed rate of 6 percent to compound interest determined in the same manner as interest imposed on underpayments of tax under section 6621(a)(2). Simple interest is accrued at the rate of 6 percent through 1995. Beginning on January 1, 1996 compound interest based on the underpayment rate is imposed on tax amounts determined under the accumulation distribution rules and the total simple interest for pre-1996 periods, if any. For purposes of computing the interest charge, the accumulation distribution is allocated proportionately to prior trust years in which the trust has undistributed net income (and the beneficiary receiving the distribution was a U.S. citizen or resident), rather than to the earliest of such years. An accumulation distribution is treated as reducing proportionately the undistributed net income from prior years.

In the case of a loan of cash or marketable securities by the foreign trust to a U.S. grantor or a U.S. beneficiary (or a U.S. person related to such grantor or beneficiary), except to the extent provided by Treasury regulations, the Senate amendment treats the full amount of the loan as distributed to the grantor or beneficiary. It is expected that the Treasury regulations will provide an exception from this treatment for loans with arm's-length terms. In applying this exception, it is further expected that consideration be given to whether there is a reasonable expectation that a loan will be repaid. In addition, any subsequent transaction between the trust and the original borrower regarding the principal of the loan (e.g., repayment) is disregarded for all purposes of the Code. This provision does not apply to loans made to persons that are exempt from U.S. income tax.

Effective date.—The provision to modify the interest charge on accumulation distributions applies to distributions after the date of enactment. The provision with respect to loans to U.S. grantors, U.S. beneficiaries or a U.S. person related to such a grantor or beneficiary applies to loans made after September 19, 1995.

Outbound foreign grantor trusts with U.S. grantors

The Senate amendment makes several modifications to the general rule of section 679(a)(1) under which a U.S. person who transfers property to a foreign trust generally is treated as the owner of the portion of the trust comprising that property for any taxable year in which there is a U.S. beneficiary of the trust. The Senate amendment also conforms the definition of certain foreign corporations the income of which is deemed to be accumulated for the benefit of a U.S. beneficiary to the definition of controlled foreign corporations (as defined in sec. 957(a)).

Sale or exchange at market value.—Present law contains several exceptions to grantor trust treatment under section 679(a)(1) described above. Under one of the exceptions, grantor trust treatment does not result from a transfer of property by a U.S. person to a foreign trust in the form of a sale or exchange at fair market value where gain is recognized to the transferor. In determining whether the trust paid fair market value to the transferor, the Senator amendment provides that obligations issued (or, to the extent provided by regulations, guaranteed) by the trust, by any grantor or beneficiary of the trust, or by any person related to any grantor or beneficiary (referred to as "trust obligations") are not taken into account except as provided in Treasury regulations. It is expected that the Treasury regulations will provide an exception from this treatment for loans with arm's-length terms. In applying this exception, it is further expected that consideration be given to whether there is a reasonable expectation that a loan will be repaid. Principal payments by the trust on any such trust obligations generally will reduce the portion of the trust attributable to the property transferred (i.e., the portion of which the transferor is treated as the grantor).

Other transfers.—The Senate amendment adds a new exception to the general rule of section 679(a)(1) described above. Under the Senate amendment, a transfer of property to certain charitable trusts is exempt from the application of the rules treating foreign trusts with U.S. grantors and U.S. beneficiaries as grantor trusts.

Transferors or beneficiaries who become U.S. persons.—The Senate amendment applies the rule of section 679(a)(1) to certain foreign persons who transfer property to a foreign trust and subsequently become U.S. persons. A nonresident alien individual who transfers property, directly or indirectly, to a foreign trust and then becomes a resident of the United States within 5 years after the transfer generally is treated as making a transfer to the foreign trust on the individual's U.S. residency starting date (as defined in sec. 7701(b)(2)(A)). The amount of the deemed transfer is the portion of the trust (including undistributed earnings) attributable to the property previously transferred. Consequently, the individual generally is treated under section 679(a)(1) as the owner of that portion of the trust in any taxable year in which the trust has U.S. beneficiaries.

Outbound trust migrations.—The Senate amendment applies the rules of section 679(a)(1) to a U.S. person that transferred property to a domestic trust if the trust subsequently becomes a foreign trust while the transferor is still alive. Such a person is deemed to make a transfer to the foreign trust on the date of the migration. The amount of the deemed transfer is the portion of the trust (including undistributed earnings) attributable to the property previously transferred. Consequently, the individual generally is treated under the rules of section 679(a)(1) as the owner of that portion of the trust in any taxable year in which the trust has U.S. beneficiaries.

Effective date.—The provisions to amend section 679 apply to transfers of property after February 6, 1995.

Anti-abuse regulatory authority

The Senate amendment includes an anti-abuse rule which authorizes the Secretary of the Treasury to issue regulations, on or after the date of enactment, that may be necessary or appropriate to carry out the purposes of the rules applicable to estates, trusts and beneficiaries, including regulations to prevent the avoidance of those purposes.

Effective date.—The provision is effective on the date of enactment.

Residence of trusts and estates

The Senate amendment establishes a two-part objective test for determining for tax purposes whether a trust is foreign or domestic. If both parts of the test are satisfied, the trust is treated as domestic. Only the first part of the test applies to estates. Under the first part of the test, if a U.S. court (i.e., Federal, State, or local) exercises primary supervision over the administration of a trust or estate, the trust or estate is treated as domestic. Under the second part of the test, in order for a trust to be treated as domestic, one or more U.S. fiduciaries must have the authority to control all substantial decisions of the trust.

Under the Senate amendment, if a domestic trust changes its situs and becomes a foreign trust, the trust is treated as having made a transfer of its assets to a foreign trust and is subject to the 35-percent excise tax imposed by present-law section 1491 unless one of the exceptions to this excise tax is applicable.

Effective date.—The provision to modify the treatment of a trust or estate as a U.S. person applies to taxable years beginning after December 31, 1996. In addition, if the trustee of a trust so elects, the provision would apply to taxable years ending after the date of enactment. The amendment to section 1491 is effective on the date of enactment.

Information reporting and penalties relating to foreign trusts

The Senate amendment generally requires the grantor, transferor or executor (i.e., the "responsible party") to notify the Treasury Department upon the occurrence of certain reportable events. The term "reportable event" means the creation of any foreign trust by a U.S. person, the direct and indirect transfer of any money or property to a foreign trust, including a transfer by reason of death, and the death of a U.S. citizen or resident if any portion of a foreign trust was included in the gross estate of the decedent. In addition, a U.S. owner of any portion of a foreign trust is required to ensure that the trust files an annual return to provide full accounting of all the trust activities for the taxable year. Finally, any U.S. person that relieves (directly or indirectly) any distribution from a foreign trust is required to file a return to report the aggregate amount of the distributions received during the year.

The Senate amendment provides that if a U.S. owner of any portion of a foreign trust fails to appoint a limited U.S. agent to accept service of process with respect to any requests and summons by the Secretary of the Treasury in connection with the tax treatment of any items related to the trust, the Secretary of the Treasury may determine the tax consequences of amounts to be taken into account under the grantor trust rules. In cases where adequate records are not provided to the Secretary of Treasury to determine the proper treatment of any distributions from a foreign trust, the distribution is includible in the gross income of the U.S. distributee and is treated as an accumulation distribution from the middle year of a foreign trust (i.e., computed by taking the number of years that the trust has been in existence divided by 2) for purposes of computing the interest charge applicable to such distribution, unless the foreign trust elects to have a U.S. agent for the limited purpose of accepting service of process (as described above).

Under the Senate amendment, a person that fails to provide the required notice or return in cases involving the transfer of property to a new or existing foreign trust, or a distribution by a foreign trust to a U.S. person, is subject to an initial penalty equal to 35 percent of the gross reportable amount (generally the value of the property involved in the transaction). A failure to provide an annual reporting of trust activities will result in an initial penalty equal to 5 percent of the gross reportable amount. An additional $10,000 penalty is imposed for continued failure for each 30-day period (or fraction thereof) beginning 90 days after the Treasury Department notifies the responsible party of such failure. Such penalties are subject to a reasonable cause exception. In no event will the total amount of penalties exceed the gross reportable amount.

Effective date.—The reporting requirements and applicable penalties generally apply to reportable events occurring or distributions received after the date of enactment. The annual reporting requirement and penalties applicable to U.S. grantors apply to taxable years of such persons beginning after the date of enactment.

Reporting of foreign gifts

The Senate amendment generally requires any U.S. person (other than certain tax-exempt organizations) that receives purported gifts or bequests from foreign sources totaling more than $10,000 during the taxable year to report them to the Treasury Department. The threshold for this reporting requirement is indexed for inflation. The definition of a gift to a U.S. person for this purpose excludes amounts that are qualified tuition or medical payments made on behalf of the U.S. person, as defined for gift tax purposes (sec. 2503(e)(2)). If the U.S. person fails, without reasonable cause, to report foreign gifts as required, the Treasury Secretary is authorized to determine, in his sole discretion, the tax treatment of the unreported gifts. In addition, the U.S. person is subject to a penalty equal to 5 percent of the amount of the gift for each month that the failure continues, with the total penalty not to exceed 25 percent of such amount.

Effective date.—The provision applies to amounts received after the date of enactment.

Conference agreement

The conference agreement does not include the Senate amendment.

F. REPEAL OF FINANCIAL INSTITUTION TRANSITION RULE TO INTEREST ALLOCATION RULES

Present law

For foreign tax credit purposes, taxpayers generally are required to allocate and apportion interest expense between U.S. and foreign source income based on the proportion of the taxpayer's total assets in each location. Such allocation and apportionment is required to be made for affiliated groups (as defined in sec. 864(e)(5)) as a whole rather than on a subsidiary-by-subsidiary basis. However, certain types of financial institutions that are members of an affiliated group are treated as members of a separate affiliated group for purposes of allocating and apportioning their interest expense. Section 1215(c)(5) of the Tax Reform Act of 1986 (P.L. 99–514, 100 Stat. 2548) includes a targeted rule which treats a certain corporation as a financial institution for this purpose.

House bill

No provision.

Senate amendment

No provision. However, section 1606 of the Senate amendment to H.R. 3448 (Small Business Job Protection Act of 1996) contained a provision that repeals section 1215(c)(5) of the Tax Reform Act of 1986.

Effective date.—Taxable years beginning after December 31, 1995.

Conference agreement

The conference agreement includes the provision in the Senate amendment to H.R. 3448 with one modification. The conference agreement repeals section 1215(c)(5) of the Tax Reform Act of 1986 effective on the date of enactment. Under the conference agreement, a taxpayer will perform two computations with respect to its taxable year that includes the enactment date. Under the first computation, the taxpayer's pre-effective date interest expense is allocated and apportioned taking into account the targeted rule, and under the second computation, the taxpayer's post-effective date interest expense is allocated and apportioned without regard to the targeted rule. These computations will not require a closing of a taxpayer's books and records and it is intended that an administratively simple approach be used in applying this rule.

BILL ARCHER,
BILL THOMAS,
TOM BLILEY,
MICHAEL BILIRAKIS,
WILLIAM F. GOODLING,
H.W. FAWELL,
HENRY HYDE,
BILL MCCOLLUM,
J. DENNIS HASTERT,
Managers on the Part of the House.

BILL ROTH
NANCY LANDON KASSEBAUM,
TRENT LOTT,
TED KENNEDY,
Managers on the Part of the Senate.

www.ingramcontent.com/pod-product-compliance
Lightning Source LLC
Chambersburg PA
CBHW081105170526
45165CB00008B/2331